DESCRIPTIVE

GEOGRAPHY OF PALESTINE.

RV RABBI JOSEPH SCHWARZ

from Jerusalem.

A DESCRIPTIVE GEOGRAPHY

AND

BRIEF HISTORICAL SKETCH

OF

PALESTINE.

BY RABBI JOSEPH SCHWARZ,

FOR SIXTEEN YEARS A RESIDENT IN THE HOLY LAND.

TRANSLATED BY

ISAAC LEESER,

ONE OF THE EDITORS OF THE NEW EDITION OF THE HEBREW BIBLE, ETC.

ILLUSTRATED WITH MAPS AND NUMEROUS ENGRAVINGS.

"For the stones thereof are dear to thy servants, and its dust they kindly cherish."
PSALM cii. 16.

PHILADELPHIA:
PUBLISHED BY A. HART,
LATE CAREY AND HART.
5610–1850.

PHILADELPHIA:

C. SHERMAN, PRINTER.

TRANSLATOR'S PREFACE.

In sending this new publication out to the world, I have but little to say, farther than that I have endeavoured to render the author's ideas as faithfully as was in my power. I had before me, for a great portion of the work, a printed Hebrew copy and a German translation in MS., the latter by various persons, and in part by the learned author, who, however, revised the whole before it was put into my hands. Notwithstanding the abundance of aid thus afforded me in my task, it was very difficult to do it full justice; as the great diversity of style naturally resulting from the co-operation of at least three persons must leave a translator often greatly perplexed. At the same time the German not rarely differed materially from the original, which also is composed not in pure Hebrew, but in the mixed dialect so usual among modern Jews; which, from the little opportunity I have had, is not so familiar to me as it is to those who have been thoroughly conversant with our modern literature by a constant perusal of the later authors of our people, and by a personal intercourse with the writers themselves. None but those who make the attempt to be their own teachers in any branch of science can know the difficulty one has to surmount, if a competent guide is not to be obtained occasionally to help the student forward. It is, therefore, highly probable, that others might have done the author more justice; but it is also not unlikely that they would have lacked some other qualification which was requisite to execute the task now before the reader.

Whenever possible, I verified the author's references, and I thus gave the spelling of the names with all attainable accuracy; in other instances I was not so fortunate; and hence it is not unlikely that some little errors may be discovered here and there, which were unavoidable, as the temporary residence of the author in New York prevented me from consulting him on all occasions in person, even where his advice may have been needed; and those familiar with literary labours can easily imagine that epistolary intercourse would have been too tedious for the elucidation of any difficulty which at the moment might have presented itself. I had, therefore, to depend on my own judgment, occasionally correcting what I thought a little erroneous; and when I deemed a statement doubtful, or not clearly understood, I put a note of interrogation in parentheses, thus (?), to call the attention to the circumstances, that the translator did not fully comprehend the author. Should the work ever be reprinted, these blemishes, together with any errors* in spelling the immense number of names entirely new to me, will be readily corrected; in the meanwhile, the reader's indulgence is asked, should he have occasion to censure once in a while my incompetency in so severe a labour as this has proved to me,—far greater, indeed, than I had anticipated.

I would merely remark, that occasionally I observed a diversity in spelling the same name in different parts of the author's book as printed at Jerusalem and the MS. prepared by him, or under his inspection. In choosing, therefore, one or the other, my judgment may have been at fault. But let me not be blamed for this, or accused of too great an ignorance of the subject; for it is one thing to know the principal outlines

* I would incidentally call attention to the following errors which I have discovered: p. 34, last line, read "Tantura, or Dardura;" p. 36, l. 15 from bottom, "Ulam;" p. 39, l. 10 from bottom, for "as" read "or;" p. 42, in note line 4, read "Belad;" p. 76, l. 9 from bottom, read "Ras al Abiat;" p. 269, the inscription should be in a continuous paragraph with what precedes and follows it, thus, "Arabic inscription, SELIMAN, &c., that is, &c.;" p. 271, l. 14 from top, for "Rabbi Meir De Rossi," read "Rabbi Azariah De Rossi."

of the geography of a country, enough for general purposes,—and quite another to be familiar with every little locality in any land, especially one so remote as Palestine. Hence the subject was generally as new to me as it is to the reader, and I had to study it as I went along. Still, I trust that no great or glaring errors will be discovered; at least I took all possible care to avoid them, and to indicate my doubts where I thought the original perhaps erroneous.

As regards the style, I purposely adhered as closely as possible to the author's words, in order to convey his meaning with the most scrupulous exactness. A freer version might have been more agreeable to the ear; but, in furnishing it, I would most likely have failed to give a correct transcript of the original.

The citations from Josephus are according to a copy the author had before him, which differs, as is evident, materially from Whiston's in the arrangement of the various books, chapters, and sections. Where I was able, without too great a search, I followed the usual copies; where this was not possible, I copied the author. The same is the case with some other quotations. I state this merely to advertise the reader that he must not suppose an error has been committed in case the book, chapter, &c., differs from that indicated in the work he is familiar with.

In proper names, where the *j* is to have the English sound, I have prefixed a *d*, thus *dj;* in all other instances, it should be pronounced as *y* in *yes*, or the liquid *i*. The diphthongs *ai*, or *ei*, should be sounded as *ay* in the monosyllable *Ay*, that is, a little broader than the long English *i*. The *a* itself sounds when long like *a* in *art*, or short as in *father*. The *e* long as *a* in *bale*, or short as *e* in *met*. The *i* long as *e* in *me*, and short as *i* in *pin*. The *u* long is sounded like *oo* in *noon*, and short as *u* in *full*. The consonants have pretty much the sounds of the usual English letters, except that *th* is always to be pronounced as *t*, the *h* being merely added to point out the derivation from *Tav*, whereas simply *t* is generally derived from *Teth*. *G* is always hard as *g* in *go*. *Z*, when derived from *Tzadé*, should of right be sounded as *ts*, or *tz*, which is the proper sound of Tzadé, otherwise it stands for *Zain*, which corresponds in sound with the English *z*, or *s* at the end of a syllable. The *Ayin*, not being readily represented by English letters, has been omitted, and occasionally only an apostrophe has been put in its place, thus *'Ütni.* *Ch* stands for the guttural *Cheth,* as in the Scotch *Loch,* and should, therefore, not be pronounced as *tsh,* the usual English sound, which is not found in Hebrew. Where a diphthong is marked with a diuresis, it should be pronounced as two syllables, thus *Seïr* read *say-eer,* &c. The final *e* should not be pronounced mute, but always as open *a,* thus *Bné,* like *Bnay.* The syllable *aim,* which occurs frequently at the end of a word, should be pronounced as *ah-yim;* and generally speaking, when two vowels come together, they should be divided into two syllables, though not marked as such; *Meir* as *May-eer, Beeroth* as *Be-airoth,* &c.

It is, however, next to impossible to convey accurately Hebrew sounds by the English alphabet; and these few directions are merely given to indicate the system I have pursued, and to give the reader some general idea of the proper pronunciation.

It would ill become me to speak much of the merit of a work on which I have been engaged for more than six months. But nevertheless, I hazard little in saying, that despite of some defects, it is one of the most useful books which have appeared for some time, and I trust that the learned author may reap from it all the benefits he so fondly anticipates. I have seldom deviated from his views, and it is only rarely that I added anything in text or note, or omitted a passage here and there. But nearly all such additions are enclosed in brackets, or marked TRANSLATOR, a privilege which the author granted me; and the omissions were only of some redundancies, not required for the understanding of the subject. The execution of the whole, in a mechanical point also, will no doubt give satisfaction, the more so, as the whole is the work of Jewish writers and artists, the drawings being executed by Mr. S. Shuster, a lithographer belonging to our nation, and whose work cannot fail to please. The maps alone are executed by non-Israelites; but they, as well as the printing, have received my own superintendence, and I have done all as faithfully as I was able. The publication has been undertaken by Mr. Hart, who is at the whole expense of it, and this is assurance enough that nothing has been omitted to do justice to the work.

It is to be hoped that this book may contribute to extend the knowledge of Palestine, and rouse many to study the rich treasures which our ancient literature affords, and also to enkindle sympathy and kind acts for those of our brothers, who still cling to the soil of our ancestors, and love the dust in which the many saints of our race sleep in death awaiting a glorious resurrection and an immortal life.

I. L.

Philadelphia, Tamuz 25th, 5610.

AUTHOR'S PREFACE.

An uncommon degree of interest has been excited in modern times towards Palestine, to an extent scarcely ever before attained. It issues forth, as it were, out of its devastation of more than eighteen centuries standing; and people seek to reanimate it through their investigations and discoveries. The learned contend for the prize of contributing the most to its elucidation by discovering and tracing out the vestiges of antiquity which it offers; and it is therefore constantly visited and travelled over by the well-informed of all nations. How much more ardently, then, must the erudite man belonging to the house of Israel feel on the subject! For should not Israel march in the advance, and serve in this matter as an example to other nations? or shall it, to whose ancestor God said (Gen. xiii. 15), "For the whole land which thou seest I will give unto thee and thy seed for ever," receive an account of its possessions—for its property the land remains, long as the time may be that its claim is not acknowledged, and its rights usurped by the hand of power—from the mouth of others?

As I now happened to live in contentment in the Holy City, this thought became the more active in me, since I had the opportunity to furnish much, more indeed than any other in this respect; because I was constantly on the spot, and had a knowledge of the languages which are necessary to carry on the discoveries and investigations, and was tolerably familiar with Hebrew literature, the most extensive and reliable source in this field of inquiry; and I was thus in a position which promised me much assistance in my labours.

I call Hebrew literature the most extensive and reliable source; and, in truth, it is this in every respect; and whoever cannot draw his information out of it in his investigations, must remain unacquainted with much, even the most interesting matter, and will therefore fail in his discoveries. It hence results, that, despite the sagacity of so many travellers, much has remained unknown; for instance, no one could hitherto indicate where to look for the Mount Hor, in Northern Palestine; Riblah, Kadesh-Barneä, Azmon, Katath, Nahallal, Shimron, Rakkath, &c.; since all the learned were unacquainted with the circumstance, that all these names were changed at a later period, as we see mentioned in Talmud Yerushalmi, and since the names into which they were changed are existing to this day. In this way, therefore, being able to draw from the source indicated, I have been permitted to discover nearly a hundred names which had hitherto remained unknown. It farther struck me, that we had no manual which could aid us in elucidating the book of Joshua, either in reading or teaching it; so that several chapters are almost left unread, and not explained in instructing. Farthermore, I found that several passages are incorrectly translated; and how, in good faith, can one expect from the learned of the West a correct explanation of the nature of the Orient? and who should feel more interested in the matter than one belonging to the house of Israel?

I therefore applied myself to compose a new geography, and I can freely flatter myself that this work does not resemble the many modern journals of the constantly augmenting visits to Palestine, in which are repeated, again and again, the old and already known facts, which are only dressed up with a somewhat changed fashion; but rarely do you find a new discovery, only some entertaining particulars, which have no value to the scholar; and all the author exhibits to the world is, that he too has travelled through the Holy Land. This work, however, is at the same time instructive, and may be viewed as a commentary on the geographical passages of the Bible, and by no means as a description of a journey of three or four months' duration,—but as the result of investigations and discoveries continued for many years with the greatest care, with many sacrifices, and not rarely with much personal danger.

I have likewise not lost sight of the labours of all preceding scholars; since I am acquainted with nearly all the works concerning

Palestine, from Flavius Josephus to the books of the most modern times; especially the celebrated work of Réland, who cites accurately the description of Palestine by Eusebius and Hieronymus.

I have also derived much information from the Arabic version of the celebrated Saadiah Gaon, edited at Constantinople in 5306 (1546), and the Persian version of Rabbi Jacob bar Joseph Tawas; likewise from another unknown edition of Saadiah of the whole Bible canon, all of which enabled me to elucidate several geographical names. I may say the same of the very rare work, Caphtore Vapherach, of Astori Pharchi, in which he gives a description of Palestine.

Having now undertaken to describe the geography of the Holy Land, it struck me that it might be advisable to give a brief account of the physical nature and history of the country, as also my studies with regard to many names beyond Palestine occurring in the Bible and Talmud, many of which are quite unknown, whilst others are shrouded in a great deal of obscurity; and I trust that I have rendered some little service in this department.

In conclusion, I cannot avoid blaming my fellow-Israelites for their neglect of this beautiful science, since they display so little interest in our country, even in a scientific point of view; and whilst they are so careful to instruct their children so accurately in the situation and nature of strange and distant lands, for instance Siberia, Australia, South Africa, &c., they appear ashamed to impart to them any information concerning Palestine and Jerusalem. But God has said: "I will heal thee again, and cure thy wounds, because they called thee the forsaken, and it is Zion for which no one careth." (Jeremiah xxx. 17.)

I, therefore, hope that my laborious efforts may attain their aim, by exciting interest and love for the Holy Land and its inhabitants, in the hearts of my brothers.

Jerusalem, in the month of Sivan, 5605.

ERRATA.

Page 17, 8th line from top, after "again," add "in Deut. xi. 24."
" 20, 13th " " for "ציני טור פרזלא" read "ציני הר ברזל."
" 24, 20th " " for "fol. 40, *a*," read "fol. 8, *a*."
" 29, 5th " " for "(King's spring)" read "(salt spring)."
" 32, 9th " bottom, for "Belad al Shem," read "al Sham."
" 34, 2d " " and other places, for "Dantura," read "Tantura."
" 34, 15th " " for "Persashath," read "Perashath."
" 36, 4th " " for "Merds," read "Merdj."
" 36, 1st " " and page 37, 3d line from top, for "Tukrath," read "Jukrath."
" 42, 9th " " for "the Great Sea," read "the Sea of Chams."
" 49, 1st, and 5th " for "Keifa," read "Cheifa."
" 51, 1st " top, and elsewhere, for "Ladschinin," read "Djinin."
" 51, 12th " " for "Al Pacha," read "Al Phacha."
" 55, 17th " bottom, for "Nakhara," read "Nakhura."
" 64, 7th " " for "Keber Mosheh," read "Musa."
" 64, 9th " top, for "Kaplar Saba," read "Kephar Saba."
" 65, 15th " bottom, for "of Chamas," read "Chamam."
" 78, 6th " top, for "Wady Saria," read "Sheria."
" 86, 9th " bottom, for "Mahmash," read "Maresha."
" 95, 7th " " for "Beth Chanin," read "Beth Chanina."
" 96, 15th " " for "of Zaba," read "of Zuba."
" 97, 14th " " for "Kirzi or," read "Kiryé a."
" 97, 4th " " for "east of the," read "south of the."
" 97, 12th " " for "Zaara," read "Zareah."
" 99, 11th " " for "קינא," read "קינה."
" 100, 15th " bottom, for "Muladah," read "Milh."
" 102, 5th " top, for "Zamea," read "Zanua."
" 116, 12th " bottom, for "Rashia," read "Rachia."
" 116, 7th " top, for "Kefar Sephuri," read "village of Suaphir."
" 117, 11th " " for "chap. 61," read "chap. 67."
" 131, 3d " bottom, for "Beth Naba," read "Beth Nuba."
" 136, 16th " " for "Karna," read "Karua."
" 151, 8th " " for "Salin," read "Salem."
" 151, 11th " " for "Pretha," read "Phretha."
" 157, 3d " " and next page, for "Adjar," read "Askar."
" 158, 8th " bottom, for "Al Sanin," read "Al Sania."
" 160, 16th " " for "Bir Namar," read "Bin Namr."
" 162, 2d " " for "Athlot," read "Athlit."
" 168, 13th " " for "Un al," read "Um al."

Page 169, 3d line from top, for "B. Shirian," read "Shiriin."

" 172, 10th " bottom, for "Kellah al," read "Kullat al."

" 172, 12th " " for "Simmiada," read "Simmaniada."

" 174, 6th " top, for "Feralthi," read "Ferathi."

" 177, 5th " " for "Jorephah," read "Jurpath."

" 178, 2d " " and elsewhere, for "Feradi," read "Ferathi."

" 179, 10th " " for "חלדון," read "חלזון."

" 179, 8th " bottom, for "אשתכא אשתכח," read "ומהכא אשתכח."

" 183, 9th " " for "Kudes," read "Kedes."

" 189, 10th " " for "of Mezobaia," read "of Zobaia."

" 189, 1st " top, for "מזגדל," read "מגדל."

" 189, 11th " " for "Vayichbach," read "Vayishlach."

" 194, 11th " bottom, for "אכזים," read "אכזיב."

" 196, 10th " " for "מצפרת," read "מצרפת."

" 197, 15th " top, for "R. Adimi," read "Abdimi."

" 200, 7th " bottom. The section beginning, "But it," &c., belongs to the next word, "Mazi."

" 205, 7th " " for "north of Jerusalem," read "south of J."

" 212, 17th " " for "Djab," read "Dehab."

" 215, 2d " " for "En Masrak," read "Mafrak."

" 230, 4th " " for "מעון," read "עמון."

" 230, 15th " " for "יעצר," read "יעזר."

" 235, 16th " top, for "of Armon," read "Admon."

" 236, 1st " bottom, for "בסנד," read "בסגר."

" 248, 4th " " for "דול," read "דוד."

" 269, 3d " " for "המערבי כותל," read "כותל המערבי."

" 274, 15th " top, for "הגדול," read "גדול."

" 288, 7th " " for "Akra," read "Akko."

" 289, 19th " " for "Konpud," read "Kanfut."

" 291, 6th " bottom, for "Zbe," read "Zaaba."

" 298, 1st " top, for "Fawas," read "Tawas."

" 298, 3d " " for "of Malacca," read "Malabar."

" 304, 11th " " for "Al Riman," read "Rimun."

" 305, 10th " bottom, for "Balul," read "Balut."

" 311, 16th " top, for "Djillan," read "Djilban."

" 311, 5th " bottom, for "Kafar," read "Kapar."

" 312, 10th " " for "Hindiv," read "Hindib."

" 312, 19th " top, for "Kulwasi," read "Kalwasi."

" 313, 7th " bottom, for "Kalaf," read "Kataf."

" 313, 5th " " for "Sartab," read "Sarnub."

" 314, 12th " top, for "Assar," read "Asfar."

" 315, 4th " " for "Pua," read "Phua."

" 315, 12th " bottom, for "Akul," read "Akub."

" 348, 13th " top, for "of the Mameluks," read "of the Greeks."

" 348, 19th " " for "Zoar," read "Zoan."

" 369, 8th " bottom, for "5071," read "5171."

" 391, 1st " top, for "1817," read "1819."

" 439, 15th " " for "Mushnem," read "Mushnun."

CONTENTS.

PART I.

CHAPTER I.

THE BOUNDARIES OF PALESTINE.

CHAPTER II.

EXPLANATION OF THE SEAS, RIVERS, MOUNTAINS, AND VALLEYS OF PALESTINE.

CHAPTER III.

A DESCRIPTION OF THE DIVISION OF PALESTINE ACCORDING TO THE TERRITORIES OF THE TWELVE TRIBES, AS GIVEN IN THE BOOK OF JOSHUA.

CHAPTER IV.

PALESTINE BEYOND JORDAN.

CHAPTER V.

JERUSALEM.

PART II.

OF THE PRODUCTS OF PALESTINE IN THE ANIMAL, THE VEGETABLE, AND MINERAL KINGDOMS.

CHAPTER I.

ANIMALS.

CHAPTER II.

THE VEGETABLE KINGDOM.

CHAPTER III.

MINERALS.

CHAPTER IV.

PART III.

A SHORT HISTORY OF PALESTINE.

ILLUSTRATIONS.

A DESCRIPTIVE

GEOGRAPHY OF PALESTINE.

PART I.

CHAPTER I.

THE BOUNDARIES OF PALESTINE.

It is difficult to determine, with any degree of accuracy, the former limits of Palestine, especially as there are apparently several contradictions in this respect in the holy Scriptures. For instance, it is said in Genesis xv. 18, "Unto thy seed have I given this land from the river of Egypt unto the great river, the river Euphrates." Again, in Exodus xxiii. 31, "and from the desert unto the river" (Euphrates); and again "from the river, the river Euphrates, even unto the uttermost sea shall your coast be." So, also, Joshua i. 4, "From the wilderness and this Lebanon, even unto the great river, the river Euphrates, and all the land of the Hittites, and unto the great sea toward the going down of the sun, shall be your coast." In Numbers xxxiv., however, where the precise boundary of Palestine is laid down by divine authority, we do not find that it was to extend from the Red Sea to the Euphrates; the most southerly points are עצמן Azmon, and קדש ברנע Kadesh-Barnea, and the most northerly, the Mount Hor הר ההר, and no mention is made of the Red Sea on the one or the Euphrates on the other side.

To reconcile this contradiction, I would offer the following suggestion: The promise of the extended boundary of Palestine is only a future prediction, and merely a reward held out in case the Israelites would live according to the will and the commandments of God, in which case they should become powerful, and so numerous that they should be compelled by their large population, gradually to extend their boundaries to the widest given limits; as we read in Exodus xxiii. 30, 31: "By little and little I will drive them out before thee, until thou be increased and inherit the land; and I will set thy bounds from the Red Sea unto the sea of the Philistines, and from the desert unto the river." The Red Sea and the Euphrates are accordingly indicated as the utmost points, which the Israelites should acquire in their most flourishing condition. But when their boundaries were fixed for them at their first entrance into Palestine (Numbers xxxiv.), these were determined in due proportion to their numbers, their population; because from the paucity of their numerical strength they were not able to take possession of, to inhabit, and to people fully the wide extent of land from the Red Sea to the Euphrates, which points should become the boundaries* of their country at a later period, when their population had sufficiently increased; and, indeed, under the reign of David and Solomon (and afterwards under Herod) the boundaries of Palestine extended thus far, although only for a very short period. But when the Israelites were, at a later period, through the mercy of God, permitted to

* To this, likewise, refers the passage of Deuteronomy xix. 8, 9, "And if the Lord thy God enlarge thy coast as he hath sworn unto thy fathers, and give thee *all the land* which he promised to give unto thy fathers: then shalt thou add three cities more for thee (for cities of refuge) besides these three," which would, accordingly give us nine such cities, to wit, three east of Jordan, three in Palestine proper, and three in the new territory between that and the Euphrates.

return to their former country from their exile to Babylon by the permission of Cyrus (כורש) King of Persia, after Palestine had been a desolate waste for seventy years, they were not able to take possession of the whole of the land after its former dimensions; but the small number of the returning exiles were only empowered to occupy a small portion of Palestine, which accordingly was comprised within narrower and different limits from any of the preceding ones. We have, accordingly, *three* different boundaries of the land of Israel at three different periods.

I. The promised limits from the Red Sea to the Euphrates.

II. Those of the conquest by Joshua from Azmon and Kadesh-Barnea at the south, to Hazar-Enan and the Mount Hor at the north, as they are described in Numbers xxxiv.

III. Those which were established when the Israelites returned from their exile under Ezra and Nehemiah, when the most northern points of their possessions were Chezib and Akko,* as I shall show more particularly hereafter.

* This will explain for us the passage in Shebiith vi. § 1 (as also Challah iv. § 8), which says that there are three different districts with reference to the laws relating to the seventh or release year, when in Palestine proper it was not permitted to sow or to reap. The country, taken possession of by the returning exiles, is given as to Chezib, whereas that conquered by Joshua is described from Chezib to the river, and from the same point to Amana, אמנה, which, according to my view, is as follows: the Chezib here mentioned, is the Achzib of Joshua xix. 29, or the village three hours (about 8 miles) distance north of Akko, now called Al Zib. Amanah is the Mount Hor, the most northerly point of Palestine, of which I shall speak more circumstantially hereafter. The *river* here spoken of cannot be easily determined. For it is not possible that the Euphrates is here understood, since, as already said, the Israelites under Joshua never penetrated that far, wherefore it cannot be taken as the boundary of their possessions. Maimonides, and the author of the

EXPLANATION OF THE BOUNDARIES OF PALESTINE,

After Numbers xxxiv. 3, &c.

"Then your south quarter shall be from the wilderness of Zin, along by the coast of Edom, and your south border shall be the utmost coast of the Salt Sea, eastward; and your border shall turn from the south to the ascent of Akrabbim, and pass on to Zin, and the going forth thereof shall be from the south of Kadesh-Barnea, and shall go on to Hazar-adar, and pass on to Azmon; and the border shall fetch a compass from Azmon unto the river of Egypt, and the goings out of it shall be at the sea."

ZIN. צין

The Targum Jonathan (יונתן בן עוזיאל) explains צין as meaning ציני טור פרזלא *Tzinay Tur Parzela,* i. e. "the iron mountain." Now, in Mishna Sukka, chapter iii. § 1 ציני טור פרזלא refers to an uncommonly close, strong,

Kaphtor Vapherach think it to be the Wady al Arish (see farther down concerning the River of Egypt נחל מצרים); but this stream is at the southwest corner, and here reference is made to a northern point. But it appears to me that the river spoken of here is the Pharpar of 2 Kings v. 12; in Arabic Fidjeh, which takes its course from the village *Dar Kanon,* which I suppose to be identical with Chazar-Enan, for Chazor is in Arabic Dar "dwelling;" Enan is easily corrupted into Kanon; the place, therefore, is the most northeasterly of Palestine proper (Numbers xxxiv. 9). Now this little stream runs from the north to the south, and forms measurably the northeastern boundary of the land of Israel, and as the Amanah is the northwestern, so is the Pharpar or Fidjeh, the northeastern limit.

The passage in Gittin, fol. 8 *a,* "How far does Palestine extend? from Amanah southward, belongs to Palestine, from that point northward, does not belong to it," refers, according to my opinion, to the country conquered by Joshua; but where the boundary points are given by *Achzib, Zib,* and *Akko,* I take the same to refer to the boundaries of the returned exiles under *Ezra.*

and hard species of palms;* the meaning, therefore, in this passage is "The wilderness of Zin, in the direction of the hard palm country," a well-known place of the desert, where this species of hard palms grew. We also find mention made at the end of Tractate *Yebamoth*, that the town of Zoar is called the "City of Palms;" the same occurs in Tosefta Shebiith, chapter vii., and in Talmud Pesachim, fol. 53 *a*. It appears, therefore, to me that חצצון תמר Chazezon-Tamar† (Gen. xiv. 7) is the City of Palms, Zoar, situated in that neighbourhood (see farther down En Gedi, עין גדי). At the southwestern termination of the Dead Sea is found a salt mountain about 150 feet high, which extends about five miles in a northerly direction, and is called in Arabic *Uzdum*. At the northern end of this mountain, is a narrow pass, in the neighbourhood of which there are ruins called *Zuari* in Arabic. To me there appears no doubt that Uzdum is derived from the ancient Sodom, and Zuari from Zoar. In Pesachim fol. 93 *b*, the distance from Zoar to Sodom, is stated as five *mill*, say in the neighbourhood of four English miles. But it is ascertained that the ancient Sodom did actually stand four English miles from the ruins of Zuari.‡ I take this pass to be "the Valley of Salt" of 2 Samuel viii. 13.

* See Rashi's exposition of צינייתא in Sanhedrin, fol. 96 *b*.

† Perhaps the Tamar of Ezekiel xlvii. 19, is the above mentioned Zoar, the City of Palms, also called Palmyra, not as *Ir hattemarim*, in Deuteronomy xxxiv. 3, is taken by many commentators for Jericho יריחו.

‡ I am, however, somewhat in doubt concerning the true position of Zoar; because, in Jeremiah xlviii. 34, Zoar is reckoned among the cities of Moab; it must, therefore, be in the Moabite country, and not on the west side of the Dead Sea. I am, therefore, induced to suggest that there were two towns bearing the name of Zoar. The village Safia, on the eastern shore of the Dead Sea, and consequently in the country of Moab, was, according to a certain tradition, formerly called Zoar, and this appears actually to be the town of this name mentioned as belonging to Moab.

Zoar is also called the "City of Salt," in Joshua xv. 62, on account of the salt mountain in its vicinity. In this mountain also must the pillar of salt (Lot's Wife) be sought for. Upon the whole, I take the entire country of the southwest portion of the Dead Sea, called in Arabic "Saideiyeh," to be that part of the desert called the Wilderness of Zin.

THE ASCENT OF AKRABBIM מעלה עקרבים

Means literally the ascent of Scorpions, so to say, a most dangerous hill. The celebrated Saadiah renders it, in his Arabic translation of the Scriptures, *Ali Akbah Akrabin*, i. e. or the country of Akbah Akrabin. The Arabs call the eastern bay of the Red Sea, Bachr Akabah; also the entire valley, from the Dead to the Red Sea, they call ערבה Araba, Al Gor, also Akabah (see farther down, art. Kikkar Hayarden ככר הירדן). It is therefore to be presumed that this ascent of Akrabbim must be sought for in this valley. And, in truth, westward from the village Chansiri, on the edge of Al Gor, not far from the Wady Kurahy, there is a fearfully high and precipitous rocky acclivity, which to pass is extremely dangerous; and I suppose this to be the Ascent of Akrabbim, here mentioned.*

The boundary line, therefore, tends eastwardly to the hill of Akrabbim, which is eastward from Zin, by which is explained, "And your south border shall be to the outmost coast of the Salt Sea *eastward*."

* I explain Judges i. 36, וגבול האמרי ממעלה עקרבים מהסלע ומעלה "And the coast of the Amorite was from the going up of Akrabbim, from the rock and upward," to refer to the city Selah, mentioned in 2 Kings xiv. 7, which was also called Joktheel, and at a later period Petra, and which is also found in this Al Gor; and this leads us to place the ascent of Akrabbim northward of Selah or Petra.

KADESH-BARNEA. קדש ברנע

No geographer or traveller has hitherto succeeded to discover a trace of this place. But I believe that, through means of our own literary treasures, I shall be able to throw some light on this obscure name, so that it will be possible to fix its position with some degree of certainty.

Our commentators Onkelos, Jonathan, and the Targum Yerushalmi, all translate Kadesh-Barnea with רקם גיעא *Rekam Gaya*. In this connexion I have also discovered that the Wady al Arish (see farther down, under *Nachal Mitzrayim* נחל מצרים), unites eastwardly with another Wady, which the Arabs call Wady Abiat (White Valley), or Wady Gaian. Another Wady, called by them Wady Bierin, is connected on the southeast with the Wady Gaian. I have scarcely any doubt but that the name of Gaian is derived from the ancient Rekam Gaya, and that Bierin is derived from the ancient Barnea; although the Arabs believe that this name is applied to the Wady because there are found in it several wells. I therefore believe that the true position of Kadesh-Barnea is to be found at the point where the Wadys Gaian and Bierin unite; and this is about 45 English miles south of Gazza.

AZMON עצמן

Is likewise unknown; still I find that Jonathan translates it with קסם *Kessam*. Now about 22 English miles southeasterly of the Wady Bierin is the Wady Kiseimi, and there is no doubt that Azmon must have stood formerly in this Wady, and was called at a later period, for instance in the time of Jonathan, by the name of Kessam.

THE RIVER OF EGYPT (NACHAL MITZRAYIM) נחל מצרים

Jonathan renders this with *Nilos*.* This, however, appears to me not to be the stream indicated, for Palestine never extended to the Nile. The more correct view is that given in Saadiah's translation, Wady al Arish, which has a northwesterly course, and falls into the Mediterranean, near the village of Al Arish, the ancient Rhinocolura.

"And this shall be your north border, from the great sea ye shall point out to you Mount Hor." (Numb. xxxiv. 7.)

The Mount Hor, הר ההר . אמנה . אמנים . טור אמנן . טוורוס אומנים . טוורוס מנוס Amanah, Amanim, Tur Amnon, Tavros Umanis, and Tavros Manis, are the different names applied to this celebrated mount. In the Song of Solomon, iv. 8, it is called Amanah; Jonathan calls it Tavros Umanis; the Yerushalmi calls it Tavros Manis, and in Talmud and Midrash it bears the name of Tur Amnon, or Amanim. It appears from Talmud Babli, Gittin, fol. 40 *a*, and T. Yerushalmi, Shebiith, chap. vi., that this mount was on the coast of the Mediterranean, and that on its summit was a town called Kapladia. We also learn from Joshua xiii. 5, that the whole mountain of Lebanon, together with the country of the Giblites (ארץ הגבלי), afterwards called Biblus, must be contained within the northern boundary of Palestine, since these districts are enumerated among the yet unconquered parts of the country. We must, therefore, seek for a point north of the Lebanon as the true site of the Mount Hor, the

* But the "Shichor which is before Egypt" (Joshua xiii. 3), is, according to my opinion, actually the Nile; because Shichor literally means the Black, which is most likely applied to the Nile, because it comes from the country of the Æthiopians, the black race known to the ancients.

northernmost boundary of Palestine. Now I found that, south of Tripoli, the Trablos al Sham, on the coast there is a promontory which runs into the sea, called in Arabic Ras al Shaka, or, during the period of the Greek domination, Theuprosopon. On this promontory is a high mountain, called Djebel Nuria, on which is the village Kalpadia, which I take to be identical with the above Kapladia, having the present appellation by a simple transposition of the p and l, a thing very common among the Arabs; as they call, for instance, שפרעם Shafram, שפעמר Shafamr. East of this mountain is the small town *Amiun*, also called Kalmiun, which I take to bear some resemblance to the former Amanah, and am certain that the Mount Nuria is identical with the ancient Hor.

"From Mount Hor ye shall point out your border unto the entrance of Hamath, and the going forth of the border shall be to Zedad." (Ib. v. 8.)

ENTRANCE OF HAMATH. לבא חמת

We find this designation often given as the northern boundary, or the northern terminus of Palestine; e. g. Numb. xiii. 21, 2 Kings xiv. 25, 2 Chron. vii. 8. It appears to me that this must be a natural boundary; and I suppose this to be Coelesyria, and means the "way which leads to Hamath;" and the road which goes to the land of Hamath actually is through the great valley which lies between the Lebanon and Anti-Lebanon. The Arabs call it Al Bakaa, which means "the valley," "the hollow;" the southern portion they call Al Bakaa tachtani, the lower valley, and the northern part Al Bakaa foki, or the upper valley; and this extends to the neighbourhood of *Hams*, and the other to the neighbourhood of Sur, Zor, or Tyre. As in the passage in question it is given as the northern boundary, the northern valley is naturally understood; but in Numb. xiii. 21, reference is made to the southern part.*

ZEDAD. צדד

In the just mentioned great valley of Coelesyria, eastward of Tripoli, is found a village, called by the Arabs Al Djededa; I believe that the ancient name of Zedad has given rise to this modern appellation.†

"And the border shall go on to Ziphron, and the goings

* The Talmud, as well as all the other commentators, explain "the entrance of Hamath" with Antiochia, or Daphné, דפני של אנטיוכיא; so also they explain Riblah, in the land of Hamath (Jer. lii. 27), with Daphné. In itself is Daphné of mythological origin. A certain nymph bore this name; and not far from Antiochia was a temple of Daphné, where there was also a laurel-grove consecrated to her. Prior to this was at this place a summer palace of Nebuchadnezzar. To this day there is a village seven English miles south of Antiochia, called Beth Alma, which means "maiden's house," so called from the fact that the above Daphné temple stood here formerly. Now whereas Antiochia was the most important city of that neighbourhood, the whole country is designated and called after it, and the land of Hamath is therefore mentioned in the Talmud by the name of Antiochia, or the temple of Daphné in its immediate vicinity.

† In Targum Jonathan are given to this passage, as an explanation, several places, the remains of which still exist. These are, לכדכור דבר זעמה ולכדכור (ולכרכוי) דבר סניגורא ודווקינוס ותרנגולא עד קסרין In this, I believe, several errors of transcribers have to be corrected: in place of כדכור (Kadkor), it should read כרכה Karakah,[a] which means *fort, castle, palace;* and to this day there are found traces of the castle of Sanigura, and the Arabs call the ruins Kallath al Sani, but to the whole district they give the name of Sagura, and it is eastward of Akko, at a distance of about 7½ English miles. So also by כרכה דבר זעמה is probably understood the old castle Kallath Saamah, situated on the Ras Abiath (the white promontory), about 7½ English miles south of Tyre. Tarnegola is the Greek *Ornithon;* Josephus calls it *Gabar,* and all these names signify the *cock.* I suppose that a temple of the idol Nergal (2 Kings xvii. 30), the god of the Cuthians, who, according to the Talmud Sanhedrin, was

[a] My copy of Jonathan reads, in fact, in one place כרכוי Karkoy, as indicated in the parenthesis.—TRANSLATOR.

out shall be at Hazar-Enan, this shall be your north border."

ZIPHRON. זפרון

Northeasterly of Damascus is a high mount called Djebl Sefira, which name I suppose to be derived from Ziphron, wherefore it is likely that the town in question must have been near this mount.

HAZAR-ENAN. חצר עינן

From Ezekiel xlvii. 17, we should conclude that Hazar-Enan must be not far from Damascus; and actually north-westerly from this place, at a distance of about 25 English miles, in the vicinity of the sources of the Pharpar (2 Kings v. 12), which the Arabs call Fidji, is the village of Dar Kanon. I take that Dar Kanon may be put for Dar Anon, because the Hebrew Hazar is the Arabic Dar, dwelling, and that Dar Anon is actually the Hazar-Enan. Perhaps the name of עינן Enan is derived from עין spring, from the fact that the source of the Pharpar is close to it, whence then the name Hazar-Enan, "the spring town."

"And you shall point out your east border from Hazar-Enan to Shepham." (Ib. vi. 10.)

SHEPHAM. שפם

Jonathan and Targum Yerushalmi explain this with Apamyam or Aphmia, which is Banias, not far from the ancient Laish or Dan. (According to Josephus, Banias was situated 3¾ English miles east of Laish.) Here is the cave of Banias, out of which the Jordan issues (see

represented as a cock, once stood here. According to Josephus (Antiquities, book xvii., § 17), the Samaritans (Cuthians) are of Zidonian origin; wherefore I conclude that this city in the vicinity of Zidon was devoted to Nergal; and hence its name of Tarnegola, Ornithon, or Gabar.—Kalkai is in the Lebanon (which see, art. Akluk).

farther down, art. Jordan.) The name of Banias is, properly speaking, of mythological origin, namely, from the Greek *Pan*, as it appears also, from inscriptions in said cave, that it was dedicated to the god Pan (see farther down, in art. Baal Gad).

"And the coast shall go down from Shepham to Riblah, on the east side of Ain; and the border shall descend, and shall reach unto the side of the sea of Chinnereth eastward; and the border shall go down to Jordan, and the goings out of it shall be at the salt sea." (Numb. xxxiv. 11, 12).

RIBLAH. רבלה

Jonathan, Targum Yerushalmi, and Saadiah all render Riblah with Daphné; and I have already said that Daphné is near Antiochia, and that the Riblah in the land of Hamath is thus correctly rendered, and not the Riblah in the neighbourhood of Banias, which Josephus several times mentions as a Daphné being near the sea of Semechonitis. I made frequent inquiries, to ascertain whether I could not find a trace of this Daphné; when at length I ascertained that there dwells on the western shore of said sea a tribe of Arabs, called the Dufni Arabs. I inquired concerning the meaning of this name, but no one could give me any satisfactory account. But there can be no doubt that this name is derived from the ancient Daphné, which must have stood where this Arab tribe have taken up their abode. Still I am not able to say whether the origin of this Daphné is likewise to be sought for in mythology or not. At least this much appears certain, that there were two places by name of Riblah, the one in the land of Hamath, the other near Banias, and that both were also known as Daphné; wherefore the former is always designated as *Riblah in the land of Hamath*. (2 Kings xxv. 21; Jer. xxxix. 5; ibid. lii. 9.)

AIN. עין

Josephus states that, between Kedesh (which see), and the sea Semechonitis, there was a city called Biri, near which was a large spring. Even at the present time this spring still exists, and the Arabs call it Ein al Malcha (king's spring); which then gives us the result that Daphné or Riblah must be eastward thereof, which then again correctly explains "Riblah on the east side of Ain."*

The boundary line of Palestine at the east was the Jordan, and the Dead Sea at the south; after the line had run somewhat southeast of this sea, to wit, to the ascent of the Akrabbim, it ran westward over the mount now called Djebl Madura, which is between the southern termination of the Dead Sea and the Wady Gaian (Kadesh-Barnea), and is probably the Mount Halak "Bald Mountain," in the land of Seir, mentioned in Joshua xi. 17; then on to Wady Gaian, Wady Bierin, Wady Kiseimi and Wady al Arish to the Mediterranean Sea, which was the western boundary line. The northern boundary was over Ras al Shaka and Djebl Nuria, then eastward through the great valley of Coelesyria towards Al Djededa, then somewhat southeasterly through the mountain

* I must notice a few errors in Jonathan. The cave of כניאס "Senias," should be *Panias;* אבלו ודמוכו should be דמעכה (1 Chron. xix. 6). In Targum Yerushalmi the following corrections should be made: מערביא מדירת עיינותא "westward of Hazar-Enan," should be מדינחא "eastward;" דגינוסר מן מערבא "west of Chinnereth," should be מן מדינחא "eastward;" דימין צפון should be די מן; טור תלגא דקיסריון should be תרנגולה דקיסריון; מערב דן should be מערת. I explain טרכון זמרא to be identical with the kings of Zimri, of Jeremiah xxv. 25, and Zimran (Gen. xxv. 2), as the father of the tribe. Josephus B. J. book iii. ch. 3, reads *Simniti,* which is evidently an error, and should be Simriti. The English translation of this passage, *Silbonites,* is also incorrect. שוקמזיי Shokmezay, is certainly the village Shikmoski, east of the sea of Tiberias, at the distance of about 15 English miles on the road to Damascus.

of Sefira, from there to the village Dar Kanon, then southerly to the village Banias, over the western shore of the sea Semechonitis to the Jordan. The southernmost points of the boundary are the Wady Bierin and Wady Kiseimi; the most northern, Ras al Shaka and Al Djededa. Palestine extends in latitude about 3½ degrees, but the longitude is uneven; at the north and south it is more than 1½ degrees, whereas in the centre, scarcely more than ½ a degree. I calculate the whole superficial space to be no more than about 600* German square miles; and if one wishes to form a square of this, it would give us only one of no more than 24½ German, or 122½ English miles.

Although the northern boundary of Palestine extended to Mount Hor, Joshua did not, for all that, take possession of the land thus far; the most northern point of his conquest was Baal Gad, which is Banias; but the whole

* I deem it my duty to explain here a most difficult passage in the Talmud, which gives the extent of Palestine. We find in Tractate Megillah, fol. 3 *a*, Sota, 49 *b*; Baba Kama, fol. 82 *b*, and Menachoth, fol. 64 *b*, that Palestine had a superficial extent of ת' פרסא על ת' פרסא a square of four hundred Parsa in breadth and length, which would make 160,000 square Parsas; each Parsa of the Talmud is, however, 3 English miles, which would then give us, 1,440,000 English square miles, which would take in more than 17 degrees of longitude and latitude, which would, therefore, extend Palestine to the Persian and Russian empires, which, in good truth, would necessarily appear too ridiculous to be entertained by the Talmudic writers. I took a great deal of pains to unravel this riddle, and I found that all these passages do not say that Palestine had actually the above extravagant extent, but only ונזדעזעה א"י ת' פרסא על ת' פרסא, which means that Palestine was shaken by an earthquake extending to four hundred Parsas, which may mean that the trembling was felt to that distance, which is actually often the case in earthquakes that they are perceived thus far, which was exemplified in the year 5597 (1837) that the earthquake which destroyed Zafed and Tiberias was felt in Bagdad and Vienna. But that the Talmudists could not have meant to assert that Palestine was actually as large is proved from Talmud Yerushalmi Taanith iv. 5, where it says that Palestine was only 40 by 40

country of Mount Lebanon,* and the land of the Giblim (Biblus) up to Mount Hor was not occupied at that time. It appears to me, likewise, that Joshua divided among the tribes only that portion of the country which had been taken possession of already, but not what was yet to be conquered, that is, only as far as Zidon and Dan. And we actually do not find among the towns of Asher and Naphtali, any more northerly than these places; so also we find among the thirty-one kings of the 12th of Joshua, none more northerly than Kedesh and Chazor. It appears, therefore, that the country north of Zidon, was for a long time not inhabited by the Israelites; in proof of which, I refer to 2 Samuel xxiv. 6, where we read that Joab, on being ordered by David to number the people, and when he for this purpose travelled through the whole country, only reached as far as Zidon and Dan, but we find no trace that he extended his journey north beyond these points. These are clear proofs that the Israelites had only conquered the land up to Zidon, although the actual boundary line extended much farther north. It was only at a later period that this

Parsas, and this corresponds exactly with my computation, since 40 Parsas are nearly 122½ English miles.

As farther proof that the assertion of the extent of 400 Parsas is by no means to be taken in a literal sense, I will mention that it occurs in *twelve* different passages, which argues that it represents an immensely great distance and nothing else. The passages are: 1. Pesachim, 95 *a*; 2. Yoma, 96 *b*; 3. Gittin, 68 *b*; 4. Kidushin, 40 *a*; 5. Ketuboth, 111 *a*; 6. Sanhedrin, 95 *b*; 7. Abodah Zarah, 17 *b*; 8. Chulin, 95 *b*; 9. Zohar Pinechas, 233 *a*; 10. Zohar Shemoth, 18 *a*; 11. Yalkut Echa Rabbethi i. 1; 12. In Piyut of Parashath Zachor, taken from Mechiltha, to Exodus xvii. 8. Now, as it is impossible that all these measurements should signify the precise extent of 400 Parsas, it follows that, as said, they denote merely a great and unknown extent.

* See Chulin, fol. 60 *b*; Senir or Sirion are mountains of Israel, wherefore the Anti-Lebanon mountains are properly reckoned to Palestine, although they are situated to the north of Dan and Zidon.

northern portion was conquered and occupied by the Israelites.

SURIA. סוריא

Under this name, which so often occurs in Talmud and Midrashim, we understand all those countries which King David had conquered beyond the boundaries of Palestine. They are considered, in some respects, equal to Palestine; in others, however, as foreign countries. (See Gittin.) The chief portion of these possessions is the country of

ARAM. ארם

This is divided into five different districts or divisions, which are

I. ארם נהרים Aram Naharayim (Genesis xxiv. 10), Mesopotamia, between the Tigris and Euphrates, and is called מאספיטמיא in Bereshith Rabba, chapter 31, and Al Djisré, the island, because it is enclosed between the two rivers just mentioned. It is also called (Genesis xxviii. 5) Padan Aram. In this district is yet the city of Ur, the birth-place of Abraham, and people point out the spot where the lime-kiln stood into which Nimrod is said to have ordered the patriarch to be cast when he made light of his idols. (See farther down, article Ur.)

II. ארם דמשק Aram Damascus (2 Samuel viii. 6) is called in Arabic Belad al Shem, after Shem, the son of Noah, whom tradition alleges to have built the city.

III. ארם צובה Aram Zobah (2 Samuel x. 8); this is the present Syria proper beyond Palestine. The city of Aleppo is called by our brothers, according to tradition, Aram Zobah, because it is alleged that the residence of the king of the country was in this city. The fort of this place and the Jewish Synagogue likewise, are evidently the remains out of the highest antiquity. This

BOUNDARY OF
PALESTINE
According to
NUMBERS XXXIV.1-15
BY
RABBI JOSEPH SCHWARZ,
of Jerusalem.
5607.
5610.
MEDITERRANEAN SEA
(OR THE GREAT SEA)
Trablos
Djedada Zedod
Thea-prosopon
Hor Hahar
Ras al Shaka
Amiun
Makmal
Baalbek
Djebl Sefira
Ziphron
Beirut
LEBANON
COELESYRIA
Dar Anon
Hazar Enan
Damascus
Bachr Murdj
ZIDON
Hermon or
Dj. Scheich
ZOR
Dj. Heish
the ladder of Tyre
Nakura
Kedes
Riblah
Sea of Merom
Zafed
Sea of Tiberias
Tiberias
Zara Zohar
HAURAN
Kelb Hauran
Kishon
Dj. Tur
or Tabor
W. Yurmuk
Adraa or
Edrei
Tantura
Caesarea
W. Krit
Salchad
or Salchah
Buzra or
Bozrah
Ramathaim
Zophim
Sebaste
Nablus
W. Kazab
Kanah
Gerizzim
Antipatris
W. Zirka Jabbok
JAFFA
Siloh
Lod
Ramle
Mizpah
Bethel
Jericho
R. Jordan
Aman
Rabbath Ammon
Hesban Cheshbon
Jabne
JERUSALEM
Beth Lehem
ASHKELON
Beth Djibrin
HEBRON
Dead Sea
W. Modjeb Arnon
GAZZA
W. Sheria
Juta
Rabbah
Rafia
Moladah
Kerak
Zuari
Ziph
Ascent of
Akrabim
Tafila or
Tophel
Djebl Madura
W. Abiat, Gaian or Kadesh
Wady al Arish
Nachal Mizraim
Buseirah Bozrah
34° 30 35° 30 36° 30
34° 30 33° 30 32° 30 31°

district was likewise called the land of *Hamath;* its Arabic name is Al Chadshass, and extends from Palmyra to Antiochia.*

(In an Arabic translation of the Scriptures, not that of the celebrated Saadiah, I found in the passage cited, Zobah given by Nezibin, which is the Nizibus beyond Euphrates; but I deem this exposition not well founded, because Zobah did not extend that far.)

These three districts were beyond Palestine proper; the two next following were within the boundary line, and considered a portion of the land of Israel.

IV. ארם בית רחוב Aram Beth Rechob (2 Samuel x. 6) is Coelesyria, and extended southward to the Wady Chasmeia. The celebrated Baal-bek is in this district, and many sections of it are now inhabited by the Druses.

V. ארם מעכה Aram Maachah (1 Chronicles xix. 6), lies east of Beth Rechob, and the snow-covered mountain of Hermon is found here. The town of Chasbeya (which see) and Abel Beth Maachah (see 1 Kings xv. 20, also called Abel Mayim, 2 Chronicles xvi. 4), belonged to this part of Aram.

THE BOUNDARY OF PALESTINE AFTER THE EXILE UNDER EZRA AND NEHEMIAH.

In Talmud Yerushalmi, Shebiith, chapter vi., occurs the following, as descriptive of the boundaries of Palestine occupied by the exiles returning from Babylon:

תחומי ארץ ישראל כל שהחזיקו עולי בבל · פרשת חומת ·
מגדל שיר ושיני דרור ושורא דעכו וקצירא דגלילא וכברתה
ובית זניתה וקובעיא ומילת׳ דביר וכוריי רבת׳ תפנים וסנפתה
ומחרתא דייתיר וממציא דאבהתא וראש מי געתון וגעתון
עצמה מי ספר ומרחשת ומגדל חרוב ואולם רבתי ונוקבת׳

* Zobah is probably the Syria *Zabal,* Mesopotamia, Apamia, mentioned in Judith iii. 1–12. [Not according to my copy.—TRANSLATOR.]

דעיון ותוקרת כרכה רבה דבר סנגרא ותרנגולא עילא' דלמעלה מן קסרין ותרכונה דמתחם לבוצרה ומלח דזרבאיי ונמרין ובית סכל וקנת ורפיח דחגרא ודרך הגדולה ההולכת למדבר חשבון ויבקא ונחלא דזרך ויגר סהדותא ורקם דגיעה וגני' דאשקלון:

A similar description is given in Siphri, section Ekeb, and Tosephtah Shebiith, chapter vi., with some divergencies, some of which are evidently errors of the transcribers, and additions, which I shall explain as far as possible.

However uninteresting this passage may appear, still it must be of importance to the learned; since by this means we shall be able to determine the boundaries and extent of Palestine at the period of its re-occupation by the Israelites under Ezra. The learned Reland quoted this passage from the Talmud Yerushalmi, but could give no satisfactory exposition of it, much as he was desirous of doing so. I, however, believe that I can explain it with tolerable accuracy, and trace the names here given.

פרשת חומת *Persashath Chomath* is evidently an improper method of writing the name of the place indicated, and should be חמת Chamath (Hamath), and, therefore, Persashath Chamath, the same as the entrance to Hamath לבוא חמת (which see), or the road which leads to the great valley of Coelesyria. In the Talmud, the phrase פרשת דרכים (Perashath Derachim) means the public highway, or cross-road; and I have already stated that this road runs southward through the valley to צור or Tyre.

מגדל שיד *The Tower of Shid.* The town of Cæsarea in Palestine is also called Shid; here, therefore, the tower of Strato. See, however, for a farther explanation, under *Ekron*, in the land of the Philistines.

שיני דרור *Shinay Deror*, should be דדור Dedor, or the fortress, the walls of Dor, now called Dantura, or Dartura (see article Dor). The word שיני *teeth,* expresses the salient points of the bastions of a fortress.

שורא דעכו *Shura Deakko,* is the wall or circumvallation of Akko. (שורא is the Hebrew שור wall; see Gen. xlix. 22.)

קצירא דגלילא *Kezira Degalila,* is the town of Kazra in Galilee. (See גבתון Gibthon, and קצרה Kazra.)

כברתה *Kabartha,* is 2½ English miles west of Shafamer (שפרעם), and is a village bearing the same name at this day.

בית זניתה *Beth Zenita.* I would prefer reading זויתה *Zevita,* which would give us the ancient Suite, 15 mill from Tiberias, destroyed by the Nazarenes in the year 4942, A. M., or 1182 C. E.

קובעיא *Kubeaya,* is north of Zafed, in the vicinity of Gish (גוש חלב), and is the village Kubea of the present day.

מילתא דביר *Miltha Debir.* Miltha, in the Chaldean, signifies *rampart, mound,* Hebrew סוללה; therefore the fortification of the town ביר Bir, which is no doubt the village Biri in the neighbourhood of Zafed.

כוריי רבתי *Kuryee Rabbethi,* perhaps בירי Great Biri. Josephus makes mention of a large town, called Biri, near the sea Semechonitis, מי מרום, the Waters of Merom, where Joshua defeated the Canaanites. (Josh. xi. 5.)—It appears to me, however, as more likely, that in place of a town, the lake or sea itself is meant, as Kuree in the Chaldean signifies a sea; therefore the Great Semechonitis, if my hypothesis be correct.

תפנים *Taphnis,* doubtlessly means Daphné, on the west shore of this lake. (See above, art. Riblah.)

מחרתא דיתיר *Macharta Deyathir,* is unknown to me.

ממציא דאבהתא *Mamzi Deabhatha,* is the village Abathia, not far from the southwestern shore of the sea of Tiberias. Mamzi means literally the way, the road, that which causes to find, which leads, or here the road to Abhatha, or Abathia.

ראש מי געתון וגעתון עצמה. *The head of the waters of Gaaton, and Gaaton itself.* I am fully persuaded that the ancient מי מגדו Mé (waters of) Megiddo, were at a later period called געתון Gaaton; therefore here the source of the waters of Megiddo, and the town Megiddo itself. (See also farther down, art. Megiddo.)

מי ספר *Mé Sepher*, would be in Chaldean the same as *coast-land;* probably, therefore, near Carmel, in the neighbourhood of Megiddo, or Gaaton.

מרחשת *Marchesheth*, in Siphri, is thus written מרעשת. *Maresheth*, is the village Marases (see מרוז Meroz), 2½ English miles northeast from Bethshean.

מגדל חרוב *The Tower of Charub.* Eastward from the sea of Tiberias is a village Kefer Charub; and near it is another by name of Megdel (Hebrew Migdal, tower). In Midrash Echah, fol. 71, col. *c*, is mentioned a place called Kafar Charub; and in the Life of Josephus, p. 524, we find Charaba in Upper Galilee.

אולם רבתי *The Great Ulan*, is the village Ulama, 5 English miles south from the above-named Abathia. It is true that we often find an Ulama mentioned in the Books of the Maccabees, as belonging to the fortified places of Gilead. Perhaps one was called the Great, the other the Little Ulama; but we cannot ascertain which of the two is meant here.

נוקבתא דעיון *Nukbetha De-iyon*, is perhaps the town עיון Ijon, of 2 Kings xv. 29, which stood in the northern part of Palestine. At this day there is, east of the Wady Chasmeia (the ancient Leontes), a narrow valley, which the Arabs call Merds I-un. A narrow valley is, in Arabic, called Nukub; Nukbetha De-iyon means, therefore, the narrow valley of I-un.

תוקרת *Tokereth.* This I take to be the Tukrath, often

mentioned in the Talmud. On the road from Zafed to Gish, near the village Kaiomeia, is found the grave of Rabbi José, of Tukrath; and, as it was customary to bury the great men of our people near the places of their nativity, it is highly probable that the town of Tukrath must formerly have stood here.

כרכה רבה דבר סנגרא *Karaka Rabbah Debar Sanegra,* is as I have proved above, p. 26, in the note to Zedad, the present Kallath al Sani.

תרנגולה עילעאה דלמעלה מן קיסרין *The Upper Ornithon above Cæsarea,* is also explained in the same note.

תרכונה דמתחם לבצרה *Tarchuna Demithcham Lebozrah,* is the country which Josephus calls Trachonitis. The Arabs call it Ledja, and it is south of Damascus. דמתחם means "which borders," or leads, i. e. the road לבצרה to Bozrah, the road which leads to Bozrah, the formerly famous city in Hauran, of which more will be said hereafter. (See also farther down, article עוץ.)

מלח דזרבאיי *Melach Dezarbayi,* is unknown to me.

נמרין *Nimrin,* perhaps the place of that name about 10 English miles west of Tiberias, or the Beth-Nimrah (Num. xxxii. 36) in the portion of Gad on the other side of Jordan (which see).

בית סכל *Beth Sachal,* is unknown to me.

קנת *Kenath,* is probably the Kanuath in the mountains of Hauran, and is mentioned in Numb. xxxii. 42. (See also בשן Bashan.)

רפיח דחגרא *Raphiach Dechagra.* Nearly all the prior commentators translate Chazor חצור, with Raphiach רפיח. I suppose that the place in question is the town of Chazor, near the sea Semechonitis. (See art. Chazor, in the commentary on the thirty-one kings of Joshua.) *Chagra* is the Arabic Chadshar, stone, therefore the "stony country;" and in fact there is found at the present day, northwest of Banias, at a distance of about 10 English miles, the village Chadshar,* and south thereof is the village Zuk; which name likewise means a high steep rock, so that the whole district is called "the stony country," which it actually is.

דרך הגדולה ההולכת למדבר *The great road which leads to the desert.* We have no data to determine either the road or the desert here meant.

חשבון *Heshbon.* See this article under its proper head.

יבקא *Yabka.* See article יבק Jabbok.

נחלא דזרך *The stream of Zerech,* evidently an error, should be זרד Zered.

יגר סהדותא *Yegar Sahadutha,* is in the land of Gilead (Gen. xxxi. 47), and is also called Mizpah. I presume that the village Al Zuf, eastwardly in the mountains of Gilead, is the Mizpah in question, since both the words rendered in English have the same signification, and are derived from the Hebrew צפה to see, to look on.

רקם דגיעא *Rekam Degaya.* See Kadesh-Barnea.

גינא דאשקלון *Gina Deashkelon,* that is, the environs, properly the angle of Ashkelon, no doubt from the Greek γωνια, wherefore it should be spelled גוניא angle.

It is very difficult to determine accurately the boundary of Palestine from these data, since they appear mostly to be merely isolated places. It is at all events certain that the northern boundary line did not extend far beyond Banias, and on the sea-coast not farther than Al Zib (Chezib); and at the present day, also, the Wady Kasmeia (Leontes) and the river Chasbeya are regarded as the western boundary of the present Palestine. Some maintain that even the Arabic name of Kasmeia is derived from the circumstance of its signifying "the separating," the dividing, or here, the river which separates Palestine, and determines the boundary line. Southward, however,

* This must not be mistaken for the Chagra in the southwest of Palestine, the ancient ברד Bared (Gen. xvi. 14), which is also rendered חגרא, and is situated in a stony country.

both boundaries, to wit, that given in Numb. xxxiv. 4, and the other marking the possession of the Israelites under Ezra and Nehemiah, are very nearly the same, since we find in the latter Rekam Gaayah, which is Kadesh-Barnea, and the environs of Ashkalon. The extent of Palestine, however, according to these data, is considerably less than that which was determined by divine command in the thirty-fourth of Numbers.

Before concluding this division concerning the boundary of Palestine, I desire to say something with respect to the hypothesis of the celebrated Astori Farchi, who for several years travelled through Palestine, and investigated its localities, till the year 5082 A. M., and was the author of כפתור ופרח, the most renowned description of the land of Israel; and this regarding his assumption respecting the Mount Hor, the extreme northwest of the boundary of Palestine. The learned author took a great deal of pains to determine this point; still I may venture to assert that his hypothesis is incorrect.

In section xi. of his description, he asserts that Mount Hor is between Antakia and Ladikieh, on Ras Zodin, and deems it identical with Djebl al Mukra, not far from Ras Basid, about a half day's journey north of Ladikieh, and believes to have found a trace of several cities of the tribe of Asher in its vicinity, for instance Umah, Afek, and Rechob (Josh. xix. 30). He also considers Hesn al Akrad, southwest of Chama, the ancient Epiphanis, as Hazar-Enan. But if we investigate the position of this alleged Mount Hor, we shall soon discover that the hypothesis is untenable; since Palestine could not have had possibly so great an extent northward, the more so as we cannot look for the country of Asher so far to the north, since, if this were so, the portion of this tribe would have been greater than that of all the other eleven tribes together; for the superficial extent from Akko, which belonged to Asher

(Judges i. 31), to the Djebl al Mukra, is considerably more than from Akko to the Dead Sea, Wady Gaian, and Wady al Arish, the south boundary of Palestine, which division would evidently be incredible, since the land was to be divided according to the population of the tribes (Numb. xxxiii. 54). Farther, we find that the towns Ladikieh, Phamiah, Arca, Arvad, and Trablos are situated south of the said mountain, which is the alleged northern boundary of the land of Israel, wherefore these towns ought to be, as a matter of course, within the limits of Palestine; but this is not the case. For in Pesikthah Rabbethi, chap. 23, it is stated expressly that Ladikieh belongs to Suria, and not to Palestine. At the end of Tractate *Challah*, it is proved that Phamiah also belonged to Suria. From Gen. x. 17, 18, it appears that Arvad, Arka, and Sin (i. e. Trablos), did not belong to the possessions of the Canaanites, consequently not to Palestine proper. It is therefore impossible to assume that the northern portion of this district should belong to Palestine, whilst the southern portion was in Suria. It is therefore necessary to assume that the Mount Hor, the northern terminus of Palestine, is south of Trablos and Ladikieh, which it actually is, according to my supposition that it is identical with Ras al Shaka. I have also mentioned that there was no city of the tribes of Israel north of Zidon; and the places in the vicinity of the Djebl al Mukra can therefore not be regarded as having been those of Asher, though the names may have some similarity. The assertion, also, that Hazar-Enan is identical with the village Hesn al Akrad, is too arbitrary and bold, without proof and authentication; since the place in question is to be sought for in the vicinity of Damascus (Ezek. xlvii. 17), and not so far northward; whereas my own idea that Dar Kanon, in the neighbourhood of Damascus, is the Hebrew Hazar-Enan, has a great deal of probability to recommend it as the correct site.

CHAPTER II.

EXPLANATION OF THE SEAS, RIVERS, MOUNTAINS, AND VALLEYS OF PALESTINE.

PALESTINE has three lakes* or seas :—1, the Dead Sea, or Lake Asphaltites; 2, the sea of Genezereth, or Lake of Tiberias; and 3, the sea of Merom, or Lake Semechonitis.

ים המלח OR ים סדום

(Gen. xiv. 3.)

The Salt or Dead Sea (Lake Asphaltites) is called in the Arabic language Bachr Lot (Lot's Sea), and is 70 English

* In Tractate Baba Bathra, fol. 74 *b*, we read: "There are seven seas and four rivers which surround (or border) Palestine, namely, the seas of Tiberias, Sodom, Chelath, Chiltha, Sibchi, Aspamia, and the Great Sea (the Mediterranean). The four rivers are the Jordan, the Yarmuch, Kirmion, and Pigah." It is farther stated there that the Jordan's sources are in the cave of Pameis, and that it runs through the lakes of Sibchi and Tiberias, through the Salt Sea into the mouth of Leviathan.—At the end of Talmud Yerushalmi, on Kilayim, these seven seas or lakes are called the Great Sea, the Sea of Tiberias, Somcho, the Salt Sea, the Chultha, Shelyith, and Apamia. But, as regards the Lake of Chamatz, it is observed that the Emperor Diocletian had it dug, and had it filled by the rivers which he conducted into it, wherefore it is not reckoned among the lakes formed by nature. This reading appears to me more correct than the first; still several corrections are necessary. Through means of literary investigations, I correct and explain the above as follows. Chultha or Chiltha signifies the Lake Phialo, which is called in Arabic Birkath al Ram. It is about 120 paces in circumference, and lies 10½ English miles east of Banias, and is the actual source of the Jordan. (See Josephus, Bell. Jud., book iii. ch. 18.) The whole country bears at this day the name Balad al Chuli, Land of Chuli. I suppose the origin of the word

miles in length, and from 15 to 20 in breadth.* Towards the south, however, it is narrow and shoal, and about 4 miles broad, and from 3 to 4 feet in depth. This sea is enclosed on the east and west by high mountains and rocks; but towards the southeast there is an extensive, fair and fruitful plain, several miles in size. It is true that the water of this sea is clear and pure; nevertheless it is more impregnated with salty matter than all other sea-waters, and is withal very bitter, somewhat sulphurous

to be חול Chul (see Gen. x. 23). This, by the way, will explain a very obscure passage in Erechin 2, where it speaks of כחולת המחוז, or the district Cholath, which was very stony and salty, and therefore unfruitful. The country is likewise called Balad al Malchi; which means "the country of salt," from the fact that the country is, so to say, covered with a crust of salt (see Tractate Ahaloth, the end of chap. iii.); whence I conclude that the present Chuli is derived from the ancient Chiltha or Chultha.—Sibchi is an incorrect reading, and should be Somcho, which is the same as the sea Semechonitis, also called Kaldayeh, which signifies "the high," identical with the Hebrew מי מרום (Mé Merom), literally the "high waters" (Josh. xi. 5). The common people call it very erroneously ים חוילה Yam Chavila, the Sea of Chavila.—Chelath or Shelyith is wrong, and should be אילת Elath, which is the Red Sea (Deut. ii. 8), which bounds Palestine at the south, since the Talmud speaks here of the country in its greatest extent.—Aspamia is also incorrect, since under this term there is always understood *Ispania*, Latin Hispania, or Spain, of which I shall speak more extensively in another place; the correct reading would be Apamia. Even at the present day there is found, north of the village Phamia (which see), the dry bed of an ancient lake, which the Arabs call Bacharea, which means "the little sea." The river Al Azy, the ancient Orontes, runs through the bed of this lake in a northerly direction.

Chamatz Lake is south of the town of Hams or Chams, and is called Bachr Chams, "the Great Sea," also Bachr Kadissa. It is formed by the just mentioned Al Azy, which runs into it, and continues its course after issuing from it. This will explain the meaning of the passage from the Talmud Yerushalmi, quoted above, that Diocletian had made it by causing rivers to run into it. (See also T. Yer. Shekalim, chap. vi.)

Yalkut to Deut. xxxiii. 23, speaks erroneously of the sea Sufni, as it should be Somcho.

* According to Josephus, Bell. Jud., book v., chap. 5, is this sea 580 stadia in length, and 150 in breadth.

in smell, and so acrid that no one can keep it in his mouth. When I made the attempt to take a little of it in my mouth, the sharp, bitter, and sulphurous taste remained perceptible more than half an hour. Salt thrown in this water remains undissolved. 100 parts of this water contain 42 parts of salts, 24 parts bitter, salty, and sour calcareous earth, and 7 parts salty natron. The weight of this water, compared to pure distilled water, is as 1211 to 1000. To institute several comparative experiments, I employed water from the Dead Sea, some taken from the Mediterranean at Jaffa, and the usual cistern (rain) water; and, on weighing them, I found that the first compared to the second as 9 to 8, and to the latter as 9 to 7. I have, however, to remark here, that I made these experiments in the month of April, at which time the Dead Sea had, on account of continued rains, taken up many streams, through which circumstance the weight of its water was much less than it usually is, and especially in the summer months, when the evaporation condenses it more than at other times. The water of this sea has also a peculiarity that nothing thrown into it will sink. Even a man, unacquainted with swimming, may confidently bathe here, for he can no more sink in this lake than in an empty vessel.* Josephus even tells† that the Emperor Vespasian had men who could not swim thrown into the Dead Sea with their hands even tied on their backs, and that not one of them was drowned. Everything which lies a little time in this water is covered with a crust of salt. On living objects, however, the skin is partially peeled off. The air in the vicinity of this sea is so impregnated with particles of salt and sulphur, that the

* The Talmud therefore remarks correctly (Sabbath 108 *b*), that a person never was drowned in the Salt Sea.

† Bell. Jud., book v., chap. 5.

clothes of persons who are a short time* on its shore are covered, so to say, with a coating of salt. Neither fish, nor worms, nor any other living things are ever found in this sea. Even those fish which swim in the Jordan, as it disembogues itself into this sea, perish the moment they touch it. If you carry this water to ever so great a distance, and place fish therein, they nevertheless die immediately. At the bottom of the Dead Sea there is found a black, fetid slime. Every morning there ascend such strong sulphurous vapours from this water, that they can be seen at a great distance. On a winter's day, at the time of the rains, I was once able to observe this from the holy city itself; for as I looked in the direction of this sea, I saw, so to say, a great cloud rising upward from the same. Should a bird fly over the surface of the water during the disengagement of these strong vapours, it would drop down dead instantly. For this reason there are but few living animals seen in the whole neighbourhood, also but few trees and plants. In the vicinity of this sea is found a species of stone-coal; there is also a species of black bitumen met with, which floats on the surface of the water, and is afterwards driven on shore. The salt, which is found in large quantities in the whole adjacent country, and especially on the seashore, cannot be used in food, because it is extraordinarily bitter, and has, moreover, the smell and taste of saltpetre. (See art. Salt.)

Although the surface of this sea is 598 feet lower than the Mediterranean, and receives the Jordan and several other minor streams, yet it never overflows its shores. This circumstance furnishes sufficient proof that this sea must have subterranean† outlets, either to the Mediterranean or the Red Sea.

* This is, however, the case only in damp and foggy weather, but not when it is hot and in sunshine.

† These unknown outlets the *Midrash* expresses by saying that the

The mountains on the shores of the Dead Sea are almost perpetually encircled by the mists ascending from its waters. These mists, which are very unwholesome, and cause the drying up of the vital powers, producing consumption, &c., have also the most pernicious influence on vegetation. It therefore happens that the fruit produced on the trees of these mountains, though to outward appearance healthy and sound, are dried up within, rotten, and filled with a carbonaceous powder. Especially is this the case with the pomegranate and lemon; which circumstance is no doubt referred to by Josephus, when speaking of the Sodom-apples, which he says fall into dust on being touched. (See also Deut. xxxii. 32.)

It is thus that the divine curse still rests on this neighbourhood, destroyed in consequence of the sins of its inhabitants. [It yet stands as the personified consequence of vice, and forms the most striking contrast in what it is now to the hopeful future promised in the thirty-sixth chapter of Ezekiel v. 8–16, 33–36, and ibid. xlvii. 1–12; the latter especially being a remarkable prophecy, promising a complete change of the whole surface of the country, as it was and as it now is, and which, if accomplished, must render Palestine indeed the highway of nations and the centre of the earth,—situated, as it is, in the midst of the great thoroughfare between the sea of India on the east, and the Mediterranean on the west.]

THE SEA OF CHINNERETH. ים כנרת

(Numb. xxxiv. 11.)

This lake, called in the Arabic Bachr Tibaria, i. e. Sea of Tiberias, because this city is situated on its western shore, is about 12½ English miles in length, and 5 in

Jordan passes through the Dead Sea into the mouth of Leviathan, to wit, the unknown terminations.

breadth,* and lies 535 feet lower than the surface of the Mediterranean. On the north, near the village Tanchum (which see), the Jordan enters this lake, and leaves it again at the south, near the village Samach (כפר צמח). It is a remarkable thing that the Jordan, which passes through this lake its entire length, does not mingle with its waters, since its course is clearly perceptible in the midst of the lake till it leaves it again, and resumes its own proper course. (Compare with Bereshith Rabba, chap. 2, and Josephus, Bell. Jud., chap. 18.)

The environs of Chinnereth are uncommonly fertile and productive; and it forms, on the whole, a complete contrast to the recently described Dead Sea. For instance, in the same measure as the water of the latter is nauseous, bitter, heavy, and salty, so is the water of Chinnereth agreeable, sweet, and light, and used, therefore, by the inhabitants of Tiberias, as drinking water. The Dead Sea is, moreover, as its name already indicates, dead; and is neither navigated by men in vessels, nor inhabited by fish or other living things. The Chinnereth, however, has all kinds of the best fish, and other species of aquatic animals; and one sees constantly an active intercourse carried on there through means of small vessels, in which, at times, the inhabitants of the other side of Jordan bring wood and other articles for sale to Tiberias. And lastly, whereas on the other district still rests the punishment sent from heaven on Sodom and Gomorrah, and the whole environ of the sea is nothing but a frightful scene of desolation, one sees near Chinnereth, as already stated, a fruitful country and one truly blessed of God, extending itself before the eye, and presenting an abundance of earthly treasures.

There prevails a calm nearly the whole year on the

* Josephus (Bell. Jud., book iii., chap. 18), gives the dimensions 100 stadia in length, and 40 in breadth.

Sea of Chinnereth; when, however, a storm does arise, which is seldom the case, it occurs very suddenly, and then, in a few minutes, the boats which may be caught out in it are generally upset. The force of the waves in that case is also so great, that many of the houses in town are thereby endangered.

WATERS OF MEROM. מי מרום OR ים סומכי

(Joshua xi. 5.)

This little lake is called by the Arabs Bachr Chit, Wheat Sea, because much wheat is sown in its neighbourhood; it is also called Bachr Banias, or improperly Bachr Chuli. It is 10 English miles south of the sources of the Jordan, and is about 5 English miles long and 3¾ broad. It is only in winter, however, that this lake has water in it, which is turbid and muddy, and in which fish are found. In summer, however, it is dried up; and it is then a swamp overgrown with weeds, and then serves the Arabs, who come hither with their numerous flocks, and encamp thereon during the whole summer, as a pasture-ground. Many canes also grow here, among which wild beasts, &c., find shelter, especially serpents and wild boars. Not far from the village Malcha, situated on its northern shore, the Jordan enters this lake. The inhabitants of the village just named cultivate the rice plant in this vicinity, which is the only place in Palestine where this plant grows. This rice, which is sent to the other towns, is quite singular in its colour and flavour; it is red in appearance, and swells in cooking to an unusual degree. The western portion of this lake is inhabited by the Duphni-Arabs, who derive their name from the town of Daphné (Riblah), which formerly stood in this district. (See Riblah p. 26.)

RIVERS OF PALESTINE.

I. JORDAN. ירדן

(Num. xiii. 29.)

The Jordan has its sources near the most northern point of Palestine, and issues from the cave of Paneas, situated about one hour's distance south of the town of Banias, whence its name *Jord* (i. e. Yored, flowing down from), *Dan* (Bechoroth, fol. 55 *a*); or יאור דן the "stream of Dan." It is at first very small, but receives afterwards an increase through the stream Dan, which has its source 2½ English miles northeast of Banias, and through the much larger one Chaspeia, called by the Arabs *Kuruni*, perhaps so denominated from the town of Korun, mentioned in 2 Maccabees xii. 21. These various streams are united in the afore-mentioned Bachr Banias, and form afterwards, at its termination, the river Jordan. The farther south the Jordan flows, the deeper and broader it becomes. It is, for example, south of the waters of Merom, about 20; 80 to the south of Chinnereth; 90 near Jericho; and near the shore of the Dead Sea, 200, nay, at times 300 paces broad. In the same manner is its depth, which amounts near Chinnereth only from 6 to 7 feet, but near Jericho and the shores of the Dead Sea, from 10 to 12. This depth, however, it attains only in the winter months (Josh. iii. 15; 1 Chron. xii. 15), whereas in summer it is only about 3 feet deep.

The Jordan, the water of which is light and good for drinking, is so rapid a stream that even the best swimmer cannot bathe in it without endangering his life. In the neighbourhood of Jericho, the bathers are compelled to tie themselves together with ropes, to prevent their being swept off by the rapidity of the current. There are the three following bridges spanning the Jordan. The first is a large stone bridge, 60 paces in length, and was built by Baldwin IV., in the year 4872 A. M. (1112), and put again in good repair in modern times by Ibrahim Pacha; it is 7 English miles south of the point where the Jordan issues from the sea of Merom, and is called Djisr Abni Jaacob, which means the Bridge of Jacob's Sons, because it is designated as the spot where the patriarch Jacob, with his family, passed over the Jordan, on his return from Haran. (But this assumption is evidently erroneous, because he pursued his journey over Sukkoth and Salem; consequently not north, but south of the sea of Chinnereth. But it is possible that Jacob took this route when he first set out on his journey to the east, when quitting his father's house.) The second is the smaller bridge south of Chinnereth, Djisr Midshama, i. e. the Bridge of the Confluence of the Waters, because it is near the confluence of the Jordan and Yarmuch—(here is also a bridge leading over the Yarmuch);—and the third is also a small structure, near the village Samach, not far from Chinnereth, and bears the name of Djisr al Knaphir.

The Arabs call the Jordan, till its entrance into Lake Chinnereth, Al Urdan; but south thereof they designate it as Al Sherian, or Al Sheriath.

II. THE KISHON קישון

(Jud. iv. 7, v. 21; 1 Kings xviii. 40; Ps. lxxxiii. 10)

Is called by the Arabs Nahr Mukata, i. e. the Stream of Slaughter—(the Mount Carmel has also the same designation, Ras al Mukata, because Elijah slew there the prophets of Baal)—and bears also the name of Keifa. It has its source south of Mount Tabor, runs southwesterly through the valley of Jezreel, runs then through a mountain ridge to the plains of Akko, near the foot of Carmel, and falls into the Mediterranean Sea east of Keifa.

Kishon, the waters of which are clear and of a greenish colour, is in summer a very small stream; but in winter, when the rains pour down torrents from the mountains of Ephraim and Samaria, it becomes so broad that the whole valley of Jezreel is covered with water, which renders it impassable for several days.

It strikes me that this Kishon is identical with the waters of Megiddo מי מגדו, mentioned in the song of Deborah (Jud. v. 19): "Then fought the kings of Canaan near Taanach by the waters of Megiddo." Taanach is 2½ English miles south of Megiddo, and both towns are situated in the valley of Jezreel; and there is no other river in that vicinity beside the Kishon, and doubtlessly it was designated as the waters of Megiddo, because it flows by that town. (In the Talmud Yerushalmi, sect. Shebiith, there is mention made, among the boundary lines of the returning exiles, as stated above, of Gaathon and the waters of Gaathon, which I hold to be identical with Megiddo and the waters of Megiddo.) It is curious that the common people call, though erroneously, by the name of the waters of Megiddo, the stream which issues near Miron, and is used to drive several water-mills, and falls into Chinnereth after passing by Zafed. This latter bears the Arabic name of Wady Amud.*

III. THE KANAH קנה

(Josh. xvii. 9)

Forms the boundary line between Ephraim and Menasseh, and has its source about 1 English mile west of She-

* Southeast of Mount Tabor there is a small river, called Al Sharer, so termed from its passing near the village of that name. It is also called Wady Biré, and falls into Jordan 1½ English miles below the bridge of Midshama. The author of Caphtor Vapherach supposes this to be the Kishon; but this assumption is quite erroneous, as Kishon must be near Carmel, as appears from 1 Kings xviii. 40.

chem, on the road to Ladshinin (En Gannim), in a large spring called Ain al Kazab, or the spring of reeds, cane or reed being called in Arabic Kazab, as in Hebrew Kaneh. It flows westwardly, and is used for irrigating the fields; and after acquiring a considerable breadth, it falls into the Mediterranean Sea south of Cæsarea. It yet bears the name of Wady al Kazab, "Cane River," and is doubtlessly the River Kanah of the Scriptures.

IV. THE CHERITH. כרית

(1 Kings xvii. 3.)

This stream is not positively known. Some suppose it to be the little rivulet Al Pacha, which flows into Jordan opposite Shechem. But this must be erroneous, because in 1 Kings xvii. 3, it says distinctly, "which is before (east of) Jordan." I therefore am led to believe that the Wady Alias (Elias' brook), which is south of Mahanaim, opposite Beth Shean (which see), is the Cherith, and bears its present name because it was the hiding-place of the prophet Elijah. (See also Yerushalmi Terumoth, chap. 8.)

V. THE SHICHOR-LIBNATH שיחור לבנת

(Josh. xix. 26)

That is, the white or glass Shichor, was anciently called Belus, and is the present *Numan* of the Arabs, and issues from the mountains near the village of Meshdl al Krum, and falls into the Mediterranean near Akko. Some think that the little stream south of Akko, called by the Arabs Ramlé Abiatz, i. e. the stream of white sand, is the river in question, since, as it is well known, the sand of this rivulet was formerly used in the manufacture of glass.*

* See Megillah, fol. 6 *a*, where (Deut. xxxiii. 19) "the treasure hid in sand" is explained to mean "white glass."

VI. THE BESORE בשור

(1 Sam. xxx. 10)

Is at present a small stream south of Gazza, and is called Nahr Sheria; it issues from the mountains of Judah, and also falls into the Mediterranean Sea.

VII., VIII. KIDRON AND SILOA קדרון ושלוח

I will explain when speaking of the holy city Jerusalem.

IX. THE GEENA גינא נהרא

(Chulin, fol. 7 *a*; Yerushalmi Shekalin vii.)

Is the name of a small river, which flows not far from Ladshinin (En Gannim), and becomes so broad in winter that it is often impassable.*

RIVERS ON THE EAST SIDE OF THE JORDAN.

I. THE JABBOK יבוק

(Gen. xxxii. 23)

Which forms the boundary between Palestine and the land of Ammon, issues from the high mountains of Hauran (which see), and divides the district of Mirad on the north, from Balka on the south; flows then westward in the plain a distance of 4 English miles, and falls into Jordan about midway between Chinnereth and the Dead Sea, opposite Shechem. The Arabs call it Al Zerka, because it passes by the fortress of Zerka, situated on the route of the pilgrims journeying from Damascus to Mecca.

* The occurrence mentioned in the cited passage of Chulin took place at the time of Pesach, at which time the Geena was in the state of being impassable.

II. THE ARNON ארנון

(Numb. xxi. 13; Deut. iii. 9)

Now called Al Mudjeb, divided the land of Moab from Palestine. It issues forth near the fortress of Katrani, also on the above pilgrim route, at the distance of a day and a half's journey east of the city of Karak (the ancient Kir Moab קיר מואב). It divides the district Balka from the just named one of Karak, and falls east of Hebron into the Dead Sea.

III. THE ZERED זרד

(Numb. xxi. 12; Deut. ii. 13)

Is not distinctly known. Some, however, say that it is the little stream known as the Wady Abné Chamad, which is north of the city of Karak, and south of the Wady Mudjeb, just named, and falls likewise into the Dead Sea.

IV. THE YARMUCH ירמוך

(Parah, ch. viii. 10; B. Bathra, 74 *b*)

Is now called Yurmuk, or Sheriath al Mandhur, also Wady Mizrib, issues out of the mountains of Djolon (the Golan of Deut. iv. 43), near the fortress of Mizrib, flows through the district of Gader (Gadara), now called Amchais, and falls into the Jordan 4 English miles south of Chinnereth. This stream, in its course through the mountain, is small and shallow, but on the plain it has a breadth of *thirty* paces.

V. THE AMANAH. אמנה

(2 Kings v. 12.)

Between the high mountains of the Djebl Heish, running from Banias to Damascus, on the road which leads to the village Midjdal (Migdal), there is found a village by the name of Beth al Djana. About 1½ English miles north of this village is found a large spring, called Al Barady, that is to say, "the cold." Its waters are clear and excellent for drinking, and it flows northeast to Damascus. This river, formerly called Chrysorrhoas, i.e. Gold River, and known in the Talmud Baba Bathra 74 *b*, as the Karmion, is the identical Amanah of the Bible, as it is actually called by all the Jews of Damascus, according to a tradition which they have preserved. Near Damascus this river divides itself in two branches; the one part flows through the city, whilst the other portion holds its course without, and is used to irrigate the surrounding country; it then runs eastwardly 18 English miles, and then falls into the lake Al Bachr Murdj.

VI. THE PHARPAR. פרפר

(2 Kings v. 12.)

On the road from Damascus to Baal-bek, not far from the village Dar Kanon (Hazar-Enan), there is a village called Fidjeh (the Figa of Parah viii. 10), north of which is the source of the stream of the same name, which flows southeasterly to Damascus, and unites with the Amanah near the lake Murdj. Now this stream is the Pharpar, as it is still called by our fellow-Israelites in the vicinity, according to tradition which they have. In case, therefore, that a divorce takes place in Damascus, they write in the letter of divorce, "at Damascus, situated on the two rivers Amana and Pharpar."

The other small streams will be explained in their proper places.

THE PRINCIPAL MOUNTAINS OF PALESTINE.

I. THE LEBANON. לבנון

This celebrated mountain, situated on the northern boundary of Palestine, derives its name from its white colour (Jer. xviii. 14), since the snow scarcely ever melts on this elevated ridge, and because its snow-covered summit, which has an elevation of more than 10,000 feet above the sea, is so high that it can be seen by those navigating the Mediterranean, as soon as they approach the island of Cyprus, although they are then at a distance of 100 English miles from the same. This mountain takes its rise south of the town of Chams, and extends south of Tripoli as the promontory of Mount Hor (הר ההר Numb. xxxiv. 7, called in the period of the Grecian domination Theuprosopon, and now Ras al Shaka), as far as the Mediterranean, and thence it runs a distance of 12 English miles to the south of Tyre, to the Ras al Nakhara, where its rocky cliffs, which are visible at a great distance, extend into the sea. On this rock is a narrow ascent, shaped somewhat like steps, by which its summit can be reached; hence it is called in the Talmud סולמא דצור, the Ladder of Tyre. (See Erubin, fol. 80 *a*, and Betza, 25 *b*.)

The highest point of the whole Lebanon range is the Djebl Makmal. North of this point, which is south of the town of Edn, is the village Beshirrai, in the vicinity of which there is a cedar forest, consisting now of about 350 cedars, which to all appearance are several thousand years old; and the largest of these measures about 40 feet in circumference, and 90 feet in height.

On the east of Lebanon there is a large valley, now called Al Bakaa, and formerly Coelesyria;* and beyond this is the eastern chain of this mountain, which is known

* See the Entrance of Hamath, p. 25.

as the Anti-Lebanon. This extends eastward to the vicinity of Damascus, where it gradually diminishes in height, and extends thus northward to the desert and the district of Chams, and southward to Dan or Laish. This range has two high peaks, one of which is called Djebl Sheich, also Djebl Theldj, i. e. Snow Mountain, and is the Mount Hermon of the Bible, and almost rivals the Makmal in elevation; the other peak is called Djebl Heish, and lies east of Dan, or Banias.

In the Bible, the term Lebanon is used to designate both of the just described chains of mountains; i. e. "Like the tower of Lebanon, which looketh to the front of Damascus" (Song of Sol. vii. 5), can only refer to the eastern range, the Anti-Lebanon; so also "And all the Lebanon, to the rising of the sun" (Josh. xiii. 5), cannot apply to the western portion, or the Lebanon proper.

II. THE HERMON חרמון

Is, as said, the highest point of the Anti-Lebanon, and is also termed in Scripture Sirion and Senir (Deut. iii. 8). Even at the present time this ridge is designated by various names; for instance, the mount northwest of Damascus is called Sanir (Senir); the one north of Chaspeia Djebl Theldj; and the one west of Baal-bek is termed Lubnan. Hence it appears that the verse quoted refers to the Djebl Heish just named, for it is north of the district of Golan, where this mount appears as a high wall, sloping down to the neighbourhood of the town Beth al Dshana, near the spring Barady or Amanah. The Bible, however, does not always understand by the word Hermon the eastern part of Lebanon only, or the Djebl Heish proper, but also the western part; as in Judges iii. 3, "And the Hivites, the inhabitants of Mount Lebanon, from Mount Baal Hermon to the entrance of Hamath," which proves that the terms Lebanon and Hermon are indifferently used, occasionally, for both the eastern and western ranges.*

THE PRINCIPAL RIVERS OF THE LEBANON.

Besides the already described Amanah and Pharpar, the following large rivers have their sources in the Lebanon and Anti-Lebanon.

I. AL AZY,

That is, the bold or the rebellious, is a large river which flows northward from Lebanon, and its name is, as I am told, partly derived from this circumstance, since all the other streams have a southern course, and partly because it is a wild and rapid water course, which tears away all the bridges which people attempt to throw over it. In ancient times it was called Orontes, but is not mentioned either in Talmud or the Scriptures. It issues out of a large meadow called Djord Dudunie, 12 English miles north of Baal-bek, takes a northerly course, by the town of Chamath (Epiphania), Phamia, and Antiochia, (Antakia), and falls south of the last into the Mediterranean.

* In Psalm cxxxiii. 3, occurs the following: "Like the dew of Hermon, which descendeth on the mountains of Zion." This verse has greatly perplexed the commentators; but I venture to give this explanation. In Deut. iv. 47, we read, "Unto Mount Sion (שיאן), which is Hermon," of course making the former a part of the latter; and assuming that the Psalmist refers to this Sion, easily corrupted into Zion ציון, the more familiar word, he means to refer to the lower height it has compared to Hermon, wherefore the dew of Hermon is said to descend on the lower mountains of Sion; and indeed we find to this day the Djebl Sanin, north-east of Beirut; and should this be the mountain referred to by the Psalm, the exposition will be quite natural and correct as I have indicated.

II. WADY CHASMEIA,

That is, the dividing or separating stream. This river, the ancient Leontes,* takes its rise south of the city of Baal-bek, flows southwesterly to the lower plain, Bakaatachtani, in the district of the ancient Beth-Rechob, and falls into the Mediterranean to the north of Tyre.

III. NAHR ABRAIM,

Formerly Adonis, flows northward of the district Kisruan, and south of Biblos, and falls there into the Mediterranean.

IV. THE ALEUD,

Also called Nahr al Kubbir, i. e. the Strong or Grand River, formerly Eleutherus, flows north of Arka (which will be more particularly described hereafter). The valley of the river forms the most northern boundary of the Lebanon, and extends from Hams (Epiphania) to the Mediterranean.

V. THE KELB (DOG RIVER),

Flows north of Beirut, and takes its name, according to some, from the circumstance that the Avites formerly dwelt in this district, and had, as their god, the idol Nibchaz, who is said to have been figured as a dog, according to the authority of Talmud Sanhedrim, fol. 63 *a*. (See also 2 Kings xvii. 31.) It had anciently the name of Licius (Lykos).

* In some ancient Arabic works, I found a river Nahr Aleud as existing between Zor and Seide (Zidon). This would place in this position the Eleitherus, which is, however, not found between Tyre and Zidon, as I shall explain hereafter. But it appears to me that this is an error of the transcribers, and that it should be Leond, or the Leontes, the same as the Wady Chasmeia in question, as this is also known in the Arabic books as Nahr Leond.

VI. THE TAMUR, OR AL KADI,

Flows at a distance of about 1½ English miles west of the city Dir al Kamr, situated between Beirut and Zidon. In winter it increases to such a size that it becomes a rapid stream, and overflows its banks to a great extent; so that travellers are often detained on its shores six or eight days, till the water returns to its former channel.

VII. THE ZABIRANI,

Is the last of these streams, and flows 5 English miles south of Zidon.

THE PRINCIPAL PLACES AND DISTRICTS OF LEBANON.

It would lead me too far to give a minute description of all the places in Lebanon and the country round about it. I will, therefore, only note those which are mentioned in the Scriptures, Talmud and other authoritative works.

Between the Lebanon and Anti-Lebanon, there is a large valley, in Arabic, Al Bakaa, or "The Valley," anciently Coelesyria, or the Chul of Gen. x. 23; it extends northward up to the neighbourhood of Chams (Epiphania), and southward to the vicinity of Tyre, near which latter place it is called Bakaa-Tachtani, i. e. the lower valley.

This great valley of the Lebanon is the בקעת הלבנון "the Valley of Lebanon" of Joshua xi. 17, and the לבא חמת "the entrance of Hamath" of Num. xiii. 21. In speaking of the battle which Joshua fought with the Canaanites at the Lake of Merom, it is said (Josh. xi. 3) that Jabin sent to the Canaanite on the east and the west, and to the Amorite, and the Hittite, and the Perizzite, and the Jebusites in the mountain, and to the Hivite under Hermon in the land of Mizpeh." Now, according to my view, is here meant the eastern valley of the Djebl Heish, mentioned above, and now called Heish Shakara; where is found, at this day, 10 English miles north of Kanitra, the village of Tel Djube, Hebrew Goba, which is similar in signification to Mizpeh, both meaning a high place whence an object can be seen at a distance. (Goba—Gibah is transformed into the Arabic Djube by changing the Hebrew Gimel into the Arabic Jim.) The most southern height of the Djebl Heish is called Tel Farash, that is, Joshua's Mount, because the Arabs call Joshua Farash, probably from the circumstance that he may have pursued the Canaanitish kings to this point. It is also said in the chapter cited, in verse 8, that the Israelites pursued their enemies (westward) as far as Zidon, and (eastward) to the valley of Mizpeh; it is farther said, in verse 17, that Joshua conquered the country from the Bald Mountain (Halak), which is in Seir, to Baal-gad in the valley of the Lebanon, under Mount Hermon, which should induce us to assume that Baal-gad is identical with the present Banias, of which we have already spoken. This district of Baal-gad was particularly noted for the criminal idolatry which was at all times practised there. It was there that the idol Baal-gad, already existing in the time of Joshua, was worshipped as late as the days of Isaiah (chap. v. 11), "Who set a table for the *Gad*" (English version, "for that troup," which, however, hardly means anything; whereas, it is highly significant when taken as the name of a heathen divinity). It was there, at Dan or Laish, afterwards called Paneas, or Cæsarea Philippi, where the children of Dan set up the image of Micah (Judges xviii. 31), and where, at a later period, Jeroboam set up one of the golden calves (1 Kings xii. 28) to mislead Israel to sin. It was there where the image of the cock-idol was worshipped by the Cutheans in the town of Tarnegola, consecrated to the god Nergal (2 Kings xvii. 30; see also Targum Jonathan; Num. xxxiv.; likewise Talmud Yerushalmi, Demai, chap. ii.); and there it was at last, where in later times, the Grecian idol Pan was worshipped, whence then the name of the town of Paneas, near which is the cave of Banias, in which there are stones bearing inscriptions having reference to the worship of Pan. The more recent name of the time of the crusaders of Belias for Banias, is founded upon the original appellation of the same Baal-gad (Joshua xi. 17).*

In this large plain, between the Lebanon and Anti-Lebanon, there also stood formerly the celebrated city Heliopolis, consecrated by the Greeks to the worship of the sun (from Helis, the sun, Polis, town), which is now known as Baal-bek† (from Baal, Belus, and Bikah, valley). This town is still famous for its remarkable ruins, which are undisputably the most gigantic in all Palestine, and are well calculated to influence every beholder with astonishment. In the remains of the ancient Temple of the Sun can be seen stones which are 60 feet in length, 12 in thickness, and 12 in height; and the simple view of these blocks causes a species of awe; as no one can imagine how human hands were enabled to erect so wonderful a structure. This colossal building,‡ erected by Solomon, it being

* This vicinity is also probably the site of Baal-Hamon, mentioned in the Song of Solomon viii. 11, where it is not unlikely that the Egyptian idol Amon (see Jer. xlvi. 23), was worshipped by Pharaoh's daughter, the wife of the Israelitish King. This idol, the Jupiter Ammon of the Greeks, was worshipped in the city Diospolis, i. e. Jupiter's town, which the Targumin suppose to be Alexandria, but which others allege to be Thebes, in Upper Egypt, where are still found the most remarkable and extensive ruins of idol temples. It is, therefore, probable that the idolatrous queen transplanted the name of Amon, changed into the Hebrew Hamon, from Egypt to the country around Lebanon, and hence, then, Baal-Hamon, the God Amon. Perhaps Baal may also refer to the idol Baal or Belus.

† The passage in Tractate Maaseroth, chap. v. § 8, שום בעל בכי translated usually (strong) "garlick, which excites tears," appears to me to be only "the garlik of Baal-bek," the *chi* being substituted for the *k*.

‡ According to Josephus (Antiq. viii. book viii., chap. 2), was the Baalath

undoubtedly the בעלת Baalath mentioned in the first book of Kings (ix. 18), was destroyed in the year 5162 (1402), by the conqueror Tamerlane;* and that which resisted his destructive inroad was overthrown 356 years later, through the terrific earthquake in the year 5518 (1758), which caused such great devastation in the plain of Lebanon and the country of Galilee.

Through a close inquiry, I have succeeded in ascertaining that Mount Lebanon is at present divided into 16 districts, of which, however, I mean to enumerate those only which are mentioned in the Talmudic writings, and which are situated south of the town of Tripoli (Trablus), in the direction of Mount Hor, the northern extremity of Palestine (Num. xxxiv. 7); but I intend to devote, in the sequel, a chapter to the countries which form the northern boundary line of the land of Israel.

TRIPOLI,

Or Trablus† al Sham (Tarpelites of Ezra iv. 9), is the Sin of Gen. x. 17, wherefore Saadiah translates it with Trablision. Even at the present time there is, north of this city, a village called Al Sini; it is also called, in the Answers of *Maharitz*, Sinim (chap. xxxvi). Trablus is distant from the sea about 1½ miles, and the river Abualia passes through it. Of our fellow-Israelites there reside at

erected by Solomon in the vicinity of Gezer of Joshua x. 33, not far from Jaffa on the Mediterranean, in the country of Ephraim. According to this assumption, it would appear that this town had the origin and derived its name from the same circumstance as that in the tribe of Dan. (See Joshua xix. 44.) But Rabbi Benjamin of Tudela thinks that the temple of Baal-bek was originally the house built by Solomon for Pharaoh's daughter in Lebanon. (1 Kings vii. 8.)

* Of which more in the historical part, which see.

† In Talmud Yerushalmi Sabb., chap. i., is mentioned that Rabbi Simeon taught in Atrubulis, by which, probably, the present Trablus is meant.

present only twelve families, although their Synagogue is a large, strong, and massive building, which would indicate that formerly there must have been here a much larger congregation. At the time of Rabbi Benjamin of Tudela, the celebrated traveller, this city was visited by a terrible earthquake, which threw down the walls of the town and many houses, and buried many inhabitants alive under the ruins of their dwellings. But in other places, also, the convulsion of nature was so great, that, as this traveller reports, more than 20,000 human beings lost their lives in Palestine through this calamity. The same occurrence is noticed by Rabbi Joseph Hackohen (fol. 22 *b*), that in the year 4930 (1170) there happened a terrific earthquake in the East, through which the city of Tripoli was overthrown, burying its inhabitants, and that Antiochia also was nearly totally destroyed by the same calamity.

Southeast of Trablus is the district Al Danie, where the above-described cedars of Lebanon are found. West of the highest peak of the Lebanon, Makmal, is the district Art Akluk, which is probably the קלקאי Kalkai often mentioned in the Talmudical writings. (See Negaim, in the beginning of chap. x.; also in Targum Jonathan, to Numb. xxxiv. 8.)

Southwest of this is the land of the Gibbim (Gebal, Joshua xiii. 5; 1 Kings v. 32; Ezek. xvii. 9), called by the Greeks Biblos, now called Djebel. East of this district, on the above-mentioned river Abraim, is the town of Aphica, which I take to be the Aphek of Joshua xiii. 4.

Between Tripoli and Biblos, on the shore of the sea, is the town of Botrus, of which Phœnician city Josephus speaks in his Antiq., book viii., chap. 7.

In the district of Al Shahar is found the village Ami (probably the village Aimi mentioned in Talmud Yerushalmi Nedarim, chap. iv., and ibid. end of Yoma).

East of the town Mar Hana, in the district of Al Shuf, belonging to the territory of Beirut, is the spring of Achab, in Arabic Ein Achab (see Parah, chap. viii. § 11), which falls into the river Abraim. In the same district is found the village Biyuth-athir, doubtlessly a corruption for Biyutar, a city referred to in Challah, chap. iv. § 10, as Bittar,* and not to be mistaken for the ancient Bethar, near Jerusalem, not far from Malcha, or the celebrated Bethar not far from Kaplar Saba (Gittin, fol. 57 *a*).

In the district of Al Djurd is the town of Batchun; it is not to be mistaken, as no doubt some have done, for the Betach belonging to the cities of Hadarezer (2 Sam. viii. 8).

Two and a half English miles south of Baal-bek is the village Rabcha, perhaps the Richpa mentioned in Maaseroth v. § 8, as the Arabs so often transpose the letters; hence Ripcha, then Rabcha.

Twenty-five miles southeast of Baal-bek is the village Sachala, where the inhabitants point out a monument, which they allege to mark the grave of Noah. That, however, but little faith can be placed in such like popular legends, will appear from the fact that also in the land of Armenia, in the vicinity of Mount Dshudi (the Ararat of Gen. viii. 4), on which the ark rested at the flood, they also point out an alleged grave of Noah. But other similar examples can be cited to prove the credulity of the people in giving currency to unauthenticated legends. So the grave of Moses is shown south of the town of Hams, near the sea and the village, where it is, is called Keber Mosheh, Moses' Grave, when it is well known that the sepulchre of this holy man is east of the Jordan (Deut. xxxiv. 6). The grave of Job is pointed out at Constantinople, also east of the Jordan (see Caphtor Vapherach, fol. 70 *b*), again in Armenia, and finally in India, not far

* In Talmud Yerushalmi, and in some other old books, I find the passage in Challah to state ביותר Beyutar, not Bittar, as we read in our books.

from the Persian boundary line, consequently in four different places.*

The northern part of Lebanon is almost a complete desert and uninhabited, and only in its southern part are there any settlements, of which, however, agreeably to my plan, I shall mention the following only.

South of Djebl Sheich, which is identical with Hermon or the Snow Mountain, is the district Al Chaspeya, in which is found the city of the same name, mentioned in Talmud Yerushalmi,—Demai, chapter ii. South of this place, is the river Chaspeya, called by the Arabs Koroni, which is the source of the Jordan, and flows to the south of the district of Dan, and unites there with the river Dan and the Jordan. West of this river, that is to say, 12½ English miles north of the sea of Merom, is the village Abel (Beth Maacha 2 Sam. xx. 14). Near this are the villages Abel al Kamach, and Abel al Krum,† which latter is not to be mistaken for Abel Keramim of Judges xi. 33, which is the land of Gilead. South of the first Abel, and north of Abel al Kamach, is the village Zeredah, where the grave of Jose of Zeredah is found. This village also has the name of Chamas. Not far from this is the village of Barthotha, in which is the grave of Eliezer of Barthotha. (Aboth i.) Perhaps this is the town of Beruthi mentioned by Josephus, which I have noticed above.

The inhabitants of Lebanon and Anti-Lebanon are mostly Druses; they are called Philistines by the Jews,

* There is a hint in Targum Echa (Lamentations) to chap. iv. 21, that Job should have lived in Armenia, as עוץ the land of Uz, where Job dwelt, is given with Armenia.

† The Jewish inhabitants of the town of Chaspeya carry their dead across the stream to Abel al Krum, because they have a tradition that the river Chaspeya formed the boundary line of Palestine, and they wish to inter the dead in the Holy Land. But this boundary line was only so after the return from Babylon, as I have shown at the proper place above.

who perhaps do this in consonance with some tradition that the present mountaineers are thus descended. These Druses are under the government of the Amir Abshir, who resides at Dir al Kamar, a town about 20 English miles northeast of Tyre. The religion of these people consists of a mixture of Christian and Mahomedan doctrines, and they are much given to immorality and general looseness of conduct. Their chief occupation consists in the production of silk and cotton fabrics; and they are also engaged in agriculture, and their wine especially is very good, and considerable quantities of cotton wool are likewise produced by them.

The Lebanon is also inhabited by a Christian sect, called Maronites, who have a convent in the town of Kanabin, in the district of Al Donie, where their patriarch, or the chief of their religion, resides. The Maronites are, however, often persecuted by the Druses, who far exceed them in numbers, and are occasionally murderously assailed by them. Only a few years back, in the year 5603 (1843) and in 5605 (1845), wars of this nature took place, in which a large number of Christians lost their lives. These Maronites, as well as the small Mahomedan population found in the mountains, are, with the Druses, under the government of the above-mentioned Amir.

In only three places of Mount Lebanon are Jewish inhabitants found: in Tripoli, as already stated, twelve families, in Dir Al Kamar eighty families, the heads of whom are mostly merchants, and in Chaspeya near thirty families. The Jews are greatly beloved by the Druses, and they are active agriculturists, like the other inhabitants of the mountains, and noted for their courage and bravery. Even the girls engaged in tending the flocks go armed with pistols and javelins, and boldly defend themselves against wild beasts and robbers. About twenty-four years ago, a Jewish girl of Chaspeya was tending her flock in the field, when a

Turk threatened to do her violence, as she was alone, and no one near to come to her aid. But she drew forth her pistol and ordered him on pain of death to desist from his attempt; and as he would not listen to her, she levelled her weapon and shot him dead on the spot. She was cited to appear before the judges; and she was not only acquitted of all blame, but much praise was publicly awarded to her for her intrepidity and courageous behaviour.

In the year 5591 (1831), when the mountaineers of the district of Sanur (which see), who occupied the fort of the same name, rebelled against the then Pacha of Akko (St. Jean D'Acre), Abdalla, and had caused a great slaughter among his troops, he requested of the Amir to aid him with some of his bravest men to subdue the rebels. The Amir assented, and sent him about one hundred Jews from Dir al Kamar and Chaspeya, who, greatly to their renown, reduced the stronghold of Sanur, which the Pacha thereupon ordered to be levelled to the ground, and it has remained in this state ever since.

The Amir is subject to the Sultan of Constantinople, to whom he pays the legal tribute, that is, when it suits him, for he is nearly independent in his mountain fastnesses amidst the towering Alps, and he need not fear the armies which his nominal sovereign might be induced to send against him. In the year 5594 (1834), when the so-called peasant war raged in the Holy Land, and the Fallahin laid waste the city of Zafed, the Amir came with his army and delivered the Jews from the power of their enemies; for at that time the Druses were on friendly terms with Ibrahim Pacha. Nevertheless, four years later, when the mountaineers were at war with their former ally, Ibrahim, they suddenly surprised Zafed, and plundered the Jews residing there. In the progress of the war, however, they were overcome by the Egyptian Pacha, notwithstanding the strength of their position, after a prolonged struggle. This occurred in 5598 (1838); and this defeat has greatly reduced their power. (Fuller particulars of these events will be found in the historical part of this work.)

THE MOUNTAINS OF GALILEE.

Having thus described the Lebanon, situated at the northern limits of Palestine, we must now notice the other more southerly mountains of the Holy Land.

In the same manner as the Hermon (Djebl Sheich) gradually expands in a chain of lower hills to the southeast, forming there the Djebl Heish; it also extends to the southwest through means of the mountains of Upper Galilee, anciently the mountains of Naphtali, and both these chains enclose the plain of the Lake Semechonitis (Waters of Merom). On the northwest portion of this lake commence the mountains of Zafed, which are a part of the southern portion of the Djebl Sheich. From the Bridge of Jacob's Sons, which spans the Jordan, there extends a plain about 4 English miles in length, and at its termination begin the mountains of Naphtali, the summit of which, called Djebl Zafed, is reached by a gradual ascent of 4 English miles in length. Djebl Sheich is thence visible in a northeast direction, and the sea of Chinnereth to the south. The descent of this mount to the south is also very gradual, and after a walk of 8 English miles, the traveller reaches the city of Zafed. On the road to Mount Tabor, about 15 English miles in length, there are constantly in view, in the plain, ranges of mountains in the distance. Northwest of Zafed, towards Tyre, there is a hilly country 30 miles in extent, which is very productive. On the west side of Zafed, on a clear day, the Mediterranean Sea, near Akko, is distinctly visible. In the direction of Zippori (Sephoris), the country is an unproductive range of hills; whereas, in the immediate neighbourhood of the just-named city, there is a very fruitful plain, anciently called the plain of Zebulun. (See Megillah, fol. 6 *a.*)* From the city of Nazareth to Tiberias, is a mountainous country; and the descent to Lake Chinnereth is by a steep road over the hills, of only 2½ miles, and from Nazareth southward to the valley of Jezreel it is 2 miles in length.

THE LAND OF GALILEE,

(1 Kings ix. 11,)

Is an elevated plain, which gradually descends westward to the level of the sea, near Akko (St. Jean D'Acre), southward to the plain of Jezreel, but terminates abruptly at the east in the level of Lake Chinnereth and the plain of the Jordan. This country is divided into

UPPER AND LOWER GALILEE.†

The former comprises, in a word, the whole mountains of Naphtali, the Djebl Zafed to the mountainous district of

* Resh Lakish said, I saw the valley of Zippori flowing with milk and honey, and it was sixteen mill long by sixteen mill broad.

† We read in Mishna Shebiith, chap. ix. § 2, "From the village of Chananiah (now Kefer Anon), where no Shikmin (see Art. *Shikmin* farther on) grow, is Upper Galilee; but south of this village, where Shikmin do grow, is Lower Galilee;" consequently the present Kefer Anon, which is about 3 English miles southwest from Zafed, is here regarded as the dividing line between the two districts in question. Josephus, however, holds the following language concerning the bounds of Galilee, Bell. Jud. b. iii. chap. 3: "Now Phœnicia and Syria encompass about the Galilees, which are two, and called *Upper Galilee* and the *Lower*. They are bounded towards the sunsetting with the borders of the territory belonging to the Ptolemais and by Carmel, which mountain had formerly belonged to the Galileans, but now belonged to the Tyrians, to which mountain adjoins Gaba (Chepha חי׳פה), which is called *the City of Horsemen*, because those horsemen that were dismissed by Herod, the king, dwelt therein. They are bounded on the south with Samaria and Scythopolis, as far as the river Jordan; on the east with Hippene and Gadaris, and also with Gaulanitis and the borders of the kingdom of Agrippa; its northern parts are bounded by Tyre and the country of the Tyrians.

Shaghar (see the foregoing note to Zedad to the name כרכה דבר סניגורא), consequently from the northwest point of

As for that Galilee which is called the *Lower*, it extends in length from Tiberias to Zebulon, and of the maritime places, Ptolemais is its neighbour; its breadth is from the village called *Xaloth* (Gineea), which lies in the great plain, as far as Bersábé, from which beginning also is taken the breadth of the Upper Galilee, as far as the village Baca, which divides the land of the Tyrians from it; its length is also from Meloth (Meroth) to Thella, a village near to Jordan." It is, indeed, difficult to ascertain the extent of Galilee from this description, since we do not know, accurately, all the names of the places mentioned therein. I presume that Baca (the *Baba* of some editions is undoubtedly an error of the press) is to be sought for in the southern part of Coelesyria, in Arabic Baaka (from בקע, a hollow, a valley), which extends to the vicinity of Tyre, and that the village had the same name as the valley in which it stood (see לבוא חמת). *Thella* is undoubtedly the ancient Tellum, now Chirbath Tillum, situated on the northwest shore of the Lake of Tiberias. Meroth (in some editions Meloth) appears to me to be the village Al Magr (the Cave), 2½ English miles east of Akko. (The Arabic Magr is the Hebrew Ma'ar מער, as Gain stands for 'Ain). Xaloth cannot possibly be the town of Kesuloth, spoken of in Joshua xix. 18, situated near Mount Tabor, since the Xaloth of Josephus is said to be the most southern point of Galilee, and can, therefore, not be sought for near Tabor. I, therefore, believe that the reading Gineea, is the correct one, in place of Xaloth, and signifies the modern Dshinin (En Gannim of Joshua xix. 21), which is actually situated on the great plain Merdj Abn Amr, the ancient valley of Jezreel or Megiddo, and can, therefore, be taken justly as the most southern point of Galilee. I think myself authorized to maintain that the reading Xaloth is absolutely erroneous, and that it should be *Cuth*, the modern Kefer Kuth, 4 English miles west of Dshinin, since I find in this name a trace of the כפר עותנה, mentioned in Gittin, fol. 76 *a*, and Yerushalmi Baba Mezia, chap. 7, Kefar 'Utna, and changing the 'Ain for Gain, would give us Gutna, which is easily corrupted into Kuth; and if this supposition be correct, then do Josephus and the Talmud agree as to the southern point of Galilee. *Zebulon:* north of the Shafamer (שפרעם) on the road to Akko, is found a spring called Ain Zabulon; perhaps there once stood near it the city of the same name, which is mentioned by Josephus in the extract I have given. Others, however, think that the town of Zebulon mentioned by Josephus, is the town of Chabul, which is situated at a distance of 5 English miles north-northeast of Akko.

Lake Chinnereth to the Mediterranean Sea near Tyre. Lower Galilee, however, comprises the mountain range of Zippori, the present Sefuri, the Mount Tabor, and the Little Hermon (Djebl Duhu), and the mountains of Gilboa, consequently the whole district, from the Jordan near Beth Shean, to Mount Carmel, and it forms the north-eastern boundary, or edge, of the valley of Jezreel.

In Upper Galilee, therefore, are situated the mountains of Naphtali, called Djebl Zafed, and in Lower Galilee, opposite Tiberias, near the village of Chittin, is the high mount, Kurn Chittin, which is, the Summit of Chittin. This mount is celebrated in history; for it was here that a great battle was fought on the 4th of July, 4947 (1187), between Saladin, King of Egypt, and the Christians, when Guy (Guidon) of Lusignan, was taken prisoner by the Mussulman king, who afterwards captured Jerusalem from the Christians, and put an end to their kingdom in Palestine. Five English miles from this mount is the one famous in the history of the prophetess Deborah (Judges iv. 6), to wit:

THE MOUNT TABOR.

This handsome mount, situated in the land of Issachar, and called by the Arabs Djebl Tur, commands a view of the most agreeable district of the whole country, and is near 3000 feet high.* On its summit, which is 1¼ English miles in circumference, was formerly a city of the same name, as will be made evident by a reference to Joshua xix. 22, and which was a fortified place even as late as the times of Josephus, when, however, it was destroyed by Titus. The Empress Helena, the mother of Constantine the Great, had

* According to the Midrash Yalkut to Deut. xxxiii. 18, it is the mountain on which the temple ought of right to have been built, on account of its being the most elegant and highest of all the elevations in Palestine, had it not been for the express revelation which ordered the sanctuary to be erected on Mount Moriah.

a monastery built on this mount; and to this day the ruins of this structure, consisting of the walls, are still existing, and on the western portion there is yet a large archway, in which the gate was. On the side of Tabor there is a forest of oak trees, in which many wild boars are found. The Turks built a fortress on this mount in the time of Innocent the Third.

THE PLAIN OF JEZREEL. THE VALLEY OF MEGIDDON.

(Joshua xvii. 16; Zech. xii. 11.)

This valley, called also Esdrelon, and by the Arabs Merdj Abn Amr, extends from east to west 20 English miles, and from north to south from 10 to 12, and is enclosed on all sides by mountains, to wit, on the north by Mount Tabor, on the south by the mountains of Ephraim (or the mountains of Samaria, Jer. xxxi. 5, 6), on the northeast by the mountains of Gilboa (1 Sam. xxxi. 1), which are 1200 feet high, and now called Galban by the Arabs, and at last, on the southwest, by Mount Carmel (1 Kings xviii. 19), at the foot of which the brook Kishon flows, which takes its course through this plain to that of Akko. This plain of Jezreel, which extends to the Lake Chinnereth, does not present, as the word would seem to imply, a perfect level throughout its extent, since it is traversed by several low ridges towards the centre, among which must be particularly noticed the Djebl Duhu, also called the Little Hermon,* which is at the distance of 2½ English miles south of Tabor. Between this and Gilboa there is a narrow valley, about 2 English miles in length, which is called by some the valley of Sharon. It was for the inhabitants of this narrow valley that the high priest prayed on the day of Atonement, "that their houses might

* Perhaps reference is made to this mount in Psalm lxxxix. 13: "Tabor and Hermon shall rejoice in thy name,"—evidently referring to contiguous positions.

not become their graves" (Talmud Yerushalmi Yoma, chap. v.), as they were in constant danger of being overwhelmed in their houses, through the mountain torrents, which, however, could not happen to the inhabitants of that Sharon which is alongside of the Mediterranean, distant from any mountain, and consequently could not suffer from such an overflow as mountainous countries alone are exposed to. This little valley extends to the Lake Chinnereth, and there is in it a village called Shirin, perhaps derived from the original Sharon. The mountains of Gilboa extend eastwardly, and separate the plain of Jordan from that of Jezreel. Beth Shean (Joshua xvii. 11) is situated in the valley Al Ghor, which is 5 English miles in breadth. 3½ miles north of Megiddo was formerly a fort and the village of Saba, wherefore the plain of Jezreel was called in the times of Josephus the plain of Saba. From this valley to the great desert near Gazza, and the Dead Sea, are a succession of mountain ridges, first the mountain of Ephraim, and then to the south the mountains of Judah. Both these chains gradually descend in the west to the level of the Mediterranean, and on the east to the plain of the Jordan and the shores of the Dead Sea.

THE MOUNT OF EPHRAIM הר אפרים

(Joshua xvii. 15)

Is the same called, according to my opinion, the mountain of Israel (Joshua xi. 21), in contradistinction to the more southern mountain of Judah. It is, however, not a single mount, as its name would seem to imply, but a long chain, several days' journey in extent, which branches out in all directions, on which were formerly many towns and villages, of which many remains are yet found at this day. The Talmud calls this range הר המלך* or טור מלכא

* In Menachoth, fol. 109 *b*, occurs "he fled to the house of the king" לבית המלך, which I suppose to be an error of the transcriber, and should

"Kings' Mount" (see Gittin 57 *b*, and Jonathan ben Uziel to Judges iv. 5). The mounts Gerizzim and Ebal (Deut. xi. 29), also Gaash (Judges ii. 9), Mount Zemaraim (2 Chron. xiii. 4), and almost all the mountains of Jerusalem, may be reckoned as belonging to the range of this mountain. Ebal lies north of Shechem, and is a naked, barren hill, 800 feet in height; but the Mount Gerizzim,* which is southwest of the valley of Shechem, is higher than Ebal, and is very fruitful, and forms the highest elevation of the whole mountain of Ephraim, which extends southwesterly to the low land near the sea שפלה (which will be more particularly spoken of hereafter), and the district of Ekron, and southeast to Beth-El, and has a breadth from north to south of two days' journey, and a length of one day's journey.

MOUNT CARMEL הר הכרמל

(1 Kings xviii. 19)

Is called by the Arabs Djebl Mukata, i. e. the Mount of Slaughter, because Elijah caused the prophets of Baal to be slain here. Just as the mountains of Gilboa extend to the northeast of the valley of Jezreel, so there are to the northwest of the same naked ridges, which form parts of Carmel, which gradually declines to the sea. (Jer. xlvi. 18.) It has its name, which signifies The Fruitful, from its fruitfulness and the abundance of its products. At its foot grow many olive trees, also many laurels, and its summit is covered with pines and other forest trees, and many kinds of flowers are also to be met with there. It is 1500 feet high, and has many caves, especially on the west side, and some allege to have counted more than a thousand of

be להר המלך to the king's mount. For proof of this correction being the proper reading, I refer to Talmud Yerushalmi Yoma, chap. vi.

* The Arabs call it Djebl Hisan, which name, I suppose, is derived from the Mount Sion mentioned in the Book of Jashar in connexion with Gen. xxxiv., in the wars of the sons of Jacob.

them. One of these, 20 paces in length and 15 in breadth, has the name of the cave of Elijah or Elisha. The Carmel affords the traveller a wide prospect: on its northern side Akko can be distinctly seen, as also the termination of the Lebanon, called Sulma Dezur, "the Ladder of Tyre," and the Ras Abiat (the White Promontory which stands in the sea); on the northeast side, Mount Hermon (Djebl Sheich) can be seen, although distant 50 English miles. The Empress Helena built on Carmel also a monastery. In the year 4987 (1227), the Christians who had come from Europe built a fort here, which is, however, now a mere ruin. The Carmel mountains extend southeasterly towards the left side of the valley of Jezreel, till they touch the mountains of Ephraim, in the neighbourhood of the village Kut, which is west of Dshinin, the ancient En-Gannim.

THE MOUNTAINS OF JUDAH הרי יהודה

(Joshua xxi. 11.)

From Jaffa there extends itself eastward, on the road to Ramleh, the highly fruitful and productive valley of Sharon, which is 15 English miles in length. Then, however, commence the mountains of Judah, which extend to Jerusalem, and the traveller has before him a constant ascent and descent on the whole road of 15 English miles, which leads to the holy city. Near Jerusalem commence the eastern mountains, which extend a distance of 12 English miles to the plains of Jordan, near Jericho.* To this range of the mountains of Judah belong all the hills of Jerusalem; for instance, the Temple Mount, Mount Zion, Mount of Olives, also the more distant ones, the wilderness of Tekoa (Zeruel, 2 Chron. xx. 16); En-Gedi (1 Sam. xxii. 2); Maon (ibid. xxiii. 24); Ziph (ibid. xxvi. 2), and Car-

* The high mountain called by the Christians Quarantania, situated northeast of Geba (Joshua xviii. 24), belongs to the mountains of Ephraim.

mel (Joshua xv. 55). These mountains, situated west of the Dead Sea, approach its shore nearer and nearer the farther they extend southward; from Gazza, however, westward, they leave the Mediterranean more and more the farther they extend to the south. Near Hebron, the mountain of Judah is 18 English miles in breadth, to wit, from here to the Mediterranean on the west 13, and east to the Dead Sea 5 miles. In general may this range be called an elevated plain; since from Hebron to Mount Seir (Deut. ii. 1), southwest of the Dead Sea, the whole road leads constantly down hill to a deep valley; so also on the south side the mountain declines gradually in a distance of 5 English miles. Near Gazza commences the great desert which extends to the Red Sea, near Mount Sinai.

THE PLAINS ON THE SHORE OF THE MEDITERRANEAN.

From Ras al Nakhura, in Talmud called Sulma Dezur סולמא דצור the Rock Ladder of Tyre, to the confines of Gazza, that is, from the north to the south of Palestine, there is a large, rich, and fruitful district of low land, which is bounded on the west by the Mediterranean, and on the east by the mountains of Galilee, Ephraim, and Judah. The Carmel divides the plain of Akko, which forms the northern, from that of Sharon and the low country (שפלה), which form the southern portion of this great level. From Tyre southward, there is a road cut out of the rocks leading over Ras al Albiat to Nakhura, where the plain of Akko is seen lying at the foot of the mount. It is said that this road is the work of Alexander of Macedon.

THE PLAIN OF AKKO

Commences at Ras al Nakhura, and extends in breadth from north to south, over Akko to the foot of Carmel. The Kishon and the Shichor-Libnath flow through the same. It is in length 5 English miles, and 15 in breadth.

THE PLAIN OF CARMEL TO GAZZA.

From Mount Carmel to Gazza, there extends itself a beautiful plain 100 miles in length and 10 to 15 in breath; and especially near Jaffa is it extremely rich and fertile, and it is this portion which is called the valley of Sharon, and commences near Dardura (the ancient Dor, Joshua xvii. 11), and in this delightful spot are met with the most beautiful flowers, red and white in colour, in greater variety than in any other part of Palestine. To the south of Jaffa, Ramleh, and Jabneh, the valley of Sharon unites itself to the valley of the Philistines, which latter portion, also exceedingly rich and fruitful, is that called in Holy Writ the low country (השפלה Joshua xi. 16; Jer. xxxii. 44; xxxiii. 13), and extends southward from Gazza to the river of Egypt, the already described Wady al Arish, where the great and fearful desert commences.

The just-mentioned beautiful plains are watered by the following little streams, most of which I have not yet described above, as they are only water-courses in winter, but dry in summer.

South of Dardura there is the Wady Kuradshe; farther south, is the Wady Zirka; south of Cæsarea is the Kanah (Joshua xvii. 9), now Wady al Kazab, already described; near Ramleh is the Wady Udshi (or the Spring of Green Waters); south of Jaffa is the Wady Rubin, which flows past the town of Jabneel (Joshua xv. 11), and is called, farther to the east, Wady Zarar. Southwest of the village Kefer Ain Karem is the valley of Elah, where David smote the Philistine Goliath: this is the view of Hieronymus; but to me it appears that there can be no doubt of the Wady Sunt, between Suweiche (the Socho of 1 Samuel xvii. 1) and Ezakaria, being the עמק האלה the valley of Elah, since Sunt is the Arabic for the Hebrew Elah, oak. West of Hebron is the Wady Azarar, which I hold to be the valley of Eshkol (Grape Valley), where the spies sent out by Moses cut a branch of the vine with a bunch of grapes attached to it (Num. xiii. 23; compare also with Midrash Tanchuma in l. c.), also the valley of Sorek, where Samson chose himself a wife (Judges xvi. 4); near Askhelon is the Wady Askelon; near Gazza the Wady Saria, also called Besor in Scripture (1 Sam. xxx. 10, see above, p. 52); and lastly, the Wady al Arish, the river of Egypt, anciently the Rhinocorura, which forms the southern boundary line of the Holy Land. (Num. xxxiv. 5.)

THE PLAIN OF THE JORDAN. בכר הירדן

(Gen. xiii. 10.)

The Arabs call the plain extending from Chinnereth to the Dead Sea, through which the Jordan takes its course, Al Gor,* which signifies a plain enclosed between mountains. This plain, termed in the Hebrew Scriptures the Circle of Jordan, constitutes the lowest portion of the

* The passage in Deut. iii. 17, מכנרת ועד ים הערבה ים המלח "From Chinnereth even unto the sea of the plain, which is the salt sea," is rendered by Saadiah "Min Ginsur ali Bachr al Gor ual Bachr al Mit," that is, from Genesereth to the sea Al Gor and the Dead Sea. In one edition I find added "al Gor ual Ordan," i. e. Al Gor and Jordan. But in Deut. iv. 49, he renders ועד ים הערבה with Ali Bachrie Tiberie, "to the sea of Tiberias," which proves that the whole plain of the Jordan, from Chinnereth to the Dead Sea, is called Gor or Arabah, since both these seas are called the sea of Gor or Arabah. This will explain an obscure passage in 2 Chron. xxvi. 7, "And God helped him against the Philistines, and against the Arabians that dwelt in Gur-Baal and the Meunim." We often find baal בעל to signify *plain*, a *fruitful land;* so that we may assume that Gur-Baal here spoken of is nothing else than the present Al Gor; and indeed there is found at this day, in this plain, a village by name of Maun, possibly the seat of the Me'unim of Chronicles. [Me'unim is legitimately derived from the singular Ma'un, and the Sheva takes, as usual, the place of Kametz, because the word is increased a syllable, and the tone is removed one syllable farther down, whence it is requisite that the first, being a changeable vowel, should be shortened, or, in other words, Ma'un becomes in plural Me-un-im.—TRANSLATOR.]

whole land, and the heat of the sun is very great here, because it is enclosed between two ranges of mountains. Near Beth Shean the plain is 5, and near Jericho 8 miles in breadth. Through the whole plain there runs a depression about 1000 paces broad, which is the bed of the Jordan. Properly speaking, does this Al Gor extend to the Red Sea, at Akaba, the ancient Ezion-Gaber* (Num.

* Through this view we can explain clearly many obscure passages in Holy Writ. For instance, Gen. l. 10: "And they came to the threshing-floor Atad, which is beyond Jordan." Now the question arises, What use was there for so circuitous a route to the east side of Jordan, when they could as easily move from Egypt to Hebron, without coming at all in that direction?—Likewise in Num. xxi. 4, it says, "They moved from Mount Hor, by the way of the Red Sea, to compass the land of Edom." If, now, they moved northward from Hor, their road lay by no means in the direction of the Red Sea, unless they made a retrogression, wherefore the Talmud Rosh Hashanah actually maintains that they made a retrograde movement. But if our assumption be correct, that formerly the Jordan flowed onward till it met the Red Sea, so that the whole Araba, the entire Al Gor to the Arabian Gulf, formed the bed of the river through which it reached the sea: then can the words דרך ים סוף "the way to the Red Sea," signify simply the Araba or Gor, equivalent to the bed, the course, the direction of the Jordan to the Red Sea. So also in Deut. ii. 1, "By way of the Red Sea;" ibid. 8, "Through the way of the plain" (Arabah). We therefore explain the passage cited from Num. xxi. 4, thus: They moved from Mount Hor through the Gor, or Arabah, to go round the land of Edom; and not that they returned to the confines of the Gulf of Arabia. We may also assume that, as the Jordan formerly reached the Red Sea, there are two "beyond Jordan" spoken of in the Scriptures, to wit, the northern part, or the course of the river till it reaches the Dead Sea, and the southern part, to wit, the ancient Jordan from the Dead to the Red Sea; so that the whole plain situated between both the bays of the Red Sea, i. e. the eastern Akaba and the western Suez, is called עבר הירדן "beyond Jordan," that is, "the east side" of the southern Jordan. We may therefore assume farther, that the threshing-floor Atad was east of the ancient bed of the river, between Egypt and Hebron, but not in the northern portion of its actual course, in the land afterwards belonging to the tribes of Reuben and Gad and half the tribe of Menasseh. As farther proof, the reader is referred to Deut. i. 1: "These are the words which Moses spoke unto all Israel on this side of Jordan, in the wilderness, in the plain (Arabah) over against the Red Sea," &c. If we examine

xxxiii. 35); since, before the destruction of Sodom and Gomorrah, through which means the Dead Sea was formed, the Jordan flowed into the Red Sea; and to this day are the old bed and former course of the river visible, and can be easily traced. The Arabs also call the southern portion of this Al Gor, below the Dead to the Red Sea, "Al Arabah."

This plain of the Jordan, the romantic beauty of which is truly astonishing, is the most agreeable district of all Palestine. It is traversed by the Jordan in its whole length. On both sides of this clear river, the water of which is very agreeable for drinking, are found the most varied trees, the green branches of which are so closely interwoven with each other, that they form the most beautiful natural arbours, under the agreeable and refreshing shadow of which the traveller passes from one to the other, as though he walked in a pleasure-garden, laid out so designedly by the hand of man. The ear of the wanderer is here delighted by the soft rushing of the Jordan, combined with the harmonious song of birds, which fill the air with natural melodies; and the eye is ravished by a view of the banks of the river, brilliant in their green ornaments, and the beams of the majestic sun, as they

the punctuation of this verse, we shall find that the pause accent, the Ethnach, is not put under *Israel*, but under *Jordan;* from which it appears that, according to the authority of the Massorah, the principal division of the verse is at *Jordan*, not at *Israel;* so that all the words following on the latter are to be taken as those used to define what is meant by "this side of Jordan," so that "the wilderness, in the plain" (Arabah), &c., would make it the ancient or southern part of the bed of the river. In verse 5, however, it says, "On this side of Jordan, in the land of Moab." This, therefore, would indicate the northern part, whence the addition "in the land of Moab" is to show that the previous "beyond Jordan," or "this side of Jordan," as given in the English version, does not refer to the land of the two and a half tribes. It is therefore but fair to assert that the assumption of Eusebius that the threshing-floor Atad was on Jordan, opposite Jericho, is entirely erroneous, as its position must be sought for in the south, near the extinct, not the actual, bed of the river.

penetrate the thick foliage; and even in the autumn, in the month of September, when I travelled through this region, I was so charmed with the whole scene that my heart, full to admiration through the incomparable beauty of this region, lifted itself up to God; and I could have exclaimed, overcome by a painful feeling at the loneliness of the scene: "My God! how is my soul bowed down within me, when I remember thee in this land of Jordan." (Psalm xlii. 7.) "Is not this whole district of the Jordan abundantly watered, fruitful, and blessed, like a garden of the Lord?" (Gen. xiii. 10.) "And still it is scarcely trod by the foot of the traveller, it is not inhabited, and the Arab pitches not there his tents, and the shepherds do not cause the flocks to lie down there." (Isa. xiii. 20.) "Still, thus speaketh the Lord Zebaoth, There shall yet be in this place, which is waste, without man and cattle, again a dwelling for shepherds, causing their flocks to lie down." "In those days shall Judah be redeemed, and Jerusalem shall be inhabited in security, and this is the name which it shall be called, *The Lord* our righteousness." (Jer. xxxiii. 12–16.)

In concluding this chapter, I wish to explain an obscure passage in Talmud and Mishna. It is said in Rosh Hashanah, 22 *b*, that fire-signals were lighted first on the Mount of Olives, then on Sartafa, next on Gerufné, then on Choran, and next at Beth-Baltin, the latter spot is also called Biram. Signal fires were also lighted on the mountains of Charim, Chear, and Geder. Some learned men believe that the latter three were situated between the other mountains; whilst others entertain the more correct opinion that they were situated in another direction from Palestine to Babylon than the first. In the Tosephta to Rosh Hashanah, there is also added as follows: "On Mount Tabor and the mountain of Machvar (see article Jaaser), likewise, were signal fires lighted."

When one stands, on a clear day, on the Mount of Olives and looks northward, he can discover the Mounts of Gerizzim and Ebal not far from Shechem. Near them, in an eastern direction, appears an indistinct prominent peak. Upon close inquiry, I ascertained that the Arabs call this peak Kurn Sartaf, i. e. the horn of Sartaf. The situation of this mount is about 6 English miles west of Jordan, east-northeast from Seilon (Silo), and distant about 24 English miles from the Mount of Olives. Wherefore I hold this point to be, without doubt, the Sartafa of the Talmud. Eastward from Jordan, at a distance of about 15 English miles in the district of Merad, at the south of Wady Redjeb, which is also called Wady Adshlun, about 3 English miles south of the old castle Kallat al Raba (Ramoth Gilead), there is found a small mountain chain called Arapun, and has near its centre a prominent peak. Without doubt this is the ancient Gerufné, since the Arabs often put *Ain* for *Gain;* hence, Arapun for Garaphun, almost identical with Gerufné. In the mountain of Hauran (which see) there is a high peak, called in Arabic, Kelb Hauran, i. e. the heart, the centre of the mountain, which is the above-mentioned Choran. Beth-Baltin is beyond Euphrates (see article Biram). On the eastern shore of Lake Chinnereth, are found the ruins of Geder. East of Kanetra, on the caravan road, over the Jordan bridge to Damascus, is found the village Tel Chara, with a mount of the same name. We may find in this a trace of the Charim of the Talmud. In a northern direction from this village, about 20 English miles south of Damascus, is the mount Djebl Chiara, probably identical with Chear.

Here, then, we have two lines from Palestine to Babylon; the first northeasterly, over Sartaf and Gerufné &c., and the other, the northern, over Geder, Charim, and Chear.

CHAPTER III.

A DESCRIPTION OF THE DIVISION OF PALESTINE ACCORDING TO THE TERRITORIES OF THE TWELVE TRIBES, AS GIVEN IN THE BOOK OF JOSHUA.

BEFORE commencing to describe this division, I wish to elucidate the 31 Kings mentioned in Joshua xii., and to determine, at the same time, to which tribe each of the respective cities belonged.

1. יריחו Jericho, a city in the portion of Benjamin, about 20 English miles east-northeast from Jerusalem, 4 English miles west of Jordan, in the valley of the Jordan or Al Gor. The district between the so-called En Sultan, also En Elisa (2 Kings ii. 22; see Jos., Bell. Jud., book v. chap. iv.), and the old castle Burdj Chadjla, about 2 English miles in length, is called by the Arabs Richa. But there is neither village nor ruin to be met with, and they know only from tradition that Jericho should have stood here. Hitherto the just-mentioned castle was always taken as a remnant of Jericho; according to my more accurate investigation, however, and the information I was able to collect, which I obtained circumstantially and correctly from the sheich of the Arabs of the neighbourhood, I must deem this view erroneous.* Jericho is called the City of Palms (Deut. xxxiv. 3, and Judges iii. 13); here was the seat of the Moabite King Eglon, and here† he was slain by Ehud, as Josephus tells in his

* See farther, article Beth-Choglah.

† Assuming this hypothesis will explain for us clearly the passage of Judges iii. 28, "And they went down after him, and took the fords of

Antiq., book v. chap. v. The whole country is now occupied by the Arabs, who dwell in tents, whose tents form together quite a considerable circle, and have almost the appearance of a village, in the midst of which the cattle are encamped at night. The adults are dressed; but the children, even those of considerable size, go completely naked, without the least covering.

2. עי Ai, namely, that in the vicinity of בית אל Beth-El. We nowhere find among the cities of the 31 Kings such a definition of Ai, as is given in Genesis xii. 8, and xiii. 3; whence I am led to suppose that there was yet another city of the same name. But I wish now to refer to the Ai of Genesis; and we find, in fact, four names for the place: 1st עי Ai; then עיא Aija (Neh. xi. 31); עוים Avim (Joshua xviii. 23); and עית Aiath (Isa. x. 28). If we now reflect that it is not likely that one place should have had four different names, we are led to suppose that there were two places called Ai; whence the diversity in writing the name. We cannot ascertain the neighbourhood where we should look for the one. But it is said in *Shemoth Rabbah*, chap. 32, that between Jericho and Ai there is but a distance of 3 mill, that is, 2¼ English miles. This Ai can, therefore, not possibly be the Ai near Beth-El, because it is more than 20 mill (15 English miles) from Richa; allusion must therefore be made here to the Ai which was near the present Richa.* About 2 English

Jordan towards Moab, and suffered not a man to pass over;" since, if this event took place at Jericho, and the whole vicinity was full of Moabites, Ehud, by cutting off their escape over Jordan to their own country, naturally must have captured many of them; whereas, if the occurrence had taken place in the country of Moab proper, to the east of the Dead Sea, the passage in question would not be easy of explanation.

* If we examine the passage cited from Shemoth Rabbah a little more closely, we shall find that it refers to a residence of a king, and can, therefore, refer only to the Ai near Beth-El, because it was here where the king in question dwelt. I suppose, therefore, that there is an error

miles southeasterly from Beitun (see Beth-El), are found, near the edge of a valley, some ruins, called by the Arabs Chirbath Medinat Gai, marking unquestionably the ancient Ai. Whence, then, Beth-El to the west, and Ai to the east (Gen. xii. 9). Joshua viii. 11, refers to the valley north of the ruins of Gai; for the Israelites lay north of Ai; the men in ambush were between Ai and Beth-El, somewhat to the south; and the inhabitants of Beth-El, in pursuing the Israelites in a northern direction, did not perceive those in ambush who were to the southward.

3. ירושלם Jerusalem (see farther down, article Jerusalem).

4. חברון Hebron (see article Hebron).

5. ירמות Jarmuth. About 7½ English miles north-northeast of Beth-Djibrin (בית גוברין which see), is the village Yurmuk, probably for Yurmuth.

6. לכיש Lachish. 12 English miles west-southwest of Beth-Djibrin are the ruins Um Lachish, without doubt the Lahchish of Scripture. The assertion of Eusebius that it was 7 mill southeast of Beth-Djibrin, appears to me erroneous.

7. עגלון Eglon. 2 English miles east of Um Lachish, are found the ruins of Adjlun; no doubt Eglon, the G having been changed into the Arabic Dj.

8. גזר Gezer.* 2 English miles east of Jaffa is the little village Gazur. It would appear, from Joshua xvi. 3, that

of the transcriber, and that it should read "between *Beth-El* (not Jericho) and Ai is but 3 mill;" and in truth there is about this distance between Beitun (Beth Aven ?) and Chirbath Medinat Gai.

* The assertion of the author of Caphtor Vapherach p. 68, that the village Ganzur, 5 English miles south of En-Gannim (Djinin), is identical with Gezer, appears to me unfounded; since, to judge from Joshua x. 33, it could not have been far from Lachish, and must have been near the sea, in nearly a straight line from Beth-Horon (Joshua xvi. 3); it can therefore not possibly be identical with Ganzur, which is north of Nablus, the ancient Shechem.

Gezer was not far from the sea, which indicates precisely this Gazur (see 1 Macc. vii. 39, 40); it therefore belonged to the tribe of Dan.

9. דביר Debir, also called קרית ספר Kiriath-Sepher (Joshua xv. 15), or קרית סנה Kiriath-Sannah (ibid. 49). Its site is unknown to me. But there is a valley in the mountains of Hebron, southwest of the town, called by the Arabs Wady Dibir, which perhaps marks the position of the ancient Debir.

10. גדר Geder. In the Wady Zarr (which see), 2½ English miles east of the mountain Modiim, I found the ruins of Gadara; probably those of Geder. It is also not unlikely that the village Djadr (by changing g in dj), 10 English miles north of Hebron, may be the ancient Geder.

11. חרמה Chormah. The actual position of this place is also uncertain; still it could not have been far from Maresha (2 Chron. xiv. 9); it belonged to Simeon.

12. ערד Arad. 22 English miles south of Hebron, and east of Moladah, is the village Tel Arad, probably on the site of Arad.*

* This is the city mentioned in Num. xxi. 1, and the vow which the Israelites made to destroy the towns belonging thereto, refers to the time when they should conquer the Holy Land; which was actually done under Joshua. "And they called the name of the place Chormah," means that the site of the place obtained that name, and that they built another city where Arad had stood, as this was left without being built on, and is not to be taken for the residence of the king of Chormah, which was the ancient Zefath (Judges i. 17), and in the portion of Simeon; this was near Michmash, and far distant from Arad, which was in the portion of Judah. The destruction of Arad is not mentioned in Joshua, because it was already referred to in Numbers. But the overthrow of Zefath and a second naming of the town from the act of destroying it (חרמה from חרם *to devote*), is another affair, the reason of which has not come down to us; as a proof, I cite the difference of the wording; in Num. xxi. 3, it says, "And he called the name of the *place*," i. e. where the city once stood, but in Judges i. 17, "the name of the *city*," &c.; the newly built town was called חרמה Chormah, instead of its predecessor Zefath; it is counted among the cities

13. לבנה Libnah, is unknown. Eusebius says only that it was in the neighbourhood of Beth-Djibrin.

14. עדלם Adullam, is likewise unknown. Eusebius merely says that it was 10 mill east from Beth-Djibrin; it should probably be northeast, since Adullam must have been near Timnah. (See Gen. xxxviii. 13; also 2 Macc. xii. 38.)

15. מקדה Makkedah is also unknown. Eusebius, however, places it 8 miles east of Beth-Djibrin.

16. בית אל Beth-El. I deem it proper to speak a little more circumstantially about this place, since it is generally assumed that there were two towns bearing this name; to wit, one belonging to the tribe of Benjamin, and situated in the neighbourhood of Jericho, consequently in the valley of the Jordan (Joshua xviii. 22); the other, however, on the border between Benjamin and Joseph (ibid. xvi. 1), on the mountain. This assertion is mainly supported by the passage (ibid. xvi. 2), "And it went out from Beth-El to Luz;" now, according to Genesis xxviii. 19, Beth-El and Luz are identical; the verse must therefore mean here from Beth-El in the valley to Beth-El on the mountain. But I maintain on the contrary that this opinion is incorrect, and that there was but one Beth-El. It appears from Genesis xii. 8, Joshua xvi. 1, and 2 Kings ii. 23, that it was situated in the mountains; and in the whole Al Gor there is no trace to be found of a single mount or a chain of mountains. It must therefore be sought for in the western mountains, those of Ephraim; wherefore it is impossible to assume that it can have been in the valley of

of Simeon, Joshua xix. 4, also to Judah, ibid. xv. 30; but Arad is not mentioned among the towns of Judah; it no doubt remained a תל עולם *Tel Olam*, "a perpetual ruin," whence then probably the present Arabic name Tel Arad, as having a trace of this fact, which has perhaps been handed down traditionally to the present inhabitants of this vicinity, and been preserved among them to this day.

the Jordan.* In rendering מבית אל לוזה I do not translate "from Beth-El to Luz," as though the ה after לוז were indicating the direction (as מצרימה instead of למצרים to Egypt; ארצה for לארץ to the earth), but "Beth-El Luzah," making Luzah (i. e. Luz with a feminine termination), the apposition to Beth-El, or "Beth-El, otherwise called Luz;" the meaning of the passage is, then, that the boundary ran from Beth-El, i. e. Luz to Archi Ataroth. We moreover find a ה at times at the end of a word without denoting the moving to a place; for example, ביטבתה Num. xxxiii. 33; לישה Isaiah x. 30; ברבלתה Jer. lii. 10; בתמנתה Judges xiv. 1. In point of fact we can discover no trace of a Beth-El in the valley of the Jordan; and the one mentioned in Joshua xviii. 22, as situated in the portion of Benjamin, is identical with that spoken of (ibid. xvi. 1) as belonging to Joseph, because it was situated on

* Nevertheless, I found a difficult passage, namely, 2 Kings ii. 2, "And they went down to Beth-El," whereas they were at Gilgal; wherefore it ought to be "And they went up," which would lead one to look for a Beth-El in the valley. Nevertheless, I found in Ruth Rabbethi chap. i. that the Beth-El to which Elijah and Elisha repaired, was the one where the golden calf was worshipped, consequently the same which was in the mountains. We must therefore explain the וירדו in this passage "They went down", as the phrase וירדתי על ההרים (Judges xi. 37), "And I will go down upon the mountains" (English version, "That I may go *up and* down"), but the words *up and* are not in the text; again וירד הסלע (1 Sam. xxiii. 25), English version, "He came down into a rock," should be "he went down to the rock," the rock being evidently the highest point; עלה תמנתה (Gen. xxxviii. 13), "Going up to Timnah," whereas in Judges xiv. 1, it is וירד שמשון תמנתה "Samson went *down* to Timnah." This seeming confusion I would thus explain: that all moving from north to south is termed going down, from the fact that in general the northern portions of Palestine are higher than the southern, which gradually sink into the level of the desert; whence then also the moving from south to north is called going up. (See Abn Ezra to Gen. xxxviii. 1.) Probably Elijah and Elisha were going southward, from the northern portion of Gilgal to Beth-El, wherefore the phrase "going down" is applicable, although Beth-El was on a mountain.

the boundary line, and is therefore reckoned as the property of both the tribes. A similar method is pursued with Jerusalem and Kirjath-Jearim (Joshua xv. 63, 68; xviii. 28), both of which are enumerated among the towns of Judah and Benjamin, because they were on the boundary. Beth-El is the city where Jeroboam introduced the worship of the golden calf, whence it was called בית און Beth-Aven, that is, instead of its being originally the house of God, it became the house of iniquity. It is probable, moreover, that the present Arabic name Beit-un, is derived from Beth-Aven. (See for farther particulars Talmud Yerushalmi Abodah Zarah, chap. iii.; Yerushalmi Shabbiith, chap. ix.; Bereshith Rabbah, chap. xxxix.; Targum Jonathan to Hosea x. 5.) In the mountains about 2 English miles northeast of Bireh (see בארות Beeroth), there is the village of Beit-un, undoubtedly the ancient Beth-El. The view of the author of Caphtor Vapherach, appears to me very obscure; for he says (fol. 61 *a.*), "South of Silo Beth-El is found; the Arabs call it Bitai, leaving out the ל (l)." The village Beita is about 5 English miles south of Nablus (Shechem); consequently north, not south of Shiloh (Seilon, or Silo), and we cannot possibly look for Beth-El so far to the north.

17. תפוח Tapuach, on the boundary between Ephraim and Menasseh (Joshua xvi. 8). At the present day the Arabs call the country between Nablus and the Jordan Balad Tapuach, as probably the town of this name was formerly in it.*

18. חפר Chepher, also called גת חפר Gath Chepher (2 Kings xiv. 25). We can deduce from Yerushalmi Shebiith, chap. vi., that this city was not far from Zippori. Now 2½ English miles southeast of Safuri there is the village Medjath (from the Hebrew מגת Miggath, changing g into dj);

* See farther, when discussing the name of Tapuach, which occurs in the book of Jashar.

and they point out there the grave of Jonah, of Gath Chepher. The modern name, therefore, has a trace in it of its former appellation, and we may therefore assume that Chepher (Hepher) formerly stood here.

19. אפק Aphek. We find that there were five towns of this name:—1, in the portion of Judah (Joshua xv. 53); 2, on the boundary between Benjamin and Ephraim (1 Sam. iv. 1); in the vicinity of the Eben Ha-ezer and Mizpeh; 3, in the portion of Issachar, in the valley of Jezreel, where the battle between Saul and the Philistines took place (ibid. xxix. 1); 4, in the portion of Asher (Joshua xix. 30); and 5, in the Lebanon (ibid. xiii. 4).* It is uncertain to which place the king of Aphek in question belonged; to judge, however, from the succession of the enumeration, which stretches from south to the north, I should conclude that it was situated in the valley of Jezreel.

20. לשרון Lasharon. I have already said, in chapter ii., that the valley of Sharon is situated on the shore of the Mediterranean Sea. About midway between Cæsarea and Jaffa are found some ruins, which are called Saran, and are probably the remains of the city here mentioned.

21. מדון Madon. 4 English miles north of Safuri (Zippori) is the village Manda. I suppose that this is identical with Madon, as the Arabs frequently transpose the letters. The author of Caphtor Vapherach remarks (fol. 67): "The Arabs likewise are in error, in calling a place in the vicinity of Zippori 'Kafar Manda,' as they maintain it to be the ancient Midian." But it strikes me that the error is merely

* Aphek, where Benhadad was defeated (1 Kings xx. 26), appears to me to have been situated likewise in the valley of Jezreel, since he was counselled to attack Israel in the plain, and not on the mountain. There is a village Fik, probably for Aphek, on the east side of Lake Tiberias; but it does not appear to me to be likely that the battle could have occurred there, since this Fik also is situated in the mountains on which Benhadad was advised not to fight.

in the naming of the place, that they pronounced it Midian instead of Madon, and this confirms me in concluding that Manda contains a trace of the ancient Madon.

22. חצור Hazor (Chazor) was the largest town in northern Palestine (Joshua xi. 10). At the present day there is a village called Azur between Banias and Meshdel, probably the remains of the old Hazor. In an Arabic version I found this passage translated "King of Cæsarea," probably meaning Cæsarea Philippi, which is Dan or Laish (which see), which is actually near Azur.

23. שמרון מראון Shimron Meron. Among the cities of Zebulun, we find, in Joshua xix. 15, the name of Shimron. Yerushalmi Megillah, chap. i., says "Shimron is the present Simuni." In our own days there is the village Samuni, 5 English miles northwest of Safuri. The author of Caphtor Vapherach, fol. 68, says: "South from the mountains of Gilboa is the town Dir Meruan, one of those belonging to the thirty-one kings." But there is a great distance between Samuni and Dir Meruan; still it is possible that the same king ruled over both places.

24. אכשף Achshaph, in the portion of Asher, which see.

25. תענך Thaanach. } In the portions of the sons of
26. מגדו Megiddo. } Joseph (which see).

27. Kedesh, in the mountains of Naphtali (Joshua xix. 37, xx. 7), is doubtlessly the modern village Kedes, 15 English miles north of Zafed.

28. יקנעם לכרמל Jokneam of Carmel. In the valley near Akko, near the Carmel, is a valley called Wady Naman, which has some slight resemblance to the ancient Jokneam. Eusebius says, "6 miles north of Megiddo is the city of Kamun," similar to Kanum; perhaps, then, this may be the Jokneam near Carmel.

29. דור לנפת דור Dor Lenaphath Dor. On the Mediterranean Sea, 10 English miles north of Cæsarea, is the village Dandura (see in the tribe of Menasseh); 2½

English miles southeast of this is the village Naphata, probably the just-mentioned לנפת, the ל being a preposition. *Naphath* does therefore appear to be a proper name, not to be translated with *coast,* as in the English version.

30. גוים לגלגל Goyim Legilgal. 19 English miles northeast of Jaffa is the large village Dshilil, probably an incorrect manner of writing Dshildshil, which is Gilgal by the usual transmutations, and belonged therefore to Dan. In an Arabic version I found this passage rendered with "the king of Al Achsab" (see Chezib); perhaps it is based upon some tradition that Gilgal and Chezib are identical. As respects the word Goyim, we find it appended to several other names, as Charosheth Haggoyim (חרשת הגוים), Judges iv. 2, not far from Chazor. So also Gelil Haggoyim (Isa. viii. 23), English version Galilee of the Gentiles, not far from Jordan.

31. תרצה Thirzah, in the portion of the sons of Joseph (which see).

THE POSSESSIONS OF THE TRIBES IN GENERAL.

The southern portion of Palestine was assigned to Judah. Near this, to the north, was Benjamin. In the possession of Judah, in the southwestern part, was that of Simeon. North of this was Dan, the territory of which extended as far as Dor (Dandura), on the shore of the sea, and formed, as it were, the wall of separation, which separated the portion of Benjamin, Ephraim, and Menasseh from the sea. Towards the north of Benjamin were the lands of Ephraim and Menasseh, which extended to the valley of Jezreel. This valley, and a part of the mountains of Southern or Lower Galilee, belonged to Issachar. Zebulun's portion was on the coast of Chinnereth, and extended towards the Mediterranean, to the south of Carmel. North of Zebulun was Naphtali, in an eastern direction, whereas Asher was on the west, on the shore of the Mediterranean, towards Zidon.

JUDAH. יהודה

(Joshua xv.)

The southern boundary of Judah I have already described, when giving the southern boundary of Palestine, with which it is identical. I wish, therefore, to make mention of a few places there omitted. It says in Joshua xv. 3, "And passed along to Hezron, and went up to Adar, and fetched a compass to Karkaa;" whereas in Num. xxxiv. 4, Hazar-Adar is given as one place, which appears here as two, Hezron and Adar. We find, moreover, in the southern part of Judah, several towns bearing the name of Chazar (Hazar), or Chazor, e.g. Chazor Chadattha, Chezron which is Chazor, Chazar Gaddah, Chazar Shual, and Chazar Susah; which leads me to suppose that we must ascribe this to the fact of its being the country of the Avim (Deut. ii. 23), who dwelt in open towns *Chazerim*, as far as Gazza. (Probably, therefore, that Adar was also one of these, or a Chazar of the Avim, hence Chazar-Adar; and Chezron was a city of the same.)

The Septuagint renders Chazar-Adar (in Num. xxxiv. 4) with Arad, and Adar in Joshua with Sanada, which I conceive to be an error, since Arad ערד was too far north to be the southern boundary of Judah and Palestine.

It, therefore, appears that the site of Hezron, Adar, and Karkaa, must have been between Wady Gaian (Kadesh-Barnea) and Wady Kisaimi (Azmon); but at the present day not a trace of these names is to be found, except the two, Gaian and Kisaimi, which enabled us to determine the probable situation of Kadesh-Barnea and Azmon.

The eastern and western boundaries of Judah are well defined, to wit, the Dead Sea on the east, and the Mediterranean on the west; wherefore, I have merely to trace the northern boundary. It says, verse 6, "And the border went up to Beth-Choglah, and passed along by the north of Beth-Arabah,* and the border went up to the stone of Bohan the son of Reuben."

Beth-Choglah was already explained when treating of Jericho. About 4 English miles north of the Dead Sea, is an old castle Burdj Chadjla; the similarity of names lets us suppose that Beth-Choglah must have been formerly in this vicinity. Hieronymus, however, says: "Beth-Choglah is 3 miles from Jericho, and 2 miles from Jordan," which would place this castle too far northwest, and consequently could not then be Beth-Choglah; but on the spot indicated by Hieronymus there is no trace of a town to be found.

Beth-Arabah is unknown; but it must have been north-west of the preceding.

Eben (stone of) Bohan Ben (son of) Reuben. The situation of this spot is on the mountain which runs west from the valley of Jordan, where I found, in the direction of Jericho, several uncommonly large rocks, of which some are well calculated to mark a boundary; but I could discover no trace to indicate the identical stone here mentioned.

Verse 7. "And the border went up towards Debir from the valley of Achor, and so northward, looking towards Gilgal, that is, before the going up to Adummim, which is

* Since, however, Beth-Arabah and Beth-Choglah are both reckoned as belonging to Benjamin (Joshua xviii. 21, 22), this passage appears very obscure; for here it appears that the boundary ran north of Beth-Arabah, wherefore it must belong to Judah and not to Benjamin. But I think that it may be thus explained: "And it run from the north to Beth-Arabah," i. e. after the line has run from the west northward, it takes the direction of Beth-Arabah, since originally the line runs from Jordan westward to Beth-Choglah, whence it runs north to Beth-Arabah, wherefore it remains beyond the boundary line, and belongs to the tribe of Benjamin, all to the south being part of Judah. This would require us to render מצפון "from the north," as צפונה or לצפון "to the north," or "northward;" which use of מ is occasionally met with, as מקדם "eastward" (Gen. xiii. 12).

on the south side of the river (should be 'the valley'), and the border passed towards the waters of En-Shemesh, and the goings out thereof were at En-Rogel."

The valley of Achor is also mentioned in a previous part of Joshua (vii. 24); it extends, accordingly, through the mountains to the valley of the Jordan, opposite Jericho.

On the mountains I found a large place, called by the Arabs, Tugrit al Dibr, and at a distance of about 1 English mile to the northwest, I saw a very high rocky hill, composed of nothing but pyrites, which they call Tell Adum. I cannot doubt but that the first is the ancient Debir, and the latter the "Height (the going up E. V.) of Adummim," or the Red Hill. This Tell is about 6 English miles east-northeast from Jerusalem. To the east of the same, I found several ruins, to wit, Akbath, Beth-Djabr, Chirbath-Gatun, which I cannot identify.

East of Azarié (see Azal) there is found in the valley, which the Arabs call Wady Chot, a handsome large spring, the Ein al Chot, which I take to be the spring of the run (En Shemesh).

En-Rogel, Gay ben Hinnom, the Valley of Rephaim, En-Neptoach, will be more particularly described under article Jerusalem.

Verse 9. "And went out to the cities of Mount Ephron, and the border was drawn to Baalah, which is Kirjath-Jearim."

Northwest of Jerusalem there is a plain about 2 English miles in extent. At its termination there is a deep valley, called Wady Zarr, also Wady Beth Chanin; the village Lifta lies in the declivity of this valley, which runs first west, then a little southward, then a little northward, and again west, and continues thus with a southern tendency, till it reaches the sea near Aker or Ekron. West-southwest of Jerusalem, at a distance of about 5 English miles, is another small valley, which at length unites with the Wady Zarr. Between these two valleys is a high plain, which, in comparison with these deep valleys, may be regarded as a mountain, and I conceive this plain to be the Mount Ephron. It is now over this point that the boundary ran, passed through the Wady Zarr, and then somewhat to the north to Baalah or Kirjath-Jearim.

Verse 10. "And the border compassed from Baalah westward unto Mount Seir, and passed along unto the side of Mount Jearim, which is Chesalon on the north side, and went down to Beth Shemesh, and passed on to Timnah."

The following are some remarkable names which I discovered in this direction. 4½ English miles west-south-west of Jerusalem, in the mountain, there is a small village called Ein Karem, which is undoubtedly the town of Karem mentioned in the Septuagint translation to Joshua xv. 61.

One English mile northwest of this point, in the neighbourhood of the village Kustel, situated on the summit of a mount, I found a ruin called Chirbath Izpa. West of Zaba (which see) I found a ruin, called Chirbath Gadran; near to this are the ruins of an old tower, an elegant palace, and other buildings. At the foot of this tower, is a large and beautiful spring, by name of Ein-Abis. About half a mile west of these ruins, on the declivity of a mount, I found the ruin Chirbath-Djeba; and 2½ English miles west of this, I saw an isolated mount, at the foot of which there is a ruin which the Arabs call Midan. It appears to me perfectly clear that this must be the Mount Modiim, which the Talmud Pesachim, fol. 93, alleges to be distant from Jerusalem 15 mill, or 11¼ English miles, which is actually the distance from Midan to the holy city. On the summit of this mount, one can see the Mediterranean to the south of Jabné and Ashdod. (See 1 Macc. xiii. 29.)

South of the Wady Zarr there are found Izfa, Chars, Ein Abis, Chirbath-Luz, the Mount Midan, and the other just-mentioned ruins, wherefore all these belonged to the portion of Judah.

North of the Wady Zarr are found Zoba, Kustel, Beth-Ula, Beth-Tiksa, Beth-Chaniné, and Nebi Smuel (improperly taken for Ramah, or Ramataim Zofim); all of which belonged to the tribe of Benjamin: it is therefore apparent that the Wady Zarr must have formed the boundary between Judah and Benjamin.

About 7½ English miles west-northwest of Jerusalem is the village Kiryé, also called Abu Gosh, because it is the seat of the celebrated sheich, or rather the captain of highwaymen, of that name, and is undoubtedly the ancient Kirjath-Jearim. About 2½ English miles west of this there is on the summit of a high mount the village Saris, which was destroyed in the year 5594 (1834), by Ibrahim Pacha, and forms the highest point between Jerusalem and Ramla. It is also mentioned by the Septuagint in the passage cited, as the correct reading should be Saris. South of this village, at the distance of about 1 English mile, is the village Kirzi or Saidé; 2½ English miles south of this there is the already mentioned Mount Midan, between the valley which leads to Kiryé Abu Gosh, and that which leads from Zaara (which see) to the village Saris. I take this to be the Mount Jearim spoken of in Joshua xv. 10, and that the land between the two valleys was called Jearim, whence then Kirjath (the city of) Jearim, and Har (mount of) Jearim. I also suppose that a trace of Seir may be discovered in Saris, and hence the Mount Seir (ibid.) to be identical with Saris, and therefore not to be confounded with Mount Seir to the east of the Dead Sea.

Two and a half English miles west of Zoba there runs a little valley as far as Kiryé Abu Gosh, and unites in the opposite direction with the Wady Zarr. There is likewise another valley extending southward from Saris to the vicinity of Zaara. I therefore suppose that the boundary line between Judah and Benjamin ran from the Wady Zarr into the little valley which extends to Kiryé Abu Gosh, from there to Saris, and then southward to Mount Midan and Kislon; again it entered the Wady Zarr, to Beth-Shemesh, which is the modern village Ein Sems, about 2½ English miles west of Mount Midan; west of Ein Sems, about 1 English mile from there, stood the village Tibna, no doubt Timnah; 7½ English miles northwest of this stood the village Akar, which is Ekron, and lies northeast of the Wady Zarr. It appears therefore that the boundary line left the Wady and ran on towards Akar.

Verse 11. "And the border went out to the side of Ekron northward; and the border was drawn to Shicron, and passed along to Mount Baalah, and went out unto Jabneel, and the goings out of the border were at the sea."

Two and a half English miles northwest of Akar is the village Jebniel, unquestionably the former Jabneel, also called Jabné (2 Chron. xxvi. 6, and Mishnah Rosh Hashanah vi. 8). The European Christians, under the government of Fulgo, King of Jerusalem, built not far from this a city, which they called Hibelim, of which R. Benjamin of Tudela speaks when he says עבלים היא יבנה Eblim which is Jabné.

The sites of Shicron and Mount Baalah are therefore to be sought between Jebniel and Akar; but I could discover no trace of them.

Jebniel is situated properly speaking in the Wady Zarr, but the Arabs call it there no more by that name, but they designate it as Wady Rubin, and it extends thence with a permanent water-course to the sea. The boundary therefore ran from Jebniel through the Wady, somewhat northerly, ending at the Mediterranean.

Josephus (Ant., book v. chap. i.) says, "To Judah belonged the northern part of Judea up to Jerusalem."

THE TOWNS IN THE PORTION OF JUDAH.

The territory of Judah is generally divided in four parts; 1, the South; 2, the Lowlands; 3, the Mountains; and 4, the Desert. (Compare Joshua x. 40; xv. in various parts.)

THE TOWNS OF THE SOUTHERN PART.

Kabzeel קבצאל Joshua xv. 21; Neh. xi. 25; its situation is entirely unknown.

Eder עדר, perhaps there may be here supposed a transposition of the letter ד and ר D and R, whence we should have Arad, (see Num. xxxii. 38), although this would overthrow my idea as given above under Chormah and Arad.

Jagur יגור; the situation of this place is uncertain. (See Tosephtah, end of Ahaloth, where, according to the reading of Rabbi Shamson the ר״ש, it says, "The borders of Ashkelon extend from the great grave to Jagur," &c.) The supposition that this is the village Dshura situated between Migdol (Meshdal) and Ashkelon, is proved erroneous, because of its being in the Lowlands, whilst Jagur is reckoned among the towns of the South.

Kinah קינא; probably Cinah, a town situated near the wilderness of Zin צין.

Kedesh קדש; this is Kadesh-Barnea, in the Wady Bierin. (See above in the Boundaries of Palestine.)

Ithnan יתנן; Hieronymus says that is in the neighbourhood of Beth Djibrin, in the direction of Hebron, 6 mill from the former; at the present time there is on the spot indicated the village Ithna; but this would place this town in the Mountains and not in the South.

Ziph זיף. 5 English miles north of Mount Madura (which see), is the narrow valley Nukab al Zapha, which name is probably derived from the town of Ziph, which once stood here.

Telem טלם. This town was situated south of Madura, wherefore this district is called to this day Tulam. I am induced to believe that in this vicinity there was yet another city of the same name, whence "and he numbered them in Telaim," טלאים with a plural termination (1 Sam. xv. 4), indicating two places called Telem; and hence then, also, the modern appellation of the whole district, Tulam, or the space between the two towns. In Midrash Koheleth to chap. v. 10, there is mentioned a Menachem Talmia, who was probably a native of Telem.

Bealoth בעלות, is probably the Kubit al Ba-ul, situated 7½ English miles southeast of Telem, and northwest of Zapha.

Moladah מולדה, is the modern village Muladah, 3 English miles southeast of Arad.

Chazar-Gaddah חצר גדה. According to Hieronymus, this town was situated in the southern part, near the Dead Sea. Perhaps he meant En-Gedi (which see).

Beer-Sheba באר שבע, is 30 English miles southwest of Hebron (Chebron), and is now called Bir-Siba.

Ezem עצם, is probably identical with Azmon (which see).

Kesil כסיל, is the same place which is represented as belonging to the mountainous part of Simeon, under the name of Bethuel (1 Chron. iv. 30), and in the conquests of David (which see) as Beth-El, in 1 Sam. xxx. 27.

Chormah חרמה. I have already said, when speaking of the 31 Kings, that Chormah is identical with the previous Zephath of Judges i. 17, and that there is the valley of Zephatha near Mareshah (2 Chron. xiv. 9). Chormah must therefore have stood in this neighbourhood, not far from Beth-Djibrin. The only difficulty in the case is that Chormah is reckoned as belonging to the South, whereas

Mareshah was reckoned among the cities of the Lowlands. It is possible, however, that the valley of Zephatha alone extended to Mareshah, whilst the town of Zephath, i. e. Chormah, was actually in the South district. At present I could find no trace of the same.

Ziklag צקלג, is also not fully ascertained; this much, however, is known, that it was north of the stream Besor (Wady Sheria), which flows 2½ English miles south of Gazza, and it must, consequently, have stood not far from the Mediterranean, and probably between the Wadys Sheria and Simsum.

Madmannah מדמנה, is probably the Levitical city Mandah, in which, according to the book of Jashar, end of Joshua, Simeon was buried. According to Eusebius, it is called Minos, and lies opposite to Gazza.

Sansannah סנסנה, is probably the village of Simsum (as the Arabs often exchange the נ n, with מ m), which is situated on the river Simsum, which runs 5 English miles northeast of Gazza, and falls by Ashkelon into the sea. I admit that, according to our assumption, all the three last-mentioned towns would belong to the Lowland, and not to the South of Judah; but the boundary lines are so little known with certainty, that it is possible that the vicinity of Gazza may have actually belonged to the South, and not to the Lowland, or the שפלה.

THE LOWLAND, OR THE VALLEY,

Commences to the southwest of Kirjath-Jearim, and west of the Mount Modiim, and extends to the Mediterranean, and southwardly to the south of Gazza. If one stands on one of the mountains west of Jerusalem, and east of the village En-Karem, he has the whole of the Lowland, with the sea, before his view. The towns of this division are:

Zorah and Eshtaol צרעה ואשתאל. Two and a half

English miles west of the Mount Modiim is, even at the present day, the village Zareah; and 2½ west of this is the village Stual, no doubt Eshtaol.

Zanoach זנוח. One English mile southeast from Zarea is the village Zamea, no doubt the former Zanoach.

En-Gannim עין גנים, is certainly identical with the village Dshinin, 3 English miles southeast of Ashkelon. A town of the same name was in the territory of Issachar.

Tappuach תפוח, is probably the village Beth-Tapa, 5 English miles northwest of Beth-Djibrin. A town of the same name was also on the boundary line between Ephraim and Menasseh.

Enam עינם, is probably the village Beth-Ani, distant 2½ English miles from Saafir (which see). Some think that this is the place spoken of as Enajim, in the history of Tamar (Gen. xxxviii. 14).

Jarmuth ירמות. See explanation of the 31 Kings.

Adullam עדלם. Ibidem.

Socho שוכו, is without doubt the village Suweiché, situated 5 English miles north-northeast from Beth-Djibrin.

Azekah עזקה. Three English miles east of the valley Saphia is the village Tell Ezakaria, which is probably the ancient Azekah, which was not far from Socho. (Com. 1 Sam. xvii. 1.)

Shaaraim שערים, is not clearly known; .but to judge from 1 Sam. xvii. 52, it must have been in the neighbourhood of Ekron and Gath.* It is probably identical with the Ir-Tarain of the Tosephtah, end of Ahaloth, as the Chald. Tarain is the same with the Hebrew Shaaraim, gates.

Adithaim עדיתים, is probably the village Eddis, 5 Eng-

* In the 1 Macc. v. 66, there is mentioned a place Shomrin, which should be Shaaraim, as it clearly refers to a city in the land of the Philistines, near Ashdod.

lish miles east of Gazza. Hieronymus also says that it was situated near Gazza.

Gederah and Gederothaim גדרה גדרתים, formed but one town, and was, as Strabo and Josephus tell us, between Ashdod and Ashkelon, and is probably the same with Beth-Gader mentioned in 1 Chron. ii. 51. Some suppose it to have been the seat of the 31 Kings (Joshua xii. 13).

Zenan צנן, is the same with Zaanan of Micah i. 11, and is probably the village Zan-Abra, situated 2½ English miles southeast of Mareshah.

Chadashah חדשה (compare with Erubin, fol. 46), is, according to the opinion of some, the town called in 1 Macc. vii. 40, and Josephus, Adasa, which, however, appears erroneous to me, since the latter lay near Beth-Choron, consequently not in the territory of Judah, but of Benjamin. I am rather led to think that it is the village Dshora di al Chadas, between Migdal and Ashkelon (see above, Jagur), which, though but a village, I fancy bears traces of the two towns Jagur and Chadashah; as in general the inhabitants of Palestine allow themselves transpositions, abbreviations, and additions in the names of the towns. At the distance of one mile from this place, in the vicinity of the sea, lies

Migdal-Gad מגדל גד at present called Midjdal (Migdal).

Dilean and Mizpeh דלען מצפה. There is, 7 English miles northwest of Beth-Djibrin, on a small mount, the village Tell Zaphi, which is probable a compound of the two names in question. According to Hieronymus, Mizpeh was north of Beth-Djibrin, which also coincides with Tell Zaphi.

Lachish לכיש. See the description of the 31 Kings.

Eglon עגלון. See ibidem.

Gederoth גדרות is probably the same with the ruins of Gadara, situated northwest of Jerusalem at the edge of the valley Zarr, which also appears to be the correct view from Chron. xxviii. 18, where this place is mentioned in connexion with Beth-Shemesh, Ajalon, Socho, and Timnah, which all were situated in Wady Zarr. (Compare Joshua xii. 13.) Geder is probably the same place.

Beth-Dagon בית דגון must not be mistaken for a town of the same name between Ramlah and Jaffa. Eusebius reports that between Jamnia (Jabné) and Diospolis (Lod), there were in his time the ruins of the village Dagon; but at present not a vestige of them can be found.

Makedah מקדה, See the description of the 31 Kings.

Libnah לבנה. Ibidem.

Ashan עשן; also called Kor-Ashan in 1 Sam. xxx. 30. Eusebius states Asan to be 15 mill west of Jerusalem; but it is now unknown.

Nezib נציב; 2½ English miles east of Beth-Djibrin is found as yet the village Beth-Nuzib.

Keilah קעילה was, according to Eusebius, 8 mill from B. Djibrin, on the road to Hebron; but it is not to be found at present.

Achzib אכזיב was at the time of Eusebius yet a village, north of Adullam, and is the same place called Chezib in Gen. xxxviii. 5. It is now unknown.

Mareshah מראשה; the ruins of this town, called Marasa by the Arabs, are yet discoverable 1 English mile south of B. Djibrin.*

When speaking of the land of the Philistines, I will treat of Ekron, Ashdod, and Gazza.

THE TOWNS IN THE MOUNTAINS

Lie in the so-called Mountains of Judah, of which we have treated above. The height of this chain is indeed

* R. Benjamin of Tudela says, that Maresha is B. Gubrin (Djibrin); but this is not so, as it is merely in its vicinity. Astori, the author of Caphtor Vapherach, fol. 69 *a*, asserts that Mareshah is near to Kefar Dichrin, north of Lud (Diospolis); but this too is erroneous, for this would place Mareshah in the mountains of Ephraim, in Benjamin's portion.

not very perceptible to the south of Hebron on the road from Jerusalem by which it is ascended; but the more precipitous are its gorges and deep valleys towards the south, east, and west. The highest points of this mountain are met with in the peaks which surround the valley of Hebron, and which have an elevation of 2664 feet above the level of the sea. The towns in the mountain district are:

Jattir יתיר is probably to be discovered in the village Yather, 15 English miles south of Hebron, and 5 north of Moladah.

Socho שוכו is at present called Suweiché, and is 3 English miles north of Yather, and 5 west of Maon.

Kirjath-Sannah קרית סנה or Debir. See the 31 Kings.

Enab ענב is the village Anab, 1 English mile northeast of Suweiché. It is in all likelihood the same place mentioned in Joshua xi. 21.

Eshtemoh אשתמה, formerly a Levitical city, now probably the village Samua, 2½ English miles east of Suweiché, and is also perhaps identical with the town of Esthomonia in Peræa, built by Herod. (Compare with Josep. Antiq., book xv. 11.)

Anim ענים is the village Ben-Enim, 2 English miles east-northeast of Hebron.

Giloh גלה is doubtlessly the large village Beth-Djalah, 1 English mile west of Bethlehem; the G, as usual with the Arabs, being changed into Dj, thus Galah, Djalah.

Arab ארב is the village Al Arab, situated on a mountain, 4 English miles southeast of Hebron.

Dumah דומה was, according to Hieronymus, in the neighbourhood of Eleutheropolis. It is possibly identical with the village Beth-Dimi, which is situated on the seashore, near Migdal. This, however, would place it in the Lowland instead of the Mountain.

Beth-Tappuach בית תפוח is the small village Tappuach,

2 English miles west of Hebron, but is not to be confounded with the town of the same name on the boundary between Ephraim and Menasseh.

Aphekah אפקה the village Abik, 4 English miles east-northeast of Yurmuk (Jarmuth).

Zior ציער is the village Sior or Zier, 2½ English miles northeast of Hebron; near it is pointed out the grave of Esau, who is called by the Arabs Sid Yusseph, i. e. Prince Joseph. According to Targum Jonathan to Genesis xlix., Esau was buried not far from Hebron.

Maon מעון the village Maun, 5 English miles south of Hebron.

Carmel כרמל is the village Al Kirmil, situated 2 English miles north-northwest of Maun on a small mount; it has an excellent water-course, called Birkat al Kirmil, in the vicinity of which is a small fort, whence the Dead Sea can be seen. (I take the Carmel mentioned in 1 Sam. xv. 12 to be this place, and not the Mount Carmel.)

Ziph זיף, the village Ziff, 2 English miles northeast of Al Kirmil, and 2 English miles southeast of Hebron. According to Josephus, it belonged to the land of the Kenites.

Jutah יוטה, probably the village Yata, 2½ English miles south of Hebron, and 3 English miles northwest of Al Kirmil.

Zanoach זנוח, probably the large village Samua, 3 English miles southwest of Maun. It is situated on a hill; it has a small fort, also the ruins of a Catholic convent. There are also at this place wells, regularly walled in, and fruitful gardens, which are well irrigated. Some, however, suppose Samua to be identical with Eshtemoh, which see.

Timnah תמנה was, according to Eusebius, 10 mill east of Eleutheropolis, and situated on a mount. There was a town of the same name in the low land near Ekron. See also Sota, fol. 10 *b*, where it says that there are two towns called Timnah.

Chalchul חלחול is the village of this name, situated on a mount, and 5 English miles north-northeast of Hebron. The grave of the prophet Gad is pointed out here.

Beth-Zur בית צור. This town and fort, celebrated at the time of the Maccabees, was the residence of several Israelites, even after the destruction of the second temple (see historical part, year 4543); but at present there is so little known of it, that it cost me some trouble to ascertain its situation. The assertion of 2 Macc. xi. 5, that Beth-Zur lies between mountains, 5 mill from Jerusalem, appears to me to be an error of the translator, and should be 15 mill. I heard the Bedouins call certain ruins, apparently those of an ancient fortress, which are situated on a mount west of Chalchul, on the road to Hebron, where an excellent spring bubbles forth from the rocky mountain walls, Chirbath Beth-Zur (Ruins of Beth-Zur); and, in fact, this point is exactly 15 miles from Jerusalem, wherefore the tradition which places the ancient Beth-Zur here seems to be well supported.

Gedor גדור. According to Eusebius, it was the Gadarah in the valley of Elah, in the vicinity of Beth-Zur, north-west of Hebron. It is at present unknown.

Maarath מערת is the village Magr,* west of Ekron. It is perhaps also identical with the Maroth (abbreviated) in Micah i. 12.

Kirjath-Baal קרית בעל, i. e. Kirjath-Jearim, which see.

The Septuagint adds yet the following names of places, which are not found in the Bible text; and although they have properly no biblical value, we will enumerate them, because some of them have been retained even to this day.

Tekoa. See article Tekoa.

Ephratha, or Beth-Lehem, which see.

* Both Maarah and Magr signify cave.

Phagor is no doubt the modern village Beth-Phagar, southeast of Bethlehem.

Etam, which see. Tatam and Thobes I do not know. Saris I have mentioned already, and is situated west of Kirjath-Jearim.

Karem is the village Ein Karem, already described.

Galem is unknown to me. It cannot be Beth-Gallim, for this is not in the territory of Judah, but near Jaffa; nor can it be the modern Beth Djallah (see Gilah), because that is already mentioned in the text.

Koulon, perhaps Kolonia (see Moza); but this belonged to Benjamin, not Judah.

Bether* is a village yet existing, 7 English miles southwest of Jerusalem. It must not be confounded with the celebrated city of this name, famous in history after the destruction of Jerusalem. (See Gittin, fol. 55 *b*, and Tosephoth Yom Tob, end of Challah.)

Manochoh is perhaps the town of Mechonah mentioned in Nehemiah xi. 28, which was at the time of Hieronymus a village between Jerusalem and Eleutheropolis (Beth-Gubrin or Djibrin), or it may be intended for Malcha (which see).

THE TOWNS IN THE DESERT.

Under this name are understood all the towns of that desert which commences on the western shore of the Dead Sea, and extends up to Zin. This district is briefly called "the Desert;" whilst those situated in the "South" of Judah are but small, and take their names from the towns nearest to them; for example, the Desert of Maon (1 Sam. xxiii. 24); the Desert of Ziph (ibid. xxvi. 12); the Desert of Jeruel (2 Chron. xx. 10), &c.

Beth-Arabah בית הערבה. See above, p. 94.

Ir-Hammelach (the City of Salt, עיר המלח). See Zoar.

En-Gedi עין גדי. Almost due east from Hebron, but a

* My copy has *Thetair*.—TRANSLATOR.

little to the south, and at a distance of 12 English miles, hard upon the shore of the Dead Sea, is a spot which the Arabs call En-Djedi, unquestionably the ancient En-Gedi, which was also called Hazezon Thamar חצצן תמר (2 Chron. xx. 2). Two English miles north of this spot there is a valley or Wady, which the Arabs call Wady al Huzazan, which I conceive to be so named from the ancient Hazezon (Thamar).

The other cities of Judah mentioned elsewhere are—

Eloné Mamré אלוני ממרה (Gen. xiv. 13). North of Chebron, and sideward from Chalchul, is a plain about 2½ English miles in length, which the Arabs call *Elon*, no doubt the ancient dwelling-place of Abraham in question.

Gerar גרר (ibid. xx. 1). This town, which was still in existence in the time of Hieronymus, was situated, as he reports, 25 mill south of Eleutheropolis (Beth Djibrin); consequently between Beersheba and Gazza, for which reason the environs of Beersheba were called in the time of the Romans "the District of Gerar." In the Talmudic writings this district is termed Gerarki. (See Yerushalmi Shebiith, chap. vi.; and Bereshith Rabbah, chap. lxiv.) At present, however, no trace whatever of this town can be discovered.

Ephrath אפרת, which is also called Beth-Lechem, (Gen. xxxv. 19), is even at the present day a large village, 3 English miles south of Jerusalem.

The Grave of Rachel קבורת רחל. 4 English miles south-southwest of Jerusalem, about 1 English mile northwest of Beth-Lehem, on the road from the former to Hebron, is found this ancient and famous monument; it is a small, low, square chapel, with a cupola, which is somewhat pointed. In the middle of the same, running east and west, is a monument, composed of several large stones, about 7 feet in length, 4 broad, and 5 in height. It was always believed that this stood over the grave of the beloved wife of Jacob. But about twenty-five years ago, when the structure needed some repairs, they were compelled to dig down at the foot of this monument; and it was then found that it was not erected over the cavity in which the grave of Rachel actually is; but at a little distance from the monument there was discovered an uncommonly deep cavern, the opening and direction of which was not precisely under the superstructure in question. In the year 5601 (1841), Sir Moses Montefiore, of London, caused the same to be entirely renovated, furnished it with a cupola, and an entrance hall, so that at present it is quite a handsome building. I think it advisable to speak somewhat more at large about this monument, since we find in the Scriptures several passages which almost seem to place it in another position than where it is. Let us first investigate the measure of distance employed in Gen. xxvi. 16, "Kibrath Eretz" כברת ארץ between the grave and Beth-Lehem, so that thereby we may be able to ascertain the true position. The Arabic version of Saadiah has mill, a mile; the Persian translation gives it with Fersh, i. e. the length of a field, an acre; Ben Seruk explains כברת as derived from כביר "a great length;" Rashi alleges it to be a Parsah, or 3 English miles; Nachmanides (Ramban) expounds it as derived from בר Bar, "a very little, insignificant," as ברי בר in Prov. xxxi. 2; and in point of fact the latter explanation does appear as the most correct, since the distance from the monument to Beth-Lehem is quite small, scarcely an English mile, and wherefore also we may take for granted that the building actually marks the grave of Rachel. Still there is one passage which offers us some difficulty; I refer to 1 Sam. x. 2, where Samuel tells Saul, "When thou departest this day from me, thou wilt meet two men near the grave of Rachel, on the boundary of Benjamin in Zelzach." This then places the sepulchre on the border of Benjamin; and still we do not find this line to be within 4 English miles north thereof. I would ask farther, since Saul travelled at the time from Ramah (Ramathaim Zophim), to his home Gibeath Saul (Kirjath-Jearim), and as Beth-Lehem and the monument are near 10 English miles southeast of Gibeah, and consequently entirely out of his way: how should he happen to meet the two men at the grave of Rachel on his return journey? In Bereshith Rabbah to Section Vayishlach, the difficulty of the grave of Rachel being on the boundary of Benjamin, is indeed touched upon, and explained in two different ways; the solution is nevertheless obscure and unsatisfactory. But in Midrash Samuel to the passage cited, there is a more correct elucidation, as follows: "When thou departest (already) this day from me, thou wilt meet (to-morrow) at the boundary of Benjamin, at Zelzach, two men, (who will quit to-morrow) the grave of Rachel;" that is to say, he was going one way and they were coming from another direction, and would thus meet on the boundary line.* If Saul and the pilgrims had both commenced their journey at the same time, it would have been impossible for them to meet at Zelzach, because the distance from there to Ramah is far greater than to the grave of Rachel; but it was probable that they should so meet if Saul set out on the day he was speaking with Samuel, and the others set out only the day following. From all this, it appears that not the grave of Rachel but Zelzach must be sought for on the border of Benjamin; whence, therefore, the three words עם קבורת רחל "by the grave of Rachel," must be taken as an explanation, giving the whereabout of the two men at the time Samuel was speaking, of whom it is said

* See also farther art. Zelzach, which is said to be, according to the same Midrash, no other than Jerusalem; and I suppose that a trace of the name may be found in that of the village *Tsellsia*.

ומצאת שני אנשים בגבול בנימין בצלצח "And thou shalt find these men at the border of Benjamin at Zelzach."

There is also a difficult passage in Sifri to Deut. xxxiii. 3, where it says that Rachel died in the land of her son (Benjamin), and still her grave is in the land of Judah. But I would explain this, that the Sifri neither said nor meant that her grave is in Benjamin's portion, but that she died whilst Jacob was on his journey from Beth-El to Bethlehem, consequently whilst traversing the territory of Benjamin, and perhaps they were still in it when Rachel was taken dangerously ill, and being near death, she might be considered dead already before they reached the land of Judah. The explanation of Nachmanides to Genesis xlviii. 7, "that she did not die on the journey, but in Ramah, a city of Benjamin, and that she was buried there," is extremely surprising. It appears that this very learned man wrote this before he lived in the Holy Land, and before he had the opportunity of convincing himself of the actual condition of the things, and the locality of the various places in question. (See also Mechiltha, chap. i.) Upon the whole, it is my conviction that the monument marks correctly the grave of Rachel, although others have without sufficient reason placed the sepulchre in another spot.

Migdal-Eder מגדל עדר (Gen. xxxv. 21), was situated, according to a well-known tradition, 2½ English miles southwest of Beth-Lehem, on a hill near the aqueduct from the spring Etam (2 Chron. xi. 6). See article En-Etam.

In the conquests of David (1 Sam. xxx.), are mentioned Beth-El, Aroer, the cities of the Kenites, and Athach.

Beth-El* בית אל (1 Sam. xxx. 27), also called Kesil

* In Echah Rabbethi to chap. i. 16, there is spoken of a Beth-El in Judah, which means that there was yet another, I presume the Beth-El in the land of the Philistines.

(Joshua xv. 30), and Bethul (1 Chron. iv. 30), was situated 17 English miles southwest of Eleutheropolis; and to this day there are discoverable in this position, on a high hill, some ruins of a fort, which, as I learned from records, are called Bethulia. Near these ruins is the village Kesi (Kesil). It appears, therefore, that this Bethulia and Kesi are the Beth-El, Bethul, and Kesil of Samuel.

Aroer ערער (ibid. v. 28), probably the modern village Arar, situated 2½ English miles south of Moladah.

The cities of the Kenites ערי הקיני. In the Greek translation of the Septuagint, there are added to these cities Zaphet, probably Zephath or Chormah of Joshua xv. 30; next Karmilos, i. e. Karmel near Ziph;* but Haleis is unknown to me.

Athach עתך (ibid. v. 30). There is at this day a valley called Athacha, north of Mount Madura. Without doubt the town of Athach must have been situated there.

Geshurites, Gezrites גשורי גרזי (1 Sam. xxvii. 8). The first name is discoverable in the modern village Adshur, which is situated 1 English mile from Dir-Dibon, on the road leading to Migdal. The latter name is to be met with in that of the village Beth-Djirsi, which lies near the Wady Simsum.

The hill Chachilah גבעת החכילה (ibid. xxiii. 19). Two and a half English miles west of Hebron, on the road to Beth-Djibrin, is the village Beth-Chachal, which has derived its name, in all probability, from this hill.

Adoraim אדורים (2 Chron. xi. 9), is at present a village called Dura, situated 4 English miles west of Hebron. It is the seat of the sheich of the district Abd Rachman, whose territory extends to Egypt.

Etam עיטם (ibid. xi. 6), is at present a little fort, called

* This is in accordance with Josephus, who represents Ziph as a town situated in the land of the Kenites.

Al Burak, and distant 2½ English miles south of the grave of Rachel. For more particulars, see farther, in art. En Etam.

Tekoa תקוע (ibid.) Five English miles south of Beth-Lehem, there are still some ruins called Thakua. Two and a half miles northeast of this place there is a separately situated mount, called Djebl Fridis, also, the Franks' Mount,* because the Franks, i. e. the European Christians, maintained themselves for some time in a fort which once stood on this mount, after they had been driven out of Jerusalem and other cities of Palestine by the rulers of Egypt. This Herod's Mount, as Josephus calls it, has the shape of a long apple, and the ruins of the ancient fortification are still visible on its summit. Some are of opinion that this mount is the Beth-Hakkerem (the vineyard-house), which is mentioned in connexion with Tekoa, in Jer. vi. 1, since to this day there are visible terraces suitable for the cultivation of the vine. Perhaps Solomon alludes to this mount in his Song i. 14, when referring to his vineyard at En-Gedi; since they are not far apart. Northwest from this mount is the cave Al Mama, 60 feet long and 6 high; and I suppose that this it was which Saul entered, when pursuing David in the desert of En-Gedi (1 Sam. xxiv. 4). West from the ruins of Thakuah are found many caverns in the depths of the mountains;

* Although it is not my purpose to discuss and censure erroneous and false views of the learned of modern and the latest times, I nevertheless cannot avoid calling the reader's attention to a gross mistake made in several modern Hebrew descriptions of Palestine, in respect to the name of this mount. I do this merely to prove that all these works are but copies of ancient writings, which, however, were not correctly understood. Now the modern learned men call this Franks' Mount הר חפשי "The Mount of Freedom" (Exod. xxi. 2), because they understood the name of Franks to signify the idea of freedom, *franco;* whereas the real meaning is "the mount of the Franks," or the strangers who came from Frankland (France), wherefore they ought to have translated it הר עם פראנקא or הר בני ארץ פראנקיא.

they are called Al Kreitun (Labyrinth), and served the inhabitants of Tekoa as places of refuge when they had to fly before the pursuing Arabic hordes, in the year 4898 (1138).*

Raphiach רפיח. Onkelos paraphrases Deut. ii. 23, "And the Avites who dwell in open places (*Chazerim*) unto Gazza," with, "in Raphiach unto Gazza." To this day are some ruins on the shore of the Mediterranean between Gazza and the village Al Arish, which are called Rapha; another proof that the Avites had extended their settlements up to that place, and in the southern portion of Palestine. (See Hezron.)

Bor-Hassirah בור הסירה "the fenced in pit" (2 Sam. iii. 26), was, according to Josephus, called Besera, and was 20 riss (2½ English miles) distant from Hebron. Perhaps we may discover a trace of the name in the modern Siar (see Zior), since it is precisely that distance from Hebron.

Lechi לחי (Judges xv. 9). Josephus reports that this place was called by the Greeks Siaron (identical with the

* This town belonged to the portion of Judah, as appears distinctly from the passage cited (2 Chron. xi. 6). The more surprising, therefore, appears the opinion of the celebrated David Kimchi to 2 Sam. xiv. 2, and Amos vii. 10, that it belonged to Asher. This hypothesis is based, however, on a misunderstanding of a passage in Talmud Menachoth, fol. 85 *b*, which says that Tekoa produced the best oil; and whereas the land of Asher produced much oil, so that it was said (Deut. xxxiii. 24), "He (Asher) dips his foot in oil," this learned commentator concluded that Tekoa must have belonged to Asher. But Tekoa, as will appear from Mishna, Menachoth chap. viii. § 3, furnished merely the finest oil, but by no means in great abundance. But the place where it was produced in such uncommonly large quantities was Gush-Chalab גוש חלב, as is told as an historical fact in the above-cited passage from Talmud Menachoth, fol. 85; and this town actually belonged to Asher, as we read in Judges i. 31: "Asher did not drive out the inhabitants of Achlab," i. e. those of the present Gush-Chalab. The error of Kimchi now arises from his mistaking Tekoa for Gush-Chalab, and placing the first in Asher, which is wrong.

Hebrew Lechi "jawbone"). Since, however, there was a spring formerly near Eleutheropolis, called Siarōn, it proves to a certainty that Lechi was near Beth-Djibrin (Eleutheropolis).

Shaphir שפיר (Micha i. 2), no doubt the village Suaphir as yet existing, situated 5 English miles southeast from Ashdod; and is perhaps identical with the Kefar Sephuria of Yerushalmi Kiddushin, chap. iii., and the Beth-Shuphrin of Vayikra Rabbah, chap. xxii.

Charsha חרשא (Ezra ii. 52), probably identical with the ruins, called by the Arabs Charsha, situated south of Wady Zarr, and at some distance from the ruins of Gadar.

Barkos ברקום (ibid. 53), the modern village Barkusia, 6 English miles northwest of Beth-Djibrin.

Jeshua ישוע (Nehem. xi. 26), the village Yesué, near the village Chulda, situated to the east of Ekron, at a distance of about 5 English miles. Here commences the so-called Lowland or plain, on this side.

Dibon דיבון (ibid. 25), the village Dir-Dibon, 5 English miles north of Beth-Djibrin.

Ir-Nachash עיר נחש (1 Chron. iv. 12), the village Dir-Nachas, 1 mile east of Beth-Djibrin.

Rechah רכה (ibid.), the village Rashia, 3 English miles south of Hebron.

Zobebah צבבה (ibid. 8), the village Beth Zaphapha, 2½ English miles south of Jerusalem.

I will now mention the following places, noticed in the Talmudic writings as belonging to the tribe of Judah:

Beth-Gubrin* בית גוברין. This formerly very large and celebrated free city, called in the times of the Greeks and Romans Eleutheropolis, from Eleutheros "free," and

* Literally "the city of the mighty," because in its vicinity lived formerly very strong and gigantic men. Jonathan translates Hebron (Gen. xxiii. 2) with קרית דגוברא "the city of heroes."

polis "a city,"* is situated 17 English miles west-north-west of Hebron, and has remarkable buildings and ruins, together with a very large and wide subterranean cave, in which there are several Christian chapels, which date from the time when Christian princes bore rule in Palestine. In the year 4557 (797), the city was destroyed by the Saracens, and it is at present but a large village, called Beth-Djibrin. This city has been almost constantly in the hands of non-Israelites, wherefore it could hardly be regarded as Jewish property; which circumstance will explain the meaning of Bereshith Rabbah, chap. 61, which comments, "And of the dew of heaven from above (Gen. xxvii. 39), means Beth-Gubrin," by which blessing this city was assigned by the patriarch Isaac to his son Esau. (See ibid. chap. 60; Shir Hashirim Rabbah, fol. 2 *a*; Koheleth Rabbah, fol. 102 *b*; Bereshith Rabbethi, chap. 10.)

Barur Chayil ברור חיל; this is the manner in which the name is given in Sanhedrin, fol. 32 *a*, and Tosephtah Maaseroth, beginning of chap. 2; but in Megillah 18 *a*, it is given as גבור חיל Gibbor Chayil, and in Yerushalmi Demai, beginning of chap. 3, as בלי חיל Blee Chayil, which, however, appears to be a mistake of the transcriber. I presume to discover in this name some historical allusion. Josephus relates in his Jewish War that the Emperor Vespasian sent a colony composed of the dismissed and meritorious veterans of his army to Emaus, 60 stadia (7½ English miles) from Jerusalem. I now consider that *Barur Chayil* refers "to the chosen men from the army," selected to occupy it, and that we find for the same reason *Gibbor Chayil* "the heroes of the army," and that it is the same with the town of Emaus. South of Saris (which see), about 7½ English miles from Jerusalem, are met with some ruins, which the Arabs call Baburaia, probably cor-

* Compare with Bereshith Rabbah, chap. 42, which says, "And the Chori (Gen. xiv. 6), is Elitheropolis."

rupted from Barureia, i. e. Barur Chayil, and that it marks the site of the military colony of Vespasian as given by Josephus.

Amus or Emius, עימאום אמאום, formerly Nicopolis, "the City of Victory," is now the village Ameius, near which is a good spring. It is 7½ English miles east of Ekron, and south of Kabab. It is, however, not to be taken for the town just mentioned; as there were two places of similar names.

Beth-Deli בית דלי mentioned at the end of Yebamoth, is the village Beth-Dulia, or corrupted into Beth-Ulia, 7½ English miles from Hebron, on the road to Jaffa.

Beth-Garem בית גרם (Erubrin 19*a*, and perhaps the הגרמי of 1 Chron. iv. 19). One and a half day's journey east from Gazza was, according to Astori, the author of Caphtor Vapherach, the village Mansul Garem; but it is now unknown.

Malchaya מלחיא of Vayikra, Rabbah 26, is the village Malcha, 4 English miles west-southwest from Jerusalem; it has an excellent spring, the water of which is light and wholesome. Here are also found a large quantity of roses.

Abus כפר אבום of Yerushalmi Sanhedrin, chap. ii., is, according to my opinion, the same with Abis, mentioned in Josephus, Bell. Jud. viii. 5, and which he places in Upper Judea; it was probably near the ruins of Gadar in the Wady Zarr. To this circumstance it is no doubt owing that the spring found there is called "the Spring of Abis." (See also above in the northern boundary of Judah.)

Imra כפר אימרא of Yerushalmi Thanith, chap. iv., is the village Beth-Imra, 2½ English miles south-southwest of Hebron.

Aryeh כפר אריה of Yerushalmi Kelayim, chap. i., is, according to ancient records, a village near Eleutheropolis.

Barkah כפר ברקא of Talmud Cheritoth (end) was, according to Eusebius, not far from Ashdod, but is at present unknown.

Darum כפר דרום of Sota 20 *b*, was the village Darum, 5 English miles southeast from Gazza, as reported by Astori; it is at present unknown.

Shachra כפר שחרא of Tosephtah, end Yebamoth, is probably the village Beth-Sachur, 2½ English miles northeast from Bethlehem, in the district of Tekoa. It may, perhaps, be the same as Ashchur, comp. 1 Chron. ii. 24, "Ashchur, the father of Tekoa." Jos. Bell. Jud. i. 1, calls it Beth-Zacharias.

Anim כפר ענים of Pesiktah Rabbah 23, is, perhaps, the above-mentioned mountain town of Joshua xv. 50, at present the village called Ben-Enim. It is also, perhaps, the same with *Oni*, mentioned in Tosephtah Ahaloth 16.

Themartha כפר תמרתא שביהודה of Tosephtah Chulin, 13, is the village Beth-Thamra, 2½ English miles southeast of Bethlehem. (See Bereshith Rabbah 6; Pesiktah Rabbethi 15.)

Etam כפר עיטם of Yebamoth, end of chap. xii., for which see article En-Etam.

PLACES MENTIONED IN THE BOOKS OF THE MACCABEES.

Kedron קדרון, 1 book, xv. 39; xvi. 9, 3 English miles west of Ekron, now the large village called Kadrun. It is remarkable that several learned men in their geographical descriptions of Palestine, have alleged, that despite of laborious investigation, they had not been able to find this place, and that there must have occurred a mistake in the transcriber by putting Kedron instead of Gedar. But it is undoubted, and easily capable of demonstration, that the author of the books of the Maccabees meant no other place than the present Kadrun, situated in the vicinity of the land of the Philistines.

Chamma חאממא, 1 book iii. 40, is the village Chamameh, 2½ English miles south of Migdal, and is situated in the Lowland, as is stated in the book cited.

TOWNS IN THE LAND OF THE PHILISTINES.

All the places designated in Joshua xiii. 2, 3, as the chief towns of the Philistines, are still known at present.

Geshur גשור now Adshur (see above, article Geshuri).

Gazza עזה is a large town, 20 English miles from Hebron, and is distant but 1 English mile from the Mediterranean. The inhabitants of this place, with the exception of a few Christians, are altogether Mahomedans. Up to the year 5571 (1811), there were found here also Jewish inhabitants, who had a handsome Synagogue, and a large burying-place, where are buried Rabbi Israel Negara, the celebrated poet, his father, and his son Moses. When the conqueror Napoleon passed through Gazza with his army in his expedition from Egypt to Palestine in the year 5559 (1799), the Jews were put in great straits, and many fled away; and they constantly diminished in number till the small remnant at length removed, in 5571 (1811), to Jerusalem and Hebron. The Synagogue became ruinous in consequence, and Ibrahim Pasha took of its stones to build a fort at Ashkelon.

Ashdod אשדוד is at present a large village inhabited by Arabs, and called Sdud; it is south-southwest from Jabné, distant 5 English miles, and but 2½ English miles from the Mediterranean.

Ashkelon אשקלון. This, formerly called the Greek city, is at present but a small village, inhabited by Arabs and Christians, and bears the name of Eskelon; it is 7½ English miles south of Ashdod on the shore of the Mediterranean. When Ibrahim Pasha was in Palestine he commenced building a tower and fort, employing the large and remarkable stones brought from the Synagogue of Gazza; but the buildings were left incomplete.

Gath גת. The situation of this place is not so well ascertained as those previously mentioned; the usual assumption that it is the town of Ramleh, situated in the territory of Dan, I hold to be quite erroneous; since it appears, from 1 Samuel xxx., that it must have been situated far to the south and west of this place. I therefore prefer the statement of Eusebius as far more correct, in placing Gath 5 mill from Eleutheropolis, sideward from Lod. At this day, also, there is found a village by the name of Gatha, 3 English miles south of Jaffa, and on the shore of the Mediterranean Sea; which is, without doubt, the remains of the ancient city of the Philistines.

Ekron עקרון, see above, Akar, in the description of the north boundary of Judah.*

* We read in Megilla fol. 6 *a*, "Rabbi Eliezer said, The prophet said (Zeph. ii. 4), And Ekron shall be rooted up; this refers to Kisri, the city of Edom, which was situated on the sands, and was a fixed nail (i. e. a dangerous place) for Israel in the Greek period. When now the kings of the Asmonean family conquered it, that day was called the day of the conquest of the tower of Shir." In another place it is called "the tower of Shid," and again "the tower of Zur." The poet, in the *Yotzer* of the 2d Sabbath Hannuckah, calls it "the tower of Nassy."[a] But it is by no means the opinion of Rabbi Eliezer, that Ekron and Cæsarea are identical; for Ekron belonged to Judah, and Cæsarea was at a great distance from it and belonged to Dan. But he explains the words of the prophet Zephaniah,

[a] This will explain an obscure passage in Talmud Chagigah, fol. 4 *b*, which reads thus: מרים מגדלא נשיא, in later editions it is even שער נשיא. Yarchi, as well as other commentators, explain this, "Miriam, who plaited the hair of the women," *Megadelah* thus meaning "to plait," *Nashi*, "women;" and in order to render it more explicit still, the later addition was made of *Seär*, "the hair." But there can be no doubt that the real sense of מגדלא נשיא (read "Migdalah Nahsi,") is the name of the above-mentioned town Kisri, or Cæsarea, which was called Migdal Nahsi; hence this Miriam who was of Cæsarea, obtained the surname "Miriam of Migdalah Nahsi." In order, however, to explain the sense farther, there arose an improper change in the passage in question; it was made to read Miriam Megadelah Dardeki (the educator of children), to show that Megadelah should not be taken for a proper name. In old and more correct editions, however, I found the addition of "Mechamemath Tannura" instead of the above.

Avin עוים. Although the name of the Avites is at present entirely unknown in Palestine, there is, nevertheless, no doubt that they once lived in the southern portion of the land of the Philistines, and had an extent of country reaching to the neighbourhood of Kadesh-Barnea. (See Raphiach and Chezron.)

Gibthon גבתון (1 Kings xv. 27) Gibthon of the Philistines. This was a Levitical city, belonging to the tribe of Dan (see Joshua xxi. 23, and xix. 44). In the latter passage it is described as between Elthekah and Baalath; it must therefore have stood between Bailin, which I take for Baalath, and Elthini, which I suppose to be Elthekah. At present I cannot find a vestige of it in that neighbourhood.*

"Ekron shall be rooted up," as having been fulfilled in Cæsarea Palestinæ, which was, indeed, uncommonly large, and always dangerous to Israel. It was also called Stratonis Tower. Astori wishes to prove from the passage cited that Ekron is Cæsarea, but his explanation is too forced and unsatisfactory.

* In Shir Hashirim Rabbethi to chap. i., v. 16, it says, that from Gibthon to Antipatris was a large multitude of towns, the smallest of which was Beth-Shemesh. In Sanhedrin 94 is said "from Gebeth to Antipatris;" in other places it reads "Geba;" but both these variations refer to Gibthon. (In Bereshith Rabbah, chap. lxi., there is "from Akko to Antipatris;" probably, however, an error of the transcriber.) In Yebamoth, fol. 62, it is also said that Rabbi Akiba had 12,000 scholars between Gibthon and Antipatris. It does not appear to me that reference is here made to the well-known Antipatris, the present Kefar Saba (Zaba, which see), for its situation to Gibthon was not such as to indicate two opposite points of a boundary line. I found, however, in Midrash Mishlé to ch. ix. 2, that the corpse of Rabbi Akiba, who was slain as a martyr in Cæsarea, was carried to Antipatris belonging to Kozrim for interment. Unquestionably must the reading "Kozrim" be erroneous, and should be Kazarah, which was in Galilee, close by Maon (which see); and to this day they point out the sepulchre of Rabbi Akiba between Tiberias and the ruins of Beth-Maon. From all this we may deduce that there was an Antipatris in Galilee, near Tiberias, and that this is the spot of which the passages cited speak; and thus Gibthon and Antipatris pro-

SIMEON. שמעון

The boundaries of the territory of Simeon are, it is true, not laid down in the Scriptures; for his portion was contained in the midst of that of the sons of Judah (Joshua xiv. 1); but as the towns which fell to this tribe are designated, the boundaries can thereby be ascertained, and this gives us the following result:

Towards the east this territory extended as far as Moladah; thence the boundary ran southwesterly to the Wady Kiseimi, i. e. Azmon or Ezem; thence it ran north to the Wady Sheria (the stream Besor), near Ziklag, for this belonged to Simeon, and lay on the northern part of this Wady; it extended then farther north to the Wady Simsum, on the northern edge of which is the village of the same name, which I suppose to be the ancient Sansannah, and reached as far as Baahath Beër, which is the modern village Beilin, situated 1 English mile north of Barkusia,—(in 1 Chron. iv. 32, it is called Baal). Hieronymus says, "Beër was 8 mill from Eleutheropolis," which suits exactly for Beilin; but this town itself, forming as it did the most northern point of the territory of Simeon, belonged to the tribe of Dan. Towards the south there were Beersheba, Moladah, Chazar-Shual, &c. In the Lowland were Attar, Ashan, Chazar-Susah, &c. But the district, however, which lay between this and the Mediterranean, remained the property of the tribe of Judah. (Judges ii. 18.)*

Having already described the greater part of the towns

perly denote two extremes of a boundary line, namely, Gibthon at the southwest, and Antipatris at the northeast, although I have not been able to discover a vestige of this place, nor the origin of its name. Perhaps it may have been derived from Antipater, the father of Herod.

* In Echa Rabbethi to ch. ii. 2, is mentioned a mountain of Simeon, which proves that this tribe must have possessed likewise a part of the mountains belonging to Judah.

of Simeon when treating of the territory of Judah, we have to notice only the following:

Beth-Hammerkaboth and Chazar-Susah בית המרכבות וחצר סוסה (Joshua xix. 5), are probably identical with the so-called "chariot cities" of 2 Chron. i. 14; and these were Madmannah and Sansannah, mentioned in the territory of Judah.

Ajin and Rịmmon עין רמון (ibid. xix. 7). The Septuagint translates these names with Thalche, which was a village at the time of Hieronymus, called Thalla, about 15 mill from Eleutheropolis, but is at present unknown.

Etam עיטם (1 Chron. iv. 32; Judges xv. 8). There is a village 2½ English miles north of Beth-Djibrin, called Gutna, as much as Utna, corrupted, perhaps, from Utma, and this from Etam. Josephus (Ant., book v. chap. i.), says, to Simeon belonged a part of Judæa, which bordered on Arabia and Egypt.

BENJAMIN.

The boundary of Benjamin is clearly laid down in Joshua xviii. 11–21. The northern line of Judah will answer to determine that of Benjamin with regard to it; and there is only this addition, that the line ran from Beth-El Luz to Atharoth-Adar, that is, the village Adara, 1 English mile south of Biri, then not far from Beth-Horon (Choron), to Kirjath-Jearim. In reading this passage of the Bible, there is an apparent contradiction. Kirjath-Jearim is described as the most western point of this territory (v. 14), and still it is said (v. 15) that the boundary extended still farther to the west (ימה). To reconcile this, our learned men have alleged that they understand this word (ימה) not as usual, "westward," but to "the sea;" but this is evidently not a correct view of the question, because in the whole circumjacent country of Kirjath-Jearim there is neither sea nor lake to be found (see Yarchi). Another difficulty presents itself in this manner: If it has represented, in v. 14, that Beth-Horon and Kirjath-Jearim formed the two terminating points of the western boundary of Benjamin, how does it happen that the towns of Nob, Chadid, Lod, and Ono, in the valley of Charashim, which lie 15 to 18 English miles west of Kirjath-Jearim, belonged to this tribe? (See Neh. xi. 31, and 1 Chron. viii. 12, to which the Chaldea Paraphrast adds דצדיאו בני ישראל ואוקדינון בנורא כד אגרו קרבא בגבעתא עם שבטא דבנימן "Which the children captured and burnt with fire when they made war at Gibeah with the tribe of Benjamin." See Megillah 4 *a*, and compare with Joshua viii. 26, and Neh. vi. 2.) The correct explanation of both the verses quoted (Joshua xviii. 14, 15), however, is as follows: In verse 14 it is not intended to define absolutely the western boundary, but only so far as the same ran in a direct line from north to south, and this is from Beth-Horon to Kirjath-Jearim. This was indeed the utmost boundary to the south, but the line did not immediately turn eastward, but went still farther westward ימה, and embraced the neighbourhood of Ono and Lod, &c.; and only from this extreme west did it bend again eastward to the spring of the waters of Nephtoach. This exposition will remove all the difficulties noticed.

THE CITIES OF BENJAMIN

Are for the most part still known. Of those mentioned in Joshua xviii. 21–28, we will notice the following:

Emek-Keziz עמק קציץ was a town probably situated in the valley Achor. (Compare with 1 Macc. ix. 62 and 64, where mention is made of Beth-Keziz. This correct reading, however, is only found in the Latin version; other copies read Beth-Batzin.)

Zemaraim צמרים. There are found at present in the

plain of the Jordan, 4 miles from the river, and north of Jericho, some ruins, called Chirbath al Zamra.

Ophrah עפרה. This town was situated, according to Eusebius, 5 mill east of Beth-El, but is at present quite unknown. It may probably have been in the vicinity of the modern village Taibi (which see).

Parah פרה lay in the valley which extends in an eastern direction to the southeast of Ramah, wherefore it is still called the Wady Pharah.

Kephar Ammoni כפר עמוני is no longer known. In 1 Macc. ix. 50, it is said "He (Bacchides) built the walls of Jericho, *Ammonai*, Beth-Choran, Beth-El, and *Parah*," no doubt including the two last-mentioned towns.

Ophni עפני. Probably the modern village Djiphni (Giphni, and this by corruption for 'Ophni), which is situated 2 English miles north of the ruins of Beit-un (Beth-El). This town is probably the *Gufnith* of Berachoth 44 *a*; the *Gufna* of Talmud Yerushalmi Taanith, chap. iv.; and the *Beth-Gufnin* of the Tosephtah of end of Ahaloth.

Gibeon גבעון, probably the village Djib (Gib), situated on a high rocky ridge, 6 English miles from Jerusalem, and 1 English mile north-northeast from Mizpeh. In the vicinity of this village is a lake, called by the Arabs Birkat Malchi, and which is already mentioned in Jer. xli. 12, "the great waters that are in Gibeon." (In Josep. Ant. B. viii. ch. 2, is mentioned that Solomon sacrificed at Hebron, evidently an error, and should be Gibeon; see 1 Kings iii. 5, where this is distinctly stated to have been the place of sacrifice.)

Ramah רמה is at present called Rahm, and lies on the road from Jerusalem to Shechem, on a small round mountain northeast of Mizpeh.

Beeroth בארות, now called Birya, is 2½ English miles north of Rahm, and is a large village.

Mizpeh מצפה lay in a northern direction, opposite to

Jerusalem, on the top of a high mount, from which there is an extended view; whence its name Mizpeh, from צפה to overlook. This town, not to be mistaken for Mizpeh-Gilead, as Kimchi has done, was the place where the prophet Samuel often assembled the people (1 Sam. vii. 5; x. 17). At present it is called Rama Nebi Samuel. (See farther, article Rama,—Ramathaim Zofim.) In 1 Macc. iii. 46 we read: "They then assembled together and went to Mizpeh, opposite to Jerusalem, for in Mizpeh was formerly a place of prayer;" perhaps referring to the custom of assembling the people, thence "gathering-place," as Synagogue in Greek means nothing but meeting-place in its original signification. Two and a half English miles northeast of Mizpeh is a village called Bir-Nabala (i. e. the pit of wickedness), in which there is a great pit, which I believe is the one in which the wicked Ishmael, son of Nathaniah, slew Gedaliah and so many others (Jer. xli. 7), and hence the name "Pit of Wickedness."*

Kephirah כפירה, probably one of the villages (Kephirim) in the valley of Ono, of Nehemiah vi. 2. (See Ono.)

Mozah מוצה is the village Kolonia, 3 English miles

* In Talmud Niddah, fol. 61 *a*, we read, "They dug on a rock in Beth-Horon, and found a pit full of human bones, and this is said to be the pit which Ishmael son of Nathaniah, caused to be filled with slain." This strikes me as extremely singular; since Beth-Horon is at a considerable distance from Mizpeh, and this tragical event occurred in the latter place. Nevertheless I found this same story in Tosephtah Niddah, chap. viii., and there it is not said that this was Ishmael's pit; it would appear therefore that this addition in Talmud Niddah is not authentic. In 1 Sam. iv. 13, we read יד דרך מצפה *Yad derech Mezapheh*, "by the way-side watching;" I almost am inclined to undertake another punctuation of this word, and to read it *Mizpeh*, and he was sitting by the wayside to Mizpeh, for the battle there spoken of took place near Eben Haëzer (v. i.), and this stone was near Mizpeh, as appears from 1 Sam. vii. 12; and Eli was therefore waiting there for early accounts of the engagement. Even the accents (נגינות) agree with the reading, and would seem to denote its correctness.

west of Jerusalem, as appears from T. Sukkah, fol. 45 *a*, that Moza is Kolonia.

Taralah תראלה is perhaps the village Thaniel=Thariel in the neighbourhood of Lod.

Zela צלע is perhaps identical with Sela, a place in the vicinity of Jerusalem. See Yalkut to 2 Samuel xxi. 14.

Gibeath-Kirjath גבעת קרית. See farther under Gebah and Gibeah.

In several passages of Holy Writ there are also spoken of the following places as belonging to Benjamin.

Anathoth ענתות (Joshua xxi. 18), is the little village Anatha, 3 English miles northeast of Jerusalem. North thereof is a stone quarry whence Jerusalem is supplied with building stone. (See Zohar end of Vayechi.)

Almon עלמון (ibid.); Bachurim בחורים (2 Sam. xvi. 5); Alemeth עלמת (1 Chron. viii. 36); Azmoveth עזמות (Neh. vii. 28), were all unknown hitherto to all inquirers into the situation of the country; but I have been favoured to discover the situation. When, in my journey of investigation through Palestine, I traversed the territory of Benjamin, I discovered some ruins of very ancient buildings on the top of a high mountain, 1 English mile northeast from the village Anatha. I made inquiry of the inhabitants of the above village concerning the name and fate of that ancient town; but no one could give me any information, until an old man, also belonging to the village, came to me and told me the following, which he gave as a tradition received in his youth from his parents: "On that mountain lay once the city of Al-Muth, the inhabitants of which rebelled against the ruler of the land, and he caused, therefore, the whole town to be demolished." I took up my Bible, which I carried constantly with me, and searched carefully into the cities enumerated in Joshua xviii. as belonging to Benjamin; but not one of them bore the name of Al-Muth. I then searched among the Levitical cities (xxi. 18) for this name, and found there the town of Almon near Anathoth, whence then it would appear that this Al-Muth, 1 English mile from Anathoth, is actually the Almon of Joshua xxi. 18. The parallel passage of 1 Chron. vi. 45, has Alemeth; compare with this ibid. viii. 36, where it says, Jehoada begot Alemeth and Azmaveth. In Ezra ii. 24, and Neh. vii. 28, Azmaveth is mentioned as close to Anathoth; consequently it is without doubt identical with Almon or Alemeth, and the latter word is corrupted by the Arabs into Al-muth. Bachurim (2 Sam. xvi. 5), is translated by Jonathan with Almon; whence it is clear that all the four names at the head of this article are the Levitical town of Almon, 1 mile northeast from Anathoth, likewise belonging to the Levites, and situated on the same mount. It is impossible now to tell why so many names were given to one locality.

Gilgal גלגל (Joshua v. 9), was, according to Josephus, 10 stadia from Jericho, and 50 stadia from Jordan. At present there is found near the Jordan a hill which appears like a heap of stones, and is called by the Arabs Galgala.

Baal-Thamar בעל תמר (Judges xx. 33). At the time of Eusebius there was a village Beth-Thamar, not far from Geba, but it is at present unknown.

Sela Rimmon סלע הרמון is the village Rimun, about 2½ English miles east of Beth-El. The whole village almost is built on a rock, whence, therefore, properly its name "the rock of Rimmon." See Tosephtah Sota, 18: "South of Jerusalem is a plain, and in the district of Geba and Rimmon are rocks and cliffs." In Yerushalmi, beginning of Berachoth, is mentioned Rabbi of Romnah, i. e. of Rimmon; in Zohar to Shemini, Rabbi Zera of the village ראמין Ramin.*

* In Midrash Echa to chap. i., v. 16, is told that Hadrian caused a large number of Jews to be assembled in the valley of Beth-Rimmon,

Lebonah לבונה (Judges xxi. 19), is the present village Lubin, 2½ English miles west of Shiloh, on the road from Shechem to Jerusalem.

In Isaiah x. 28–34, occurs the following: "He (Sanherib) is come to Aiath, he is passed to Migron, in Michmash he hath laid up his carriages; they are gone over the passage; Geba is a night-lodging for us; Ramah trembleth, Gibeah of Saul is fugitive. Lift up thy voice, O daughter of Gallim; cause it to be heard in Laish (or 'listen Laish'), O poor Anathoth. Madmenah is moved; the inhabitants of Gebim gather to flee. Even this day will he rest in Nob; he will shake his hand against the mountain of the daughter of Zion, the hill of Jerusalem."

Aiath עית, i. e. Ai. See in the 31 Kings.

Migron מגרון. About half an English mile south of Beitun (Beth-El), are found some ruins, which the Arabs call Burdj Magrun (i. e. the town or fort of Magrun); and they are undoubtedly remains of the town of Migron.

Michmash מכמש. The village Mikmas, 2 English miles

and had them there all slain, so that their blood flowed into the river Kypros. I take this river to be the present Wady Mudiah, which flows to the east of Rimun. Josephus (Bell. Jud. book i., chap. xvi.) makes mention of this Kypros, and relates that King Herod, in honour of his mother Kypros, built a castle of the same name near Jericho. Astori, in reference to the passage cited from the Midrash, thinks Kypros to mean Cyprus, and explains the matter allegorically, that the slaughter was so great that the course of the blood could, as it were, be traced through the sea as far as the island of Cyprus. But the Midrash speaks distinctly of a river, not an island Kypros. Still I found in Yerushalmi Sukkah 5, "the blood ran through the sea (בים) to Kypros;" but I think it ought to be כים *like* a sea, not בים *into* the sea. Upon the whole, there is some trouble in reconciling all the difficulties connected with this event. The Yerushalmi (loc. cit.), also Esther Rabbethi (introd.), say that this tragic event befell the inhabitants of Alexandria in Egypt; and if this be so, the river cannot be the Wady Mudia; but in Esther Rabbethi there is not the addition "that the blood ran like a stream as far as Kypros."

north of Djeba (Gibea), in the vicinity of which are the ruins of a place called Zanua, which would then argue that the correct reading in Menachoth 83 *b*, should be זנוחא מכמס Zenucha of Michmas, as the place where the best wheat grows; not as it is in many of our copies, since both the names as given by me still exist at this day.

Maabrah מעברה, the passage. It is the same narrow path through which Jonathan, son of Saul, went over to attack the Philistines (see 1 Sam. xiv. 4); but the names of the rocks there mentioned, Bozez and Seneh, are now unknown.

Geba גבע. See farther down.

Bath-Gallim בת גלים is the modern village Beth-Djallin, situated between Ramleh and Jaffa, and was the birth-place of Paltiel, the son of Laish (1 Sam. xxv. 44). The assertion of Eusebius, that Gallim lies near Ekron, is entirely incorrect, since Senacherib never penetrated thus far. On the contrary, the whole of the towns mentioned in Isaiah x. 28–32, as reached by the Assyrian king in his expedition against Judah, are north of Jerusalem, in the territory of Benjamin.

Laish and Madmenah ליש ומדמנה are no more known. The former is perhaps the city of Leasa, mentioned in 1 Macc. ix. 5–15, whence Judah pursued Bacchides to the mountains near Ashdod.

Gebim גבים was, according to Eusebius, Ophni, situated near Geba; but it appears to me to have been identical with *Gob*, where the Philistines fought with Israel (2 Sam. xxi. 18). The parallel passage to this, however (1 Chron. xx. 4), reads *Geser*. It is possible enough that Geser and Gob are identical, or that they were two places situated near one another.

Nob נוב is the present village Beth-Naba, distant 17 English miles northwest from Jerusalem.

Gebah, Gibeah, Gibath-Binjamin, Gibath-Shaul, גבע

גבעה גבעת בנימן גבעת שאול. Geba and Gibea denoted one and the same place, for in Judges xix. it is always called Gibeah; still in xx. 30 we find Geba; also in v. 33, "the cave of Geba." So also in Joshua xviii. 24, the word is also Geba. It is also called Gibath-Binjamin (1 Sam. xiii. 2), also Geba-Benjamin. This proves that both names signify one and the same place. Its situation must have been very near to Ramah (Judges xix. 13), and is no doubt the modern Djeba, 2½ English miles east of Rahm. We find, however, another town of the same name, to wit, Gibeah or Geba, on the frontier between Judah and Benjamin, in the neighbourhood of Kirjath-Jearim. In 1 Sam. x. 15, it is called Gibeah; but in xiii. 3, it is termed Geba, also Gibeath-Shaul, or Gibeah of Saul; for this was his birth-place, from here his she-asses ran away, from here he went out to seek for them, and returned thither after consulting with Samuel. So also it is said in Isaiah x. 29, "Gibeah of Saul is fled." We find that Kirjath-Jearim is reckoned, in Joshua xv. 60, among the cities of Judah; but in xviii. 28, among those of Benjamin. It must therefore have been situated, as a matter of course, on the boundary line, so that it was sometimes considered as belonging to the one, and at others to the other tribe. I therefore investigated carefully the situation and surrounding country of Kirjath-Jearim, and found that it is situated on the declivity of a mount, which is south of the same. Close to the village, in a northwest direction, is a height; and it appears evident that Geba must have stood upon it. Both Kirjath-Jearim and Geba formed but one continuous town. Kirjath-Jearim was at the south, and Geba at the north, and the boundary line ran through both; so that it is still visible at this day, namely, because the boundary line ran along the road which leads to Jaffa. Geba was thus a city of Benjamin, whilst Kirjath-Jearim is assigned to both Benjamin and Judah. It appears to me even that, owing to their geographical connexion, their names *Kirjath-Gibeath* (Joshua xviii. 28), are put in the construct state,* so to say, placed in connexion as far as language can do it; for the first was in a measure Gibeath-Kirja (i. e. Gibeah of Kirjah), and the latter Kirjath-Gibeah (i. e. Kirjah of Gibeah). If it is now said in 1 Sam. vii. 42, "And the men of Kirjath-Jearim came and fetched up the ark of the Lord, and brought it unto the house of Abinadab in Gibeah" (therefore afterwards called the "Hill of God," ibid. x. 5), "And it came to pass while the ark abode in Kirjath-Jearim," &c.,—this, however, will not appear as a contradiction, if we reflect that both formed but one city. (See Bemidbar Rabbah, chap. iv., which says distinctly that Gibeah and Kirjath-Jearim were but one town.)

"The sons of Benjamin were at —— Ananiah, Chazor, Ramah, Gitthaim, Chadid, Zeboim, Neballat, Lod, and Ono, (in) the valley of Charashim." (Neh. xi. 32, 35.)

Ananiah עננית is probably the village Beth-Chanina, situated 3 English miles north of Jerusalem on the road to Mizpeh.

Chazor חצור. 3 English miles northeast of Beth-El, not far from the plain of Jordan, are yet seen the ruins of Tell-Chazor, and if this be the city in question, it was beyond the limits of Benjamin, as given in Joshua. In the vicinity thereof, was the city of Ephraim, mentioned in 2 Chronicles viii. 17. Perhaps this Chazor was

* To those persons not acquainted with Hebrew, it may be enough to state that, when two nouns in Hebrew are related to each other as possessor and possessed, the first, or the possessed, is put in the construct state—not as in English, where the genitive form is attached to the possessor. So we say in Hebrew, עיר דוד the city of—David. Many times this word is changed, either in vowels or consonants; particularly is the latter the case in feminine nouns ending in ה, or the end syllable *ah*, which is changed in ת or *ath*. So Kirjah, city, becomes Kirjath, city of, and so with all others.—TRANSLATOR.

identical with the town Baal-Chazor, of 2 Samuel xiii. 23, near Ephraim (Ephrain).

Gitthaim גתים, perhaps the present Ramleh, which is also called Gath, as I have learned from several Jewish documents, which favour the idea that Ramleh has been built on the site of the ancient Gath, which is also mentioned in 2 Samuel iv. 3. The opinion advanced by others, that Ramleh should be the former *Gath*, in the land of the Philistines (Josh. xiii. 3), is erroneous. (See above, article Gath.) There was formerly a large and famous city named Gith, 5 English miles west of Shechem, situated on a singly standing but not high mountain, not far from the plain of the sea; and there is at present on the spot the village Kirjath-Djid (Gith); but as it was situated in the territory of Ephraim, it cannot be identical with this Gitthaim, which belonged to Benjamin.

Chadid חדיד is the village Al Chadida, situated 5 English miles east of Lod, on the summit of a round mountain. In the first book of the Maccabees xii. 38, and xiii. 13, mention is made of Adida in the Lowland; see also Erechin chap. ix. § 6, and Eduyoth, chap. vii. § 5. The position assigned in the Maccabees agrees then with what I have advanced, that the so-called Lowland or valley extended up to the mountain of Lod.

Zeboim צבעים is the village Zuba, situated on a high mount, 3 English miles west of Jerusalem. In Challah iv. 10 is mentioned the Mount Zeboim. This place had a very strong fort, which was destroyed by Abraim (Ibrahim) Pacha in the year 5594 (1834).

Neballat נבלט is no doubt, according to my opinion, the large village Beth Naballa, 5 English miles south of Ramleh.

Lod לוד, also called Lydia and Diospolis, is now the large village Lidi, 2½ English miles northeast of Ramleh.

The Christians point out here the grave of their Saint George, which name the town also bore during their reign in Palestine.*

Ono אונו is entirely unknown now; but it was situated as the Talmud, end of Ketuboth, mentions, 3 mill from Lod. (See also Zohar Vayetzé, 151 *a*, and Pinchas, 117 *a*.)

The valley of Charashim גי החרשים. In Talmud Yerushalmi Megillah, chap. i., is related that Lod and Ono lay in the valley of Charashim, and in fact constituted the same.

Azel אצל (Zech. xiv. 5; 1 Chron. xiii. 38, ix. 44). I believe that this is the village Azaria instead of Azalia, changing ל l into ר r (as also is done in Ezek. xix. 7), which is situated southeast of the Mount of Olives. Perhaps the name of this village may be derived from Azel, son of Elasah, belonging to the tribe of Benjamin (1 Chron. viii. 37). In the Talmud, this place is named Hutzal, in the portion of Benjamin (Megillah v. 6). A town of the same name was in Babylonia, as appears from

* Rabbi Benjamin, of Tudela, in his travels says ומשם לשרגוג והיא לוז, this is an incorrect reading and should be לשנק' גורג והיא לוד "And from there to sact. Georg, which is Lod." In Semachoth chap. ii. § 4, it is said "the son of Gorgos in Lod," which I presume refers to the Georg in question. This city was for a long time the seat of the most learned men after the destruction of Jerusalem; so that we generally understand under the terms Chachme Negeb, or Dahrom, (חכמי נגב and חכמי דרום) "The wise men of the south," which often occur in the Talmud and Midrashim, especially in Talmud Yerushalmi, the learned men who dwelt at Lod. This will explain a somewhat obscure passage in Baba Bathra, fol. 25 *b*, "He that wishes to become rich should turn northward, but if he desires to be wise let him turn to the south." Now it appears from Josephus that the land of Galilee was one of wealth, extraordinarily populous, and famous for its agriculture and industry, consequently the seat of riches, just as the south, the Dahrom, or Negeb, was the seat of learning. The Talmud then, means, if one desire wealth, let him go into the northern country, into Galilee; but if he wishes to become learned, let him go south to Lod, and acquire the wisdom there dispensed.

Yoma, fol. 52 *b*.* See also, farther down, my description of the Mount of Olives.

Gimso גמזו (2 Chron. xxviii. 18), is the village Djimsi, 2½ English miles east of Lod, on the way to Jerusalem. Nahum Ish Gimso was a native of this place. (Taanith 21*a*.)

Anab ענב (Joshua xi. 21), is the village Anabah, 3 English miles east of Ramleh.

Shaphir שפיר (Micah i. 11). We have already remarked in the description of Judah, that southeast of Ashdod there is a village Suaphir; but also 2½ English miles northwest of Lod, there is a village named Saphiriah, which is probably the one meant in Micah. Nevertheless, nearly all the places mentioned by this prophet lie in the northwest part of Judah.

Aphek אפק (1 Sam. iv. 1; vii. 12); there is not a vestige to be found any more of this city, which must have been situated in the neighbourhood of Mizpeh.

Beth-Kor בית כר (ibid. vii. 11) is probably the modern village Karna, near Ramalah, which is a village situated on a mountain, 2 English miles west of Beeroth, and not to be mistaken for Ramleh. But it is also possible that Beth-Kor was situated on the Wady Kurava, which unites with the Wady Luban (Lebona), and extends as far as the Wady Udshé. (See article מי הירקון Mé Hayarkon.) Probably it is the Kuria mentioned in Jos., Bel. Jud., book v. chap. iv.

We will now notice the following towns belonging to Benjamin, mentioned in the Talmudic writings.

Keni קני (Ahaloth xviii. 9; Yerushalmi, end of Teru-

* In Talmud Kethuboth, fol. 3 *a*, is said "Hutzal of Benjamin in the land of Babylon." I, however, believe that "of Benjamin" is an erroneous addition, since the passage refers to the country of Babylon. And, in truth, I found in old editions, the correct reading הוצל בארץ בבלי "Hutzal in the land of Babylon."

moth; Zohar Tazria, 42 *b*, as Keni near Lod) is probably the village En-Keni, about 2 English miles east of Lidi; in the immediate neighbourhood thereof, is the cave in which Rabbi Simeon Ben Yochai and his son lived in concealment; as it appears clearly from the introduction to Tickuné Zohar, that it was in the environs of Lod. This is also asserted in Talmud Yerushalmi Taanith, chap. iv., and in Pesiktah Rabbethi, 32. It is, therefore, quite erroneous to show this cave in Upper Galilee, near Pekiin, as it is said in the book Shibeché Yerushalem.

Kefar-Dichrin כפר דכרין (Gittin, fol. 57 *a*) was a city situated on the Tur Malka, "the King's Mountain." It was probably identical with the town of Beth-Zachara, mentioned in 1 Macc. vi. 32, and elsewhere, and in Josephus' Antiquities and War of the Jews, since *Zachar* is the same as the Chaldaic *Dichrin*, both signifying *male.* Astori found yet, 2½ English miles north of Lidi, in the mountains, a village called Dachrin, but it is now unknown.

Pekiin פקיעין (Chagigah, fol. 3 *a*, Sanhedrin 32 *b*,) was between Jabné and Lod, but is now unknown.

Be-Tray בי תרי (Sanh. 95 *a*) is probably the village Bi-tharis, 1 English mile east from Lidi.

Kubi קובי (ibid.), is probably the village Kubab, 3 English miles southeast of Ramleh.

Zalmon צלמון (Yebamoth, 122 *a*; end chap. iv. Mishna Kelaim; Tosephtah Parah, 8; Torath Cohanim to Bechuckotai). In Greek authorities I find the following indication of this place: "Zalominé is a town in the vicinity of Diospolis (Lod), but the particulars are not any more known at present." It is possible, however, that the ruins of Calomon (for Zalomon), situated 1 English mile west of Kuneisa, on the shore of the Mediterranean, south of Chaifa, are the remains of the city in question.

Josephus' Antiq., b. v. chap. i., says, that the portion of

Benjamin extended from Jerusalem to Beth-El; elsewhere he says, that it extended to the Great Sea (Mediterranean). He consequently contradicts himself with what he says concerning the position of the land of Dan.

DAN דן.

It is true that the boundaries of the territory of Dan are not given in the Scriptures; but they can be determined with tolerable accuracy from the towns of this tribe, as enumerated in Joshua xix. 40–48. Through means of Josephus, who in various passages calls Jabné (Jamnia) a city of Dan, and gives Dor (Dandura) as the most northern, and Ashdod as the most southern towns of the same, we can easily fix the northern and southern boundaries. It appears also, from the description of the territory of Simeon, that the present village Beilin, the Baalath* of the Bible, was the most northerly point of

* In Yerushalmi Sanhedrin, chap. i., it says: "We find that the public announcement of the year and the monthly determination of the feasts and festivals (קדוש השנה וקדוש החדש) by the Sanhedrin (which would only take place in the territory of Judah), were made in Baalath, which sometimes belonged to Judah and at others to Dan. Eltheké, Gibethon, and Baalath, belonged to Judah; Baalah, Jyim, and Ezem, belonged to Dan. How could they then make the announcement in Baalath? Because the houses belonged to Judah, the fields, however, to Dan." This passage contains much of interest in a geographical point of view, so that I deem it proper to discuss it somewhat at length. It appears strange that Eltheké, &c., should be ascribed to Judah, and Baalah, &c., to Dan, when the reverse seems to have been the case, on reference to Joshua xv. 29 and xix. 44. Again, if Baalath belonged to Judah, the determination of years and festivals could legally take place there; the question, therefore, in the passage cited appears most surprising. There can, therefore, be no doubt but that a transposition has taken place in the passage before us, and that it ought to be read correctly "Eltheké Gibthon, and Baalath belonged to Dan, and Baalah, Jyim, and Ezem, to Judah." We can deduce from this passage of the Yerushalmi that the Baalah of Joshua

this tribe; it lay therefore on the boundary between Simeon and Dan, and was thus the most southeasterly point of the latter. The boundary ran thence westward to Ashdod, on the Mediterranean, and on the other side from Baalath over Beth-Shemesh, the modern En-Sems, to Ajalon, now Jalo, and turning northwesterly it ran between Lod and Ramleh, for the former belonged to Benjamin, and then northerly over Djilil, Kefar-Saba, &c., to Dandura, the ancient Dor. It will thus appear that the territory of Dan was situated between the Mediterranean and the portions of Benjamin and Ephraim, so that the western parts of these tribes could by no means have extended to the sea. What is said therefore in the description of the limits of the sons of Joseph, "And the goings out thereof were to the sea," (Joshua xvi. 3, 5,) means only that the boundary ran in a straight line, without turning to the north and south in the direction of the sea, but not that it ever touched the same. Josephus, by the by, contradicts himself, in extending the land of Ben-

xv. 29, is different from Baalath[a] of ibid. xix. 44, since the former was quite to the south, and that the second, which was also called Baalath Beër (Ramoth Negeb), was in the portion of Simeon, and was on the boundary between this tribe and Dan, but is still considered by the Yerushalmi as a city of Judah, because originally all the part of Simeon was included in that of his powerful brother, so that the cities of the former are also considered as belonging to the latter. We learn farther from this that the frontier towns are often considered as belonging to one and again to the other tribe, and that in a measure the possession of them was alternately determined, since the text says, "Sometimes to Judah, at others to Dan." Again, that occasionally the division of these boundary towns was so, that the town itself, the buildings, as the Talmud has it, belonged to one, whilst the fields, meadows, and environs belonged to another tribe; which exposition will enable us to unravel many obscurities in the divisions of the tribes.

[a] I believe that Baalath is Baalah in the construct state, and is, so to say, an abbreviated phrase, and that the other noun belonging to it is to be understood. Thus Baalah of Bear. The *Kametz* in Joshua xix. 44, is only because it concludes the verse.—TRANSLATOR.

jamin to the Great Sea, whilst he alleges that the coast belonged to Dan.

We will now mention the following of the towns of Dan:

Zoreah and Eshtaol צרעה אשתאל. See above, page 101.

Ir-Shemesh עיר שמש. See above, page 104.

Shaalabbim שעלבין is no longer known. In the time of Eusebius there was a village in the vicinity of Sebasta (Samaria), called Shelbin. If now the territory of Dan extended so far as Dor, as Josephus reports, then is it easy to conceive that this tribe had some possessions up to the immediate vicinity of Samaria. The next mentioned town, Ajalon, is certainly a considerable distance from Samaria; but it is by no means unusual to enumerate several towns together, although they lie far apart from one another.

Ajalon אילון is the modern village Jalo, 11 English miles from Jerusalem, and 2½ English miles from Gibeon; wherefore the assertion of Rashi to Joshua x. 12, that Ajalon is far from Gibeon, is not borne out by the fact. East of Lod, on the road to Gimso, there is a large valley running between two high mountain peaks, of which one points to the south, the other to the north. On the southern mount, there is the just-mentioned Jalo, opposite to which lies, on the northern mount, the village Beth-Ur, which is Lower Beth-Horon of Joshua x. 10, and xvi. 3. Above the same, is a narrow pass which leads to a village lying on the summit of a steep mount, and is now called Beth-Ur Fok, which means Upper Beth-Horon (Joshua xvi. 5); but this appellation seems to me erroneous, since this place must have been much farther removed from Lower Beth-Horon; it would be more correct* to take it for "the descent to Beth-Horon" of Joshua

* This narrow pass is also mentioned in Sanhedrin, 32 *b*, and Tosephtah *b*, Niddah 8, also in Bereshith Rabbah 73, where it speaks of Rab Huna of

x. 11. From this peak one can see Gibeon to the east and Ajalon to the west. It would then appear that Joshua must have stood here when (x. 12) he called out in prophetic inspiration "Sun, stand still in Gibeon, and moon, in the valley of Ajalon."

Elon אילון. Although not any more known, it is nevertheless mentioned in 1 Kings iv. 9, along with Shaalabbin, Beth-Shemesh and Beth-Chanan.

Eltheké אלתקה, also called Elthekon (Joshua xv. 59), is perhaps the village Althini, not far from Beilin (Baalath).

Baalath בעלת גבתון. See above, page 122.

Jehud יהוד is the village Jehudia, 7½ English miles southeast of Jaffa.

Bené Berak בני ברק. There is a spot, 5 English miles northeast from Jaffa, which the Arabs call Barak, perhaps the former site of the town, although there are no ruins to be found at it. The assertion of Eusebius that this town should have been situated near Ashdod, is incorrect.

Gath-Rimmon גת רמון was situated, according to Eusebius, 12 mill north of Eleutheropolis, on the road to Lod. It is at present unknown.

Mé Hajarkon מי הירקון, i. e. the waters of disease; this place was, according to my opinion, near the Wady Udshi, which descends from the mountains of Lod. Wady Udshi

Beth-Horon. In Yoma, chap. vi. § 9, it says: "It is a distance of 3 mill from Jerusalem to בית חדודו Beth Chidodo;" but the Yerushalmi to this passage and Maimonides read "to Beth-Horon." I confess that this reading cannot be correct, since Beth-Horon is much farther than 3 mill from Jerusalem. Josephus says the distance is 100 stadia, about 12 English miles; and Beth-Ur is actually thus far from Jerusalem. The correct reading, therefore, is Beth-Chidodo, the name of a town or place now unknown, but which was probably southeast of Jerusalem, near the valley of Kidron, the rocky defiles of which was the place whither the scapegoat (שעיר המשתלח לעזאזל) was sent on the Day of Atonement, of which I may, perhaps, speak more hereafter.

also signifies the stream of pain, nearly synonymous with the Hebrew appellation of the town, which was also most likely applied to the river near which it stood.

Jaffa יפו. This is a small town, surrounded with a wall and defended by a small fort. It is situated on the Mediterranean Sea, and forms the harbour of Jerusalem.* When I arrived in Palestine in the year 5593 (1833), there lived not even a single Israelite in this place; at present, however, are found here near *thirty* families. That many Israelites lived here in ancient times, is proved sufficiently by many passages in the Talmud; for instance, in Yerushalmi, end of Moëd Katone, and Pesiktah Rabbethi 15, we find mentioned R. Acha, of Jaffa; in Yerushalmi Pesachim, chap. i., R. Phineas, of Jaffa; in Talmud B. Megillah, fol. 16 *b*, R. Adda Demin Jaffa; in Vayikra Rabbah, R. Nachman, of Jaffa, and Pesiktah Rabbethi 17, R. Tanchum, of Jaffa. This town was totally destroyed in the year 5358 (1598); but was subsequently built up again. When Napoleon returned this way in the year 5560 (1800), after his unsuccessful expedition against Akko (St. Jean D'Acre), he caused, in his anger at his defeat, the walls of Jaffa to be battered down. (For farther particulars, see historical part.)

Bené-Elam and Bené-Charim בני עילם בני חרים (Ezra ii. 31, 32), is perhaps the village Charim ben Elim, situated on a bay of the sea, 8 English miles north-northeast of Jaffa. The inhabitants point out here the grave of the high priest Eli, contained in an elegant building; but no one acquainted with the Bible, can have the least doubt

* In Yoma, fol. 38 *a*, we read, "When they arrived at the harbour of Akko," i. e. at the time they carried the gates made for the temple from Alexandria to Jerusalem. I can scarcely believe that it was necessary to run so far north as Akko for this purpose, and I venture therefore to read Jaffa in its place; and in truth, the Talmud Yerushalmi for Yoma, in the same narration, has נמלא של יפו "The harbour of Jaffa."

of the incorrectness of assuming this monument to be what is alleged for it. For, why should Eli, who died at Shiloh (1 Sam. iv. 18), have been carried hither to be buried? This error appears to me to have arisen from an incorrect interpretation of the name of the town Charim ben Elim. It is evidently a compound of Bené-Elam and Bené-Charim, both of which places, as is apparent from the others mentioned in Ezra ii., must have been situated in the neighbourhood of Jaffa. The people now changed Elam into Eli, and thus originated the false legend that the grave of Eli the high priest was existing there. On this grave, over which is built quite an elegant structure, there is a large tombstone, inscribed on one side with a Hebrew, and on the other with a Samaritan, inscription. It is well known, the Samaritans call themselves all priests, and their chief they called "high priest." It is, therefore, highly probable that this grave encloses the bones of one of these; perhaps his name may have been Eli, whence then the origin of this error becomes doubly apparent. The Samaritans, however, go constantly to this grave to perform at it their devotions; but every one who is truly pious, will guard himself against being misled by legends of so little credibility as this. Near this place are some ruins, which are probably the remains of Apollonia, mentioned in Josephus' Antiquities and the Jewish War.

Ataroth, Beth Joab עטרות בית יואב (1 Chron. ii. 54). On the road from Jerusalem to Jaffa, 1½ English miles west of Saris, is the village Al Etron (incorrectly pronounced Latrun), and is no doubt the ancient Ataroth. Three-fourths of an English mile north-northeast of this is Beth-Joab, near which is a large spring called Bir-Joab.

From those places of Dan mentioned in the Talmudic writings, we will describe the following.

Kefar Saba כפר סבא (Yerushalmi Demai, chap. ii.), is

still a village, situated 3 English miles north of Djilil, or Gilgal (Joshua xii. 23). In this Kefar Saba is found a monument, which the Arabs call "the sepulchre of the sons of Jacob;" but I could not ascertain the reason of so naming it. This town was also called Antipatris (see Yoma, 69 *a*, and Gittin, 76 *a*); and Josephus relates of it, that Herod had it built up, and gave it the name of Antipatris, in honour of his father Antipater.

Bither ביתר (Gittin, 57 *a*). Of this formerly celebrated city, which was situated 10 English miles north of Kefar Saba, there remains nothing but some ruins. There is also a village of the same name 7½ English miles south-west of Jerusalem.

Kisarin קיסרין also called Cæsarea Palestinæ (Megillah, 6 *a*), is at present the miserable village Kisarié, and is situated on the Mediterranean, 7½ English miles south of Dardura. It was built by Herod, called the great, and named Cæsarea, in honour of the Roman emperor, Augustus Cæsar. This formerly famous seaport town, and the largest in Palestine after the destruction of Jerusalem, is now totally destroyed; and there is nothing visible of its former elegance, except large and still remarkable ruins, the interiors of which are filled up with the huts of fishermen. When Ibrahim Pacha undertook considerable repairs on the fortifications of Akko, he caused some large stones from the ruins of Cæsarea to be brought away for the purpose. In order to distinguish this place from another of the same name at the foot of the Anti-Lebanon (Cæsarea Philippi), this one was called Cæsarea Palestinæ.

Pundeka פונדקא (Yerushalmi Demai, ch. ii., "from Pundeka to Kefar Saba"), is the present village Phunduk, 5 English miles east of Kefar Saba. Also 2½ miles north north-east of Sebasta (Samaria), there is the village Phundokomi. It will appear from the passage just cited from the Yerushalmi, that there were two towns called Pundeka; and these are no doubt the two villages Phunduk and Phundokomi.

Zerifin צריפין (Menachoth, 64 *b*), the present village Zaraphan, 2½ English miles north of Ramleh, on the road to Jaffa. Another village of the same name, Zeraphan Athikah, i. e. the old Zeraphan, is in the vicinity of Ekron.

Kushta קושטא (Sanhedrin, 97 *a*), is probably the village Al Kustani, situated in the Lowland, 5 English miles southwest of Ekron.

Ramleh רמלא, i. e. sand, in Arabic, so called on account of the large quantity of sand found on the road from Jaffa to this place, lies 10 English miles southeast of Jaffa, in the Lowland. It is therefore quite erroneous to assume that this town is identical with Ramathaim-Zofim, which was on the mountain of Ephraim. Not less surprised was I to find it stated, in a description by a non-Israelite, that in olden time no mention whatever occurs of Ramleh, the more so since the Mahomedan historian Abulfeda relates that it was built in the year 63 (i. e. 4435 A. M., or 675 C. E.) by Soliman Ebed al Maliki. This is evidently a mistake; because Ptolemy already speaks of Ramleh in his description of the country. The error of the author quoted may have arisen from a rebuilding of the town by Soliman.

THE SONS OF JOSEPH.

"And the lot of the children of Joseph fell from Jordan by Jericho, unto the water of Jericho on the east, to the wilderness that goeth up from Jericho throughout Mount Beth-El, and goeth out from Beth-El Luzah, and passeth along unto the borders of Archi to Ataroth, and goeth down westward to the border of Japhleti, unto the border of Beth-Horon the nether, and to Gezer; and the goings out thereof are toward the sea." (Joshua xvi. 1–3.)

In explanation of this passage, I will remark that only

the southern boundary of Ephraim and Menasseh, as it limits in this direction the territories of both, is designated with the common name of "the boundary of the sons of Joseph." In describing, however, the other boundary lines, the names of both the respective tribes are mentioned. (See Joshua xvi. 5, and xvii. 7.) By the Water of Jericho is understood the spring called En-Sultan, which is the same with that known as the spring of Elisha, which, as mentioned above, page 83, has its source northwest of Jericho; and as it spreads itself like a stream, it is called here "the water of Jericho." Since now the northern border of Benjamin is the southern one of the sons of Joseph, we can take it for granted that the Ataroth here mentioned is the same with Ataroth-Adar of Joshua xviii. 13, or at least that they were two places situated close by each other. At the present time there are two villages called Atarah, one of which is 1 English mile south of Beëroth, and the other 7½ English miles north of Beit-un (Beth-El). It appeared to me at first doubtful which of the two was the Ataroth of the Bible; but upon closer investigation I convinced myself that this position must be assigned to the first, and that the second was merely an arbitrary appellation, of which no trace can be found in antiquity. The assertion of Eusebius, that Archi-Ataroth is 4 mill south of Sebasta, appears to me quite erroneous.

Japhlet יפלט, though not known at present must still have been situated between Atara of Beëroth and Beth-Ur, i. e. Beth-Choron.

Gezer גזר. See the 31 Kings, page 85.

Lower and Upper Beth-Horon (Choron). These two places, as appears from Joshua xvi. 3 and 5, must have been a considerable distance apart, and we have already remarked above, p. 140, that the first was near Jalo (Ajalon). In order to determine the site of the second, the following will, I think, be sufficient. In the book of Jashar to Gen. xxxiv., it is alleged that Beth-Horon was not far from the town of Gaash; and the remains of Joshua are interred, as is well known, from Joshua xxiv. 30, at Timnath-Serach, now, no doubt, the village Kefar Charas, as the burial-place of Joshua is called Timnath-Cheres in Judges ii. 9, and it is at the same time described as north of Mount Gaash. (The grave, moreover, of the great leader of the Israelites, ornamented with a handsome monument, is pointed out at Kefar Charas.) Consequently Beth-Choron must have been in the immediate vicinity of this place. And indeed there is, 3 English miles north of it, a village named Chavara, and the similarity is sufficiently strong to authorize us to suppose it to be the ancient Upper Beth-Choron. It is probable that the Persian Satrap of Moab, Sanballat, the Choronite (Neh. ii. 10), was a native of this town.

The position of the frontier towns of verses 6 and 7 is correctly given by Eusebius, as follows:

Michmethah was 15 mill from Shechem, and 6 mill from Beth-Shean; Taanath-Shiloh* 10 mill east from Shechem, in the vicinity of Jordan, and Janocha, 12 mill east of Shechem, and Naaran (1 Chron. vii. 28), at present called Neama, was 5 mill from Jericho.

But the meaning of the various Bible passages is not that the boundary line ran westerly from Beth-Horon to Michmethah, for the latter was not in a western direction from the former, but at a distance of more than 20 English miles in a northern course; and the western border is first defined only farther down in verse 8. I rather think the proper meaning to be that the border did not run in a straight line from Beth-Horon to Michmethah, but at first

* According to Yerushalmi Megillah, chap. i., Taanath-Shiloh is identical with Shiloh. If this be so, then the statement of Eusebius is incorrect, and should be in that case 15 mill southeast from Shechem.

somewhat westerly, and then it turned northeasterly, till it touched Michmethah; thence to the south, to the east of Taanath-Shiloh, and then farther southeasterly to the Jordan. The western border, however, went (verse 8) from Tappuach to the stream Kanah, which flows to the west of Shechem, and falls into the Mediterranean, in the southern vicinity of Cæsarea Palestinæ, and it was this river which separated Ephraim from Menasseh. Josephus relates that the possessions of Ephraim extended from Beth-El to the valley of Jezreel; for Michmethah was not far from this valley.

MENASSEH.

Of the cities of the sons of Joseph, Menasseh and Ephraim, we will enumerate the following (see Joshua xvii. 11):

Beth-Shean בית שאן, called in Talmud Be-shan, and in the times of the Greek rule, Scythopolis, i. e. town of the Scythians, is situated 10 English miles south of Tiberias, and at a distance of 2 English miles from the Jordan, and is at present but a small village of 200 inhabitants, who live in about 80 small and low houses. Still there are seen the ruins of ancient Roman buildings. At the time of Astori it was yet a large city, where many Israelites lived.*

Jibleäm יבלעם (called Bileam in 1 Chron. vi. 55, and Belama in Judith viii. 3), is probably the modern village Jabla, which is southwest of Beth-Shean, and about 2 English miles south of the village Kafra.

* In 1 Kings xxii. 39, there is spoken of ובית השן אשר בנה commonly rendered "And the ivory house which he built;" it may perhaps stand for ובית שאן, "And Beth-Shean which he built." Shên in Hebrew means *tooth,* and par excellence that of the elephant, or *ivory;* hence the reading as it is would give us an ivory palace; but if it be a contraction for Shean, it would say that Ahab rebuilt Beth-Shean.

Dor דאר, is the present small village Dardura, or Dandura, 10 English miles north of Cæsarea, on the sea-shore. It has now but 50 inhabitants, and the ruins of an ancient fortification.

En-dor עין דור, is the village An-dar, 3 English miles northeast of Jezreël.

Thaänach תענך (mentioned as the Levitical town *Aner* in 1 Chron. vi. 55), is the modern village Thanak, and is situated in the valley of Jezreel, 2½ English miles south of Ladjon (Legion or Megiddo), on the river Mekadé or Kishon.

Megiddo מגדו, at present called Ladjon (from Legion, an army corps), wherefore the Romans so called it, is also situated on the Kishon, for which reason this stream is called the "Waters of Megiddo" (Judges v. 19), as has been said above in the description of the rivers of Palestine.

The Three Nepheth (English version, three countries), שלשת הנפת, probably three places of the same name, which were all situated in the neighbourhood of Dor (Joshua xii. 23), which would appear also to have been the case from the fact that even now there is a village called Naphatha 2½ miles southeast of Dardura.

Kamon קמון (Judges x. 5), is at present unknown; but was situated, according to Eusebius, in the valley of Jezreel, 6 mill north of Megiddo.

NAMES OF THE TOWNS OF THE SONS OF JOSEPH.

Shomerone (Samaria) שמרון (1 Kings xvi. 24), was formerly the capital and residence of the kings of Israel, commencing with Omri. Its situation is on the Mount Shomerone, 5 English miles northwest of Shechem, and is at present but a small village, Sebasté. This name, which also occurs even in the Talmud (Erechin, chap. ii.), is derived from the Greek σεβαστος (Sebastos, synonymous with Augustus); it was so called by Herod I., in honour of Augustus Cæsar, when he adorned it with magnificent and large edifices. Even at this day several remarkable ruins can be seen near Sebaste (among which is a colonnade of sixty marble columns), which no doubt date from the time of Herod.*

Tirzah תרצה (1 Kings xiv. 17). This former place of residence of Jeroboam, son of Nebat, king of Israel, is now the village Tarza, and is situated on a high mount east of Samaria.

Shechem שכם (Gen. xii. 6), is at present a city without walls, and is situated, south and north, between the mounts Gerizzim and Ebal. In the time of the Romans, it was named Flavia Neapolis, whence it is called, in the corrupted dialect of the country, Nablus.† Here live twenty Jewish families, and many Cutheans, who live nowhere else in Palestine. But I shall speak of this sect in another place. To the east of Shechem, at the distance of about 2 English miles, is the village Abulnita, where Joseph lies buried. (Joshua xxiv. 32.)

The hill of Phinehas גבעת פינחס (ibid. 33). Five English miles southeast of Shechem is the village Avartha, i. e. inheritance (compare with Talmud Baba Bathra, 111 *b*), in which the grave of Phinehas is. The grave of his father, Elazar, is close by it, on a high mountain. Below the vil-

* In Megillath Taanith, chap. vii., is mentioned באו לים בוסטי "they came to the sea of Busté," which is evidently an error, as no such place or sea is known; it should read, however, לסבסטי "to Sebasté," and the corruption is no doubt owing to the carelessness of a transcriber, by first dividing the word into two, and then adding a useless letter.

† In Midrash Rabbah to section Massay מסעי, we read שכם בהר אפרים זהו נפולין "Shechem, in the mountain of Ephraim, is Napulin," which is a faulty reading, and should be נפוליז Napulis, Neapolis, or Nablus. In Talmud Yerushalmi Abodah Zarah, chap. v., it is said, "Rabbi Ishmael went to Napulis when the Cuthians came," &c.; whence it will be seen that the Talmudists already made use of this word to denote Shechem.

lage, in the midst of olive trees, is the grave of Ithamar. These sepulchres are ornamented with large monuments.

Thimnath-Serach תמנת סרח (Joshua xxiv. 30), is the village Charas, 5 English miles south-southwest of Shechem. There are found the graves of Joshua, his father Nun, and Caleb, all of which are marked with large monuments.

Shalem שלם (Gen. xxxiii. 18), is the village Salin, 5 English miles east of Shechem.

Pirathon פרעתון (Judges xii. 15), "is probably the modern village Pretha, on the mountain of Amalek, 5 English miles west of Shechem." So says Astori; but at present it is quite unknown.

Shamir שמיר (Judges x. 1). This town was probably situated 5 English miles northeast from Samaria, on the same place where now are found the ruins of the fort Sanur, the *n* being substituted for the *m*.

Shiloh שילה (1 Sam. i. 3). Ten English miles north-northwest of Sela-Rimmon is the village Thurmassia (Talmud Yerushalmi Barachoth, chap. ii., R. Jacob of Thurmassia), not far from which are found the ruins of Seilon or Shiloh. In the time of Astori Hapharchi, the town of Shiloh was yet standing; and there was a vault, which was named Kubah al Sechina, i. e. "the vault of the holy residence," synonymous with אהל מועד "the tabernacle."*

* In Talmud Zebachim, 118 *b*, also in Yerushalmi Megillah, chap. iv., we read: "A narrow strip of land went out from the portion of Joseph into the territory of Benjamin, and on this stood the altar of Shiloh." To one who knows the situation of the territories of Joseph and Benjamin, it must appear extremely strange to maintain that Shiloh, which, with all its environs, is situated in the portion of Joseph, should have stood on a strip of land, as here described. I therefore assert boldly that an error has occurred here in transcribing, and that the reverse would be the proper reading—"A narrow strip of land went out from the territory of Benjamin into the portion of Joseph," &c. I found, moreover, that such

Thebez תבץ (Judges ix. 50), is the village Thubaz, 7 English miles northeast of Shechem.

RAMAH IN THE MOUNTAIN OF EPHRAIM. RAMATHAIM-ZOPHIM.

Since there prevail so many erroneous opinions with respect to this town, the birth-place of the prophet Samuel, I am induced to speak of it more at length than usual.

In the village Ramé Nebi Smuel, 4 English miles northwest from Jerusalem, is found a monument, which is said to mark the resting-place of Samuel. Over it stood formerly a Christian church, but now a Turkish mosque, with a high tower, whence the muezzin calls the people five times every day to their devotions with a loud voice. The lower part of this mosque is a very old massive structure, having its origin at the time of the Christian supremacy in Palestine; but the upper portion and the tower are more modern, and the work of the Turks, and were constructed under Mahomed Pacha, who resided at Jerusalem in the year 5385 (1625). I ascended once to the top of the tower, and was well rewarded for the exertions I made by the magnificent and wide prospect which offered

errors in transcribing are by no means remarkably scarce. For instance, it is said of the site of the altar at Jerusalem, in Yoma, fol. 12 *a*, "A strip went out from Judah to Benjamin," on which it stood; and in Siphri to Deut. xxxiii. the reverse is stated, "from Benjamin to Judah," one of which assertions must needs be erroneous. And we may assert this with regard to Shiloh, that an error is evident in the statement as it now reads. I also found latterly, quite to my satisfaction, that Kimchi to 1 Samuel vii. 7, cites the above passage as I have corrected it, which proves that it is well founded. The circumstance of this narrow strip's going out from Benjamin, will now explain the difficulty which I noticed when speaking of Hazor in the tribe of Benjamin, that the modern Chirbath-Tell-Chazor does not lie in that, but in the territory of Joseph. But as now this strip commenced near the vicinity of the town Sela-Rimmon, and extended to Shiloh, it will place the Chirbath-Tell-Chazor precisely in the portion belonging to Benjamin, although it is within the territory of Joseph.

itself to my view. I saw on the one side the long line of the Mediterranean, on the other the whole plain of the Dead Sea; the southern mountains near Chalchul (which see, page 107); the mountains of Shechem, &c.; in short, such a prospect as I had scarcely ever enjoyed before. In the interior of the mosque, where the Arabs keep a perpetual light, is found the form of a grave-hillock, over which is the monument, over which is spread a handsome green cover. Under this stone a cavern is said to exist, in which, as is alleged, rest the remains of Samuel and his parents, Elkanah and Hannah. This spot is also honoured by the devout of our own brother Israelites, and is visited, especially on the 28th and 29th of Iyar of every year. (Comp. Orach Chayim, chap. 580.) It is nevertheless not to be disputed, that it is erroneous to take this monument as the one which marks the grave of Samuel; because Ramé is in the centre of the cities of Benjamin, near Gibath-Shaül; and it appears from 1 Samuel xv. 1, that the prophet was buried in his home at Ramah, in the mountain of Ephraim (ibid. i. 1). This mountain, it is true, extends itself widely both in length and in breadth, even into the territories of other tribes, for instance, Menasseh, Issachar (Judges x. 1), Benjamin, Dan, and as far as the Lowland of Judah. Still it can be easily proved that Ramah did not lie near Gibath-Shaül, because

1. When Saul went out to seek the stray asses of his father, he only arrived, on the third day after leaving his father's house, at Gibath-Shaül, at Ramah (1 Sam. ix. 20). The question now would arise, how could he spend the time of three days in roaming over a space of but a few miles in extent, that is in case the present Ramé should mark the residence of Samuel?

2. David fled from before Saul, and went to Samuel at Najoth in Ramah (1 Sam. xix. 18). If now Ramah had

been close to Gibath-Shaül, the residence of his mortal enemy, David would surely not have fled thither.

3. It appears from the commentary of Ramban to Genesis xxxv. distinctly, that this eminent and learned man knew positively the situation of Ramah, and he places it two days' journey from the grave of Rachel, which is, however, but 10 English miles from Gibeah. Consequently Nachmanides paid no attention to the various fables which were no doubt current in his time also on this subject.

It is, therefore, evident that the alleged grave at Ramé Nebi Smuel, can by no means be the real sepulchre of the prophet Samuel, since this place is, as I have already stated above, page 126, the ancient town of Mizpeh, in the land of Benjamin. This erroneous opinion, however, had its origin, as many other similar fallacies, in that period when the Christians came into Palestine, and obtained the government of it, when the holy monuments were pulled down, and others again erected on spots chosen at pleasure; and then they gave them such arbitrary names as the fancy of the moment dictated; through which means great confusion and false opinions have originated, and these have, alas! survived even to our day.

In the same spirit does Rabbi Benjamin, of Tudela, report, that when the Nazarenes took and conquered Ramah from the Mahomedans, "they found there the grave of the prophet Samuel, near the Synagogue; that they then took him away from here and carried him to Shiloh, where they reinterred him, and built over his remains a church, which they called after this prophet." I deem it perfectly useless to prove that this traditional legend is both fabulous and improbable. In order, however, to determine the proper position of Ramah, i. e. Ramathaim-Zophim, we will, in the first place, endeavour to ascertain the districts which Saül passed over in his journey from Gibeah to Ramah, where he was anointed king over Israel. We are told (1 Sam. ix. 4, 5): "He passed through Mount Ephraim, the land of Shalishah, the land of Shaalim, the land of Jemini, and came at length to the land of Zuph."

Shalishah שליישה. As late as Eusebius' time, there was a town called Beth-Salisa, 15 mill north of Lod. Nevertheless, I believe that I may place the land of Shalishah with greater accuracy in the valley of the Jordan, the modern Al Gor; since, according to the assertion of the Talmud, Sanhedrin, fol. 12 *a*, the vicinity of Shalishah produces and ripens the first and earliest fruit in the whole land, and this is actually the case at the present time in Al Gor. The same is said in Tosephtah Shebiith, chap. 7, and Bereshith Rabbah, chap. 99; that the neighbourhood of Jericho (Al Gor) ripens its fruits first of all. We also read in Midrash Shemuel to chap. xiii., "Shalishah is Beth-Ramtha," and, according to Yerushalmi Shebiith, chap. vi., Beth-Ramtha is synonymous with Beth-Charim. So also is it said in Talmud Shabbath, fol. 26, that from En-Gedi to Ramtha is found the Balsam shrub (אפרסמון). The latter place is the same with Beth-Ramtha, which King Herod called Livias; it was situated on the north-eastern shore of the Dead Sea, or beyond Jordan, and consequently in the valley of this river. This position appears to me more correct than that of Eusebius.

Shaalim שעלים seems to me identical with Shuäl, of which it is said (1 Sam. xiii. 17, 18): "And the spoilers came out of the camp of the Philistines in three companies; one company turned unto the way to Ophrah, unto the land of Shuäl; and another company turned their way to Beth-Horon; and another company turned to the way of the border that looketh to the valley of Zeboim, towards the wilderness." The first division, accordingly, took their course northeasterly to Ophra (which see); this lay 5 English miles east of Beth-El, and consequently Shuäl must have been in the same vicinity. The second went southwesterly to Beth-Choron (which see), and the third, southeasterly to the valley of Zeboim. There are uncommonly high masses of rock near En-Gedi (see above), on the western shore of the Dead Sea; from the top of these one beholds this lake, which has a depth of fifteen hundred feet, bathing the rocks beneath. These appear to me to be "the rocks of the wild goats" mentioned in 1 Samuel xxiv. 2, and represented as being near the wilderness of En-Gedi. Between them there runs a valley, in which the ancient Zeboim (Gen. x. 19) may have been situated, wherefore it is termed the valley of Zeboim, which town must, however, not be mistaken for the one of the same name in Benjamin (Neh. xi. 34).

Jemini was, as is well known, the patronymic term for Benjamin, consequently the land of Jemini means the territory of this tribe in general. Zuph (from צפה Zaphoh "to behold") is probably applied to the high and elevated environs of Ramathaim, called thence Zofim "of the watchmen," because it offered a wide prospect. If we now pursue Saul on his journey which he took in company with his young man, we shall have the following route: From Gibeah (or Kirjath-Jearim or Gibath-Shaül) they travelled northward to Lod, which was already in the land of Ephraim; from there to Shalishah, in the valley of Jordan; thence they turned northward to Shaalim; then northwesterly to Jemini; again to the northern part of Benjamin, near Lower Beth-Horon, and thence, at last, farther to the north, till they reached Zuph, i. e. Ramathaim-Zofim or Ramah.

After I had positively convinced myself, that Ramah must have been several days' journey from Gibeah, and that its position must have been to the north of Shechem, I sought to ascertain whether some traces could not be now found of this birth and burial-place of Samuel; and I am pleased to state that I succeeded in quite a satisfactory manner. 3¾ English miles west of the fortification of Sanur, the Shamir of Judges x. 1, there lies, on a high mount, in an opposite direction to the valley of Jezreel, the village Ramé, unquestionably the Ramah of Samuel. It is said in the book of Judith, iv. 6, 7: "And the high priest Jehoiakim wrote to the inhabitants of the large field (or plain) situated opposite to Jezreel, near Dathaim (or as other readings have it *Bamathaim*), to occupy the (approaches and) passes of the rocks which are on the sides of the mountains on the way to Jerusalem, through which the enemy would have to pass into the land of Judea." There can be no question but that an error has crept into the translation, and that instead of Dathaim or Bamathaim, places not otherwise known, we should read Ramathaim (Zofim); for there is no spot where the road from Galilee to Judea has to pass between mountains and rocky cliffs but precisely here, and it is likewise opposite to the valley of Jezreel. We have already stated above that the mountains of Ephraim extend to this valley, and, among other portions, included part of Issachar; and so the Judge, Tola, a man of Issachar, lived in Shamir, in the mountain of Ephraim (Judges x. 1). I also suppose that Ramah, the birth-place of Samuel, who was a Levite, was one of the Levitical cities belonging to Issachar, which is called Jarmuth in Joshua xxi. 29, and Ramoth in 1 Chron. vi. 58. (See Kimchi to 1 Sam. i. 1.)

Another proof that Ramah must have been near Shechem can be derived from the following passage of 1 Sam. xix. 22: "Then went he (Saül) also to Ramah, and came to the great well which is in Séchu." My labours to ascertain the position of the town of Séchu, led me to the following results: Southeast from Shechem is as yet a village called Adjar; not far from it, on the road to Jerusalem, is a large well, which is 100 feet in depth, and called "Jacob's Well," and it is said of it that at its bottom is found the cupola of a destroyed church. Near it are the ruins of the large buildings which the Empress Helena, the mother of Constantine, had caused to be erected in honour of the place. It now strikes me that this village Adjar can be none other than the ancient Sechu, and that the so-called Jacob's Well is the same great well where Saul made inquiries concerning the whereabouts of David and Samuel on his journey to Ramah.

Bezek בזק (Judges i. 4), is the modern village Abzik, 5 English miles south of Beth-Shean.

Zelzach צלצח on the boundary of Benjamin (1 Sam. i. 2). According to the Talmud it is identical with Jerusalem. To me, however, it appears a compound noun from צל shade and צח rock; and actually there are found southeast of Jerusalem large masses of rocks, which mark almost accurately the boundary line of Benjamin. It is also possible that the name of the village Tseltsia (for Zelza), situated 3 English miles west of Shiloh, is derived from the ancient Zelzach.

Arumah ארומה (Judges ix. 41), is the village Ramin, 2 English miles west of Samaria (compare Zohar Shemini, fol. 39 *b*).

Ophrah עפרה (Judges vi. 11), is perhaps the village Erafa, situated north of the fortification of Sanur, the modern name probably having arisen by transposing the letter f and r.

Jeshanah ישנה (2 Chron. xiii. 19), is the village Al Sanin, 2 miles west of Beth-El.

Ephrain עפרין (ibid.), was situated east of Beth-El, in the valley of Jordan. According to Hieronymus, it was distant 20 mill north of Jerusalem. At present it is unknown. (See Menachoth, 83 *b*, and above, Chazor, in Benjamin.)

Birzaith ברזית (1 Chron. vii. 31), is the village Bir-Sith, still existing, 2 miles north of Djifni (Ophni). It must not surprise us that this town, situated in Ephraim, is also reckoned to Asher; because we often find that the possessions of one tribe encroach on those of the other, which also is the case with Japhlet mentioned along with Bir-Sith. (See 1 Chron. vii. 31–33, and Joshua xvi. 3.)

Gath-Rimmon גת רמון (Joshua xxi. 25, and called Bileam in 1 Chron. vi. 55) appears to me to be identical with Hadad-Rimmon in the valley of Megiddo of Zechariah xii. 11. This Levitical town of the tribe of Menasseh, situated 2 English miles west of En-Gannim, and south-east of Legion (Megiddo), in the valley of the latter, the environs of which extended to Megiddo itself, was called in the time of the Romans Maximianopolis. At present it is but the village Kafer Guth. The site of this village agrees accurately with the description given in the book of Judith vii. 3, "And they encamped in the valley near Blema (i. e. Bileam), which is opposite to Jezreel." In the Talmud it is called Kefar Uthni (see Gitten, fol. 76 *a*), and it is said in Bechoroth, 55 *a*, that מכפר חנינה לכפר עותני ל"ב מיל "from Kefar Chaninah to Kefar Uthni is 32 mill, and that Zippori (Sephoris) lay between them." This agrees also exactly with the position of Kafer Guth, which is near 32 mill, each mill being reckoned as always, in the Talmud, of eighteen minutes' walk, or about 24 English miles, from Kafer Anan (which see), and Sephuri is moreover midway between the two.

Abel-Mecholah אבל מחולה (Judges vii. 22), was according to Eusebius 16 mill south of Beth-Shean, on the bank of the Jordan. Perhaps, however, it may be identical with the present village Methshalon, situated 2 English miles southeast of the fortress of Sanur.*

* According to Yarchi to Ketuboth, 105 *b*, the prophet Elisha was of the tribe of Gad, consequently his birth-place (Abel-Mecholah), must then have been east of Jordan, in the land of that tribe. But I can find no passage which authorized Yarchi to make this assertion.

Zerarah צררה (Judges vii. 22, and Zorethan צרתן in 1 Kings vii. 46), although not known at present, must still have been, to judge from the passages cited, south of Beth-Sheän, opposite the ruins of Sukkoth, which are situated on the east side of Jordan.

Of the places belonging to the sons of Joseph mentioned in the Talmudic writings, we will notice the following:

Akrabbah עקרבה. See farther down, at the end of this chapter.

Assiri אסירי (Tosephtah Mikvaoth, chap. iv.), probably the village Assiri, situated in a southern direction, opposite to the village Djeba (i. e. Geba, which, however, is an arbitrary name, having neither Biblical nor Talmudical origin), 5 English miles north of Shechem.

Kefar Nimrah כפר נמרה (Midrash Echa, 72 *a*) is the village Bir Namar, 2 English miles southwest from the just-named Djeba.

Yathmah יתמה (Orlah, chap. ii. 5), is the present village Yathmah, 5 English miles south of Chavara, i. e. Beth-Horon.

Bedan בדן (ibid. iii. 7, Kelaim, xvii. 5; Yerushalmi Demai, iii.) Northeast of Shechem there is a valley, which is known as Wady Al Badan.

Perech פרך (ibid.) That part of the just-named valley which extends to the southeast close to the Jordan, is now called Wady al Farchi. Jos., Bell. Jud., book ii. chap. xxi., mentions a Capharecho, probably the Perech in question.

The Valley of the Spring Socher בקעת עין סוכר (Menachoth, fol. 64 *b*). Between Salin, i. e. Shalem, and the village Abulnita, famous for possessing the grave of Joseph, lies the village Askar, where the spring En-Askar rises. Here commences a fruitful plain, opening towards the east, and extending to the Jordan, which appears to me to be the plain or valley in question. The spring, which gives it the name, is also called, in Yerushalmi

Abodah Zarah, chap. v., En Kushith עין כושית, "the spring of the Moors." I have already mentioned, when speaking of Ramah, that the well of Jacob is considered holy by the Christians. I therefore also believe that idolatry may have fixed its abode near the spring of Askar, to which, probably, the contemptuous name also refers. In Bereshith Rabbah, chap. 98, it is said ברכת שמים מעל זו אזכרות שבבעל, which passage no commentator has as yet been fortunate enough to decipher. But I believe that reference is here made to the Valley of Socher, since בעל in the Talmudic dialect stands for בקעה מישור "plain, or valley" (see 2 Chron. xxvi. 7); and as this vicinity, which belonged to Joseph, is exceedingly blessed and fruitful, it may be assumed that Jacob, in blessing him, had reference to this valley,—therefore "the blessing of heaven above means Askar in the plain;" so that אזכרות stands for אסכרות "the springs of Askar."

Kefar Dichrin כפר דכרין (Gittin, fol. 57 *b*). This considerable and large town is, besides the passage cited, often referred to in Talmud and Midrashim. It was situated on Mount Ephraim, the Tur Malkah, "King's Mountain" of the Rabbis. At the time of Astori there was a vestige of it remaining in the village Dachran, situated a few miles north of Lod, in the mountains; at present, however, it is unknown. It might be believed that it was identical with the town Beth-Zecharias, often mentioned by Josephus, as both have the same signification, only that it appears from several passages of this author, that Beth-Zecharias was not as far north, but more to the south, in the part of Judah; which circumstance induced me to state already that I suppose Beth-Zecharias to be the present Beth-Sachur, not far from Beth-Lehem. (See Jos., Bell. Jud., book i., chap. i.)

In the book of Jashar to Gen. xxxiv., speaking of the wars of the sons of Jacob, the following names occur:

Chasar חסר, probably Chazor in Benjamin (Neh. xi. 33).

Sartan סרטן. Here prevails, without doubt, an error in the transcriber, and it should read Sartaf, this name being applied to the town because it lay near the Mount Sartaf, situated 5 English miles west from the Jordan.

Arbelio ארבליו. "And they heard that the men of Arbelio had gone out to them." By this name cannot by any means be meant the town of Arbel, in the land of Naphtali; for this place was situated near Chinnereth, and was, therefore, too far out of the way for the sons of Jacob; and it is of their then sojourn of which the book of Jashar speaks in the passage referred to. But probably it should read Archelio ארכליו, with כ instead of ב; and reference is had, no doubt, to the town of Archelais, which, as Josephus relates (Ant., book xvii. 13), was a day's journey from Jericho. The assertion of this historian, that Archelaus, the son of Herod the Great, was the builder of this city, may be explained to mean that the king in question improved materially this very ancient city of Archil, having some resemblance to his own name, and, so to say, had it completely restored. (See also Rimmon in Zebulun.)

Ethanim אתנים appears to me should read Machanaim (compare with Yalkut). This was on the east side of Jordan, and was opposite to where the sons of Jacob were at the time.

Shiloh, Gaash, Beth-Choron, Tappuach, and Har Sion, have been described in their proper places.

Castra קסטרה. In Echa Rabbethi, chap. i. 17, "Castra and Cheipha were perpetual enemies;" in Midrash Samuel, chap. xvi., is Kazra, which is an erroneous reading, and should be Castra. Compare with Baba Kamma, fol. 98 *a*, "in Castra," or on "the King's Mount." The place now called Chirbath (ruins of) Athlot, situated at the foot of Carmel, on the sea-coast, north of Dardura, and south of Cheipha, was formerly called Castrum Peregrinorum. I have no doubt that this is the place referred to in the above quotations. Astori did not know of this Castrum, and therefore corrected Castra into Cæsarea, which, as will be seen, was by no means necessary.

Taba טאבא, stated in 1 Macc. ix. 50 to be in the vicinity of Beth-El and Jericho, is no doubt the village Taibi, which is 7 English miles west of Nama (Naarah), and situated on the highest point of the mountains of that neighbourhood. Between it and Nama flows the stream Duga (Fish River; compare with Ezek. xlvii. 9). Here, therefore, seems to have been situated the village Dagun, of which Josephus speaks in his Bell. Jud., book i. chap. i.

Maabartha מעברתא (see Yerushalmi Taanith, chap. iv). According to the account of Josephus (Bell. Jud., book v. chap. iv.), Neapolis or Shechem was also called Maabartha.

A BRIEF REVIEW OF THE POSSESSIONS OF MENASSEH, AND OF THE SONS OF JOSEPH IN GENERAL.

The most northeasterly point of Menasseh extended to Beth-Shean, situated on the borders of Issachar; but the northwest boundary touched Mount Carmel, which itself belonged to Asher. This will explain the meaning of Joshua xvii. 10, &c., "And they met with Asher on the north, and with Issachar on the east. And Menasseh had in Issachar and Asher Beth-Shean and its villages, and Jibleam and its villages," &c. To the southeast the line ran up to Tappuach (to the east of Shechem—see the 31 Kings), and to the southwest to the river Kanah, south of Cæsarea; so that Menasseh was situated north of Ephraim. If we now contemplate carefully the possessions of the sons of Joseph, we shall see that it had two prominently protruding points, to wit, to the northeast and northwest—so to say, in the form of two horns, between the points of which Issachar stood. Perhaps Moses alluded to this conformation of their territory when he blessed Joseph, and said (Deut. xxxiii. 17), "And his horns are as the horns of the reëm," i. e. the wild ox. Josephus relates that the possessions of Menasseh extended from the Jordan to the Great Sea near Dor.

ISSACHAR.

The territory of Issachar, which was enclosed on three sides by Menasseh (to which probably Jacob's prophecy, "Issachar is a strong-boned ass, couching between the stables," Gen. xlix. 14), extended on the east to the Jordan, near the southern shore of Lake Chinnereth, and on the north to Mount Tabor; from here the boundary ran over Kesulloth and Abez, to the vicinity of Mount Carmel, and the southern extreme appears to me to have been Remeth, i. e. Ramathaim-Zofim, in Mount Ephraim. To this tribe belonged the whole of the plain of Jezreel. Josephus states that the possessions of Issachar extended from Jordan to Mount Carmel.

The towns of Issachar were the following:

Jezreel יזרעאל, no doubt the village Serain, which is 3 English miles north of En-Gannin (Djinin). The name of Serain has undoubtedly been put for Serail, abbreviated for Jezreel; and the change of *n* for *l* is nothing uncommon; as Beth-El becomes Beth-en or Beit-un, and Beth-Djibrin is also called Beth-Djibril. About 1 mile east from here is a mount called Djebl Djulud,* from which descends an un-

* This enables me to expound an extremely obscure passage in the Bible (Judges vii. 3), which no commentator has hitherto been able to elucidate: "Now therefore go to, proclaim in the hearing of the people, saying, Whosoever is fearful and afraid, let him return and depart early from Mount Gilead." It appears almost like a riddle to decipher, how they should depart from Mount Gilead, which is on the east side of Jordan, whereas, the camp of the Israelites was in the valley of Jezreel, at a very great distance from the said mountain, with which it stood in no connexion whatever. But there can be no doubt, that the Mount Gilead referred to, is the Djebl Djulud, and that only a false pronunciation has

named rivulet, which runs southerly, in the direction of the mountains of Gilboa. Near Serain commences the valley

obtained, putting Djulud for Djilead, i. e. Gilead. The rivulet which descends from it, is also doubtless the stream mentioned (ibid. v. 45), where the people were mustered, and it was likewise near this mount where the battle of Gideon took place. The learned Astori says in his work, fol. 67 *b*: "To the east of Jezreel, as far as a horse can run (a stadium), is a spring, near which the Israelites encamped in the (last) war, under Saul. It rises south of Mount Gilboa, and is called En Djilud. The Arabs say, that there also took place the fight between David and the giant Goliath; but herein they are mistaken." This was probably merely an incorrect tradition, and an exchange of *Goliath* for *Gilead.* The author went carelessly over the ground without noticing whether this traditional name Djilud or Goliath was of any importance or not, or whether also the name of the mountain Djebl Djulud had in it a trace of the former Gilead. Still, all this proves that there was a Mount Gilead likewise on the west side of Jordan.

Whilst on the subject, I will explain another obscure passage, to wit, 1 Kings xxi. 19: "On the spot where the dogs have licked up the blood of Naboth, shall the dogs lick up thy blood also." Again it says (ibid. xxii. 38): "And they washed out the chariot in the pool of Samaria, and the dogs licked up his blood." Naboth was stoned to death in Jezreel, and still it is said, as if in fulfilment of the prophecy, that Ahab's blood was licked up in Samaria; how was this? Kimchi, it is true, notices this difficulty; but believes that the water of this pool ran to Jezreel, where the dogs licked it up, dyed as it was with the blood of the deceased king. But whoever knows the relative positions, and the nature of the country of Samaria and Jezreel, will easily understand the impossibility of taking Kimchi's opinion as at all solving the difficulty; for Sebasté is more than 16 miles from Sarain, and then it is not to be supposed that the water should run upward from the former to the latter place, from a low to a high level. It therefore will appear evident that the word במקום translated "on the spot," should not be thus rendered, but with "in place of," "in punishment for,—the dogs having licked up the blood of Naboth, they shall lick thy blood also." We also find in Hosea ii. 1, והיה במקום "And it shall come to pass that *instead* of people's saying of them," &c. The difficulty in question is thus entirely removed, although it is quite surprising that all translators have failed in understanding, and all have mistranslated this passage. It will therefore be seen what interest and benefit a correct geography of Palestine must have for a true exposition of Holy Writ.

of Jezreel, named now Merdj Abn Amer. The Greeks called Jezreel "Esdrela," whence the plain was named Esdrelon.

Kesulloth כסלות, is the village Aksal, 2½ English miles west from Mount Tabor.

Shunem שנם is no doubt the village Sulim (again exchanging the l for n), 2½ English miles in a direct northern line distant from Sarain. At the time of Astori they yet professed to know the site of the house of the respectable woman who entertained Elisha so hospitably. (2 Kings iv. 8.)

Chapharaim חפרים. Eusebius and Hieronymus speak of the village Aframa, i. e. Chapharaim, about 5 mill north from Legion (Megiddo); but at present it is unknown.

Shion שיאון is probably identical with the modern village Sain, situated between Deburi=Daberath, and Jafa, i. e. Japhia (Joshua xix. 12).

Harabbith הרבית. There is, 3 English miles west from Beth-Shean, a village called Arubuni, in which I find a trace of the ancient Harabbith. Hieronymus says: "3 mill west from Beth-Shean, is the village Eraba," which I suppose to be the present Arubuni. Bereshith Rabbah, chap. 33, probably alludes to the same place when speaking of the town of Arabi in the vicinity of Beth-Shean.

Kishion קשיון. Astori writes, fol. 67 *b*, "2½ miles south from Aksal is Kishion, near which the river (Kishon) has its source." At the present day the Arabs call the village near which the sources of Kishon are, and which is to the southwest of Tabor, "Sheich Abrik," i. e. chief Barak, in allusion to Barak, son of Abinoam (Judges iv. 6), because he overcame on the banks of this stream the army of Sisera. Not far from this village is the village Muzr; it appears, therefore from the statement of Astori, that Sheich Abrik is the ancient Kishion. In 1 Chronicles vi. 37, among the Levitical cities, it is called Kedesh.

Abez אבץ is probably the village Kunebiz, also called Karm En Abiz, which lies 3 English miles west-southwest from Aksal.

Remeth רמת. See Ramathaim-Zofim.

En-Gannin עין גנים. This is the present large village Djinin, about 20 English miles north from Nablus, on the road from the latter place to Tiberias. In its vicinity is a small stream, called En-Djinin. (See also second chapter, article Ginai.) In 1 Chronicles vi. 58, this town, one of the Levitical cities, is called Anem ענם equal to Annim ענים. This shows the transmutation of ע Ayin into ג Gimel, as in Arabic the Gayin is put for Ayin.

Tabor תבור. Josephus relates that in his time there was a town with a fort on Mount Tabor, which probably had the same name as the mount itself. The present ruins on it are the remains of a church built by the Empress Helena.

Beth-Shemesh בית שמש i. e. house of the sun; I presume this to be identical with the small village Kaukab al Chama "the star* of the sun," which is 3 English miles north from Beth-Shean, and near the Jordan. Astori relates, "Beth-Shemesh, of Issachar, is south of Zippori (Sefuri), and is called Shumshi;" but I believe that, more correctly speaking, this Beth-Shemesh, near Sefuri, belonged to Naphtali (Joshua xix. 38), and not to Issachar.

THERE BELONGED FARTHER TO THE PORTION OF ISSACHAR

Daberath דברת (Joshua xxi. 28); this is the village Diburi, 1½ English miles west from Tabor. This town was also reckoned as belonging to Zebulun (ibid. xix. 12), which proves that the boundary lines of both tribes passed

* This will explain for us an obscure passage in Pesiktah Rabbethi, chap. 16: שאלתי את ר"ר א' מן כוכבה "I asked the Rabbi—one from Kochabah," which I hold to refer to some learned man from the city of Kochabah, probably the present Kaukab al Chama.

near it, wherefore it is often viewed as belonging to both. In the Life of Josephus it is called Dabarith.

Meron מראון. (See description of the 31 Kings.)

Beth-Eked בית עקד (2 Kings x. 12). Eusebius says: "15 mill from Legion (Megiddo), in the plain of Esdrelon, may still be seen the ruins of this town," but at present it is quite unknown.

Aphek אפק (1 Kings xx. 26) is probably the modern village of Fukua, 2 English miles east from Djinin. (See also description of the 31 Kings.)

Dothan דותן (Gen. xxxviii. 17) is the village Dutha, 6 English miles south from Djinin; near it is shown the pit in which Joseph was cast before being sold by his brothers.

Meroz מרוז (Judges v. 23), probably the village Merasas, 2½ English miles northwest from Beth-Shean. (See also Maresheth in first chapter, page 36.)

Beth-Hashitta בית השטה (Judges vii. 22), is probably the little village Shitta, 1 mill west from Djebl Duhu, i. e. the little Hermon.

NAMES OF PLACES IN THE PORTION OF ISSACHAR OCCURRING IN THE TALMUDIC WRITINGS.

En-Tob עין טוב (Pesiktah Rabbethi, chap. 41; Talmud Rosh Hashanah, fol. 25 *a*), is the village Un al Taibé, which is between Tabor and Beth-Shean. Near this is the rivulet Wady Tubeni, i. e. En Tob, the spring Tob, which descends from the mountain of Gilboa. I believe that the oft-mentioned Tibaon טבעון (Machshirin, chap. 1; Talmud Megillah, 24 *b*) was identical with En-Tob, and that the change of appellation arose from a mere transposition of the syllables. In Pesachim, fol. 53 *a*, are spoken of אהיני דטובני a species of dates, from the vicinity of *Tubeon*.*

* I cannot again avoid to refute the view of a modern writer. I have read in the preface of a medical work, composed in the Hebrew language מרפא לעם "The People's Physician," where the author quotes a passage

Serunia סרוניא (see Yerushalmi, end of Kilaim; Bereshith Rabbah, chap. i.; Zohar Tazria; also called in Yerushalmi Sanhedrin, chap. vii., Beth-Shirian (בית שיריין) is no doubt the small village Sirin, situated on a mount between Tiberias and Beth-Shean, 2 English miles northwest from the Jordan bridge Midshama. At the foot of the mount, is the valley Sarané. (See second chapter, article Valley of Jezreel.)

Neürin נעורין (Chulin, fol. 5 *a*), is the village Nuris, about 2 English miles southeast from Serain. The Naaran of 1 Chron. vii. 28, is *not* to be mistaken for this, for it is the same as Naarah of Joshua xvi. 7, and is the present Naami.

Kapra כפרה (Yerushalmi Megillah, chap. i.; Yerushalmi Shekalim, chap. v.), is the village Kaparah, situated 5 English miles southeast from Mount Tabor. Astori took this place for Chafaraim (which see); but this view appears to me incorrect.

Naïm נעים (Bereshith Rabbah to Gen. xlix. 15), is the village Nain, 1 English mile southwest from En-Dor.

Thineam תנעם of the same passage, is the village Thenna, 1½ English miles northeast from Um al Taibé.

Pislon פסלון, the valley of Pislon of the same passage. Between the Little Hermon and the mountains of Gilboa

from Nidda, fol. 22 *b*, in the following words: "Rabbi Elazar, son of Zadok said, My father brought two cases from Tibeon to Jabné, &c.; the people asked my father, he asked the wise men, and they asked the physicians," &c.,—that he understands by *Tibeon* nothing else than Thebes, in Greece, and that hence our wise men obtained their medical knowledge from that country, since they sent their medical problems (שאלות) to Thebes for solution. This notion rests upon the erroneous mistaking Tibeon in Palestine for Thebes in Greece; since it appears clearly from Erubin, 29 *a*, that the city in question was near Ardiska, and it can be proved positively from Tosephtah Terumoth, chap. ii., that the latter was unquestionably in Palestine; consequently the author has no proof whatever, that our wise men obtained their medical knowledge from Greece.

is a small valley, at the end of which, in the vicinity of the Jordan, is the village Phasal, in which I believe to discover a trace of the ancient Pislon, after which this valley is named.

Kefar Barkai כפר ברקאי (Pesachim, 57 *a*, also end Kerithoth), is the village Barkin, 2 miles west from Djinin, and is also probably the Barkeas mentioned by Josephus (Bell. Jud., book iii., chap. iv.)

Kefar Thamartha כפר תמרתא (Megillah, 16 *a*), is the village Thamra, 1½ English miles east from En-Dor.

Ulam אולם (Siphri to Balak; Yerushalmi Sanhedrin, chap. x.; Yerushalmi Shebiith, chap. vii.), is the village Ulama, 1 mile north from Sirin. (See 2d chapter, under this name.)

Gebul גבול (Kethuboth, 112 *a*; Yerushalmi Challah, chap. iii.), is the village Jebul, 3 English miles northeast from Beth-Shean, and is probably identical with the town of Gabala, in Lower Galilee, which was built by Herod, as reported by Josephus, Antiq., book xv., chap. ii.

ZEBULUN.

Although the boundary line of this tribe is described in Holy Writ, I found it, nevertheless, difficult to ascertain it with accuracy, because, despite of all my efforts and investigations, I could not discover the greater part of the names mentioned in the Scriptures when describing them. I mention only as many of the towns as I could ascertain, and will afterwards seek to determine the principal points of the boundary.

Jokneam יקנעם. See above, in the description of the 31 Kings.

Kisloth-Tabor and Daberath כסלת תבור דברת, have already been described in Issachar. (See above, p. 167.)

Japhia יפיע is the village Jafa, situated 2 English miles northwest from Aksal.

Gath Chepher גת חפר. See above, in the 31 Kings, p. 89.

Rimmon רמון is the village Rumané, about 3 English miles northeast from Safuri. According to my view, this place is identical with the Levitical town Dimnah, described in Joshua xxi. 35 as belonging to Zebulun, the ר Resh being exchanged with ד Daleth, from a similarity of the form—a procedure not unusual in other names, as דעואל and רעואל, Deüel and Reüel (Num. i. 15, and ii. 14). In proof of this supposition being correct, we find this same town called, in 1 Chron. vi. 62, *Rimmono* רמונו; wherefore I think that דמנה Dimnah is equal to רמנה Rimnah, and the vowels are changed to suit the new conformation of the word. About 2 English miles west from this village, and 1 English mile north from Safuri, are found the ruins of Rumi. In respect to this I have to observe, that we read in the commentary of Moses Alshech to Shir Hashirim, cap. vii., v. 6, "Even at this day there is found, near Zippori, a town called Romi, where the Emperor Antoninus sojourned, and gave it this name, after his own capital in Italy." I believe that these ruins of Rumi occupy the site of the somewhat late town Romi; and it is also possible that its name was also derived in part from Rimmon, in the vicinity of which it was erected, and was thus, so to say, a second Rimmon, and had in this manner a double signification, and gives us, at the same time, a vestige of the ancient Rimmon.* (See also the description of the cities of the sons of Joseph, article Archelio, which is mentioned in the Sepher Hajashar.)

* Several learned men have therefore adopted the opinion that the city Romi, so often mentioned in Talmud and Midrashim, does not always mean Rome in Italy, but the then newly built up Romi in Palestine, since it was several times the place of sojourn of several Roman emperors. This view would explain, indeed, several obscure passages in the Talmud; but it cannot be always taken as correct, which is proved by a passage in

Kattath, Nahalal, Shimron, and Yidalah קטת נהלל שמרון ידאלה cannot be traced any more in the modern names of the country. But fortunately I found an explanation of these names in Yerushalmi Megillah, chap. i., where it says that Kattath is the modern Katunith, Nahalal the modern Mahalul, Shimron is Simunii, and Yidalah is Chirii; and I was enabled to find out all these places.

Kattath or Katunith. (End of Sota is mentioned Rabbi José Katnutha, so called, probably, from being a native of this place; as we also find him described in Tosephtah Sota, 15, as R. José, son of Katnuth, a native of Ketuntha or Katunith.) By closely investigating the matter, I found that the town of Kana is called, in the Chaldean, Katna, which has the same signification with Katunith. Now, 1 English mile northeast from Rumani is the village Kana el Djelil, i. e. Kana of Galilee, to be distinguished from a town of the same name near Tyre. This proves to my mind that it is the Kattath of the Bible.

Nahalal or Mahalul (see also Yerushalmi Maasser Sheni, chap. v.), is no doubt the modern village Malul, 2 English miles southeast from Semunie.

Shimron or Simunii (see also Bereshith Rabbah, 81) is the village Semunie, situated 3 English miles southwest from Sefuri. It is also probably identical with the Simmiada mentioned in the Life of Josephus.

Yidalah or Chirii, no doubt the village Kellah al Chiré, 6 English miles southwest from Semunii.

Beth-Lehem בית לחם is the village of that name, about 7 English miles south from Shaf-Amer, and the same distance west from the village Nazara (Nazareth). All the

Yerushalmi Horiyoth, chap. iii., from which it clearly appears that Romi there spoken of, and which occurs in a narrative mentioned also in Talmud Babli, Gittin, fol. 58, and which is taken by many scholars for Romi in Palestine, must have been beyond the confines of the Holy Land, and, consequently, Rome proper, in Italy.

villages near Nazara, are for the most part inhabited by Christians, who point out there to the traveller, many relics and antiquities.

THERE BELONGED ALSO TO ZEBULUN

Kitron קטרון (Judges i. 30). The Talmud Megillah, fol. 6 *a*, says, "Kitron is Zippori," which is the village Sefuri, situated on a mount 7 English miles southeast from Shafamer. According to Echa Rabbethi to chap. ii. 2, there is a distance of 18 mill, i. e. 13½ English miles, from Tiberias to Zippori. In the Græco-Roman period, it was called Dicepolis (see Jos., Bell. Jud., b. iii. chap. iii.*)

Madon מדון. See above, in the account of the 31 Kings, where I maintain that Madon is the present Kefar Manda. In Shemoth Rabbah, chap. lii., the name of Madon is still retained; but otherwise we find nearly everywhere either Manda or Mandon. So in Vayikra Rabbethi, chap. i., is mentioned Rabbi Issachar, of Kefar Manda; and the people there show to this day the grave of this worthy Rabbi. In Tosephtah Yabamoth, chap. x., the name of Mandon is applied to the place. All this proves that Madon, Manda, and Mandon, are synonymous. It is about 5 English miles north of Sefuri and 4 English miles northwest of Rimuni.

In Talmud and Midrashim, the following places are mentioned :—

In Yalkut to Genesis xlix. 13, it is said that the towns in which the great Sanhedrin had their seat, after the destruction of Jerusalem, were nearly all, with the exception of Jabné, in the portion of Zebulun, to wit: Usha

* In Taanith, fol. 24 *b*, it is said "There came so heavy a rain that the water from the roof-gutters of the town of Zippori flowed into the Digluth=Chidekel or Tigris." This is evidently an erroneous reading, and should be Mechusah, which was in Babylonia, not far from the Tigris. I found this name introduced in the old editions, which is thus incorrectly given in the modern ones as Zippori.

אושא; Shafram שפרעם; Beth-Shearim בית שערים, Zippori צפורי, and Tiberias טבריא. The situation of these places was as follows:

Usha, which is also mentioned in Tosephtah Mikvaöth, chap. vi., is the village Usa, situated 6 English miles west-northwest from Feralthi; for which, see under Naphtali.

Shafram is the modern large village Shafamer (derived from the original name by transposing *m* and *r*), situated 7 English miles east from Chepha, and west of Manda. In this village live about thirty Jewish families, who have an old Synagogue. Between this and Usa, is the grave of the martyr Rabbi Jehudah ben Baba, who was slain there, as appears from Talmud Abodah Zarah, fol. 8 *b*.

Beth-Sheärim is no doubt the modern village Turan (= to the Chaldean תערא Taara, which is the Hebrew שער "Shaar" gate), 5 English miles east-northeast from Sifuri. Astori calls the place Ashara; but this name is no longer in use. It is probable that תורן Turan, which is mentioned in Talmud Sabbath, 120 *b*, means no other than Beth-Sheärim, as it was then called.

Zippori. See above, article Kitron.

Tiberias. See farther down, where I shall speak more at length of this town.

In Bereshith Rabbah to Genesis xlix. 13, it is said, "'And his border shall be unto Zidon,' means Zebud, of Galilee, according to one authority, and Bigdal Riv, according to the other." The first זבוד דגלילה is undoubtedly the modern village Sibdia, situated 5 English miles northeast from Sur (Tyre), since Upper Galilee extended, as already said in the description of Galilee, to the vicinity of Tyre. As to Bigdal Riv (בגדל ריו), it is extremely difficult and obscure of elucidation; but I have no doubt that here again is an error of the transcriber to be corrected, and that for בגדל ריו we should read מגדל רוי Migdal (or Tower of) Revi, and signifies the modern village Burdj al Rui, i. e. fort or tower of Rui, situated on the sea-coast between Zidon and Ras Zarfand (see article Zarephath). This would give us the result that Zebulun extended to the northeast of Tyre and the south of Zidon.

Old Kazerah, near Zippori, קצרה ישנה של צפורי of Erechin, ch. ix. § 6; it was, according to Yerushalmi Erubin, chap. v., scarcely 70 cubits from Beth-Maun. It is true that at present the name of Kazerah is no longer in use; but its former site is readily ascertained; since the grave of the renowned martyr Rabbi Akiba, as is generally well known, was at Kazerah, as I have already stated above, in a note to Gibthan, and it is pointed out, about 2 English miles northwest from Tiberias, on the mountains between Medjdl and Kallath Abn Miun.* In Midrash Samuel,

* The meaning of the word Kazerah I believe to be the same as that of קסטרה or גסטרה; since this town is called in Talmud Bab. Shabbath, 121 *a*, גסטרה של צפורי Gasterah of Zippori, whereas in Yerushalmi Shabbath, chap. xvi., Yerushalmi Nedarim, chap. v., and Yerushalmi, end of Yoma, it is uniformly termed Kazerah of Zippori. The proper meaning of Kazerah, Gasterah, Kasterah, is, according to Rashi, to the above passage of Shabbath שלטון, prefect, superintendent, overseer, or manager. In Latin, the word Castrum means a camp, a place where soldiers stay over night, or take up their temporary abode; (and this term in various changes or abbreviations has become incorporated in various modern names of towns, as Lancaster, Chester, Doncaster, Winchester, &c.—Tr.) The Romans built a fortified camp for their soldiers near Zippori; and as there was already a town in the neighbourhood, this was called the Old, whilst the modern erection became known as the New Kazerah, Gastera, or Castrerah, of Zippori, the change in the pronunciation being merely required to make the Roman word appear in the usual Hebrew dress. It appears to me that the town mentioned in Kiddushin, 76 *a*, as הישנה של צפורי Hayeshanah, i. e. the Old of Zippori, means no other than our Kazerah, although Rashi considered it as a proper name, which is incorrect, because the definite article ה is never applied to proper names as such, and besides this, the name in question does not occur in this locality. There is a town Jeshena mentioned in 2 Chron. xiii. 19; but it was not in Galilee, but near Beth-El, and is the modern Al Sania. (See the cities of the sons of Joseph.)

chap. xxvi., is mentioned Rabbi Isaac ben Kazeartha; and the probability is that his father was from Kazerah.

Shichin שיחין was, according to Sabbath, 121 *a*, near Zippori, and was an uncommonly large and important city, as appears from Echa Rabbethi to chap. ii. 2; at a later period, that is, after the destruction of Jerusalem, it also was reduced to a mere unimportant village, and is hence called Kefar Shichin in Sabbath, 150 *b*, and in end of Yebamoth it appears as Kefar Shichi. Josephus, in Bell. Jud., b. ii. chap. xxv., mentioned Soganes near Sephoris, which is without doubt the Shichin of the Talmud. I am almost led to believe that it is identical with the Sochoh of 1 Kings iv. 10, which was gradually changed into Shichin.

Guftha or Gubabtha גופתא גובבתא is mentioned in Yerushalmi Megillah, chap. i., where we read of Rabbi Jonathan, secretary of the town of Guftha; also in Yerushalmi Shekalim, chap. vii. In Talmud Babli Erubin, 64 *b*, it is called Gufthi. It would appear, from Midrash Koheleth to chap. xvi. 10, that this place was 3 mill, or 2¼ English miles, from Zippori;* but at present I could discover no trace of it.

The Old Jodephath יודפת הישנה of Erechin, chap. ix. § 6, was an uncommonly strongly fortified town, and was situated near the modern Jafa, the Japhia of the Bible; Josephus defended it (Jotapata) long against the Romans, as he has circumstantially narrated in the third book of the Wars of the Jews. I believe we discover a resemblance

* I believe that this will elucidate a passage in Bereshith Rabbah to Gen. xlix. 13, where some remarks are made concerning the birth-place of the prophet Jonah, and it is asserted of Gath-Chepher אולין גובבתא דצפורי that it is Gubabtha of Zippori. The commentators seem at fault to explain the meaning of this passage; but it strikes me that it is probable that our Gufthi and Gath-Chefer were the names of the same town, as it is clear that both refer to a place near Zippori. It is therefore probable that the modern Meshad (see in the 31 Kings, art. Chepher), must be the site of the town in question.

to this name in the modern village Djepatha or Depatha, which is about 1½ English miles south of Jafa. I must at the same time notice an opinion common among our people, though erroneous, in their calling the castle near Zafed, Jorephah, which is, by the by, also an erroneous spelling of the word, since they exchange the D with R, and there can be no doubt that the real name should be Jodephath; since it appears from the passage just cited from Josephus, that Jotapata or Jotapha was by no means in the vicinity of Zafed. The Rabbi Menachem Jodephaah of Zebachim, 110 *b*, derived his name probably from this place.

Maün מעון of Zebachim, 118 *b*. In Tosephtaha Shebiith, chap. vii., it is said that Maün is in Lower Galilee. In the Life of Josephus, § 12, is mentioned Beth-Maus, as being 4 stadia (½ English mile) from Tiberias. The same is asserted by Astori, and he found the place still inhabited when he visited it. The present Kallath Aben Miun, which is west of Medjdl, at a distance of about 1 English mile, does not, according to my view, occupy the exact site of Maün, as it is too far to the northwest. I cannot here avoid to notice the opinion of the learned Astori, who endeavours to prove in his work, fol. 66 *b*, that this Maün is the same Maön whither David fled before Saul (1 Sam. xxiii. 25). As David did not enter Galilee in his wanderings, it is not necessary to employ any arguments to disprove Astori's opinion; but I may surely express my astonishment that one so learned should commit such an error.

Kefar Shubethi כפר שובתי of Bereshith Rabbah, chap. lxxxv., is the modern village Kefr Sabth, situated on a mountain, 5 English miles southwest from Tiberias.

Rebitha רביתא of Chulin, 60 *a*, is probably the village Rabuthia, situated at a distance of 3 English miles from the northwestern shore of Lake Chinnereth, which receives, to the north of Medjdl, the Wady Rabuthia, which has its source in the environs of Feradi and Kefr Anan.

Senabrai סנבראי of Yerushalmi Megillah, i. (R. Levi of Senabra, Yerushalmi Shebiith, ix.), is the Sennabris mentioned in Josephus, Bell. Jud., b. iii., chap. ix., as being 30 stadia, or about 4 English miles, south of Tiberias. Even at the present day there are found in this vicinity traces of ruins called by the Arabs Sinabri.

Amos עמוס (Koheleth Rabbethi, fol. 106 *b*). Josephus speaks of Emaus in Galilee, not far from the hot spring of Tiberias; but it is at present unknown. (See farther, art. חמת.)

Hatulim or Chatlim הטולים · גרסת הערוך חטלים (of Menachoth, 86 *b*), is the modern village Al Chatli, east from Mount Tabor, and not far from the river Jordan.

The town of Laban (the White Town), in the mountain עיר לבן בהר, of Menachoth, 86 *b*. I have ascertained from ancient documents, that the town of Nazareth was called the White Town, since the houses thereof, as also the whole environs, the soil and stones, being calcareous, have all a white appearance; and as it is situated on a mountain, it is undoubtedly the town in question.

Beth-Rimah בית רימה of Menachoth, 86 *b*, is probably the modern village Ramé, 1½ English miles east from Usa.

Garsis גרסים Erubin, 21 *b*. (Rabbi Joshua from Garsis.) Josephus mentions this place, and calls it a city of Galilee, 20 stadia (2½ English miles) from Sephoris. At present no vestige of it can be found.

The Gulf of Kantir גולפא דקנטיר of Zohar Bereshith, 56 *b*; "on the other side of Lake Chinnereth is the village Kantir, consequently the place in question means the gulf or harbour of Kantir;" thus reports Rabbi Menachem de Lozano, in his Maärich; but it is at present unknown.

I believe now to be able to state the following, as ascertained, in regard to the possessions of Zebulun. In the blessing of Jacob concerning him (Gen. xlix. 13), he said, "Zebulun shall dwell at the haven of the seas," not "sea," as in the English version. The whole prophecy of Jacob always refers to the possessions in the Holy Land; and the plural ימים "seas" says plainly that Zebulun should have the coasts of two seas in his territory, which would then give us the respective shores of the Mediterranean and Chinnereth. I found farther proof that Zebulun was bounded by both seas, from the following: in Tractate Megillah, 6 *a*, it is said that the purple shell (Chalazon חלזון) is only found in the territory of Zebulun; in Tractate Sabbath, 26 *a*, it is said that this shell is only to be met between Tyre and Cheifa,* which is also confirmed by experience at the present day. It is also stated in Yalkut to Deut. xxxiii. 19, that the fishing for the purple snail took place only on the coast of the Great Sea, in the territory of Zebulun.

There are, besides this, several contradictory statements made respecting the possession of the Lake Chinnereth. It is said in Zohar Behaalotecha, 150 *a*, and in several other passages besides those already cited, that this lake belonged to Zebulun, and that several of the towns already named—for example, Tiberias—were situated on this lake. Nevertheless, in Baba Kamma, 81 *b*, it says that this lake, and even some land lying south of it, belonged to Naphtali. It is also asserted in Megillah, 6 *a*, רקת זו טבריא of Joshua xix. 35, "Rakkath is the (later) Tiberias;" and since Rak-

* To this is found a contradiction in Zohar to Exodus xiv. 25, וים כנרת הוה בעדבה (דזבולון) אשתכא אשתכח חלזון לתכלתא "And the sea of Chinnereth was in the portion of Zebulun, and thence was obtained the purple shell for the Techaleth" (the *blue* of Exod. xxv. 4). The same is said in Zohar Terumah, 149 *b*, that the purple shell is found in Chinnereth, which belonged to Zebulun. But I could not find the least evidence that this shell is ever found in Chinnereth. The learned Rabbi Jacob Emden, mentioned in his work מטפחת הספרים, already, that this passage is most surprising.

kath is reckoned in Joshua to Naphtali, it would appear that the Lake Chinnereth in the vicinity of Tiberias belonged to Naphtali. In Yalkut to Deut. xxxiii. 23, it is said that the lake of Tiberias, as also Semechonitis, belonged to Naphtali; and in Baba Bathra, 122 *a*, it is likewise stated that the district of Genisur (Genezareth) was in Naphtali. It appears, therefore, that Chinnereth was considered as belonging to both tribes, as was the case with frontier towns, as has been noted above, at Baalah, in the land of Dan.

The southern boundary line of Zebulun went, therefore, westward from this lake to Mount Tabor,—the mount, however, and town of the same name, belonged to Issachar,—then ran farther to Doberath, which town belonged to both Zebulun and Issachar; thence somewhat northerly, towards Shion, which belonged to Issachar; thence to Mount Carmel to the river Kishon, which flows there (Joshua xix. 11), to the vicinity of Akko, which district belonged to Zebulun, according to Baba Bathra, 122 *a*, though Akko itself belonged to Asher. At the northeast, Zebulun extended to Tanchum (Kefar Nachum), since it was situated on the boundary between Zebulun and Naphtali; thence the line ran westwardly to Kitron (Sifuri); thence it extended, in a long and narrow strip, to the vicinity of Zidon; so that a small part of this territory touched the Mediterranean, whereas the greater portion of this coast belonged to Asher, as will be shown hereafter.

Josephus says that Zebulun extended from Chinnereth to the Great Sea, near Mount Carmel.

NAPHTALI.

It is necessary first to explain the position of the towns of Naphtali, and then the territory in general. It is said in Joshua xix. 33, "And their coast was from Chelef, from Aylon Bezaanannim, and Adami Hannekeb, and Jabneël, unto Lakkum, and the outgoings thereof were at the Jordan." But of all the names of these places, there is not a vestige left at present in the country. Fortunately, however, I found an explanation of them in Yerushalmi Megillah, chap. i., where it says that Bezaanannim is אגני הקדש Agné Hackedesh; so it is also commented in Jonathan to Judges iv. 11, עד מישר אגניא דעם קדש "to the plain Aganiah, which is near Kedesh." Now the meaning of Agné in the Chaldean is "swamp, moor" (see Rashi and Kimchi, in the passage cited); and the commentary of Jonathan then translates the verse "the swampy country which is near Kedesh." But I have already stated above, in the second chapter, that Semechonitis is only filled with water in the rainy season, but is at other times a large swamp. There can therefore be no doubt that Aylon Bezaanannim was between this swampy lake and Kedesh.

It is farther said in Yerushalmi Megillah, that Adami is Damin (דמין). Now this would give us the village Damé (= Damin), 5 English miles west from the south-west point of the sea of Tiberias. It is also said, in the same passage, that Hannekeb is Zeidatha (ציידתא). I suppose to find a trace of this name in that of the village Hazedhi, 3 English miles north from Al Chatti. It is stated there farther that Jabneël is Kefar Yamah, i. e. the village by the sea. I thought at first to have found a correct elucidation concerning the site of this Jabneël, since Josephus says, in his Bell. Jud., book iv., chap. i., "The Lake Semechonitis is 30 stadia broad and 60 long, and extends to Jabné." This would seem to indicate that Jabneël, Jabné, or Kefar Yamah, was situated on the north-west shore of Semechonitis. But I afterwards found, in other and more correct editions, instead of Jabné, "to Daphné," which really appears the correct reading, for the reasons given in the first chapter, article Riblah.

I therefore believe that this Jabneël was situated on the southern shore of Lake Chinnereth, and that it is the Jamnia or Jamnith in Upper Galilee, mentioned by Josephus in the Bell. Jud., book ii., chap. xxv., and in the Life of Josephus.

Aznoth Tabor אזנת תבור, although now unknown, was situated without doubt not far from the east side of Mount Tabor.

Chukkok חקק, probably the village Jakuk, 10 English miles northeast from Tabor. Here is pointed out the grave of the prophet Habakkuk.

Haziddim הצדים. In Yerushalmi Megillah, i., cited above, it says: "Haziddim is the same with Kefar Chittai," which is without doubt the village of Chittin, situated 5 English miles west-northwest from Tiberias. Near it is a steep and high mountain, called Kurn Chittin (see above, second chapter, page 71). This Kefar Chittai is also mentioned in Bereshith Rabbah, 65; and in Chagigah, chap. v., § 6, "Rabbi Jacob from Kefar Chittai." We also read in Yerushalmi Megillah, i., that Zer, the next mentioned town in Joshua xix. 35, was near the above; wherefore, although now unknown, it must have been near the modern Chittin.

Chammath חמת. In Talmud Babli, Megillah, 6 *a*, it says, that Chammath is the same with Chamtan; and ibid. fol. 2 *b*, it says, "From Chamtan to Tiberias there is a distance of 1 mill." I presume this to be identical with the Emaus of Josephus, and that its situation was near the present hot spring of Tiberias; for although it is more than a mill from Tiberias, it must be observed that this is now situated farther to the north than it was in the time of the Talmud. I farther believe that Chammath is identical with the Levitical town of Naphtali חמת דאר Chammath Dor, literally "the hot springs from fire,"

(דאר = דאור*), in reference to the hot springs found there, of Joshua xxi. 32. In 1 Chron. vi. 61, it is called חמון Chammon.

Rakkath רקת is, according to Megillah, fol. 6 *a*, the later Tiberias.

Chinnereth כנרת is called in the same passage Genussar גנוסר, and was still standing in the time of Astori, and at present the ruins of Gansur can be seen 2½ English miles northwest from Tiberias. Josephus, in his Bell. Jud., b. iii., chap. xxxv., paints in an extraordinary manner the productiveness of the plains of Genussar גנוסר, and says that it is 30 stadia long, and 20 broad; but at present all is deserted and wasted. It is scarcely thirty years ago when this plain was like a garden of God, the fruits of which were pre-eminent in the whole country for their size and superior excellences; but the Arabs of the vicinity became engaged in a civil war, and destroyed everything, from mutual motives of revenge and infuriated passions, so that not a vestige remained.

Adamah אדמה, I believe identical with the present village Dama, situated 5 English miles west-northwest from Zafed. In Orlah, chap. ii., we read of Rabbi Dosthai from Kefar Dama, and in Menachoth, 99 *b*, of Ben Dama בן דמא, so called, perhaps, from being a native of this place, "a son of Dama."

Chazor חצור. See above, in the 31 Kings.

Kedesh קדש, is the village Kudes, situated on the mountains of Naphtali, 5 English miles northwest from Lake Semechonitis, and 20 miles north from Zafed. It was formerly one of the cities of refuge (Joshua xv. 7). Here are shown the graves of Deborah, Barak, Abinoam, Jaël, and Cheber.

En-Chazor עין חצור is undoubtedly the village En-Azur,

* This would require a Chaldee construction, in which the Daleth is the preposition "of the."—TRANSLATOR.

about 3 English miles south from the village Azur. (See above, art. Chazor.)

Migdal-El-Chorem מגדל אל חרם, 8 miles east from Akko, is the village Medjdl al Krum. I suppose this name to be an incorrect pronunciation of Migdal-El-Chorem.*

Beth-Anuth בית ענות. Eusebius says: "15 mill east from Sephuri is the town Bathanea." I think it ought to be "north from Sephuri;" since even at the present day there is a village called Baineh, 1 mile northeast from the village Medjdl al Krum. I take Baineh to be Beth-Ené = Anath. In proof of the correctness of this supposition, this place is called in Yerushalmi, end of Orlah, "Bainah," whereas in Tosephtah Kelaim, chap. i., it is called Beth-Ana, which shows the identity of the two names.

Beth-Shemesh בית שמש. At the time of Astori, there was a village, 2½ English miles south of Sephuri, called Sumsi, which he supposed to be Beth-Shemesh of Issachar (Joshua xix. 22); but it is my opinion that it was identical with the Beth-Shemesh of Naphtali (ibid. 38), although the position assigned it by Astori would seem to place it beyond the boundary of this tribe. (See farther, the description of the possessions of Naphtali.)

Charosheth-Hagoyim חרשת הגוים (Judges iv. 2); I take this to be the village of Girsh = Chirsh, which is situated on a high mount, 1 English mile west from the Jordan bridge, the Djisr abné Jacob. Jonathan explains this name with "fort, castle;" and in truth the village of Girsh is well calculated to have been an ancient fort. It was nearly totally destroyed through the earthquake of 5597 (1837).

Tishbi תשבי (1 Kings xvii. 1). In the book of Tobith, chap. i. 2, it is said: "Tisbi, a city in Upper Galilee, east of Kedesh, in Naphtali, and north of Asher;" the latter

* The author takes these three words to be one name; but the accentuation seems to point out that Migdal-El means one, and Chorem another place.—TRANSLATOR.

position appears obscure and incorrect, and ought to be "east of Asher." It may have been the birth-place of the prophet Elijah. But he is called the Gileadite; wherefore this Tishbi of the prophets, must have been east of Jordan. Josephus calls Cheshbon, in the territory of Reuben, "Tisbunis;" this place was a Levitical city (Joshua xxi. 39; 1 Chron. vi. 66). As Elijah was, according to some, a priest, it is likely enough that he was born in a city of the Levites.

"And Naphtali touched on Judah on Jordan towards the east" (Joshua xix. 34). This passage appears extremely difficult, since it assigns Judah possessions so far north in Palestine. But I think to be able to explain it in the following manner. We read in 1 Chronicles ii. 21, "After this Hezron, the son of Perez, the son of Judah, took the daughter of Machir, the father of Gilead, for a wife, when he was sixty years old, and she bore unto him Segub. Segub begat Jair, who had twenty towns in the land of Gilead. And he took Geshur and Aram with the towns of Jair from them, with Kenath and the towns thereof, sixty cities. All these belonged to the sons of Machir, the father of Gilead." Aben Ezra says to Numbers xxxii. 42, "Jair, son of Menasseh, belonged to the family of Judah, since Hezron took the daughter of Machir for wife, and begat Segub, who begat Jair, who had possessions in the land of Gilead, consequently his family name was derived merely from the mother's side." In Baba Bathra, 112 *a*, it is said, "Jair married a wife with many possessions and goods; she died, and he inherited the whole property." From all this we may deduce that all the possessions of Jair, "the Chavvoth Jair," beyond Jordan, properly speaking, belonged to Judah, and these separate towns were situated in Gilead, on the east side of the Jordan, opposite the territory of Naphtali. The passage in question then says that Naphtali was bounded on the east by that part of the possessions of Judah situated in Gilead, through inheritance from the female line of Machir, but has no reference to the territory of Judah proper, situated at the south and to the west of Jordan; and thus is the difficulty removed.

In Talmud and Midrashim the following names occur:

Zefath צפת of Yerushalmi Rosh Hashanah, chap. ii.; the description of which in detail shall be given hereafter.

Miron מירון mentioned in Zohar to Shemini, fol. 39 *a*, also in end of Haazinu, and probably the Mero (instead of Meron), of Josephus' Bell. Jud., book ii. chap. xxv., and the Ascent of Beth-Meron מעלת בית מרון of Rosh Hashanah, fol. 18 *a*, is the village Miron, situated on a mountain, 5 English miles to the west of Zafed. In this place and its environs are many vaults and graves, where many of our ancient learned men of blessed memory repose; especially one cave, where are deposited the remains of the celebrated Hillel and many of his disciples; another, where the equally famous Shamai and his wife lie interred. There is also found there a most ancient Synagogue, as also an unroofed college (Beth-Hammidrash), beneath which are the graves of Rabbi Shimon ben Jochai (the alleged author of the Zohar), and of his son Rabbi Eliezer. On the 33d day of Omer, on the 18th of Iyar, there is held here every year a general popular festival, which is attended by our brothers of Israel even from Damascus, Aleppo, Bagdad, Cairo, Constantinople, &c. At night the houses are illuminated, burning torches are carried about, and they have religious dances, and innocent and modest amusements of all sorts, and you often will find several thousand Israelites in attendance at this festival, which is called הילולא דר' שמעון בן יוחאי Hilula derabbi Shimon ben Jochai, that is "Rejoicing feast of Rabbi Simeon." It appears to me that the origin of this festival is owing to that on this day, the

33d of the Omer, the day of his death, the Great Idra* was delivered by him to his scholars, as is told in Zohar, end of Haazinu, and it is consequently a festival for the Cabbalists.

Kefar Chananiah כפר חנניא of Shebiith, chap. ix. § 2, is called כפר חנן Kefar Chanan in Midrash Neëlam to Vayera, fol. 115 *a*, also in Zohar Vayiggash, fol. 216 *b*, and is the modern village Kefr Anan, 5 English miles west-southwest from Zafed. There is a Synagogue here, but it is in ruins.

Ferathi פרתי of Bereshith Rabbah to Vayechi (Rabbi José from Ferathi), is the modern village Ferady, 1 mile north of Kefr Anan. They point out here the grave of Rabbi Nachum, of Gimso, and in a cave, that of Rabbi Ishmael.

Kefar Sami or Simaï כפר סמי או סימאי. This place is termed Sami in Tosephtah Gittin, i., Samai in Gittin, fol. 6 *b*, and Sama in Midrash Koheleth to chap. vii. 26. Yerushalmi Challah, chap. ii., mentions that a river is found near this village. Now this points the place to be the modern village Samai, about 1 English mile south from Miron, near to which flows the Wady Leiman, in a southerly direction, and after turning it falls into Lake Chinnereth, near the former town of Tanchum, where it is called Wady Amud. This, therefore, must be the river mentioned in the passage cited as being near Samai.

Shizur שיזור is the modern village of this name, 3 English miles west from Kefr Anan; near it are the graves of Rabbi Shimeon, from Shizur, of the high priest Rabbi Ishmael, son of Elisha, and Rabbi Shimeon ben Elazar.

* This is a lecture, if it may be so called, by Rabbi Simeon to his scholars, and is, like the whole of the Zohar, greatly esteemed by his followers, among whom may be classed all the followers of the Cabbalah, the mystical philosophy of the Jews, and the modern Hassidim.—TRANSLATOR.

Kaparah קפרה is the modern village of the same name, 5 English miles west from Medjdl al Krum. Here is the vault of Rabbi Elazar, of Kaparah, and another of Bar Kaparah. It is probably the town called Kaprath in the Life of Josephus.

Sichnin סיכנין of Siphri, to Haazinu; Rosh Hashanah, 27 *a*; Zohar Balak, 186 *a*, is the village Sichni, situated 5 English miles south from Medjdl al Krum. They point out here the graves of Rabbi Yehudah and Rabbi Shimon of Sichnin.

Achbarah עכברה of Baba Mezia, 84 *b*, is the village Echbara, 1½ English miles west-southwest from Zafed.* In Josephus' Bell. Jud., book ii., chap. xxv., it is called Achebariana.

Biri בירי of Baba Mezia, 84 *b*, and Pesachim, 51 *a*, is the village Birya, about 1 English mile north of Zafed.

Kefar Tanchum or Nachum כפר תנחום או נחום in Midrash Koheleth, 85 *a*, it is called Kefar Nachum; in Midrash Shir Hashirim, 17 *b*, Kefar Tanchumin; in Yerushalmi Terumoth, at end, and in Yerushalmi Taanith, i., Kefar Techumin. At the time of Astori, it was yet standing, under the name of Kefar Tanchum, about 1¼ English miles east from Genussar. At present it is destroyed; the site is nevertheless well ascertained, and bears the name of Kefr Tanchum. They point out there the graves of Nahum the prophet, of Rabbi Tanchum, and Tanchuma, who all repose there, and through these the ancient position of the village is easily known. It is close on Chinnereth, and 2½ English miles north of Tiberias.

Kerazim כרזים of Menachoth,† 85 *a*, is no doubt identical

* I found a most singular explanation in the book Aruch, art. Achbarah, where he explains the passage in Baba Mezia, 84 *b*, בני עכברה with שכונה "the neighbours," since the word is evidently the name of a place, whence the correct rendering should be "the inhabitants of Achbarah."

† The assertion of Rashi to this passage from Menachoth that Kerazim

with the ruins called by the Arabs Karsaim, about 2 miles southwest from the above Kefr Tanchum.

Arbel ארבל of Aboth, i. § 6; Yerushalmi Peäh, vii., and Yerushalmi Berachoth, i., is identical with the ruins of Irbel, 1½ English miles northwest from Tiberias. They there point out the grave of Nitai of Arbel (Aboth, i. 6), and even that of Dinah, daughter of Jacob, and, between the laurel trees found there, the sepulchre of Seth, son of Adam, and that of Rabbi Zera.

Migdal, also Migdal Detzibaya* מגדל · מגדל דצבעיא of Midrash Echa, ii. 1, Bereshith Rabbah to Vayichbach, and Midrash Shemuel, chap. iii., is the village Medjdl, about 1 English mile northwest from Tiberias. This town is also called by the Christians, Magdelenia, and I doubt not but that this name is alluded to in the Talmud. For it is said in Pesachim, fol. 46 *a*, מגדל נוניא, "Migdal Nunia is 1 mill from Tiberias;" now there is either an error of transcribing in putting the *n* for *l*, or a mere actual substitution of one of these *liquid* letters for the other, as is often done in other cases, as Beth-en for Beth-el; Djibril for Djibrin; Serain for Serail; whence I think it undoubted that Migdalnunia is no other than Magdelenia.

Teliman טלימאן; from certain documents I have learned that the just-named Migdal was also called Talmanuta; and I believe that this name too is discoverable in the Talmud, that it is identical with Teliman here cited, which occurs in Yerushalmi Demai, ii., as מערת טלימאן "the cave of Teliman," or, as I think, identical with the cave of Talmanuta.

was not far from Jerusalem, is not correct, since its true position was in Galilee, and Tosephtah Menachoth, 9, also controverts Rashi's statement in this respect.

* This name is perhaps somewhat akin to the one mentioned as the surname of one of David's heroes in 1 Chron. xi. 37, Juasiel the Mezobaite, or of Mezobaia.

Pethugtha פתוגתא, so it is called in Vayikra Rabbah, chap. v.; but the פרוגייתא Perugaitha of Sabbath, 147 *b*, is an incorrect reading; it is no doubt the village Fatigha, situated in the valley called Wady Sisaban, in a line due east from Zafed.

Gamla גמלא of Mishnan Erechin, chap. ix. § 6; Yerushalmi Maccoth, chap. ii.; and Tosephtah Maccoth, chap. ii. It is stated in all these passages to be situated in Galilee, whereas Josephus places it in the district of Golan (Golanitis), on the east side of the Jordan. But I have learned from Bedouins and other Arabs, that about 5 miles south of Hunin, which is 6 miles north of Kedesh in Naphtali, the ancient Gamla should have stood on a mountain, according to a certain tradition. It is true, I could discover no trace of the town; still the tradition has a great air of probability to recommend it.

Neburia נבוריא of Midrash Koheleth to chap. vii. 26; Yerushalmi Berachoth, chap. ix.; is probably the ruined village Nebarti, 7 miles south of Kedes. They point out there the graves of Rabbi Joshua, of Kefar Neburia, and of Rabbi Eliezer, of Modai.

Safsufa ספסופא of Yerushalmi Terumoth, chap. viii., is the village Safsaf, between Meron and Zafed.

En-Kachal עין כחל is a name often mentioned in the preface to the work Emek Hamelech, and signifies a beautiful and large spring, existing under this name, at the present day, on the road from Tiberias to Zafed, northwest from the sea of Chinnereth.

Concerning the possessions of Naphtali in general, I can only speak when I have described and explained the towns belonging to Asher, wherefore I will then give the synopsis required.

ASHER.

Of the cities mentioned as belonging to Asher, in Joshua xix. 24–31, I have been able to ascertain what follows:

Chelkath חלקת is probably the modern village Jerkat or Jerka, about 2 English miles east from Kefr Jasif (see Achshaf). It strikes me that the *r* in Jerkat is substituted for *l*, as this is often done in other names, as has been remarked above, art. Azel, in Benjamin. In 1 Chron. vi. 60 (English version 75), this Levitical city is called Chukkok.

Chali חלי. We read in the book of Judith vii. 3 : "They encamped—as far as Chalon,* opposite to Esdrelon." Perhaps that Chali and Chalon designate the same place, and its situation must therefore be sought for near Mount Carmel.

Beten בטן. Eusebius says: "This is 8 mill east from Akko;" but this should evidently read northeast, or else if it be as the text of Eusebius reads it, it would place Beten in the midst of Naphtali.

Achshaph אכשף. This is given in the Septuagint with Keaph, which is as much as Cheifa. But Hieronymus says that Achshaph is the town of Chasala, in the neighbourhood of Tyre, on the river Leontes. Astori believes it to be Arsuf (at present destroyed), on the sea-coast, in a direction west of Samaria (Sebasté). But all these opinions have much that is objectionable in them. I rather am inclined to believe that it is identical with the modern village Kefr Jasif = Chasif = Achsif = Achshaph, 5 English miles northeast from Akko. At present no Jews are residing there; but they left it but a short time ago, and an ancient Synagogue is still in the place, and is in good repair. The burial-ground of the Jews of Akko is in this village, because Akko is not considered as belonging to the Holy Land, since it was not repossessed by the exiles returning under Ezra, as has been already noticed in our first chapter.

Alammelech אלמלך. The little stream Nahr al Melchi flows south of Shafamer, in a westerly direction, and falls, near Cheifa, into the Mukata (Kishon). Its name would

* This is the Latin reading, and is no doubt correct.

almost seem to indicate that it is called after the ancient Alammelech, which stood on its banks.

Amad עמעד is probably the village Al-Mead, 2 English miles north from Kefr Jasif.

Mishal משאל is at present unknown. Eusebius merely remarks that it is on the sea-coast, not far from Carmel.

Beth-Dagon בית דגון. About 9 English miles northwest from Zafed is a village called, in the language of the country, Beth-Shan. But, upon strict inquiry, I found that the proper pronunciation should be Beth-Djan, that is undoubtedly Beth-Dgan, as the Arabs often put their Dj for the Hebrew G; wherefore I would identify this village with the Beth-Dagon of Scripture.

Beth-Haëmek בית העמק appears to me to be the modern Amuka, i. e. the deep, synonymous with the Hebrew Emek, it being situated in a valley. This village is 12 miles north-northwest from Zafed, on the road to Kedes. It is also probable that it is referred to under Kefar Amiku of Taanith, 21 *a*.

Cabul כבול is the large village Kabul, 5 English miles north-northeast from Akko. They point out here the graves of R. Abraham Aben Ezra, and of R. Shelomoh Ibn Gebirol. It is mentioned in Pesachim, fol. 51 *a*, and Vayikra Rabbah, chap. xx.

Ebron עברון is no doubt the present village Ebra, situated south of Kallat Shakif, which lies in the valley of Kasmeia. Among the Levitical cities it is called Abdon.

Rechob רחוב. I have read in some books that its position was about 7½ miles east of Tyre, on the river Leontes, in the present Wady Kasmeia; but it is now unknown.

Chammon חמון is called Ammon in Yerushalmi Demai, chap. ii., and is probably identical with the village Hamani, situated 1 mile west of Kanah.

Kanah קנה, is the village of this name, 3 English miles southeast from Tyre (Sur).

Zidon Rabbah, the Great Zidon צידון רבה is at present called Saida, and is a small, pretty town with a small harbour. Here live about fifty Jewish families, who have a handsome Synagogue. Without the town is shown the grave of Zebulun, son of Jacob, over which is a cupola with an outer court. The Arabs call him Sheich Saida, i. e. chief of Sidon; this would argue that this town belonged to Zebulun and not to Asher, and that the boundary of the former reached this town; since he would not have been buried here, if it were not in the territory assigned to him. South of Latrun (see Atroth-Beth-Joäb) is a village also called Zidon, whence then the name of Great Zidon, to distinguish it from the smaller synonymous town situated farther south, near Latrun.

Zor, Tyre צור is the present small unimportant town of Sur, 20 English miles south of Saida. It was in ancient times situated on an island, which, since the time of Alexander of Macedon, is a peninsula. Without the town there is a large monument, which the Arabs call Sidna Chur, i. e. "The Prince Chiram," and maintain that Hiram, King of Tyre, lies buried here. It would appear that it is a long time since Jews lived here. When Zafed, that is the part inhabited by Jews, was plundered and nearly destroyed, in 5594 (1834), by the Arabs and Bedouins, there arrived at Sur a ship from Barbary, North Africa, filled with Jewish pilgrims, who purposed settling in Zafed; but when they learned that it had been destroyed, they nearly all remained in Sur; but in the course of five or six years, the greater portion having died away, the remainder settled in other places, so that at present not a single Jew is found in Sur. As its former name was Tyrus, the vicinity was named Tyrusia; and hence I believe that the Tursia so often occurring in Talmud and Midrashim, is no other than this district of Tyre; hence the Tursiim means Tyrians. In Megillah, 26 *a*, it is said, "A Synagogue of the Tursiim was in Jerusalem." There was another one of the kind in Lod, as mentioned in Vayikra Rabbah, chap. xxxv. In Pesiktah Rabbethi, chap. xv., it is stated, "Rabbi Nachum taught in Trissia," &c., which probably also means in the vicinity of Tyre, or Tyrusia. On the coast of the Mediterranean, 14 English miles south from Tyre and 2 English miles north from Zib (Achzib), there is an extremely steep, high, and narrow promontory, which stretches into the sea; it can be seen at a great distance, and it is ascended as it were on a ladder, that is to say, the path leading to its summit is cut out in steps, similar to a staircase, hence its name, "the Ladder of Tyre," סולמא דצור Sulma Dezur. In Arabic it is termed Ras al Nakura. (See also Erubin, 80 *a*, and Beza, 25 *b*.)

Chosah חסה, which Eusebius states to be a city between Zor and Achzib. At present there is a village, called Al Busa, perhaps a corruption from Chusa, 2 English miles northeast from Zib, and is possibly the Chosa of Scripture. 1 English mile south of Saida (Zidon) there is indeed the village Al Chasia, which is more similar to Chosah than Busa is; but it cannot be identical with it, as it is too far to the north.

Ramah רמה is probably the village Ramis, 5 English miles southwest from Kedes.

Achzib אכזים; in Talmud and elsewhere, it is briefly called Chezib כזיב, and is the modern village Zib, situated on the sea-shore, about 5 English miles north from Akko. Here also is to be noticed a singular statement of Astori in saying, fol. 65 *a*, "This Achzib is the place mentioned in the history of Judah, son of Jacob, in Genesis xxxviii. 5;" but this opinion is erroneous, since that Chezib was in the land of Judah, not far from Adullam (which see).

Aphek אפק may probably be identical with the village En-Fit, also called En-Fik, situated about 3 English miles southwest from Banias.

Rechob רחוב. Some have believed that Eusebius, in saying that Raüb is 4 mill from Beth Shean, referred to Rechob of Asher. But this cannot be correct, since Beth-Shean was not near this tribe; but it is to be sought for in the Lower Bakaa, not far from the river Wady Kasmeia, in the direction of Banais or Laish (Judges xviii. 28). It strikes me, however, that Eusebius meant "Araba" or the town of Harabbith, belonging to Issachar (which see).

There also belonged to Asher the following places:

Akko עכו (Judges i. 31). In Arabic Aka signifies, "hot sand;" and the place may have derived its name from the fact that the whole line of shore to Cheifa, 8 English miles in length, is in a measure a sandy desert, which becomes very hot in the summer. It seems that this town was already in ancient times destroyed, and dwindled down to a village, since we often find it called Kefar Akko, that is, the village of Akko; for instance, in Tosephtah Sotah, chap. i., and Bereshith Rabbah, chap. xxx., also in Sotah 34 *b*. It is also possible that reference is made to a village of the same name with the town, which may have been situated near Akko. At present there are here about forty Jewish families, who have a small but very ancient Synagogue. In the time of the Romans it was known as Ptolemais. Its fortifications are extremely strong. It was during the great part of the period of the Franks, that is, whilst the Europeans possessed the country, the residence of their kings. It suffered much in 5592 and 5600 (1832 and 1840), through the bombardment and capture of the Egyptians and Europeans; but it has been speedily restored and rebuilt, and is again very strongly fortified. It has been often captured. In 4398 (638) it was taken by the Calif Omar from the Greeks, when the whole country came under the power of the Saracens. In 4864 (1104) it was taken by Baldwin I. from the Saracens; in 4947 (1187) it was recaptured from the Christians by Saladin,

King of Egypt; in 4951 (1191) it was taken by Richard Cœur de Lion, and Philip of France; and in 5051 (1291) it was finally captured by Serapa, King of Egypt, on which occasion 60,000 Christians lost their lives. In 5559 (1799) a contest was waged here between Sir Sydney Smith, who was in the city, aiding the Turkish Pacha, and Napoleon Bonaparte, the commander of the French army, who besieged and had at length to retire without taking it. In 5592 (1832) it was captured by Abraim (Ibrahim) Pacha, of Egypt, who conquered at that time all Palestine and Syria, and carried Abd Alla Pacha a prisoner to Alexandria. In 5600 (1840) it was again taken by the military expedition of the English and Turks, from Abraim Pacha, since when the whole of Syria and Palestine has remained under the power of the Ottoman Porte. [It is called, in the European dialects, St. Jean d'Acre. TRANSLATOR.]

Zarephath צרפת (1 Kings xvii. 9). The ruins of this place are found close upon the sea, 6 miles south of Saida. One mile east from this, on a high mountain, is the village Surafend, probably of a later date than the town itself. It is possible that the passage משרפת מים כל צידונים (Joshua xiii. 6), untranslated in the English version, is synonymous with Zarephath, that is, "purifying," from Zaroph צרוף, "to purify,"—no doubt so called from the fact that salt was made here from sea-water; wherefore we may assume that משרפת is put* for מצפרת.

About 1 mile north of Dor (Dandura) is a village, likewise called Surafend; whence it is possible that the definition of 1 Kings xvii. 9, "to Zarephath, which belongs to Zidon," refers to the fact that there was another city of the

* May it not also be merely synonymous, and not exchanged?—and that Missrephoth Mayim merely means places where the (sea) water was boiled, subjected to fire, or, so to say, burnt out, and thus be a legitimate derivation from שרוף Sahrofe, "to burn?" This derivation does not, however, gainsay the identity of the name with Zarephath.—TRANSLATOR.

name, which may have been the modern Surafend, near Dor.

In Talmud and Midrashim the following names occur:

Cheifa חיפה, of Sabbath, 26 *a*, Tosephtah Yebamoth, chap. vi., and Shemoth Rabbah, chap. xiv., was called Purpureon during the dominion of the Greeks and Romans, because the purple shell* was often found and taken in the vicinity. (See the passage cited of Talmud Sabbath.) Josephus, in his Bell. Jud., book iii., page 2, calls this town "Caba, a city of the horsemen," because King Herod's cavalry was stationed here. It is at present an insignificant little town, at the foot of Carmel. Not far from it the Kishon (Mukata) falls into the sea. About forty Jewish families, who have an old Synagogue, reside here at the present time. In their burying-ground are the graves of Rabbi Adimi of Cheifa, and Rabbi Isaac Napcha (Smith?).

Shikmonah שקמונה, of Demai i., Baba Bathra, 119 *a*, was, according to Josephus, between Cæsarea and Akko; but it is at present unknown. Some believe it to be identical with Cheifa.

Turi טורי, of Midrash Shir Hashirim to chap. viii. 7, Midrash Samuel, chap. iii., Yerushalmi Baba Mezia, chap. ii., is either the village Tireh, between Akko and Shafamer, or the village Turia, south of Carmel, not far from Merdj aben Amer.

Gush-Chalab גוש חלב, of Menachoth, 85 *b*, Shemoth Rabbah, chap. v., Siphri to Haazinu, and Zohar Acharay Moth, fol. 63 *b*, was destroyed at the time of Rabbi Chiskiah and Rabbi Jesa (see Zohar, 71 *a*). Josephus, in his

* I must call attention to the fact that the blood, or the dyeing material of this shell, produces a red dye; and that still, both in Scripture and Talmud, this colour is always given as blue תכלת. But it appears from Talmud and other documents, that through certain preparations and mixing, the original red colour was changed into a blue. This remark is extremely interesting, as this explains the incongruity which otherwise would make erroneously the blood of the chalazon of a blue colour.

Bell. Jud., book iv., chap. iv., calls it Gischala, a fortified town in Upper Galilee. It was the birth-place of the chief John (Paritz Yochanan), who is so famous in the siege of Jerusalem by the Romans. It is the Achlab אחלב of Judges i. 31, mentioned as belonging to Asher. Oil was produced here in great abundance (see also article Tekoa, page 114). It is now the village Gish, also called Gish-Chalab, and is 5 English miles northwest from Zafed. There are shown here many graves of our departed learned men, among others, those of Adrammelech and Sharezer, the sons of Sancherib (2 Kings xix. 37); and near these the graves of Shemaiah and Abtalion (Aboth i. § 10), who were descended from the first-named princes, who, after slaying their father, are said to have embraced Judaism, having witnessed the slaughter of the Assyrian army before Jerusalem, and seeing that the Holy City was under the protection of God. (2 Kings xix. 35; Gittin, 57 *b*.)

Upper Tarnegola, above Cæsarea, תרנגולה עילא דלמעלה מן קסרין (Targum Jonathan to Num. xxxiv. 9, 10; Yerushalmi Shebiith, chap. vi.; Yerushalmi Demai, ii.) Pliny, v. 19, mentions Zarephta and Ornithon, meaning, undoubtedly, Zarephath and Tarnegola, Ornis in Greek being synonymous with the Hebrew Geber, and Chaldean Tarnegol = cock. The Gabara often mentioned by Josephus, Gabara and Gischala (Life of Josephus, page 525), is no doubt the same place. It is certain that this place had an idol image of a cock, which was worshipped here, דווקנים דתרנגולה "the image of the cock" (Jonathan to Num. xxxiv. 9, 10); farther, that the Nergal נרגל mentioned in 2 Kings xvii. 30, which was represented under the image of a cock (see Sanhedrin, 63 *b*), was the idol of the Cutheans, who were properly of Zidonian descent, as they themselves asserted, in their letter to Antiochus (Jos., Antiq., book xiii. chap. xvii.); that this worship was peculiar to the Zidonians, wherefore they had a city dedicated to it in their territory, to wit, the town of Tarnegola, and that their descendants, the Cutheans, worshipped the same idol in Judæa, after their emigration thither. The exact position of this ancient town is not known; I however heard from the Bedouins and Arabs, that they knew the name of Gabara by tradition, and that it is said to have been situated northwest from Banias, not far from the valley Wady Kasmeia (Leontes). This assertion has a great deal of probability to recommend it, since this position will place Tarnegola north of Banias, the former Cæsarea Philippi, which would therefore explain the definition, Tarnegola above Kisrin (Cæsarea). The same definition is given by Jonathan to the word דן Dan, in Gen. xiv. 14, דן דקיסריון "Dan of Kisarion," which proves clearly that already in the time of Jonathan, Dan or Banias was defined by styling it Kisarion, i. e. Cæsarea.* In Pesiktah Rabbethi, chap. iii., there is spoken of, R. Eleazar, of סרונגלה Serongala, which must be incorrect, and should read Tarnegola, or R. Eleazar, a native of this place; and this mention in this late book proves that this name must have been known at a later period than the Talmud.

In Yerushalmi Demai, ii., the following names are mentioned, Yedut, &c., to Chamas.

Yedut יעדוט is probably the village Djudeidé = Yudeidé, 1½ English miles northwest from Kefr Jasif. I deem it to be the town Gedud = Djedud (by changing G into Dj), mentioned in Negaim, chap. vi. 94. Also, 3 English miles west of Chaspeia, there is a village Judeta. In the vicinity of Zidon there is a mount called Djebl Djudud, similar to Gedud or Gedut. This mount is much visited by Christian pilgrims. There is pointed out the grave of Aholiab son of Achisamach, of the tribe of Dan. (Exodus xxxi. 6.)

Susita סוסיתא of Bereshith Rabbah, chap. xxxi. and

* It is also probably identical with the Kisrin in Upper Galilee, mentioned in Sukkah, 27 *b*.

xxxvii., "from Susita to Tiberias," of Echa Rabbathi to chap. i. 17, "Susita, for the most part a heathenish town (as said in Yerushalmi Rosh Hashanah, ii.), was always at enmity with the Jewish inhabitants of Tiberias." It appears from Pesiktah Rabbethi that Susita was near Geder. In Yerushalmi Shebiith, vi., it is said that "the land of Tob," of Judges xi. 3, is Susita. Literally the meaning of the word is, "the horseman's town," from Sus סוס horse. Josephus calls the place Chephus or Chephon, perhaps derived in some manner from the Greek Hippos, also denoting horse. There can be no doubt but that this name is also used in the Talmudical writings; for instance, in Megillah, 24 *b*, בני חיפני וביישני "the men of Chephon and Beth-Shean." Bereshith Rabbah to Vayechi has Rabbi Isaac of Chefinos. The place is at present unknown, but it must have been on the southeastern shore of Lake Chinnereth.

Nob נוב is the village Naba, 1 mile south from Usa; and probably identical with Niphapha, mentioned in the Life of Josephus.

Chaspeya חספיא has already been spoken of in the description of the Lebanon.

Kefar Zemach כפר צמח, is the present village Semach, on the southeast point of the Lake Chinnereth. The earth hereabout contains some gypsum (sulphate of lime), and they make here remarkably fine water-jugs.

Bazath בצת is the village Baza north of Akko.

Rosh Mé ראש מי. This I suppose to be the village Ras el Ain, "the Spring Head," equal to Rosh Mé, "the Water Head," 2 miles south from Sur. But it nevertheless seems more correct to seek for its site at the village Mes, on the road from Banias to Chaspeya.

Mazi מזי, is perhaps the village Ramis, 5 miles southwest from Kedes.

Berin ברין is the village Beroï, between Medjdl al Krum and Akko.

Ammon אמון, see above, under Chammon.

Karaka debar Hazareg, or debar Sanagera, כרכה דבר הזרג also in several passages כרכה רבה דבר סנגרא, which, as has been already stated in Chapter I., is undoubtedly the present destroyed city Kallat al Sani, 4 English miles south from Zafed, the vicinity of which is still called Shaghur, which has an evident resemblance to Sanagera.

Chamas חמס is without doubt the village Chamsin, 2 miles east from Chezib. Near this place flows a little stream, which falls into the sea south of Chezib; I suppose this to be the Nahar Deroma Shel Chezib נהר דרומה של כזיב of Tosephtah Shebiith, iv.: "The south river of Chezib."

Kefar Zumaria כפר צומריא of Toseph. Shebiith, iv., is the village Simuriéh, 3 English miles north from Akko. In some copies of this Tosephtah, the reading is Kefar Zemach.

Kefar Signah in the valley כפר סיגנה בבקעה of Menachoth, 86 *b*, probably the village Sagan, in a valley northwest from Gish-Chalab, and is in all likelihood identical with the Sagani of Jos., Bell. Jud., b. iv., chap. i., and the Como-Sagana of the Life of Josephus.

Arab ערב is the village Arabi, 10 English miles east from Cabul, and is probably the place referred to in 2 Sam. xxiii. 31. There is also a village of the same name, 3 miles northwest of Nablus, the sheich of which had for several years lately a war with the sheich of Nablus; for the former was the so-called Mudier, i. e. head chief, over Nablus and its vicinity at the time of Abraim Pacha, but was deposed when the country came again under the government of the Sultan of Constantinople, and had thus to quit Nablus, and became therefore a deadly enemy of the sheich who was put in his place; the consequence was a war between these chiefs, so that it was a long time impossible to travel in that neighbourhood. It appears from Yerushalmi Sabbath, chap. xvi., that our Arab was in Galilee, wherefore I hold it to be the first-named Arabi, and not the one near Nablus (Shechem in Ephraim).

In these parts of Palestine are likewise situated Dan, Laish, Banias or Panias (Talmudicé Pamais) דן ליש בניאס פמאיס. I have already treated of these names. 4 English miles west from Banias, they point out some ruins, which are said to be those of Dan or Laish. Josephus also states that this was the distance between Dan and Banias. In Banias, they point out the grave of the prophet Ido, and over it stands a large Butum (Sycamore?) tree; also the grave of Shebuel, son of Gershom, son of Moses, and a cavern in which is the sepulchre of Abayé and Raba. About 3 mill north of Banias, there is a mount, on which is an old building having several cupolas. There is a tradition that the "covenant between the pieces" with Abraham (Gen. xv. 9) was made on this spot; the Arabs call it Meshhad al Tir, i. e. the covenant or testimony of the bird (turtle-dove?), in reference to the "bird" referred to, ibid. v. 10.

Zeredah צרדה. North of the just-named mount, on the road to Chaspeya, is the village Chamam, 3 miles west from which is the village Zarada. They point out here the grave of José ben Joëzer, of Zeradah. (Aboth i. § 4.)

Barthotha ברתותא. The ruins of this place are found not far from Chamam. Here is shown the grave of Rabbi Eliezer, of Barthotha. (Orla i. § 4.)

Abel, or Abel Beth-Maachah אבל אבל בית מעכה of 2 Samuel xx. 15, and 1 Kings xv. 20; but in 2 Chronicles xvi. 4, it is called Abel Mayim* אבל מים. The dis-

* It is extremely surprising that the Targum of Rabbi Joseph to the passage cited from 2 Chronicles, translates Abel Mayim with "Abel Mimaarab," Abel at the west; whence it must be inferred that he read מִיָּם Miyam, of the west, instead of מַיִם Mayim, water.

trict of Maachah, which lay beyond Jordan, extended to this place. (See above, page 33). About 14 miles north fromLake Semechonitis, on the road to Chaspeya, is the village Abil; not far from it is another village Abel al Kamach, and still another Abel al Krum, which is supposed, though erroneously, to be Abel Keramin (of the vineyards) of Judges xi. 33. I therefore believe that the above Abil is identical with Abel Beth-Maachah; and since it is near the Wady Chaspeya it is termed Abel of the Water. As this district has three towns, all called Abel, it appears to me to be that called in Vayikra Rabbah xvii. "Abelim" האבלים "The Abels." It also appears that there must have been an Abel not far from Zippori, since it is said in Erubin, 87 *a*, "An aqueduct led from Abel to Zippori;" but it is difficult to believe that the modern village Abilin, 6 English miles northwest from Sifuri should be meant here.*

Haberim הברים of 2 Samuel xx. 14, not far from Abel Beth-Maachah. We find that in that vicinity, many places were known as Biri, Beeroth, Birya. Josephus says: "Between Kedes and the Sea Semechonitis, is the town of Biri." Again, he says, that Joshua conquered the princes of Canaan, near the town Berote, near the Sea Semechonitis. In Yerushalmi Shebiith v. is named a town of Birya near Tafné, i. e. Daphné. Wherefore I am inclined to think that this neighbourhood was termed the Berim, i. e. the plural form of Ber, or the district of the various cities of Bir, or Ber, as above with Abelim.

* In Bereshith Rabbah, chap. xxxiii., it is said: "Three springs of Palestine and vicinity, remained not closed up after the flood (Gen. viii. 2). The springs at Tiberias, Abeleni, and the one of the Jordan, issuing from the cave at Pamais." The spring of Abeleni is unknown to me; but in Sanhedrin, 108 *a*, the reading is Geder, Tiberias, and the large spring of Biryam, not far from Euphrates. (See farther, article Biryam.) All these three are hot springs; and, therefore, the reading of Talmud Sanhedrin is no doubt correct, but not that stating Abeleni and Pamais.

Kefar Likitia כפר לקיטיא of Echa Rabbethi to chap. i. 16. We may discover a trace of this name in that of the ruins known as Tell Kati, which are held to be those of Dan, or Laish.

Kefar Kurenis כפר קוריינים, of Vayikra Rabbah, xvii., (named Kefar Karnaim כפר קרנים in Ruth Rabbethi and Pesiktah Rabbethi, xvii., which is an incorrect reading) "they went out from Kefar Kurenis and passed through the whole of Abelim," &c., which is in the neighbourhood, as said, of Abel Beth-Maachah. Northwest from this district, on the other side of the Wady Chasmeia, is a stream named Nahr Zaherani, which falls south of Saida into the sea. There is also a village called Dar Zaherani; and as Z is often exchanged for K, I take this name to be put for Kaherani, or our Kefar Kurenis.

Yarchi ירחי of Baba Mezia, 85 *b*, "Samuel Yarchinai" (of Yarchi) is the modern village Yarchi, west of Medjdl al Krum.

THE POSITION OF THE TERRITORIES OF NAPHTALI AND ASHER.

I have stated already that the Lake Chinnereth belonged both to Naphtali and Zebulun. Tanchum was on the frontier between both tribes; thence the boundary line of Naphtali ran northward along Jordan, the Lake Semechonitis, and Dan, or Laish; thence westward to the land of Asher, (which, therefore, was west of Naphtali); then the line ran east of Gish, between Dama, i. e. Adama, which belonged to Naphtali, and Gish; thence south to Shafamer, which was in Zebulun; thence the eastern boundary line ran north of Ramin to Tanchum and Lake Chinnereth.

Asher's territory was west of Naphtali, and had, therefore, nearly the whole coast of the Mediterranean from Carmel to Zidon, only that Zebulun had a narrow strip on the sea-coast, as already stated above. To the south, Asher extended, in part, to the Merdj Aben Amer (the Valley of Jezreel), to the southeast of Cheipha, where it touched on Menasseh (Joshua xvii. 10), and even on Issachar, as has been stated in the definition of the boundary of that tribe.

Josephus states that Naphtali possessed Upper Galilee, up to Mount Lebanon and the sources of the Jordan; Asher, the valley of Mount Carmel, as far as Zidon.

But it is impossible at present to designate with absolute correctness the precise boundary lines of every tribe; since the same were not very strictly defined, and since many places and towns were held in common, and are to be considered frequently as belonging to one and then to the other tribe, as I have already clearly proved.

In concluding this chapter, I must explain a Mishna of Maaser Sheni, chap. v., § 2.

The fourth year's produce of the vineyard (as also of trees), as stated in Leviticus xix. 24, could not be redeemed for money, like the second tithe (Deut. xiv. 25); but had to be carried to Jerusalem, if it had been grown within a day's journey from the Holy City. Now the question arises, "Which are the points defining this distance?" The answer is "Ailath to the south; Akraba to the north; Lod to the west, and the Jordan to the east." In Beza, 5 *a*, it is given incorrectly, "Ailath north, and Akraba south," and ought to be corrected as above. I was myself a long time unable to decipher what is meant by Ailath, notwithstanding my indefatigable inquiries, as I could not find either in our or other literature or tradition any place of this name situated a day's journey north of Jerusalem; till at length it struck me, and this quite correctly, that it could mean no other than Eleutheropolis, and should stand for Ailath-polis, with an interpolated ר R, or Ailather-polis. Thus, for example, a little river, north of Trablus (Tripoli), is called in Arabic Aluut, but in the western languages Eleuther, with *r* superadded. I doubt not that אילת Ailath, (or Elath?) is an abbreviation for אילתרפולים Ailetheropolis or "city of freedom." Wherefore it is called in Bereshith Rabbah החורי "the free" (Gen. xiv. 6), which is synonymous with its Greek appellation, and is also identical with the modern Beth-Djibrin (which see).

Akraba is the Akrabathena often mentioned by Josephus; even at this day there are ruins, about 6 miles east from Chavara (Beth-Horon), called Akrabéh.

I would merely remark that we cannot take the direction of these places as absolutely due south and west, since Ailath is southwest, and Lod northwest from Jerusalem, whereas Akraba is almost due north, say north by east. The distance also is not quite alike to all four points from Jerusalem: to the Jordan it is about 25, to Akraba 32, to Lod 22, and likewise to Beth-Djibrin 22 English miles.

CHAPTER IV.

PALESTINE BEYOND JORDAN.

NATURE OF THE COUNTRY IN GENERAL.

I HAVE already stated in the second chapter that the Djebl Heish was the most northeasterly point of the tribes to the west of Jordan, as it is the most northwestern for those on the east side of the same river. From the foot of this mountain there extends to the eastward a large elevated plain to the district of Hauran. On this table land, south of the Jarmuch, ירמוך which falls into the Jordan in an eastern direction from Mount Tabor, commence the mountains of Gilead. South of this range there is another elevated plain, which touches to the west on the valley of the Jordan, to the east on the desert of Arabia, and to the south on the Arnon or Wady el Modjeb. This plateau, however, extends yet farther south to Al Kerak (Kir Moäb); but here begins a high mountainous country, extending to the Wady Ahsa, which falls into the southeast point of the Dead Sea. There commences the Djebl* Seïr (Mount Seir הר שעיר), also called Sarra, which extends to the Red Sea at Akabé, situated on the eastern termination of the same.

Josephus calls the territory east of Jordan by the general name of Peræa.

* This name Djebl as denoting Mount Seir is already used by Jonathan; for in Deut. i. 2, he translates הר שעיר with טורא דגבלא—the mount of Gebla, closely allied to the Arabic Djebl.

The following are the countries situated east of Jordan and on the borders of Palestine:

EDOM; MOAB; AMMON; MEDIAN AND KENI; BASHAN; GESHUR; MAACHAH, ARGOB, AND AMALEK.

EDOM אדום

Is situated south and southeast of Palestine, and extended to the Red Sea.* In the times of the Romans it was called Petræa, because the capital, the large city of Sela (i. e. Rock), was also called Petra (Stone).

I will now mention the names of the yet known remains and vestiges of the former towns of this country:

Sela סלע, or the Jokteël of 2 Kings xiv. 7, is situated about 3 English miles east from Mount Hor, the so-called Djebl Hauran, in a narrow valley called Wady Musa, 2½ miles in circumference, and enclosed between uncommonly high rocky cliffs. A narrow pass, a mile in length, but scarcely wide enough for a loaded camel to get through, brings us from the Arabah (see chapter second, article District of Jordan) into this valley. This rocky gorge, consisting of immense masses of rock, seems to have been formed by the hands of nature, and not by means of human labour. A little stream comes down from the cliffs, and passing through this gorge, enters the Arabah. Within these rocky walls, which are 500 to 600 feet in height, are found ruins of houses, palaces, temples, theatres, which are as old as the time of the Edumeans themselves or that of the Romans; and there are discovered in every direction heaps of stone, marble columns, uprooted pillars, &c.; and

* It appears that at a later period the Edomites moved and spread themselves farther to the north; for we find them in the vicinity of the Euphrates, as we are told in Bereshith Rabbah, chap. lxxiv.: "When David went to Aram Naharayim and Aram Zoba to war, he encountered on the way Edomites and Moabites." It is farther said in the work cited, chap. lxxv., "The Edomites were afraid of the Barbarians and Germanians." Germania is a district in Asia Minor, as I shall prove in another part of the book. (Is it perhaps Caramania?)

in the walls also there are found houses, columns, graves, and temples, hewn out of the rock, and though they have existed already in all probability far more than a thousand years, everything looks as bright and clear as though it had been only the work of modern times.

The prophet Obadiah no doubt alluded to the strong position and the security of Edom, when he said, "The pride of thy heart hath deceived thee, thou that dwellest in the clefts of the rock, whose habitation is high," &c. (verse 3).

The Arabs call this country Gabal, which some suppose is derived from Obal (Gen. x. 28), who is said to have settled here, and first corrupted into Abal, and then Gabal.

Buz בוז (Jer. xxv. 23). There is a village south of Petra, called Basta, which is supposed to be the ancient Buz.

Bozrah בצרה (Gen. xxxiv. 33; Isaiah xxxiv. 6; Jer. xlix. 13; Amos i. 12), was anciently one of the principal cities of Edom. At present there is left but an old castle, called Bezeira, about 30 miles north from Petra, situated on a mountain; near it are some large ruins. A town of the same name was also to be met with in the district of Hauran.

Teman תימן (Gen. xxxvi. 11, 15; Jer. xlix. 7, 20; Amos i. 12; Obad. i. 9; Job ii. 11), is said to be the present large village Maän, situated about 5 miles east-southeast from Petra, on the road which the pilgrims follow from Damascus to Mekka. In its environs are many handsome fields and gardens. (See also Tosephtah Sanhedrin, chap. xii., and Taanith, iii., § 7, Rabbi Shimon of Teman.) But to me it appears more probable that Maän is the

Maön מעון of 1 Chron. iv. 41, and 2 Chron. xxvi. 7; "the Meünim" (English version Mehunims, incorrect), since this town or district appears to have been in Al Gor. (See above, "The Valley of Jordan.")

Tophel תפל, of Deut. i. 1, is probably the small town Tafila, 6 English miles north of Bezeira.

Dedan דדן, of Ezek. xxv. 43, is the village Dehana, 5 miles south-southwest from Bezeira.

Ezion Gaber עציון גבר of Deut. ii. 8, is the modern small town of Akaba, on the eastern termination of the Red Sea.* It has a small castle. Josephus (Antiq., book viii., § 2), calls the place Birinzi.

Elath אילת (ibid.) East of Akaba are found some ruins, which are called Eila. In the times of the Romans, the Red Sea was called the Elanitic Gulf.

Hor Hahar, the Mount Hor הר ההר (Num. xx. 25), is the high mount Djebl Harun†, i. e. Aaron's Mount, about 8 English miles west from Maän; there is a convent on it. In a cave of this mount is the supposed grave of Aaron. The walls of the cave are covered with inscriptions, which appear to be Hebrew, but written so indistinctly and unintelligibly that their contents cannot be guessed at or deciphered.

About 6 English miles north-northwest of Tafila is a small town called Chanziri, celebrated for the battle which Abraim Pacha fought there in the year 5594 (1834), with

* It is curious and surprising that the inhabitants of Aden, in the southern part of Arabia, not far from the straits of Bab al Mandab, where the Red unites with the Persian Sea, suppose this town to be Ezion Gaber, and that they write in their contracts עציון גבר דמתקרא ערן "Ezion Gaber, which is called Aden." There can be no good foundation for this traditional assumption of the identity of these two cities, since the Israelites never entered Arabia (Yemen) on their journey from Egypt to Palestine.

† There is a chain of mountains running almost uninterruptedly from this Djebl Harun to the Dead Sea and the country of Moab; so that the whole may be regarded as one uncommonly long range. This will explain an obscure passage of Siphri to Deut. xxxiv.: "This mount had four names, the Mount of Abarim, Nebo, Hor, and Pisgah,"—not that they are the selfsame elevation, but various peaks, all belonging to the same chain.

the Bedouins of that vicinity, and where he was defeated by them, although he conquered them at a later period.

I wish in this place to explain several names which occur in the itinerary of the Israelites through the desert, which will be the more interesting, as I have succeeded in discovering several things which remained unknown to other travellers.

Etham אית‎ם (Exod. xiii. 20), is that part of the desert which lies north of the Red Sea, near Suez, and is called at the present day Ethia = Etham.

Baal-Zephon בעל צפון (ibid. xiv. 2). Not far from Suweis (Suez), at a distance of 1 mile to the north thereof, is the village Tell Kalsum (the Red Sea being called in Arabic Bachr al Kalsum), near which is a place called Bir Zufis, which evidently has a strong resemblance to Zephon.

Marah מרה (Exod. xv. 23). At a distance of two days' caravan journey, about 25 English miles, south of Suez, on the shore of the Red Sea, is found a spring, the water of which is bright and clear, but exceedingly bitter. It is called En Chavara, and supposed identical with Marah, i. e. "bitter."

Elim אלים (Exod. xv. 27). One day's caravan journey south of En Chavara, on the sea-shore, is a valley called Wady Taibé, whence a rocky headland runs into the sea, which bears the name Ras Zelima, in which I think to discover a strong resemblance to Elima, or Elim; wherefore we may assume it to have been situated in Wady Taibé.

Sinai, Choreb סיני חורב (Exod. xix. 11). Three days' journey southeast from Wady Taibé is the large mountain range of Djebl Tor. Here are found two mounts, of which one is about 6000, the other about 7000 feet above the level of the sea. At the foot of the latter, to the south, is a large and broad plain. One of these mounts is supposed to be the celebrated Sinai or Horeb; and the probability is in favour of the latter, because it must have been in the large plain "where Israel encamped opposite to the mount." (Exod. xix. 2.)

Paran פרן (Num. x. 12), is no doubt the Wady Phiran, where formerly the town of Pharan stood; this valley is to the west of Elath, opposite to Djebl Serbal. Nevertheless it is certain that the wilderness of Paran must have extended much farther than this in a northern direction, since we read in Numbers xii. 16, "They removed from Hazeroth (Chazeroth), and encamped in the wilderness of Paran;" and ibid. xxxiii. 18 it says: "They removed from Hazeroth and encamped at Rithmah," which consequently must have been in the wilderness of Paran, which then must have extended as far as Wady Rithimath (see farther, article Rithmah). Josephus, Bell. Jud., book iv. chap. ix., even asserts that the desert of Paran extended to the neighbourhood of the Dead Sea.

Di-Zahab די זהב (Deut. i. 1), is undoubtedly the village Djab, the Hebrew Zahab, not far from the shore of the eastern arm of the Red Sea, in an eastern direction, opposite to the Djebl Tor.

Rithmah רתמה (Num. xxxiii. 18). About a half day's journey south from Wady Kiseima (see Azmon, chap. i.), is found a valley calley Wady Rithimath. *Rothem* literally means a Broom-bush; hence, Rithmah, the country of the Broom-shrub; and there actually grow many broom-bushes near the Wady Rithimath. It appears probable, as Rashi already said, that Rithmah is identical with Kadesh-Barnea, and the distance between Wady Gaian (Kadesh-Barnea) and Wady Rithimath is actually quite small.

Chazeroth חצרות (ibid. 17), is undoubtedly identical with the spring called En al Chuteroth, about a half day's journey distant from Wady Rithimath, in an eastern direction. The change of Z and T is easily accounted for.

Kibroth-Hataavah קברות התאוה (ibid. 16). The celebrated Saadiah translates this name in his Arabic version with Kabur al Shahava "the grave of desire." One day's journey to the south-southeast from the En al Chuteroth, is another spring named En al Shahava, "the spring of desire;" which leaves no doubt of the identity of the place.

Moseroth or Moserah מסרות מסרה (ibid. 30, and Deut. x. 6), undoubtedly identical with the Wady Muzera, one day's journey south from Wady Rithimath.

Luz לוז of Judges i. 26. One mile south from Wady Muzera, and almost connected with it, is the Wady Luzan. It is possible that this was the Luz in the land of the Hittites; and it appears from Zohar to Terumah, fol. 269, that this town of Luz was situated beyond Palestine proper.

Béné-Jaakon בני יעקן (Num. xxxiii. 31). 10 English miles south from Wady Muzera is the Wady Anaka, and in its vicinity a mount of the same name, which bears an evident similarity to Jaakan, by transposition of the *n* and *k*.

Chor-Hagiddgad or Gudgodah חר הגדגד (ibid. 32) and גדגדה (Deut. x. 7) is undoubtedly the Wady al Gudhagid, one day's journey from the former Wady Anaka.

Jotbathah or Jotbath יטבתה יטבת (Num. xxxiii. 32) is very probably the Wady Taibé, which is on the western shore of the northern point of the Red Sea, opposite to Akaba.

Abron עברון (ibid. 34). I am inclined to believe that this name signifies "ferry," being derived from עבר, "to pass over," or the place of passing from the western shore of the Red Sea to the eastern, since Jotbath was on the former and Ezion-Gaber on the latter side of the Gulf of Elath. It is possible that the people either actually crossed this arm of the sea, or that it was a station whence the passage was usually made by other travellers.

Kadesh, En-Mishpat קדש עין משפט (ibid. 36, Gen. xiv. 7). About 10 English miles south from Petra, is found a large and important spring, which the Bedouins call En al Sedaka = Zedakah, i. e. the Spring of Justice, and is unquestionably the ancient En-Mishpat, since Zedakah and Mishpat are often synonymous, meaning *justice, equity, rectitude.* This Kadesh is also called Rekem, as in Onkelos to Genesis xiv. 7, and Numbers xx. 1; so also in Mishna Gittin, chap. i., § 2, "From Rekem in the east." Now this Rekem cannot be the same stated by Rabbi Gamliel in § 1, "From Rekem and Chagra," which is Kadesh-Barnea in Rekam-Gaia, since this is in the south of Palestine, and not in the east, wherefore "Rekem in the east" must be Kadesh, En-Mishpat. This name of Rekem, as given to this Arab town, called by the Greeks Petra, is derived, as Josephus states in his Antiquities, book iv. chap. vii., from Rekem, the prince of Midiam (Num. xxxi. 8). And it is actually the case that this spring is but 10 miles distant from Petra, whence it is then clear that the environs thereof were called Rekem.*

* It is, therefore, an erroneous assumption of several eminent writers to consider Kadesh-Barnea as identical with Kadesh, En-Mishpat; since I have sufficiently proved that the former is the modern Wady Gaian, and the latter without any doubt, the En al Sedaka, which is at a very great distance from Wady Gaian. Even the learned Abn Ezra makes this mistake in his commentary to Numbers xx. i.; and the celebrated Rashi to Deuteronomy i. 46, asserts the same and brings a proof from the book *Seder Olam*, from which it appears that the Israelites were in the fortieth year of their pilgrimage at Kadesh-Barnea, which is called in Scripture En-Mishpat, and that, consequently, both names designate the same place. But I did not find in Seder Olam, in the passage cited, the two words וחזרו לקדש "And they returned to Kadesh," and are merely an inference of Rashi, as nothing is said by Seder Olam to establish the identity of the two Kadesh of Deuteronomy i. 2, 19, and ibid. 46. In fact, Rashi himself revokes his opinion, since he says to Numbers xxxii. 8, "There were two Kadesh."

The above is all which I could trace out of the names mentioned in the route of the Israelites through the desert; but it is at present impossible to explain the actual relation of these encampments, since some of the distances are but from seven to ten miles, whereas others are from twenty to thirty. Of ten encampments from Rithmah to Moseroth (Num. xxxiii. 19–30), I could not find the least trace; but I believe that they must have been in the large, very stony, and mountainous desert of Azazimath, which extends eastward from Wady Rithimath and Wady Mazura, to the vicinity of Mount Madura, and is actually the most naked and impassable desert of the whole surrounding country.

Nebajoth נביות (Gen. xxv. 13). Josephus calls the inhabitants of the land of Nebajoth "Arabs," and says their territory extended from the Red Sea to the Euphrates. In 1 Macc. v. 24, 25, and ix. 35, they are styled "the inhabitants of the east side of Jordan." But, as a rule, it is impossible to give with any certainty an accurate description, or to assign the true position of the territories of nomadic nations, since they never have any settled home, and move about at pleasure within a wide range.

Kedar קדר (ibid. and Jer. xlix. 28). It is also impossible to state the exact position of the country of this nomadic tribe. It is mentioned in connexion with Nebajoth, and the kingdom of Hazor. It must therefore have been in the eastern desert of Arabia, and extended, like the former, from the Red Sea up to the Babylonian territory.

Jishbak ישבק (Gen. xxv. 2). It is probable that this tribe inhabited the country around the mount and village of Shobek, which are about 6 miles to the north of Petra.

Masrekah משרקה (Gen. xxxvi. 26). There is, 8 miles south from Petra, a town called En Masrak, which is possibly the Masrekah of Scripture.

MOAB מואב

Was situated to the northeast of Edom, and extended from the modern Wady Ahsa, which has a northwestern course, and falls into the southeastern point of the Dead Sea, to the Wady Modjeb (the Arnon of the Bible). The present name of the country is Belad al Kerak, and is even now a fruitful country (Isa. xvi. 9, 10). Especially the wheat produced here is very excellent, and is carried in considerable quantities to Jerusalem for sale. The names of the localities of Moab known at present are the following:

Ar Moäb ער מואב (Num. xxi. 28, and Deut. ii. 29), was also called Rabbath Moab, that is, Rabbah belonging to Moab, and in the time of the Greek and Roman supremacy Areopolis, is at present the village Rabba, 15 miles north from Al Kerak (which see). There are found close to it ruins, which measure more than a mile in circumference.

Kir Moab קיר מואב (Jerai. xv. 1), is the present town Al Kerak, which is situated opposite to the southeast termination of the Dead Sea. It is the largest town in the whole vicinity, and is well fortified, and built on high rocks, in front of a deep and narrow valley, which some suppose to be the valley of the stream Zered, which falls into the Dead Sea. It is connected with a very strong fort, which I suppose to be the Mizpeh Moab of 1 Sam. xxii. 3. In the year 5594 (1834), when the Arabs and Bedouins of this neighbourhood had rebelled against Abraim Pacha, they took the fort through treachery and deception, and slaughtered many of the garrison; but some time after, the rebellion was quelled, and the Arabs were sufficiently punished and humbled. The Pacha was even determined to demolish and destroy the fort; but he could not succeed, since it is, so to say, a large boulder of rock, a solid mass of stone. It can be seen, by means of a spy-glass, even at Jerusalem, on a clear day. It would appear that Kerak was formerly inhabited by Jews, since one can observe Hebrew inscriptions on the stones of several houses.

One and a half miles north from Kerak, the Wady Sufsaf, a small river, falls into the Dead Sea. I have scarcely a doubt but that this is the "Willow River" נחל הערבה of Isa. xv. 7, and Amos vi. 14, since Sufsaf in Arabic signifies willow; hence it is literally the same as Nachal Ha'-arabah, Willow River. (See Sukkah, chap. iii., § 3.)

Sela סלע (Isa. xvi. 1). North of the Wady al Ahsa is a village called Al Pietra, a name probably of Roman derivation. It is unquestionably the just-named Sela (rock, Petra), of Moäb.

Eglaim אגלים (ibid. xv. 8), is the village Agala, 7 miles south of Ar.

Ham הם (Gen. xiv. 5). We may perhaps trace this name in that of the village Humeimath, situated 1 mile north of Ar.

Besides the above, I shall speak of other names in the territory of Moab when treating of the towns of Reuben and Gad.

AMMON עמון

Extended from Arnon to Jabbok, the Wady Zurka of modern times. In Deut. ii. 37, we read: "Only unto the land of the children of Ammon thou camest not, unto any place on the river Jabbok, nor unto the cities of the mountains," &c. I suppose this mountain of Ammon to be the one which extends to the south of Hauran, and I shall speak at length of it when discussing the latter range. We can find but extremely few vestiges of the ancient names of places in the land of the Ammonites, and I shall describe

Rabbah or Rabbath Ammon, the largest town of the country, when discussing the cities of Gad.

MIDIAN מדין.

It is difficult to designate exactly the land of the Midianites, since we find traces of this people in many places. Josephus says, that Moses came, in his flight from Egypt, to the city of Midian, on the shores of the Red Sea, which was so called from Medan, the son of Abraham. And even at the present day there is a village to the south of Akaba called Median. We find the hordes of Midian came as far as Gazza (Judges vi. 4), into the land of Moab (Gen. xxxvi. 35, and Num. xxv. 6); in the land of the Amorites (Joshua xiii. 21), and in Edom, to wit, Rekem near Petra. See Kadesh, En-Mishpat, page 214.

Descendants from the Midianites were

THE KENITES קני

Of Judges iv. 11; 2 Kings x. 9; and 1 Chron. ii. 55. They were all descendants of Jethro, the father-in-law of Moses (see farther, art. "Children of Rachab"). We find also Kenites who did not belong to the house of Israel, who, to distinguish them from the former, are called Shalmaii, as it is given in Onkelos and Jonathan to Num. xxiv. 21, and Gen. xv. 19. The Kenites spoken of in 1 Sam. xxvii. 10, and xxx. 29, belonged probably to the first class, that is, to those adopted among the Israelites.

AMALEK עמלק.

The chief residence of this tribe must have been on the mountain of Seïr, as is plainly told in 1 Chron. iv. 42; as also in Gen. xiv. 7,* consequently not far from Petra. It is likewise said in 1 Sam. xv. 7, "And Saul smote the Amalekites from Havilah till thou comest to Shur, that

* But here it is said, "the whole field of the Amalekite," which would denote a low and level country.—TRANSLATOR.

is over against Egypt," and also in 1 Kings xi. 16 (see Baba Bathra, fol. 21 *b*), that Amalek* was embraced in the territory of Edom. Nevertheless we can trace it in a more northerly direction; for instance, the Mount Amalek in the land of Ephraim (Judges xii. 15). West of Kirja, Kirjath-Jearim, is even to this day a district called Bné Amlek; and even a Mount Seïr is spoken of in Joshua xv. 10. Not far from Djifni (see עפני Ophni or Benjamin), north of Ramla, is the village Amalek. The Armenians are usually called by the Eastern Jews Amalekim, perhaps owing to a tradition that they settled in the north, where the present Armenians are found. Nay, we find Amalekites even in Persia, since Haman was an Agagite, which means a descendant from Amalek; and according to the Second Targum to the Book of Esther, Haman was a native of India, but an Amalekite by descent; for it says to chap. viii. 13 המן בר המדתא מהנד״א הוה ומן זרעי׳ דבית עמלק הוה "Haman the son of Hamdatha was from India, and was also from the descendants of the house of Amalek." Josephus says, the possessions of Amalek were on the mountain of Seïr, and in the vicinity of the Arabian Petra.

BASHAN בשן.

We understand under the general term Bashan, the following districts: Geshur, Maachah, Argob, Salchah, Golan, as appears from Deut. iii. 8–14, and 1 Kings iv. 13.

Onkelos and Jonathan render Bashan with Mathnan מתנן (see Joshua xii. 4), and the Arabic version of Rabbenu Saadiah has instead of this Al Bathni.

Argob is rendered by Onkelos with פלך טרכונא "the District of Tarchona;" by Jonathan with טרגונא Targona; by Targum Yerushalmi with אטרכונא Atarchuna; and by Saadiah with Al Chut Modjeb.

* It was a tribe of the great Idumean nation.—TRANSLATOR.

Maachah is rendered by Onkelos and Jonathan with אפקירוס Aphkeros, and Geshur and Maachach with Korvé and Antikeros by Jonathan.

Salchah is given by Jonathan with סלווקיא Salwakia.

Josephus, in his Ant. b. xiii. chap. xv., and in his Bell. Jud., b. i., chap. iv., says that Golan and Seleucia are in the vicinity of Lake Semechonitis; in another place he styles Og, King of Bashan, "King of Gaulonitis and Gilead." He also says, in Bell. Jud., b. ii., chap. vi., that the Emperor Augustus gave to one of Herod's sons, Antipas, the land of Perea and Galilee, and to the other, Philip, Batanea, Trachonitis, and Auranitis. He also says that Batanea was next to Trachonitis.

I will therefore now proceed to explain the nature and position of this district, and divide it into five parts.

1. Golan גולן, the modern Djulun, extends from the southern shore of the Lake Chinnereth to Banias; in this district lay the canton of Argob חבל הארגב, in which were sixty cities fortified with high walls, &c. (Deut. iii. 4, 5). Even up to the present time there are found here uncommonly many, near three hundred, ruins of former towns, forts, towers, villages, theatres, and temples, both from the most ancient period when the Israelites yet dwelt there, and that of the dominion of the Greeks and Romans. No wood is found in the whole district; everything is built of hard basaltic rocks, the cutting of which is exceedingly difficult.* You scarcely find a trace of wood anywhere; even the bolts of the houses and the nails are made of

* In Prov. xxvi. 28, it says, ופה חלק יעשה מדחה "and a flattering mouth worketh ruin;" here Jonathan translates Midcheh with Tarchenutha. Perhaps the true meaning of this word is "a laborious, profitless striving," which one has, so to say, to expect in dressing basaltic rocks, literally a repulsion, a rebounding, and a flying off, like ונדחה ידו "And his hand glideth off" ("fetcheth a stroke," English version); whence this part of Bashan is called Terachona, "the hardstone land."

basaltic stone. It is at present but little inhabited, and the inhabitants that are there, live in the ruins. Here were the villages of Jaïr חות יאיר the possessions of Judah which bordered on Naphtali (Joshua xix. 34). Here also was the city of refuge, Golan (Deut. iv. 43). According to Talmud Makkoth, 9 *a*, it was situated just opposite Kedesh in the mountain of Naphtali, likewise a city of refuge, in a due eastern direction. But on the spot thus indicated, now called Tell Hara, I could find no trace whatever of the city of Golan.

2. Jetur, at present called Djedur, and formerly Ituræa, lies to the east of Djulun, and extends northwardly up to the district of Damascus, and to the northwest to the mountain of Hermon. The name of Jetur was probably derived from the son of Ishmael, mentioned in Genesis xxv. 15. I think also that the Arabic name Djedur bears a strong resemblance to Geshur גשור, since it and Maachah were comprised in this district. In the eastern portion of it is the village Machadj, which is very much like Maachah; not far from it is another village, called Sekara, also one called Kerath, and another named Kiria; it may be thought perhaps that these words have a trace of Aphkeros, as Maachah is given by Onkelos, and Korvé and Antikeros as Geshur and Maachah have been called by Jonathan.

3. Uz (Utz) is at present called Al Ledja. It lies south of Damascus, and extends to the mountains of Hauran. The Romans called it Trachonitis, which proves that the canton of Argob extended thus far, since Argob is explained by calling it Trachonitis. In the eastern part of this district, not far from Mount Hauran, is the town of Djuba, which, perhaps, was the cause that Saadiah translates Argob with "Mudjeb."

In this district a severe battle was fought in the year 5593 (1833) between Abraim Pacha and the Arabs and

Bedouins of the vicinity, who caused a great slaughter in the army of the Pacha; since they were thoroughly acquainted with the country, its defiles and caverns, which knowledge they duly employed to deceive the Pacha's army, who were entirely unacquainted with the same.

4. The mountains of Hauran, at present called Djebl Hauran. The name appears to me to be derived from the Chaldean חור Chur, "hole, cavern," since there are many caves in this neighbourhood. It is already mentioned in Ezekiel xlvii. 17, חורן *Chavran*, English version, Hauran, as also in Rosh Hashanah, 22 *b*, and Yerushalmi Abodah Zarah, chap. iii.—Josephus calls this mountain Batanea. This district has but few inhabitants, and these are Druses, whom I have already mentioned in the description of Lebanon. This mountain district has in part a productive soil; but to the east thereof commences a great desert, which extends to the Euphrates.

5. The plain of Hauran, is called at present Sachl Hauran. It is the Auranitis of Josephus, and lies to the southwest of the mountain of Hauran; it is a fruitful country, produces corn, vegetables, and an abundance of cotton wool. It is this place which is mentioned in Deuteronomy iii. 10, as "all the cities of the plain, and the whole of Gilead and the whole of Bashan to Salehah and Edreï."

I will next explain the names of the towns which are yet discoverable.

Salchah סלכה (Deut. iii. 10, Vayikra Rabbah, v.) At the foot of the eastern portion of the Hauran Mountains, is the town Zalchath, with a fort; it is, however, now destroyed, and is entirely without inhabitants. It appears that these ruins must date from the Jewish period, since the style of architecture of the ruined edifices is nowise of the Roman and much less of a later time.

Edreï אדרעי (ibid.) is probably to be sought for in the

very large ruins called Draä, which are found in the plain of Hauran, not far from the strong fort of Mizrib. (In Yerushalmi Berachoth, v., is mentioned Rabbi Tanchun of Edreï.)

Kenath or Nobach קנת נבח (Num. xxxii. 42), is probably to be discovered in the village Kunath, situated in the mountain of Hauran, one day's journey north from Kelb Hauran (for which, see end of chap. ii.), near which are found the large ruins of many buildings of Roman architecture.

Karkar קרקר (Judges viii. 10); I suppose this to be the village Al Kerak, situated 5 miles south from Al Churak (see next article).

Ashteroth-Karnaim (i. e. Ashtaroth of the Horns or mountain peaks) עשתרות קרנים (Gen. xiv. 5, and Joshua xii. 4.) It appears from Sukkah, fol. 2 *a*, that this place was situated between two high mountain peaks. Astori supposes that Al Churak, which is 8 miles northeast from the ruins of Draä, is identical with Ashteroth-Karnaim; others, however, think it to be the old and strong castle of Al Mizrib, situated on the route of the pilgrims from Damascus to Mekka. Near it is the source of the Jarmuch (which see). More will be given when speaking of the cities of Menasseh.

Bozrah בצרה (Abodah Zarah, 59 *a*; Yerushalmi Shebiith, vi.; Yerushalmi Bikkurim, iii.; Midrash Shemuel, xxv.; Vayikra Rabbah, viii.) I believe that the Basar mentioned in 1 Maccabees v. 26, is identical with this Bozrah, and that it is the present Buzrah, which is on the plain of Hauran, and almost the last inhabited place in the district, for here commences the great desert which extends to the Euphrates. Near it are very large and numerous ruins, and it has but few inhabitants. Astori says in his work Caphtor Vapherach, fol. 71 *a*, "Bezer, in the wilderness (Deut. iv. 43), is half a day's journey east from Edreï; people call it Bozrah." But this view is entirely wrong, since this Bozrah belonged to the tribe of Menasseh, as will be shown farther down, in the territories of the trans-Jordanic tribes, whereas Bezer belonged to Reuben. This city of refuge is said, in Talmud Makkoth, 9 *a*, to have been situated just opposite Hebron, in an eastern direction, whilst Bozrah lies opposite to Djinin (En-Gannim), which is to the north of Shechem. (See Bezer.)

Zohar צחר. This name occurs in Hilchoth Terumoth, of Maimonides i. § 9. Josephus, Ant., book xiii., chap. xv., makes mention of Zahara; and we should conclude that formerly it must have been a very large city. It may be the modern Al Zahara, situated one day's journey north of Salchah; it has but 200 inhabitants, though the ruins there are several miles in circumference.

POSSESSIONS OF THE TRIBES OF REUBEN, GAD, AND HALF MENASSEH.

Before entering on the division of the territories of these tribes, I must first explain the land of

GILEAD. גלעד

We often find that this term designates all the territory of Palestine situated on the east side of Jordan; and in point of fact the mountain of Gilead ramifies throughout the whole of this territory. This mountain extends on the east as far as the plain of Hauran, on the west to the Jordan valley, on the north to the Jarmuch, and on the south to the country of Balka, which lies to the south of the Jabbok, through which cause all the trans-Jordanic tribes had possession in Gilead. This also will explain Deut. iii. 12: "And I gave to the Reubenites and the Gadites the half of the Mount Gilead, with its cities; but the remainder of Gilead, and all Bashan, the kingdom of Og, I gave to the half tribe of Menasseh." The highest points of this mountain are the Djebl Djelad,* which is south of the Jabbok, and the Djebl Osha, which is about 1½ miles north of Tsalt (for which see in the tribe of Gad). The Arabs point out on the latter the grave of Hoshea, whence its name. But this legend is not authentic. The mountain of Gilead is very productive; there are found on it good pine and oak forests, and many varieties of fruit trees.

The mountains of Jazer and Machvar, the mountains of Abarim (יעזר מכור הרי העברים), which lie in the southern part of Belka, appear even higher than the mountains of Gilead,—not that they actually are so, but because Belka is an elevated plain, and is consequently higher than the land of Gilead; wherefore even the lower elevations of the higher plateau appear higher than the most lofty of the lower plain of Gilead. The Djebl Atara, situated about 9 miles to the south of Cheshbon, is the highest point of this Jazer range. (See also article Nebo.)

REUBEN. ראובן

The territory of this tribe was entirely in the south, as appears quite plainly from Joshua xiii. 16, and that Arnon

* The Arabs call likewise the whole chain Djebl Djelad. It is also known by them as Djebl Gidj. This will elucidate an obscure passage of Midrash Shemuel, chap. xxx., which no one has been able to decipher. It is said, in explanation to 2 Sam. xxiv. 6, ויבאו הגלעדה "'And they came to Gilead,' this is Gidsh גרש." There cannot be any doubt but that, at the time the Midrash was written, Gilead bore already its present name. I found in the Arabic translation of Saadiah, Gilead often rendered with גרש Gidj, only that it is incorrectly written Girsh. I presume that the version in Arabic characters is a copy of the Constantinople edition, which appeared in square Hebrew characters; and as D ד and R ר in this alphabet are very much alike, the copyist mistook the form; whereas the Arabic D and R are very different in their appearance, so that no change could take place between Girsh and Gidsh.

was its southern boundary,* which separated it from Moab, of the possessions of which the Israelites were prohibited to touch the least (Deut. ii. 24). To the east Reuben was contiguous to the territory of Ammon (ibid. 37); and I believe that the mountain chain extending from Rabbath-Ammon to Kerak, over which the general route of the pilgrims to Mekka leads, was the eastern boundary of the territory of Reuben. To the west it bordered on the Dead Sea (Salt Sea); and to the north it appears to me to have extended to the little mountain which lies in the plain of Cheshbon, to the northwest of that place (properly speaking, to the Wady Cheshbon), which was not far from Nebo, as will be explained hereafter.

The names of towns still to be traced out are—

Aroër ערער. On the northern bank of the Modjeb, at a distance of about 15 miles from the Dead Sea, are found some ruins called Arar; they lie nearly opposite to Hebron, only a little more to the south.

Medeba מדבא, no doubt identical with the ruins Madeba, which are more than a mile in circumference, and are situated about 5 miles south-southeast from Cheshbon.

Cheshbon חשבון is the modern village Chasban, nearly opposite to the northern extremity of the Dead Sea, at the distance of 14 miles. On a high hill near it are found large ruins, and one discovers yet the traces of ancient pools (see Song of Solomon vii. 4). The environs of Heshbon are, properly speaking, an elevated plain, situated

* The Arnon, or the modern Wady Modjeb, therefore, separated Moab from Israel; and it separates at present the northern country of Al Belka from the southern Al Kerak. The Arabs call Al Belka also Belad al Kafer, i. e. the land of the unbelievers, because many Christians lived here formerly. In short, I often hear them call the ruins which belong to the Christian period, Heida min Zeman al Kafer, i. e. This is still from the time of the unbelievers. Ruins from the Greek period, especially destroyed towers and fortifications, they call Rum Kalleé, "Greek Fort," because Greece is styled by them *Al Rum*.

between the mountains of Jazer and the Djebl Atara, through which the Wady Zirka (Jabbok) flows; and the passage of Joshua xiii. 16, "Cheshbon and its towns, which are in the plain," refers probably to this plateau. Nevertheless, one has a high point of view, with a wide prospect, when standing near the ruins on the above-mentioned hill; to the west there is seen the valley through which the Wady Chasban flows, the Jordan, the Dead Sea, even Jerusalem, and especially Bethlehem, can be distinctly observed; to the north the view rests on the ancient Ramoth-Mizpah (which see), and to the south the whole country of Moab.

Dibon דיבון. Two miles north from the ruins of Arar are found the ruins of Dhiban, which is possibly the same with the Dimon דימון of Isaiah xv. 9.

Beth-Baal-Meon בית בעל מעון is the village Maïn 2 miles south-southwest from Chasban. Hieronymus says, "Medba lies opposite to Hesban, and the town of Baal Maüs (probably Beth Meön), is in the district not far from Hesban." This agrees with my statement.

Jahzah יהצה is probably the village Jazaza, to the southwest of Dhiban.

Kedemoth קדמות is at present unknown. Jonathan says to Deut. ii. 26, "The wilderness of Kedemoth," מנהרדעא דסמוך למדבר קדמות "from Nehardea which is near the wilderness of Kedemoth," which is a most singular statement, since Nehardea is in Babylonia, to the east of Euphrates. Perhaps we may suppose here a slight error in transcribing: 5 miles east from Mount Arapun (see end of second chapter), which is situated in the district of Wady Adjlun, is a little stream called the Wady Nahady נאהאדי; and I suppose that we should read in the passage quoted from Jonathan מנהאדעא, and that Kedemoth might have lain near it; but this would bring this town into the territory of Gad, whereas it is stated to be in Reuben.

Kirjataim or Shavay-Kirjataim שוה קריתים קריתים (Gen. xiv. 5); no doubt the ruins of Kiriat, 1½ miles southwest from Mount Atara.

Sibmah שבמה is at present unknown. Astori, fol. 70 *b*, says: "One day's journey east from Jazer is Sibmah, which is called Shahbah." But this appears to me incorrect, since Shahbah is in the territory of Gad, and Sibmah was in Reuben.

Zereth-Hashachar צרת השחר is at present also unknown. In Yerushalmi Berachoth, viii., is mentioned Rabbi Jochanan of Kirzejon: he may have been perhaps a native of Zereth-Hashachar, since the Chaldean Kirzea is synonymous with the Hebrew Shachar, and means the early morning, or morning dawn.

Beth-Hajeshimoth בית הישימות is probably identical with the ruins of Bteh-Jisimuth, situated on the north-easternmost point of the Dead Sea, half a mile from the Jordan.

There belonged to Reuben in addition the following:

Lesha לשע (Gen. x. 19), is translated by Jonathan with Kaldeha קלדהא, which is unquestionably an error of the transcriber, and should be קלרהא Kalraha (or Kalirha); the same is said in Bereshith Rabbah to this passage, and Yerushalmi Megillah, i. Josephus, however, says that Herod rebuilt the town of Lesha and called it Kalirrhœ, (contracted Kalrah, or Kalirha); it was situated at the foot of Pisgah, and had hot springs, which fall into the Dead Sea. And now at this day there are found on Wady Zirka, where it falls into the Dead Sea, ruins of this place, as also the hot springs.

Mattanah מתנה (Num. xxi. 19), was, according to Eusebius, 12 mill east from Medba. It is at present unknown.

Abel אבל (ibid. xxv. 1). Josephus says that Abela is 60 stadia (7½ English miles) from Jordan. The same is said in Yoma, 75 *b*, "from Beth-Hajeshimoth to Abel-Hashittim is 3 paras;" and Beth-Hajeshimoth is, as said above, near Jordan, which therefore makes the Talmud and Josephus agree in respect to the distance of Abel from Jordan. Hieronymus says, "Abel is in the mountains of Phagor (Peor פּעור, the ע given with g) which lies north of Livias." But it is at present unknown.

Elala אלעלא (ibid. xxxii. 37), is identical with the ruins El Al, 1 mile north from Hesban.

Bezer בצר (Deut. iv. 43). Jonathan explains this with כותירין Kevathirin, which is very obscure. But to the southeast of Arar, not far from Wady Modjeb, is an isolated high mount called Djebl Kuwetta, which evidently resembles the Kevathirin of Jonathan; and it would therefore appear that Bezer must have stood here formerly, as this mount is also just opposite Hebron, to the east, and agrees with the position of this city of refuge as given in Makkoth, 9 *a*.

Nebo נבו (Deut. xxxii. 19). This is the mount whence Moses overlooked Palestine, wherefore it appears to have been a high mount whence there is a wide prospect. It is not possible at present to identify it with certainty. Generally Mount Atara is taken for Nebo: it forms indeed to the west, fronting the Dead Sea, a very high mount; but on the east it appears and is by no means as high. I however cannot doubt that the assumption is incorrect, and that the true Nebo must be looked for farther to the north. It appears from Sotah, 13 *b*, that it was situated 4 mill = 3 English miles, within the borders of Gad, although the town of Nebo is reckoned as belonging to Reuben; whilst at the same time the grave of Moses was in the portion of Gad, as we may assume from Deut. xxxiii. 21 כי שם חלקת מחקק ספון "For there is the burial-place of the Lawgiver hidden." (See also Onkelos and Rashi to the passage.) I therefore believe that the same is certainly to be sought for among the mountains which lie northwest of Hesban, and between which the Wady Hesban flows, and falls into the Jordan to the northwest of Jisimut, at a distance of about 6 miles from Hesban. Eusebius says, "Nebo is 6 mill west (probably meaning northwest) from Hesban;" which agrees exactly with my hypothesis.

Minith מינית (Judges xi. 33) is probably the village Mindja, 5 miles east from Hesban. In 1 Maccabees v. 26, there is mentioned "Mageth Chasban." I doubt not that an error was committed here in copying from the original text, which was to a certainty in Hebrew language and characters, by substituting the גּ G for נ N, and that Mageth is nothing else than Maneth, an easy corruption from Minith.

GAD גד.

The towns of this tribe were as follows:

Jazer יעזר. Eusebius says that this place is 15 mill north from Hesban: it existed even still at the time of Astori; but at present there are ruins, called Seir, on the spot indicated, which leaves no doubt the Seir is derived from Jazer. Near it there rises the spring called Wady Seïr, and I believe that Jeremiah alludes, in chap. xlviii. 32, where he speaks of the sea of Jazer, to water pools which were probably supplied from this spring. A collection of water is often called a sea in Hebrew, as the brazen sea which Solomon made, 1 Kings vii. 44.

Rabbah or Rabbath, of the sons of Ammon רבה and רבת בני מעון (Deut. iii. 11) was called Philadelphia in the time of the Roman supremacy. Eusebius says: "It lies 10 mill northeast from Jazer." At present it is a small village called Aman, near which are very large ruins.

About 8 miles northwest from Aman are found the ruins of Zafit; Josephus says that Jephtha (Yiptach) was buried in the town of Zaphea, or, as other readings have it, Zibia. Perhaps this is the ruined Zafit; or it may be the place called the wine-press of Zeëb, spoken of in Judges vii. 25.

Aroër ערער is the village Ira, situated near Aman. So we also read in Joshua xiii. 25, "Aroër, which lies before Rabbah."

Ramath-Mizpah, also called Mizpeh-Gilead (Judges xi. 29), רמת מצפה · מצפה גלעד, is the present Tzalt, and is a moderately-sized town with a strong fort. The town is situated on a high mount, and its houses and public buildings are erected in the form of terraces on the same. In the town is a considerable spring, the water of which can be conducted under ground into the fort. The environs of Tzalt furnish much and excellent wheat, which is some of the best of all brought to Jerusalem. Many insist that this town is the city of refuge Ramoth-Gilead; but this was somewhat farther to the north, opposite to Shechem. (See also farther, article Ramoth-Gilead.)

Machanaim מחנים. Astori says, "A half day's journey from Beth-Shean, in a direction just opposite, is the town of Machna, which is Machanaim;" but it is now unknown.

Beth-Harim בית הרים. Yerushalmi Shebiith, vi., says, "Beth-Ramtha is Beth-Harim." In Sabbath, 26 *a*, is mentioned, "From En-Gedi to Ramtha." Josephus, Bell. Jud., book i. chap. 3, calls it Beth-Ramtha, and says, "Herod called it Livias." Some suppose it to have been near where the Wady Seir falls into the Jordan; others where the Jabbok joins the same river.

Beth-Nimrah בית נמרה. From the mountains which are near Tzalt, descends a small river which is called Wady Nimrin, and joins the Jordan opposite to Beth-El

(Beitun). About 1 mile east from the Jordan, alongside of this Wady, are found the ruins of Nimrin. According to Astori, Beth-Nimrah was called at his day Namr, and was about 2½ miles south of Jazer. At present there are found some ruins called Naur, which are 5 miles to the south of Seir: are we to assume that Namr is the same with Naur? But as Astori's account stands, it appears incorrect; for Beth-Nimrah was in the plain (Joshua xiii. 27) without doubt, in the valley of the Jordan, and his statement would bring it in the mountains. In Peah, chap. iv., § 5, is mentioned Beth-Namr, i. e. Beth-Nimrin.

Sukkoth סכות. At the time of Astori, there remained yet some traces of this town to the east of the Jordan, near its bank, in a southeast direction from Beth-Shean. Extremely curious, however, is the fact, that the Bedouins call certain ruins to the west of Jordan, 1 mile south from Beth-Shean, by the name of Sukkoth; since the town mentioned under this name in Scripture, was on the east side of Jordan. It is, therefore, evident that we cannot trust all the traditions of the Bedouins.

Zaphon צפון. In Yerushalmi Shebiith, vi., it is said that Zaphon is identical with Amatha, which is probably the Omatho often mentioned by Josephus, which was in the vicinity of Ramoth-Gilead, not far from Jordan. At present the Bedouins call a certain spot near where the Wady Redjib joins the Jordan by the name of Amathéh, and it appears to me to mark the site of Zaphon correctly.

Botnim בטנים. Eusebius simply says that Bathnia is in the portion of Gad, but gives us no farther account of its position. It is, therefore, entirely unknown.

There belonged also to the tribe of Gad the following:

Ramoth-Gilead רמות גלעד (Deut. iv. 43); it is also called Ramah (2 Kings, viii. 29). I take it to be identical with the modern Kallat al Rabat, which is situated on one of the highest points of the mountain of Gilead, not far from the Wady Redjib, and west of Adjlun. It is even at this day a strongly fortified place, which can be seen at a great distance, and it can be perceived even as far as Mount Taibi (see Ophrah, in Benjamin), in a northeastern direction.

Kamon קמון (Judges x. 5), is the village Kumima, 7 miles east-southeast from Beth-Shean.

Abel-Keramin (of the vineyards) אבל כרמים (ibid. xi. 33). Eusebius says that 6 mill from Philadelphia is a village, in the vicinity of which there are many vineyards, whence its name; but at present it is unknown. Some suppose, erroneously, that this is Abel al Krum in Lebanon, as I have stated already. The whole district of the Jordan was formerly often called Arabah (Arabia), whence I believe that Abel Arab of Pesachim, 72 *a*, is the same with the town in question.

Tob טוב (ibid. xi. 3). I have already above, in mentioning Susita, proved that Tob, Susita, and Chefus are all names of the same place. The inhabitants are called by Josephus Tubanians. (See also 1 Macc. v. 13.) I have stated before that the town of Susita was situated on the southeastern shore of Lake Chinnereth. It belonged to the Decapolis (i. e. the Ten Towns).*

* Under Decapolis are understood the *ten* towns of Palestine, the inhabitants of which, in the time of Herod, were not Jews, but Greeks, Romans, and the like. They were united under some sort of constitution and similarity of laws, although at a distance of each other, under the name of Decapolis. They were—Damascus, Philadelphia, Raphana, which was not far from Ashtaroth Karnaim (1 Macc. v. 37); Beth-Shean; Geder; Chefas (Susita); Dion (now unknown); Pellam, which lay not far from Geder, now unknown; Garasas, now the immense ruins called Djerash, 15 miles southeast from Kallat al Rabat, which equal those of Baal-bek and Palmyra or Tadmor; and Kanatham, Kenath. Some suppose that Laish (Cæsarea Philippi), Beth-Gubrin (Beth-Djibrin), Kefar Zemach, Karnaim, and Abila Batanea, at present the large ruins Abel, on the bank of the

Jabesh-Gilead יבש גלעד (ibid. xxi. 8), is the modern village Jabes, on the Wady Jabes, which falls into the Jordan. It is 10 miles east from Jordan, in a direction opposite to Beth-Shean.

Bithron בתרון (2 Sam. ii. 29). Astori says that this place was called in his day Al Atrun, and was south of Machanaim. It is, however, now unknown.

In Talmud and Midrashim, the following places are mentioned:

Geder גדר (Rosh Hashanah, 23 *b*, Erubin, 61 *a*, Sanhedrin, 108 *a*, "the spring of Geder;" Yerushalmi Orlah, i., mentions improperly גדודה "Gedudah," i. e. to Gedud; it should be גדרה "to Geder;" likewise in Tosephtah Taharoth, vi., instead of בית גדי וחמתן Beth-*Gedi* and Chamthan, should read גדר "Geder"), is undoubtedly the place now known as the extensive ruins of Umcheis, which are 8 miles from the southeast shore of Lake Chinnereth, and 1½ miles from the southern bank of the Jarmuch. Close by it is a hot spring. At the time of Astori, Geder was yet in existence; and he paints it with its hot spring, pools, and extraordinarily remarkable buildings, which were unusually strong: he says, moreover, that according to tradition, Og, king of Bashan, had his residence here. At present there is scarcely the least trace of its former beauty and elegance.

Migdal-Geder מגדל גדר (Taanith, 20 *a*, and Massecheth Derech Eretz, in which work it is always called מגדל עדר or גדוד, which should be גדר, since Migdal Eder, or Shepherd's Tower, is quite in a different direction, whereas the transaction spoken of must have taken place near Tiberias, not far from a sea, Chinnereth, and a river,

Jarmuch, perhaps Abel Arab, as said above, should be reckoned among the Decapolis. It appears from the Yerushalmi and Tosephtah that in all these mentioned towns there dwelt many heathens.

(either Jarmuch or Jordan). It was probably near Geder, but is at present not known.

Regib רגב (Menachoth, 85 *b*), is the village Redjib, 9 miles east from Jordan, on the Wady Redjib, which has its source in the mountain which lies to the northeast of Kallat al Rabat, and joins the Jordan opposite to Shechem. Eusebius says, "Regeb is 15 mill west from Garasas" (see above, note to Decapolis), which agrees with the village Radjib. I do not think that Regeb is derived from Argob, although in the Samaritan text it is for חבל הארגוב, i. e. Regeb רגב.

Kefar Akabiah כפר עקביה (Yerushalmi Nazir, at end). Southeast from Lake Chinnereth, on the road to Damascus, is En-Akabi, also Chan-Akabi. (See Jos., Ant., book xiii. chap. xxiv.) There is also, south of Zafed, a village called Akabi, where are shown the graves of Armon and Akabiah, son of Mahallalel.

Eglon עגלון was yet in the time of Astori inhabited by many Jews, and was even later, as I have learned from Jewish documents, a place of importance. It is the present village Adjlun, 1 mile east from Kallat al Rabbat; it is situated on the Wady Redjib, which is also called Wady Adjlun, and passes by this village.

THE POSITION OF THE POSSESSIONS OF GAD AND MENASSEH.

From the above we learn that some of the towns of Gad were not far from the Lake Chinnereth. Consequently the territory of this tribe extended to that lake; and I presume that the Jarmuch formed the boundary line between Gad and Menasseh. In an eastern direction, all the land between Wady Chesban, the boundary line between Reuben and Gad, and the Wady Jarmuch, even as far east as the plain of Hauran, belonged to the latter tribe, as appears clearly from 1 Chron. v. 11: "The children of Gad dwelt opposite, in the land of Bashan, as far as Salchah." The Midrash Yalkut to Deut. xxxiii. 20, also says that the portion of Gad extended very far to the east.

To Menasseh, however, belonged all the remaining places from Jarmuch to the mountains of Hermon and the great desert, which extends to the Euphrates, that is, the greater part of Bashan. I must now notice the few names of places which have not yet been described, and which belonged to Menasseh.

Ashteroth-Karnaim I have already noticed it is true; I have, however, to cite the opinion and statement of the celebrated Saadiah Gaon, who translates Ashteroth-Karnaim with Al Znamin. Now at the present day even there is found a place called Zunamein, on the pilgrims' route to Damascus, 1½ days' journey south from the same, and half a day's journey east of Kaneitra. I suppose this also to be the fort in the land of Gilead, mentioned in 1 Macc. v. 26, since Gilead denotes also other portions to the east and north besides Gilead proper.

Chalamish חלמיש. In Echa Rabbethi, to chap. i. 17, it is said, "Chalamish was always at enmity with Navéh." I learn from old books that Zanamin is identical with Chalamish; so that Zanamin, afterwards known as Salamin, was also called Chalmish [i. e. rock, which would well suit to the appellation of Karnaim, "rocky points, peaks"].

Navéh נוה of Echa Rabbethi, i. 17, Tosephtah Sukkoth, iv.; Midrash Koheleth, fol. 88; "R. Palti of Navéh;" "Midrash Ruth, 49;" R. Shiloh of Navéh, is the village Nová, on the above-mentioned road, 1 day's journey south from Zunamein.

Shukmezi שוקמזי of Jonathan to Num. xxxiv. 11, is probably the village Ashmiskin, 9 English miles southeast from Nova.

Bashchar בשכר of Sabbath, 139 *a*, I suppose to be identical with the Basgar in Arabia בסגר של ערבי"א mentioned in Echa Rabbethi to iii. 7. Josephus, Antiq., b. xiii., 6, says that Jonathan the Maccabee was murdered in Basga, in the land of Gilead; in 1 Macc. xiii. 23, that place is called Basgamé, all which names no doubt refer to the self-same place.

ADDENDUM.

In 1 Kings iv. 9 are mentioned Makaz, Shaalbim, &c. The Septuagint translate Makaz with Michmas, which I suppose to be incorrect; since Shaalbim is near Samaria, consequently far from Michmash. Otherwise is the situation of Makaz unknown.

Aruboth (ibid. 10), I hold to be the town Rabitha, in the portion of Zebulun, the present village and Wady Rabutia.

"In Asher and Aloth" באשר ובעלות (ibid. 16), I think should be rendered in Asher and *Bealoth*, i. e. Baal-Gad or Laish, and that the ב (in) before Asher also is the preposition understood for Bealoth; I prefer this construction since we find nowhere any mention of a town called *Aloth*. Bealoth is put without question for Baalath, which has been sufficiently described before.

CHAPTER V.

JERUSALEM ירושלם—ARABIC, THE HOLY, AL KUDS.

ITS FORMER AND PRESENT CONDITIONS.

SITUATION.

To the east of the city is the Mount of Olives (Olivet), elevated 2555 feet above the level of the Mediterranean Sea; between it and the city is a deep narrow valley, called the valley of Kidron; it commences at the north-east, where there is a little plain, and extends to the south of the spring En Rogel, where the valley obtains a larger extent and forms a little plain or level piece of ground.

To the south and west there is likewise a valley, large and deep, called the valley of Gichon;* more southwardly, looking eastward, it bears the name of the valley of Rephaim,† and extends to the just-mentioned little plain, or the level near the spring Rogel, where, therefore, both the valleys Kedron and Gichon unite. Jerusalem is thus surrounded on three sides with deep valleys, entirely so on

* It appears to me that the stream Gichon, which rises at the Upper Pool (see farther, under En Shiloach, "the spring of Siloah"), once flowed through this valley to that of Kedron, near the En Rogel. Here also was the שדה כובס the washer's or fuller's field, whence the valley is called מסילת שדה כובס "the way or the course (of the water) into the fuller's field." (Isaiah vii. 3.)

† I hold that Emek Rephaim is synonymous with the עמק הפגרים Emek Hapegarim, the valley of the corpses of Jer. xxxi. 40, since it appears, from Psalm lxxxviii. 11, that Rephaim signifies the same with Pegarin, i. e. the dead body.

the south and east, partially at the west, whilst at the north and the northwest there is a plain.

Between the valleys of Kedron and Rephaim, and to the west of the spring Shiloach, there is a small narrow valley, running in a northern direction, and is partly embraced within the limits of the city at the northwest; I refer to the valley Gé Ben Hinnom גי בן הנם. Josephus, Bell. Jud., b. vi., chap. v., calls it Tyropœon, i. e. Cheesemakers' Valley. It also separates Mount Moriah from Zion.

Moriah, also called the Temple Mount, is 2280 feet in height, and lies to the west of Kedron, and at its west side is the northern part of the valley Ben Hinnom, consequently that portion called Tyropœon; as the first name is applied to that part which lies beyond the limits of the city, but not to the northern division, which is within Jerusalem. Mount Zion is 2381 feet in height; it lies to the southwest of Moriah, and to the south of the city.*

We will now say something concerning the boundary line between Judah and Benjamin (Joshua xv. 7), which we broke off above, and refer to this passage.

The En Rogel mentioned in Joshua xv. 7, is unquestionably the well which is one hundred and twenty-two feet deep, and covered over with a very ancient cupola, and bears now the name of Bir Juab (the well of Joab). I am unable to determine whence this name is derived; but the Arabic† version already gave the above with Bir

* The passage of Psalm xlviii. 3, הר ציון ירכתי צפון "The Mount Zion, on the sides of the north," is extremely obscure, since Zion is at the south; we must therefore explain it as though it read 'וירכת "and the sides," meaning, first Zion the upper city, and then the lower town or the northern part, or Jerusalem proper, as will be spoken of more hereafter. (See also Pesiktah Rabbethi, 41, and Zohar to Vayiggash, fol. 206, where this remarkably irregular passage is already discussed.)

† I greatly doubt whether this version is by Rabbi Saadiah Gaon רבנו סעדיה הגאון; for I think that the Pentateuch alone is the genuine work of Saadiah; and although he translated the entire remainder of

Juab. This well, or rather spring, is found in the southern part of the Kidron valley, and near it is the abovementioned Sedé Kobes, whilst En Rogel may signify the same idea, that of fuller's or washer's spring, since the washing or fulling of cloth was performed with the feet; hence Rogel is fuller, a washer with the feet, from *Regel*, foot. Jonathan also renders En Rogel with עין קצרא Ein Katzdah, "The fuller's spring."

The northern line of Judah now ran from this spring upward through the valley of Hinnom, turned then to the west, up to Mount Zion, which lies to the west of this valley, (Ps. xv. 8, "and goeth up to the top of the mount, that lieth before the valley of Hinnom westward;" at that time this mount was not yet called Zion, which name was not applied to it before the time of David, wherefore it is described briefly as "the mount.") To the south of Mount Zion is the valley Rephaim, the most southern part of the valley of Gichon. I made diligent inquiry to ascertain by what name the Arabs call it, and I learned that it is in their language Wady Rafaath, i. e., Rephaim; the plural of Rafa in Arabic being Rafaath, as Rephaim is the plural of Raphé in Hebrew. I felt, therefore, convinced that my view on the subject was quite correct. I mention this thus circumstantially, since nearly universally, although erroneously, this valley is taken for the Gé Ben Hinnom.

Although Joshua defeated the King of Jerusalem (Jos. xii. 10) it nevertheless appears that the city was not at that time taken possession of by the Israelites. It was

Holy Writ, the other portions of the usual Arabic version are the work, for the most part, of later writers. Nevertheless, there is found in the very ancient Al Aleppo (Chaleb), which is said to have been built already in the time of David, an Arabic translation of the entire Holy Bible in manuscript, which is universally held to be the work of Rabbenu Saadiah.

captured only after Joshua's death (Jud. i. 8). But the Jebusites were not finally conquered till the time of David and Joab, who were the first to capture the City of David, the fort of (Mezudath) Zion. It appears that it did not lie on the top of the mount, but on the declivity of the same, towards the valley of Hinnom; since we read of a going down to the fort of Zion (2 Sam. v. 17); and an "ascending" from the same to the valley of Rephaim is also spoken of (ibid. 19).* The Millo מלוא (ib. v. 9) was on the eastern declivity of Mount Zion, towards the spring of Siloah (שלוח). In 2 Kings xii. 21, we read בית מלא היורד סלא, "they smote Joash at Beth-Millo, which goeth down to Silla." I explain the last word to mean Shiloach, exchanging ס for ש and א for ח, such an exchange of letters being quite common, and that it means at the Millo which leads down to Shiloach.

In the same neighbourhood, to the southwest of the temple mount, was also the house of Solomon, built for his wife, the daughter of Pharaoh, whence a staircase led to the temple. (See 1 Kings x. 5; 2 Chron. ix. 4, and Neh. iii. 15.)

THE GATES.

Of the extent and the position of the walls and gates of Jerusalem of the ancient period, we know but little; we only find in 1 Kings ix. 15, that Solomon built the walls of the city; but we find no vestige to determine how far it extended to the south and north. Of the gates but little is mentioned; we only find in 2 Kings xiv. 13, that "Jehoash, king of Israel, broke down the wall of Jerusalem from the gate of Ephraim to the corner gate, *four hundred cubits*." It is probable that this breach re-

* It is possible that the house of David בית דוד of Yoma, 77 *b*, was situated in a valley or hollow, as it would also appear from the passage in 1 Samuel v. 17–19 (which see).

mained open till the time of Uzziah (2 Chron. xxvi. 9), and Hezekiah (ibid. xxxii. 5). We also find mention made of a gate between the two walls near the king's garden (ibid. xxv. 4); but beyond these data we know nothing.

But at the rebuilding of the city by Nehemiah, we have a more particular description of the walls and the gates, which probably, therefore, existed previously; since it appears likely that everything was built on the former site, to the former extent, and after the ancient dimensions; I will, therefore, investigate the probable previous position of the gates enumerated by Nehemiah.

He tells, in chap. ii. 13, 15, "And I went out by night by the Gate of the Valley, even before the Dragon Spring, and to the Dung Gate, &c., then to the Gate of the Spring (fountain, English version), and to the King's Pool, &c., and then I went up in the night by the brook, &c., and turned back and entered by the Gate of the Valley."

I scarcely doubt but that the Dung Gate was at the south, near the valley of Hinnom, or the Tyropœon;* so we read also in Jeremiah xix. 2, "Go out into the valley of Ben-Hinnom, which is before the gate Charsith" (East Gate, English version). Jonathan renders חרסית with Kikaltha קיקלתא the Chaldean for "dung," which clearly proves that the Dung Gate was near the valley of Ben-Hinnom. We are also told that the Valley Gate was one thousand cubits distance from the former (Neh. iii. 13),

* This Greek name of Josephus can also be explained, since this Dung Gate is called in Nehemiah iii. 13, ש׳ השפות, the Gate Shephoth instead of האשפות Ashpoth, of ii. 13. Now the word שפות Shephoth is used in 2 Samuel xvii. 29 to signify "cheese," whence we can conclude that the gate was also called "the cheese gate," or the gate of the cheesemakers, whence again we may assert that the name Tyropœon, "valley of the cheesemakers" of Josephus, finds it origin in the Scriptures.—[The English version of Charsith with "east," is probably derived from חרס "the sun," thus the gate of "sunrise."—TRANSLATOR.]

consequently the Valley Gate must have stood in a northwest direction from the other, for to the east we find no other valley at the distance of one thousand cubits (two thousand feet). I consider the Valley Gate to have led to the valley of Rephaim, which encompassed Mount Zion altogether at the south and partly at the west. Between the two gates just described, was the Dragon's Spring, which is now totally unknown. Southeast from the Dung Gate, stood the Gate of the Spring or Fountain, probably not far from the Lower Spring of Siloah. There also was the King's Pool, which exists at this day, as will be farther mentioned at the explanation of the pools of Jerusalem. There was farther, in this vicinity, the Gate between the two Walls by the king's gardens, of 2 Kings xxv. 4. Even at the present time, are found in that neighbourhood, near the village Selivan, several gardens, which are abundantly watered from Siloah. There were also the steps which led to the temple, as I have stated above, when speaking of the Millo.

I will next describe the supposed situation of all the gates mentioned by Nehemiah:

At the south there were, 1. The Dung Gate, also called the Gate between the two Walls; east of the same was 2. The Gate of the Fountain.

At the west, 3. The Valley Gate; 4. The Corner Gate, properly northwest from the first, at a distance of four hundred cubits.

At the north, 5. The Gate of Ephraim, also called the Gate of Benjamin, in Jeremiah xxxvii. 13, since it led into the territory of both Ephraim and Benjamin. 6. The Prison Gate (Neh. xii. 39), the site of which can be accurately determined even at present by means of a tradition which defines the position of the prison, the grotto of Jeremiah, or otherwise called the Archer's Court חצר המטרה: it was situated near the Bab al Amud (which see). To the east of this gate were the towers Meäh and Chananel מאה וחננאל of Nehemiah xii. 39.

At the east were, 7. The Sheep Gate (properly at the northeast). 8. The Old Gate, also called the Middle Gate (Jer. xxxix. 3), since, according to the assertion of Yerushalmi Erubin, v., it bore different names, to wit, שער העליון the Upper Gate; the East Gate שער המזרח; the Middle Gate שער התוך, and the Old Gate שער איתן. 9. The Water Gate (Neh. viii. 1, "Upon the broad street, before the Water Gate," is explained by the Talmud to mean "the Temple Mount" הוא הר הבית). 10. The Fish Gate (at the southeast), of 2 Chronicles xxxiii. 14, is explained in the Chaldean translation of Rab Joseph with מזבני כוורי "where fish are sold, or the fish market," and was probably near the pool of Shiloach; and 11. The Horse Gate, of Jer. xxxi. 40, and 2 Kings xi. 16, and xxi. 11.

Ophel,* of Neh. iii. 26, was quite at the southeast, above the lower spring of Shiloach. It was an uncommonly strong fort, the former position of which is still known from tradition. The following statement is extracted from

* The passage in Zephaniah i. 10, יללה מן המשנה "A lamentation from the *other* gate," is given by Jonathan with מן עופא Opha; wherefore Rashi expounds it with משער העופות "from the poultry gate," a most singular name, since I could not find any trace of a gate so called in any position. I hold it, therefore, as certain that here is an orthographical error, and that עופא should read עופלא 'Ophla, or the Ophel described above; and it actually well suits to the description, Mishné, or "the double," which signifies then the two walls (2 Kings xxii. 14), or the double wall החומתים, as also Rashi states to the passage cited, and as I shall describe more fully hereafter. This certainly does not confirm Rashi's explanation of poultry gate; but my hypothesis is confirmed from the fact that several editions of Jonathan have the correct reading מן עופלא, instead of מן עופא. From Yerushalmi Taanith, iii., it appears plainly that Ophel was in the valley of Kidron. See also Taanith, 22 *b*. The commentary of Rashi and Tosephoth to this passage, however, concerning "Ophel," does not appear very clear to me.

the travels of Rabbi Benjamin, of Tudela: "There is found a large spring, the one called Shiloach, in the valley of Kidron; over this spring stands a large building (בנין גדול), which dates from the days of our forefathers," מימי אבותינו. The Italian Itinerary of the year 5282, of which I shall speak more hereafter, says: "On the summit of the mount, at the foot of which is the source of the Shiloach, stands a building, where formerly was a village with houses having cupolas. It is said that here stood the mint of King Solomon." At present this spot is called Ophel, and is done so, without doubt, according to a correct and true tradition.

The number of the gates just given, as also the course and circuit of the walls of Jerusalem as they were in the time of Nehemiah, continued thus till, as Josephus relates, the city was enlarged towards the north, and supplied with new walls. When it was rebuilt, after the destruction in the reign of Hadrian, it was done on a much diminished scale, and with less gates. I could find nowhere any reliable accounts of that period, which give us any information respecting the then size, gates, and wall of Jerusalem. Only of a much later time, the year 4930 A. M. (1170), Rabbi Benjamin, who then travelled through Palestine, relates "that Jerusalem had four gates, the gates of Abraham, David, Zion, and Jehoshaphat, which is east of the temple." The Gate of Abraham probably denotes the one leading to Hebron, "the city of Abraham," as at this day they call the gate leading to Hebron Bab al Chalil, "the gate of the beloved," as Hebron itself is termed Beth al Chalil, "the house of the beloved," referring to Abraham,* the man universally beloved. The Gate

* After careful investigation, however, I found that the Arabs do not apply the name of Chalil to Abraham, but to Isaac, since they call so every one whose name is Isaac; and I believe that this epithet is given solely to Isaac, and only denotes him, as in Gen. xxii. 2, את בנך יחידך אשר אהבת

of David appears to be the western one, which stands near the Kallai, that is, the so-called fort of David מגדל דוד. The Zion's Gate is the modern one of the same name; and the Gate of Jehoshaphat is the eastern entrance, which is near the valley of Jehoshaphat, i. e. the valley of Kidron. It would thence appear that, at the time of Rabbi Benjamin's visit, Jerusalem had no gate on the north side.

In the year 5282, an Italian of Leghorn, whose name is unknown, travelled through Palestine. His investigations and remarks are, it is true, but briefly and simply given, but are nevertheless here and there interesting, and are attached as an appendix to the small work, שבחי ירושלם "The Praises of Jerusalem." The traveller relates, "Jerusalem has six gates: 1, Bab al Sebat, the Gate of the Tribes, i. e. the one through which the pilgrims entered when they went three times a year to Jerusalem, on the festivals of Passover, Weeks, and Tabernacles; 2, Bab al Amud; 3, Bab al Katun, since in its neighbourhood much cotton was spun and worked up; and three other gates, not far from Zion." Even at the present day the eastern gate is called Bab al Sebat; the northern one is called Bab al Amud; and the three near Zion are termed the small southern gate, not far from the ancient Dung Gate, the Zion's Gate, and the Western Gate, which opens on the road to Jaffa. But the Bab al Katun is unknown; yet it may perhaps be the one now walled up, somewhat to the east of Bab al Amud. This then proves that, before Sultan Soliman erected the present wall of the city, in the year 5287 (1527), it had the gates of the present day. At present Jerusalem has five gates: 1, at the south, on Mount Zion, the Zion Gate, also called Bab al Chalil, and Bab

"Thy son, thy only one, whom thou lovest." He lived, as his father had done, in Hebron; whence it may properly be called Beth-Chalil, "the house of Isaac" (the beloved).

Nebi David, gate of the prophet David, from the fact that King David lived at Zion, and is entombed there also; 2, the gate situated to the east of the first, at the foot of Mount Zion, the so-called Little Gate, near the site of the ancient Dung Gate, and also named Bab al Megarbi, for מערבי, by changing Ain into Gain, because the interior of the city, in the vicinity of this gate, is occupied only by Mahomedans, who have emigrated hither from Africa (i. e. the western country, hence "the gate of the westerns"). When the Arabs and Bedouins rebelled against Abraim Pacha in 5594 (1834), he had this gate closed and walled up; but it was again opened when, in 5601, Palestine reverted to the Sultan of Constantinople. 3, At the east, the Bab al Sebat; 4, at the north, the Bab al Amud, "the column gate," because it has a colonnade attached to it; 300 paces to the east is a small walled up gate, but it is not known when and why it was closed; and 5, at the west, the Bab al Jaffa, which opens on the Jaffa road.

On the eastern side of the city wall, just opposite the great mosque on the temple mount, called Al Sachara, can be seen two large gates, close to each other, which are walled up; they are called by our brethren שערי הרחמים "the gates of mercy." They are already mentioned in Massecheth Soferim, 19, and are said to have been built by King Solomon, as is also believed by Astori and Rabbi Emanuel Riki, authors of the book עטרת אליהו "the Crown of Elijah." But I have no doubt that they belong to a much later period, since we perceive on the stones figures, drawings, and ornaments, of the Arabic fashion; and their style and character is such that they must to a surety have been erected by the Arabs. The tradition may perhaps be owing to an idea that here once stood the "gates of mercy," erected by Solomon, but they can by no means be themselves the remains of that high antiquity. I moreover found traces of the oldest period only on the following places: the Mourning Wall, or the כותל המערבי the west wall of the temple, of which I shall speak more circumstantially hereafter; the southwestern corner of the city wall; and the lower portion of David's Tower מגדל דוד Kallai. These three are actual remains of that high antiquity, on which is impressed the seal of truth; but all the other remains are the works of later periods.

WALLS.

We nowhere find, except in Josephus, any mention of this subject, and although I searched our books everywhere with much accuracy and care, I could find but very meagre and unsatisfactory notices of the same. But Josephus gives us a circumstantial description of them. He says, in his Bell. Jud., b. v., chap. iv., and in several other passages, that Jerusalem was encircled with three walls; but when the city was protected by deep and impassable valleys it had but one. He says, moreover, in another passage, that Jerusalem consisted of four mounts, that is to say, it was built on four mounts; to wit, Mount Zion on the south; Mount Moriah on the east; Bezetha on the northeast (properly instead of Beth-Zetha, or Beth-Chadetha, "new town," חדתא changing ח ch into צ z, or as others think Beth-Zoah בית צואה, which see), and Acra חקרא the fort, on the northwest. He says farther, in another place, Jerusalem was divided into the Upper, Lower,* and New Town (Bezetha); that farther, the Tyropœon extended from without in a northern direction

* The שוק העליון ושוק התחתון upper and lower markets often mentioned in the Talmudic writings, for instance, in Tosephtah Chulin, iii. (In Talmud Chulin, 62 *a*, for שוק העליון we find גליל העליון Upper Galilee, or, Upper District?); also in Tosephtah Sanhedrin, finis, which proves that already in the time of Jeremiah, the divisions of Upper and Lower Town were in use. See also Echa Rabbethi, to i. 16.

through the city and separated Zion from Moriah and Acra.

Concerning the walls he tells circumstantially (Bell. Jud., b. v., chap. iv. § 2): "Now of these three walls the old one was hard to be taken, both by reason of the valleys, and of that hill on which it was built, and which was above them, &c. Now that wall began on the north, at the tower called *Hippicus*, and extended as far as the place called *Xistus*, and then joining to the council-house, ended at the west gallery (cloister) of the temple. But if we go the other way westward, it began at the same place, and extended through a place called *Bethso*, to the gate of the Essenés, and after that it went southward, having its bending above the fountain Siloam, where it also bends again towards the east, at Solomon's Pool, and reaches as far as a certain place which they called *Ophlas*, where it was joined to the eastern gallery (cloister) of the temple. The second wall took its beginning from that gate which they called *Gennath*, which belonged to the first wall; it only encompassed the northern quarter of the city and reached as far as the tower *Antonia*. The beginning of the third wall was at the tower Hippicus, whence it reached as far as the north quarter of the city and the tower Psephinus, and then was so far extended till it came over against the monuments of Helena, which Helena was queen of Adiabené, the daughter of Izates; in her days it extended farther to a great length, and passed by the sepulchral caverns of the kings, and bent again at the tower of the corner, at the monument which is called the *Monument of the Fuller*, and joined to the old wall, at the valley called the *Valley of Cedron*."

He farther says, that as the population of Jerusalem increased, and when also the weakest and most exposed part of the city, Bezetha, to the north of the temple, was built up, King Agrippa, at the time of Claudius Cæsar, caused it to be surrounded with a very strong wall, 25 cubits high, and 10 cubits broad, and strengthened with ninety towers. Several years were consumed in erecting it. Here also stood the high tower Psephinus, from which one had a view as far as Arabia, Judæa, and the Great (Mediterranean) Sea. Josephus also relates in another place that the first wall has sixty and the second but fourteen towers.

Before proceeding with an explanation of these data of Josephus, I find it highly necessary to trace out, if possible, the position of the ancient Hippicus, since it is given by Josephus as the starting point of his description; and it has therefore first to be ascertained before we can properly define the position of the walls as given above.

No investigator has hitherto been able to give even a mere approximation to a definition of the part of the city where this tower formerly stood, and it is universally put, although quite arbitrarily, by all the learned who desire to describe the ancient walls of Jerusalem, on the *western* side thereof, that is to say, on the spot occupied by the modern Kallai, the so-called Tower of David, whence it has become at present in a measure the fashion to call the Kallai by the name of Hippicus, and the walls of Jerusalem are thus traced from this starting point. No one has hitherto been able to controvert this hypothesis, because there were no counter proofs that Hippicus had not stood on this spot.

I am therefore greatly rejoiced that I have succeeded, by means of a careful investigation of our faithful and credible writings, to obtain reliable data as to the true position of the Hippicus of Josephus.

The Targumist Jonathan Ben Uziel, a scholar of the famous Hillel the Elder (Sukkah, 28 *a*), lived in Jerusalem at the time of King Herod, who erected this tower in honour of his general, Hippicus, who had fallen in battle; consequently we must accept his explanation on this subject as correct, credible, and perfectly reliable. Now, on referring to the מגדל חננאל Tower of Chananel of Jer. xxxi. 38, and Zech. xiv. 10, we find that Jonathan renders it with מגדל פיקוס Migdal Pikus, evidently Tower of Hippicus, whence it is perfectly clear that this tower must have been erected on the site of the ancient Chananel tower; for who could know more about it than this learned man, who lived on the spot when Herod built this structure?

If we now investigate carefully the position of the Tower of Chananel, as given in Nehemiah, we find it placed to the northeast of the Prison Gate, or Jeremiah's Grotto חצר המטרה, also called the Archer's Court, so that the northern boundary of Jerusalem would naturally extend from the Tower of Chananel, on the northeast, to the Corner Gate at the northwest (Jer. xxxi. 38). Wherefore it is subject to no doubt, but that we must seek for Hippicus in a northern direction. It farther appears, from Jos., Bell. Jud., book vi. chap. vi., that the three strong towers, of which Hippicus was one, were situated on the northern side of the city, and not far distant from the fort Antonia, which was confessedly to the north of the temple. In a northerly direction, above the Grotto of Jeremiah, is found a high rocky hill, since it is at the foot of this hill that the grotto is, properly speaking, cut out of the rock; and here is an unusually favourable site for a tower, and one may even trace some vestiges which betoken that at some time a strong building or a fort must have stood here; wherefore I am almost positive that I may freely assume that Hippicus was erected on this spot.

It is a most difficult problem to determine anything accurate and certain from the above description of Josephus; since with all our exertions we could scarcely discover any remains of all these ancient walls; wherefore we must be satisfied with something "probable," or "not unlikely."

I would therefore hazard the following opinion: The first wall of Josephus is undoubtedly the one which was built by Nehemiah, in whose time the fort or tower of Antonia was still outside of the city; so that the northern wall of the temple, that is to say, that of the temple mount, which was, according to the authority of the Talmud, as I shall discuss more circumstantially hereafter, 500 cubits, or 1000 feet, in breadth, formed at the same time part of the northeastern wall of the city, which extended yet farther to the north; so that the eastern city wall only commenced, properly speaking, from the northwest corner of the temple mount, and extended then to the Tower of Chananel, which was exactly opposite this point of the mount, in a northern direction, and was thus the proper northeast termination of the city wall. The part where afterwards the fort Antonia stood, and which was to the north of the temple mount, was therefore outside of the city; and it was only at a much later period, at the time of the Maccabees, that this fort was connected with the city and united with the temple. Hippicus, not far from Jeremiah's Grotto, is therefore exactly north from the northwestern corner of the temple mount, or the wall of the temple, since we comprise under the words *temple, temple wall, temple buildings,* the whole of the temple mount, with all its buildings, walls, &c. This now will explain the assertion of Josephus, that the first wall extended from Hippicus to Xistus, which, accordingly, must have been situated between the temple mount and the northeastern termination of the wall, that is to say, from north to south, and terminated at the western gallery or cloister, which means at the northwestern corner of the temple mount; but that from this point onward, the wall of the temple mount formed also that of the city. On the other side, that is, in a western direction, the wall extended from Hippicus towards the upper Gichon, then ran southwardly around Mount Zion, then northerly, and again southerly, and formed the double wall (חומתים); ran next around the fountain of Siloah, thence past the lower pool, till it reached the Ophel, and terminated finally at the eastern gallery of the temple. This was the circuit of Jerusalem at the time of Nehemiah, and in this wall must we look for all the gates mentioned in the same authority.

The second wall was erected at a later period, and I presume that it is the same which Jonathan the Maccabee caused to be built within the city, in order to separate Acra, where his enemies, the Grecians, were posted, from the other parts of Jerusalem, as Josephus tells us. At that time, however, the fort of Antonia was already united with the city and the temple. I suppose, also, that this wall ran from east to west, and that the Gate of Gennath was between the Valley and the Corner Gate, although it must have been a later structure than the time of Nehemiah, as it is not mentioned by him; and that from this point the wall ran in a northeasterly direction, till it reached Antonia, or, more correctly speaking, to where the first wall came in contact with the fort of Antonia, or it may have passed the first wall, so that it (the second) reached as far as this point. This wall therefore separated Acra at the north from the other parts of Jerusalem.

The third was a structure of a still later period; it also commenced at Hippicus, ran to the north in a somewhat western direction, and bent then easterly till it touched the valley of Kidron; extended next to the south to the northeast corner of the temple mount, or more correctly speaking, to the eastern part of the fort Antonia; since this tower was already connected with the temple, as we understand by "the old wall near the valley of Cedron," of Josephus, the fort of Antonia.

I will next mention the few vestiges which I have been able to find of the several names mentioned by Josephus.

Bethso is probably, as I have stated already, synonymous with בית חדתא Beth-Chadetha "the new town." Some derive it from Beth-Zoah, "dirt or dung." According to the assertion of the Yerushalmi Sanhedrin x. and Vayikra Rabbah xxxvi., the vicinity of the upper spring of Gichon (Isaiah vii. 3) is considered as a place of filth, impurity, and uncleanness, and might, accordingly, mark the site of Beth-Zoäh; but Josephus places it at the northeast, not at the west, as this hypothesis would do.

Gennath. In Maasseroth ii. § 5, we find mentioned a Ginnath Veradim גנת ורדים, "a rose garden" in Jerusalem, which was situated to the west from the temple mount, according to the Tosephoth Yom Toba on the passage; and it is probable enough that this Ginnath, garden, is identical with the Gennath of Josephus.

Monuments of Helena. Josephus, Antiq., book xx., chap. ii., says that the sepulchral monument of this queen was 3 stadia (about one-third of a mile) from Jerusalem. More than this is not known of this structure.

Sepulchral caverns of the Kings. In Erubin, 61 *b*, is mentioned "the great cavern of Zedekiah." In Midrash Tanchumah to Numbers iii., it is placed at 12 mill or 8 English miles, and in Midrash Rabbah to the same passage at 18 mill or 12 English miles from Jerusalem. The traveller from Leghorn of the year 5282, already quoted above says: "Not far from the Bab al Amud, is the cave of Zedekiah, which extends under ground to the mountains near Jericho. Several persons told me, that they themselves had walked a mile in the same. It is so spacious that a man on horseback with a lance in his hand, can ride through it quite comfortably." I now believe that this cave of Zedekiah, wherein it is probable that at a later period graves and caverns had been cut out of the rock, may denote the sepulchral caverns of the kings of

Josephus. The present sepulchral monument, or rather the cave in which it is, is that of the rich Kalba Seboa, who is mentioned in Gittin, 56 *a*, and which is five-eighths of a mile north from the Bab al Amud,* is held to be the cave of Zedekiah, and consequently identical with the sepulchres of the kings. About half a mile to the northwest of the cave of the Kalba Seboa, there is a sepulchral cave, consisting of two chambers, one above the other, and cut out of the solid rock; in both the chambers, there are about seventy niches hewn out in the rocky walls thereof, and the whole presents a very beautiful and remarkable work of antiquity.† It is commonly called the Cave of the seventy Sanhedrin שבעים סנהדרין, and is supposed by some to be the sepulchral caverns of the kings of Josephus; but this hypothesis is without any satisfactory proof, and even the name it bears of "the cave of the seventy Sanhedrin" is also quite arbitrary. This name probably was given to it, because it has about seventy niches, although they are quite empty, which may have led people to suppose that seventy elders were buried here. But who, and of what time were they? as there were always seventy such elders in Israel. I could find no trace for this appellation in our ancient writings, and only found it in quite recent works.

As Josephus makes no mention of an eastern wall, it appears, as was said already, that the eastern wall of the temple (i. e. of the temple mount) formed likewise the

* In the year 5607 (1847), the Arabs, on digging near this grave, found a deep vault full of gigantic human bones, which excited the astonishment of every one at the great stature of the persons, the remains of whom they were. The Pacha forbade farther digging, and the cave was again closed up.

† Since I have inspected this beautiful vault with its niches cut in the walls, I understand clearly the Mishna of Baba Bathra vi., § 8, which describes the ancient manner of forming sepulchral vaults with their niches one above and alongside the other.

eastern city wall, as it is still the case at the present day; he says likewise in another place, that the arches, vaults, and outbuildings of the eastern temple wall extended beyond the valley of Kidron, as it passed beneath them. The fact that the eastern wall of the city and temple were the same, may be derived also from Talmud Zebachim, 116 *b*, and Tosephtah Kelim, i.

It is true, that Josephus does not state in the passage quoted, that the city wall passed over the valley of Kidron, and reached to the southern part of the Mount of Olives; but it is stated in another place (Jewish War, book v., chap. vi.), that "Simon held in possession the upper town, the great wall as far as Kidron, and from the old wall all the part which extends east of Siloah, up to the palace of Monobazes, and the spring of Siloah;* Akra, the lower town, as far as the Palace of Helena, the mother of Monobazes" (Izates).†

That what Josephus terms "which extends east of Siloah," is already, without doubt, on the Mount of Olives. We find, likewise, in 1 Maccabees xii. 37, "The wall which was to the east, beyond the valley of Kidron, had fallen down, and they built therefore this part of the wall, and called it *Caphnatha*." I presume that this word is derived from the Chaldean word *Caphnaioth* (כפניות דקלים) which is synonymous with *Zini*, a species of palms, as stated in chapter i., article Zin. This name, however, signifies a spot on Mount Olivet, as I shall state more particularly hereafter, which was not far from Beth-Pagi

* In another passage, Josephus tells that the spring of Siloah, outside of the town, was in the possession of the Romans. Simon, therefore, could not have occupied the spring of Siloah itself, but only the wall and the part of the city which was not far from the spring, which being out of the circuit of the walls, was in the possession of the enemy.

† They point out, even at present, a large ruin north of the temple mount, in the district called Bab al Chotta, which the Jews call, from a tradition they have, "the Palace of Helena."

בית פגי; the name was derived from the circumstance that there, on the declivity of the mount, were found some olive trees and palms פגי תאנים וכפניות דקלים, "The *Pagé* of figs, and *Caphnaioth* of dates;" hence Caphnatha and Pagi.

It is also stated distinctly in Shebuoth, 16 *a*, likewise in the Tosephtah cited there, that a part of Mount Olivet, naturally referring to the southern part thereof, in the vicinity of the spring of Siloah, was actually within the city wall. A part likewise of the just-named Beth-Pagi was within the city, as I shall prove farther down. At the present day even you can find traces of a wall, which ran in a southern direction, near the village Selivan, which is on the declivity of Mount Olivet, close to the Siloah spring.

I have not succeeded, as I must confess, to discover many remains of the ancient walls, although I have read much in the works of several moderns, that they had actually discovered many remains, whilst they at the same time describe the direction of the walls according to their own assumed ideas, explain and expound the words of Josephus in many ways, setting out from the erroneous assumption that the modern Kallai is identical with the ancient Hippicus, and fix the course of the walls from this principle, and then fancy they can discover remains of antiquity, and endeavour to impose their belief on others. I have no doubt, that no learned man, who is a friend of truth, will or can contest my proof that Hippicus must have been on the north, and not at the west, since the Migdal Chananel occupied a northern position. Although this view must upset some darling scheme of certain scholars, the fact cannot be gainsaid, unless men are determined to dispute altogether the correctness and truth of the learned Jonathan, who lived at the time when Hippicus was built.

The present city walls occupy only in a few places the

site of the ancient ones. Only the southeastern, and nearly the entire western appear to me to stand on the old sites; whereas the present northern, northwestern, and southern walls stand where none other was before. The modern Jerusalem is therefore considerably smaller than the ancient one. Josephus also says, that the ancient city was 33 stadia in circumference, that is 4⅛ English miles; whereas at present it is but 3 miles, to wit, 5152 ells (each of a little less than 3 feet, or 1 yard English); the ancient city extended farther to the north, and a little less to the south than the present.

I believe that I may therefore boldly maintain that it is clearly proved, from what has been said, that the alleged grave of Christ is quite wrong; as it must have been indisputably without the city, at a distance at least of 100 paces, or 50 cubits, according to Baba Bathra, ii., § 9, whereas, the so-called holy sepulchre is pointed out as being in the city, not far from the ancient temple, exactly opposite to the northwest corner of the temple mount; although many pious men, who believe in all the Christian legends, take all possible pains to place it beyond the limits of the ancient city; and maintain, therefore, that this alleged position was beyond the first wall; that Hippicus is the present Kallai, and that the first wall ran from the Kallai to the temple from west to east. This idea is so ridiculous, that it deserves no refutation; for Jerusalem must have had, in that case, a truly wonderful shape and size; for it could not have been more than 150 cubits (300 feet) in breadth from south to north, excluding Zion, if the northern line extended from the Kallai to the temple. It appears even from 1 Kings xviii. 17, that the city wall extended in the time of Hezekiah to the vicinity of the Upper Pool, since those stationed on the wall could hear the speakers who stood there. Any one therefore endowed with common sense must accordingly acknowledge, that the alleged locality of the so-called holy sepulchre rests on an impossible idea, and that the whole matter is nothing but a fabulous tradition of the pious but deceiving Empress Helena, and of her equally deceptive priests, who discovered this grave, and had a structure erected over it.

MORIAH, THE TEMPLE MOUNT הר הבית.

This mount, which rises 141 feet above the valley of Kidron, and 2280 above the level of the sea, appears as a mount only on the east and the south sides, on which it is bounded by the valleys of Kidron and Rephaim; but on the north and west sides it is level with the other ground near it. This is owing to the many destructions which Jerusalem has had to endure, which caused the depressions on these two sides to be filled up with rubbish and ruins.

According to Middoth, ii., § 1, it was 500 cubits, say 1000 feet long and broad. But I found, by actual measurement, the present breadth from east to west 995 feet, and the length from north to south 1498 feet. The discrepancy is, however, easily accounted for; since the present place includes the space once occupied by the fort Antonia, which was to the north, and which being now united and included in the temple mount, makes this a third longer than it originally was.

This mount, therefore, now forms on its summit a flat and roomy place of the above dimensions, i. e. 1498 feet long by 995 in breadth. It is called

MEKOM HAMIKDASH, מקום המקדש

That is, the site of the ancient temple, in Arabic, Al Charim, "The Holy." It is enclosed on all four sides with a high wall and buildings; and the southern and eastern parts of this enclosure form, at the same time, the city wall in these directions. The western part is the well-known and revered fragment of the wall of the holy temple mount, and is named the כותל המערבי Kothel Hama'arabi, i. e. *the west wall.* It is sixty feet in height, and has twenty-three rows of stone. The nine lower rows consist of large stones, three to four cubits long, and two cubits broad and high. The upper fourteen rows, however, consist of smaller stones; and hence it would appear that this upper part belongs to a later period, and was perhaps built by Caliph Omar. It is also called "the mourning wall," since thousands of Israelites constantly deplore there and weep for the fall of Jerusalem. It is touching to see how every Jew bends his head, moaning and reverentially, at the foot of this holy wall, and lifts up his tearful eyes to heaven, and exclaims, sobbing, "How long yet, O Lord!" This spot is visited by travellers of all nations; and no one can ever quit the place unmoved, and with indifference. It is no vain fancy! I have indeed often seen there non-Israelitish travellers melt into tears. No one can describe the feelings experienced on this sacred spot. One paints to himself in spirit the former exalted state of the Israelitish people in the highest degree, and then feels suddenly that it is sunk into the dust and robbed of its glory; but his imagination places again before him the future exaltation—he feels himself inspired, and exclaims, "Surely this is the gate of heaven!" (Gen. xxviii. 17.) This wall is visited by all our brothers on every feast and festival; and the large space at its foot is often so densely filled up, that all cannot perform their devotions here at the same time. It is also visited, though by less numbers, on every Friday afternoon, and by some nearly every day. No one is molested in these visits by the Mahomedans, as we have a very old firman from the Sultan of Constantinople that the approach shall not be denied to us, though the *Porte* obtains for this privilege an especial tax, which is, however, quite insignificant.

In the midst of this plain מקום המקדש is a square platform, fourteen feet in height, in the middle of which stands the large mosque Al Sachra, i. e. the hard stone, referring to the אבן שתיה which is in the midst of it. It was built in 4397 (637) by Caliph Omar. This octagonal building is sixty feet in length, and has on four sides entrances and outer halls. On each of these four sides there are six windows, but seven on the other four. A large cupola is extended over the whole building, and is ninety feet high and forty in diameter; it is covered over with square leaden plates. In the walls, near the windows, there are introduced glazed bricks, green, red, black, and white-coloured, which reflect in many beautiful rays the solar light, and give the building a magnificent appearance. The inner walls are painted white; and there are in the interior twenty-four columns, each twenty feet in height, and sixteen of which support the great cupola. The interior middle portion of this mosque is enclosed and barred off by means of an iron railing. The Mahomedans go as far as this railing to perform their devotions, with their faces turned to the south. Within this railing is a small wooden enclosure, wherein is the Temple Stone אבן שתיה Eben Shetiyah, or "foundation stone" (Yoma v., § 2). It is a large, round, white stone, which is about thirty feet in circumference, and is covered over with red satin cloth. It is only fastened to the floor on one side, and is propped up below with pieces of wood, that it may not fall down; but beneath it the soil is dug away, and it appears to hang in the air. Its elevation from the floor is about ten feet. (Compare with Yoma v., § 2, where it is said that it was elevated but three fingers' breadth from the floor, which affords, therefore, a clear proof that the temple mount has been dug down about ten feet.) The Mahomedans reverence this stone as a holy object, alleging that it came from the garden of Eden, and that Abraham sat upon it when he was about sacrificing his son Isaac. They even go so far as to point out the traces of five of Abraham's fingers. Beneath this mosque there are in all directions subterraneous caverns and passages; but no one ventures to investigate, or even to enter them.* One large subterranean passage leads from this mosque to that of Al Achsa, i. e. The Farthest, the most northern mosque, since the Arabs have three especially sacred mosques, one in Mekka, the second in Medina, and the third in Jerusalem, which is the farthest to the north. Under the term Al Achsa, or the most northern mosque, that of Al Sachra is included, as they are considered to form but one mosque. Al Achsa is situated in the southern end of the temple place, and is a large and very long building, and is called by the Jews מדרש שלמה "the School of Solomon," though I could not ascertain whence the name is derived. Near this mosque is a very large cavern, wherein are found columns and ruins, equalled only by those of Baal-bek and Tadmor (Palmyra). There is also met with there a large stone sarcophagus, having a large and broad stone cover. No one knows what it contains, and none have yet ventured, or rather been able, to open it. It appears that all these ruins and remarkable monuments of antiquity date from the period of King Solomon.

On all sides of the temple place, are seen Mahomedan dervishes, who come from Barbary, in Africa (who have this prerogative above all the dervishes, owing to a distinction which they once obtained in a siege and battle at Jerusalem), armed with spears, standing sentinel day and

* If we note carefully the position of the mosque Al Sachra, we shall find that it is situated nearest to the west end of the temple mount, somewhat more distant from the northern end, farther yet from the eastern, and the farthest from the southern part of the same. See Tosephoth Yome Tob to Middoth, commencement of chap. ii.

night, to prevent any profane person, i. e., any one but a Mahomedan, from entering on this holy spot.

The Mount of Olives or Olivet הר הזתים also הר המשחה, Arabic, Djebl Tur, forms the highest elevation of the whole environs of the holy city, from which it is separated only by the valley of Kidron. It is 2555 feet above the level of the sea, and it has three summits. On the acclivity of the southern summit, near the village of Selivan, which part is called in Scripture הר המשחית "The mount of vexation or corruption" (2 Kings xxiii. 13), is a spot which the Arabs call Beth-Hana, probably the בית הינא Beth-Hina, of Pesachim, 23 *a*, also called כפר הינו Kefar, i. e. village of Hinu, in end of Ketuboth. Some consider the village Azaria, which is half a mile southeast from the Mount of Vexation, as Beth-Hina or Bethaniah; but it is unquestionably the same with Azal,* as I

* This gives me an opportunity to explain a passage in the Bible which many learned men have attempted, but not succeeded to elucidate satisfactorily. It is Zechariah xiv. 5, ונסתם גיא הרי כי יגיע גי הרים אל אצל ונסתם כאשר נסתם בימי הרעש בימי עזיה מלך יהודה. We find in several Oriental copies instead of וְנַסְתֶּם Venastem, "you will fly," וְנִסְתַּם Venistam, "and it shall be stopped up." Jonathan has the same reading, and explains it in the same manner in his Chaldean Paraphrase (see also Kimchi). If this be assumed, however, we cannot explain the גיא הרי "valley of my mountain," nor what relation the splitting of the Mount of Olives in twain has to do with the earthquake in the time of Uzziah. But I think I have found the key to this passage, and will quote for this end the following passage from Josephus, Antiq., book ix., chap. x., being a part of the history of Uzziah: "The king was highly nettled at this, and threatened to put them to death if they spoke a word more. Immediately the earth trembled, and the roof of the temple opened, through which a beam of the sun darted full upon the face of the king, who from that instant became a leper. This prodigy was followed by another: near a certain place before the city, named Erogê, the one half of a mountain that looked westward was torn from the other half, and rolled for the space of four furlongs, till it stopped to the eastward of it, by which means the road was blocked up, and the king's gardens covered with rubbish." I do not doubt but that this remarkable event is alluded

have stated in the description of Benjamin; whereas Beth-Uhana marks more correctly the ancient Beth-Hina. Not far from this Beth-Hina (Bethania) was Beth-Pagi, which partly belonged yet to the city, as appears clearly from Pesachim, 63 *b*, and Menachoth, 95 *b*, and Sanhedrin, 14 *b*; and that the city wall extended partly also as far as this spot, was said already above. A spot a little to the south of this is called, by the Bedouins and Arabs who reside there, Dir Zini, probably identical with the Zini of the "iron mount" of Sukkah iii., § 1, referring to a species of palm which grew there on the Mount of Olives, and synonymous with Caphnatha, also denoting a palm tree, as was also stated above. According to the passage cited from Talmud Sukkah, there grew also a species of hard palm צִינֵי הר ברזל, near the valley of Ben-Hinnom.

At the foot of the central Mount of Olives, just opposite the temple mount, and where the Jewish burial-place is, there is pointed out an uncommonly large square stone, covered over with a roof, supported on columns, which marks, according to popular opinion, the grave of the prophet Zechariah (2 Chron. xxiv. 21). I could, however, find nowhere any proof for the correctness of this tradition, which appears to me the more singular, since

to in Zechariah, and that גיא הרי Gé Harai, is by transposition nothing else than the Erogé for Gé-oré, of Josephus, Hebrew Gé Harai, or that it was called both Gé Harai and Harai Gé; and I actually once saw an edition of Zechariah which read ונסתם הרי ג״א, and if we could depend on this, it would argue in favour of the correctness of Josephus' legend of the mountain of Erogé, i. e. Harai Gé having been split and closed up the king's gardens. We should then translate: "And it (the way) shall then be closed up through Gé-Harai; for Gé-Harai shall come to Azal; and it (the way) shall be blocked up as it was blocked up in the days of the earthquake, in the days of Uzziah, King of Judah." Azal is, as said above, the modern Azaria, and the distance from Olivet agrees exactly with Josephus' legend; 4 furlongs, stadia, being half a mile, which is the distance between Erogé on Olivet and Azal, to which it was carried by the earthquake.

this monument appears to belong to the Gothic style of the middle age, and not to that gray period of antiquity. Near this is found a large cave with tall columns, which represent windows, by which I mean that through the space between the columns, which are placed close to the sides of the cave, the light is shed into the interior from without. This cave is called בית החפשית, English version, the "several house" of 2 Kings xv. 5. Near this, again, is a very handsome square structure, hollow within, and cut out of the rock; the upper part gradually diminishes till it forms, so to say, a pointed roof. It is called יד אבשלום "Absalom's Monument" (2 Sam. xviii. 18); but I can scarcely adopt this traditional nomenclature; since the "King's Valley" עמק המלך where Absalom actually constructed his own monument, was not near Jerusalem, but in the plain of Jordan, as, according to Bereshith Rabbah to Genesis xiv. 7, the valley of Siddim, Sukkoth, ha-Melech (King's), and Shaveh, are all one and the same, or the modern Al Gor; wherefore we must look for Absalom's column in that neighbourhood. I also found in Josephus, Antiq., book vii., chap. ix., that this monument was a marble column in the King's Valley, and two stadia* from Jerusalem. But this monument, now called that of Absalom, has nothing in common with that of Josephus, for it is neither a column nor is the material marble.

THE SPRING (FOUNTAIN) OF SILOAH עין שילוח EN SHILOACH

Is also called גיחון Gichon, in 1 Kings i. 33, which is given by the Chaldean paraphrase of Jonathan with Shiloach. This spring is found near the village of Selivan in a deep rocky cavern, on the foot of a rocky mount, on which formerly the Ophel stood. It first runs under ground in a southwestern direction, then issues forth near

* I presume it ought to read two hundred, and Al Gor is actually 200 stadia or 25 English miles from the holy city

the lower pool (which see), waters the gardens of the village Selivan, and is gradually lost in its farther course. This spring also existed in David's time, in its present position in the valley of Kedron, as we read in 1 Kings i. 33, "And carry him *down* to Gichon," and v. 35, "Then ye shall come *up* after him." But we find also mentioned an *upper* Gichon spring, in 2 Chron. xxxii. 30, which was situated undoubtedly near the upper pool (which see); the water of this upper spring, Shiloach or Gichon, ran southwardly through the Wady Djurad, where the modern pools are, and turning to Zion, passed through the Wady Rephaim, which, as I have already stated, was the Pass to the Fuller's Field, down into the Kidron valley, where it united with the Lower Siloah near En-Rogel. From the above it will appear that there were two springs of Siloah, the upper one of which, however, does not exist any more at the present day.

We find in Holy Writ that Hezekiah caused the Upper Gichon to be stopped up (2 Chron. xxxii. 2, 3, 30), and had the water brought into the city* (2 Kings xx. 20).

* The passage of 2 Chron. xxxii. 3, seems to contain a contradiction; it is said there that it was Hezekiah who stopped up the waters of the Upper Gichon spring, and led them westward down to the city of David. If now, he stopped up all the wells, springs, and water-courses (ibid. 3, 4), that the kings of Assyria should not find any water, why should he then conduct the water of the Upper Gichon to the west, in the direction of the city of David, unquestionably without the town, that they might nevertheless find water? It is said farther, in another passage, that Hezekiah conducted the water *into* the city, which no doubt refers to the water of the Upper Gichon, which he covered up so that it should not run without, and only diverted its course into the city; and still it is related as above, that he led the water down to the city of David, not *into* the city itself? It is at the same time to be remarked that the water of the spring took this course already before the time of Hezekiah, since it could run in no other direction, than into the valley of Kidron; what need was there then of conducting it again?

I therefore boldly maintain that the passage has another meaning, and

I gave myself a great deal of trouble to find out if possible the position of this subterranean water-course. I investigated many cisterns, and I discovered at length that the water of the cistern, which is situated between the temple mount and Kallai, in the direction where formerly was situated the Tyropœon of Josephus, was exactly like the water of the Lower Siloah spring in taste, weight, and purgative quality. The owners of this cistern also assured me that even in a continuous long absence of rain the water is scarcely ever entirely dried up in it. Whence I would clearly conclude that it must stand in some connexion with the subterraneous channel of the Upper Gichon. About 25 paces from my present dwelling, is the bath called Chamam al Shaafé, on the western declivity of the temple mount. There is found a very deep cistern, the water of which is just like that of the spring of Siloah; and I think it therefore certain that the former aqueduct of Hezekiah is now below the surface of the ground in this direction; although it formerly ran uncovered through the city, as we read in Yerushalmi Chagigah, i., that the Shiloach ran through the middle of the city (Jerusalem). The learned Azulai mentions in his שמות הגדולים "The names of the Great," fol. 30 *b*, that as late as the time of the great Cabbalist Rabbi Chayim Vital, who lived in 5340 (1580), one could hear near the Kallai or David's Tower, a strong subterraneous rushing of running water, which was represented as the ancient aqueduct of King Hezekiah.

that וישרם למטה "he led them downward," does not refer to Hezekiah at all, but to the spring of Gichon itself, which is of the masculine gender in Hebrew; and I would therefore translate it "And he, Hezekiah, stopped up the source of the waters of the Upper Gichon, which (spring) conducted them westward as far as the city of David;" which would therefore be merely a description of the nature of the spring, which poured its water into the Kidron valley; [whence Hezekiah may have led it into the city itself.—TRANSLATOR.]

This investigation also proves that though both springs are somewhat far apart, one being in the valley of Kidron, the other on the height of Gichon, they must still have but one source, since the water of both is exactly of the same nature and quality.

THE SPRING ETAM עין עיטם, OR NEPHTOACH נפתוח.

(Joshua xv. 9.)

In the Scriptures we nowhere find any mention of a spring Etam, but of a city of that name in 2 Chron. xi. 6: "He built Beth-Lechem, Etam, and Tekoa." This town, therefore, must have been situated not far from Beth-Lechem and Tekoa. Josephus places it at 60 stadia, 7½ English miles from Jerusalem, and says that in that vicinity there are many springs and an aqueduct, which goes to Jerusalem. It must therefore have stood without question near the old Castle of al Burak, where is a large spring, the water of which is carried hither (Jerusalem), through means of canals. Josephus, Bell. Jud., book ii., chap. xiv., makes the direction and course of this aqueduct to be 300 stadia, or 37½ English miles, and in his Antiq., book xviii., chap. iv., 200 stadia, or 25 English miles; but both data are evidently wrong, and must be errors of transcribing; for the direct distance is but 60 stadia, and if we even allow much for the curves of the aqueduct, which are naturally deviations from the direct line, it could hardly have been longer than 100 stadia. This aqueduct extends now from the spring Etam near Al Burak, towards Beth-Lechem, then in a northerly direction to the vicinity of Jerusalem, turns then somewhat southwesterly from Zion, passes the Wady Djurd and turns towards Mount Zion, encompasses the same on the south, then on the east; turns next to the north, and entered the city near the small southern gate Bab al Megarbi, runs to the temple mount, near the great mosque Al Sachra, where it issues forth through a tubular box, near the Mahomedan court-room Al Machkamé, in an outer hall. As the Mahomedans were engaged this year, 5605 (1845), in clearing a space near the West Wall המערבי כותל, they came accidently to a large subterranean cave, and a spacious and ancient structure, in which is a large reservoir of this Etam aqueduct, whence the water passes into the tubular box. Sultan Soliman conducted this Etam water also to the buildings on the west side of the temple mount, and to several other places; and there are still seen in all directions on several of these ancient tubes Arabic inscriptions.

SELIMAN ABN ALIM SENA 943 AL CHADJRA,

That is, Seliman, son of Alim, in the year 943 of the Chadjra (Hegira), or the Mahomedan era, which is 5297, A. M. (1537). Such a tube, constructed out of large, strong stones, and covered with ornaments, and supplied with the above inscription, is near my residence, which is situated on the western part of the temple mount.

These tubes are without water already these forty years; and only in the Machkamé the water flowed at the time I came hither, in the year 5593 (1833); but a year later, when the Bedouins and Arabs rebelled against Abraim Pasha, these barbarians went in their fury so far as to cut off and thereby destroy this beautiful and beneficent most ancient aqueduct. It remained useless till the year 5604 (1844), when the pasha of our city had the above fountain again restored; and even the one near my house was also repaired in the year 5607, and I was rejoiced to be able to obtain the water from it.

It appears that this aqueduct existed already in the time of Joshua. It is probable that an opening was made in it to the west of Mount Zion, so that passers by might draw water from it. The same is the case at the present day in many places, and I have seen a large one to the west of Mount Zion. I therefore believe myself authorized to assume that this aqueduct was called, on the spot in question, Mé Nephtoach מי נפתוח, "the opened water" (see Joshua xv. 9), as Rashi also explains in this passage, "this means the spring Etam." It is also probably referred to in 2 Sam. v. 8, "Whoever smiteth the Jebusites and toucheth the aqueduct;" which means who shall be able to cut off and destroy the supply of water, which furnished this necessary of life to the Jebusites, who will then be compelled to yield through the want of water.

It is also the same which was led into the outer court of the holy temple, and supplied it with the water necessary for the then sacrificial service, as said in Pesachim, 64 *a*. The Sea of Solomon ים שלמה of 1 Kings vii. 44, also received its water from this aqueduct, for which see Yoma, 37 *a*.

Let us quote here the description of the ambassadors of Ptolemy, king of Egypt, which they gave to their master after their return home from their journey to the holy city Jerusalem:

"The temple has its front to the east, and its back to the west; its whole floor is covered with marble. At the depth of nearly five-eighths of a mile under ground are found a number of aqueducts, which are constructed with an astounding degree of artistical skill. They are lined with lead, carefully closed up, and covered over with earth to a great depth. These artificial channels and aqueducts run under ground, in various directions, to all parts of the temple. In the floor of the sanctuary, and near the pavement, are constructed many secret openings, which can be opened and shut up at pleasure, and which cannot be observed by any one, without it be the priests and the temple servants. If these orifices be now opened, the water rushes in from all sides, and the marble floor of the sanctuary is washed clean of the blood of the sacrifices, if it be ever so much, and thus cleansed of itself, and in the easiest manner. There can be, moreover, never a want of water in these artificially constructed tubes, as it is conducted hither from a large natural spring (Etam), which to a certainty can never dry it.

"I cannot omit also to report to thee, O my king, that the people showed themselves ready with remarkable kindness to conduct me to the chief point of this aqueduct. One day, namely, I was conducted half a mile outside the city of Jerusalem,* when one of those who accompanied me told me to stand still and to listen awhile; and when I heard the fearful rushing of the water beneath my feet, I thought to myself how magnificent must be the work of this aqueduct." (See Meöre Enaim of Rabbi Meir De Rossi, fol. 15 *a*.)

We have also to remark that this aqueduct extends somewhat up hill from the valley below, and reaches even to the middle of Mount Zion. This is owing to the fact that the spring, the source of this aqueduct, near Burak, lies somewhat higher. This was already remarked by our wise men in Talmud Yoma, 31 *a*: "Abayé said, This proves that the spring Etam must lie about twenty-three cubits higher than the floor of the temple, since the water in the aqueduct could be conducted this height above the floor."

POOLS.

There are in the holy city and its environs the following five pools:

I. The Upper Pool of 2 Kings xviii. 17, Isaiah vii. 3, and xxxvi. 2. It is called by the Arabs Birkat Mamuli. It is about 500 paces west from the Kallai, and is about

* The spot here spoken of was probably the opening in the aqueduct, the Mé Nephtoach, which is about half a mile from the city.

100 cubits (200 feet) long and broad, and 15 cubits (30 feet) deep.

II. The Lower Pool of Isaiah xxii. 9, also called (ibid. 11) the Old Pool, likewise the Siloah Pool in Nehemiah iii. 15. It lies in the valley Ben-Hinnom, where the Siloah (Shiloach) issues out of the rocky mount, the ancient Ophel, and then falls into the pool, which is considerably smaller than the first, and then comes out again from the same.

III. The Pool of Hezekiah. This was constructed by Hezekiah, and produced by conducting the water into the city (2 Kings xx. 20). This pool, which is within the city, to the northeast of the Kallai, is of the same size with the Upper Pool, and is connected with it by means of a canal, which supplies it with water.

IV. The pool which lies to the east-northeast of the Bab al Sebat, which appears, however, to be a modern structure, as no mention is made of it either in the Scriptures or the Talmud.

V. The pool which is to the north of, and near to the temple mount, and in which, in ancient times, as Josephus reports, the animals destined for sacrifice were washed.

Besides these five, there are yet found two ruined pools to the northwest of Mount Zion, in the valley called Wady Djurad, which is situated between the heights of Gichon and Wady Rafaat. The northern one was constructed in the year 693 of the Chadjra (Hegira), or 5051, A. M. (1291), by Sultan Mahmed ben Kialian, as I have learned from the inscriptions on the walls of this pool; hence its name Birkat Sultan. The southern, however, was built by Sultan Soliman, in the year 943 of the Chadjra, i. e. 5297, A. M. (1537), and bears the name of Birkat Seliman.

Water is found only in the first three which I have mentioned; the other four are entirely empty, and partly ruinous.

Kallee, taken outside of the City.

Kallee, taken within the City.

Published by A. Hart Philadelphia

THE FORT KALLAI

Is situated on the west side of the city, near the Jaffa gate, not far from Mount Zion, wherefore it is universally supposed to be the Tower of David, Migdal David מגדל דוד; the Fort of David, Mezudath David מצודת דוד; or the City of David, Ir David עיר דוד; which is nevertheless an error, as I have said already that the Tower of David must have been situated not far from the Siloah spring. The Kallai is a strong castle, with a deep ditch and strong towers, and is situated on the highest elevation in the city. The stones in the foundation wall do indeed denote a most ancient structure; but the superstructure is evidently far more modern, and could not have been erected before the European princes came into the Holy Land and conquered it, as I shall more fully discuss in the historical part of this work. There are documents which state that this fort was built by men of Pisa, in Italy, who passed into Palestine in 4999 (1239). It appears to me that the ancient foundation walls of this structure are the remains "of the house of the heroes" בית הגבורים of Nehemiah iii. 16, or of the "corner of the armory house" עלות הנשק המקצוע of ibid. 19.

INHABITANTS.

Jerusalem contains more than 32,000 inhabitants, to wit, 7,500 Jews (6,000 Sephardim and 1,500 Ashkenazim; under the first are understood all the natives, and the immigrants from Turkey, Asia Minor, Persia, Arabia, and Barbary in Africa; and under the latter the immigrants from Germany, Holland, Hungary, Poland, Russia, Galicia, or other European countries), 15,000 Mahomedans, i. e. Arabs and Turks, and 10,000 Christians, i. e. Greeks, Armenians, Latins (Spaniards and Italians), Russians, and Germans.

SOME ACCOUNT OF THE SYNAGOGUES AND SCHOOLS,

ישיבות AND בתי מדרשים.

There are five large Synagogues in Jerusalem, which have existed already for several centuries. Four belong to the Sephardim congregation, and one to the Ashkenazim, or rather to the Germans, since, when it was founded, the name of the Polish, Russian, or Galician Jews was not known. I shall, however, speak more in detail of the last mentioned in the sequel.

Among the first four is the so-called Zion Synagogue. It is the oldest and largest; and if a common tradition is to be believed, for which, however, I know of no proof, it was the former college (Midrash) of Rabbi Yochanan Ben Zakkai. See, concerning this, Echa Rabbethi, which says that the בית הגדול of 2 Kings xxv. 9, "the great house," or "the house of the great," is (i. e. on this spot stood at a later period, and was again burnt) the College of Rabbi Yochanan Ben Zakkai. The other three were built at a much later period.

All these four Synagogues form, properly speaking, but a very large single building, since they stand near one another, so that one can walk from one into the other, and the centre one, the smallest of all, has no entrance from the street, and you have to reach it through either of the three others. On my arrival, in the year 5593 (1833), I found them in a most miserable and lamentable condition, since they were at the time greatly out of repair, and almost threatened to tumble in, and were useless in rainy weather, inasmuch as they were roofed in with nothing but old and rotten boards, and our brothers could not obtain the permission from "the pious faithful" to drive as much as a single nail to fasten anything in the building without being first authorized by the *most worthy* persons in authority, and such a favour, not to mention to permit the making of repairs, and much less to rebuild the Synagogues, could not be granted in order not to commit a terrible sin against Allah and his Nebbi (prophet); independently of which, the *silver* to procure the consent was not easily obtainable in Jerusalem.

But in the year 5595, Abraim Pacha of Egypt, who understood and was able to instruct and convince his people "that even the Nebbi had grown more tolerant in modern times," gave the permission to rebuild anew from the foundation all these four Synagogues, and they are accordingly at present four fine buildings. Their situation is opposite to the south-southwest corner of the temple mount, on the declivity of the former Tyropœon.

Besides the above five Synagogues, there are a great many smaller and private ones, which have been founded quite recently, and public and private schools ישיבות and colleges מדרשים, by which are understood public libraries, large collections of nearly all the accessible Hebrew books of modern and (more especially) of more ancient times, and manuscripts likewise, where every one is permitted to enter and make use of the literary treasures.

For the most part there meet, in each Yeshibah or Beth Hammidrash, societies who study and discuss together a particular subject, for instance, a מסכתא or Treatise of the Talmud; and they have usually one person, and this the most capable and learned, as teacher or chief, called ראש הישיבה Rashé Hayeshibah.

These Yeshiboth are foundations instituted by our worthy brothers in Babel, Asia Minor, Turkey, Italy, Barbary, Holland, Germany, England, and Poland; (and why should not America follow the example?) They devoted a sufficient capital, the proceeds of which will be enough to support a Yeshibah, together with the society meeting therein.

It is but lately that I obtained from the respectable firm of the Messrs. Landauer, of Hürben near Augsburg in Bavaria, a permanent capital, which will always procure me the rent for my own residence and Yeshibah.

Several Yeshiboth have at the same time a Synagogue, which is also the case with mine.

In the principal Yeshibah there is also the seat of the high court בית דין הגדול, which has to decide on the gravest and most important proceedings.

The following are the principal Yeshiboth and Bathé Hammidrash in Jerusalem; besides which there are several unnamed smaller ones. The name given to them, bears generally an allusion to that of the founders; and as female names are also met with, it proves that worthy ladies were likewise founders of these institutions.

1, Beth-El בית אל; 2, Beth Jaacob בית יעקב; 3, Chesed Leäbrahan חסד לאברהם; 4, Nevéh Shalom נוה שלום; 5, Berith Abraham ברית אברהם; 6, Kissay Eliyahu כסא אליהו; 7, Keneseth Yisrael כנסת ישראל; 8, Kedushath Yome Tobe קדושת יום טוב; 9, Orach Chayim אורח חיים; 10, Damesek Eleazer דמשק אליעזר; 11, Ruach Eliyahu רוח אליהו; 12, Bné Yitzchak בני יצחק; 13, Toledoth Yitzchak תולדות יצחק; 14, B'né Moshéh בני משה; 15, Aholé Zadikim אהלי צדיקים; 16, Chayim Vachesed חיים וחסד; 17, Kinnor Naim כנור נעים; 18, Pirché Kehunnah פרחי כהונה; 19, Kehunnath 'Olam כהונת עולם; 20, Emeth Leyaakob אמת ליעקב; 21, Magen David מגן דוד; 22, Beth Aharon בית אהרן; 23, Dath Yehudith דת יהודית; 24, Ohel Rachel Ubeth Yehudah אהל רחל ובית יהודה; 25, Sukkath Shalom סכת שלום; 26, Eduth Bihoseph (my own) עדות ביהוסף; and 27, Or Hachayim אור החיים.

These colleges and schools are all in Jerusalem; but there are several, although as might be expected in less numbers, in Hebron, Zafed, and Tiberias.

Among those mentioned above, are several which have been in existence many hundred years, and of their founders we may say in the words of the Psalmist (cxii. 6) : לזכר עולם יהיה צדיק "The memory of the righteous shall remain for ever."

THE SYNAGOGUE OF ASHKENAZIM—ARABIC, DIR ASHKENAZI.

I deem it worth while to speak more circumstantially concerning this structure, since it will lead us upon much that is historically interesting. By the term Synagogue is not meant a single building, but an entire large court, which forms as it were a whole street, which contains within its circuit many houses and buildings, and is constructed after the style of a monastery. Through perusal of documents and investigations made on the spot, I came upon the result, that this old building is the same Synagogue which was built in the year 5027 (1267), at the time of the celebrated Nachmanides (Ramban רמבן); since he says, in his letter to his son in Spain, as I shall mention hereafter in the historical part: "We found a very handsome ruinous building with marble columns and a pretty cupola, and we made collections in order to restore the same to serve as a Synagogue, and commenced to build on it." This building, with a handsome cupola and marble columns, is still existing close by the present Synagogue; it was taken away from the Synagogue, as I shall tell hereafter, and is called at present Al Maraga, and is used as a raisin mill, in which raisins are crushed and ground in order to boil them into a syrup. At the time of the founding of this Synagogue it was limited to this single building; but at a later period, when the number of the Jews increased, all the houses contiguous to it were incorporated with it, and all denominated the Synagogue of the Ashkenazim. It was for a long time the only Synagogue in Jerusalem where divine worship was held. It would appear that the old Sephardim Synagogue, that of Zion, was in ruins, since neither Nachmanides, nor other describers of the country, mention the least about it. As late as about 5346 (1586), both congregations, the Sephardim and Ashkenazim united, worshipped there together; and only at the time when it was taken by violence from the congregation, and they were compelled to choose themselves another place in the court as a Synagogue, which has been preserved up to the latest period, the Sephardim separated from the Ashkenazim, the former probably restoring their ancient and former Zion Synagogue, since which time the other remained with the Ashkenazim, whence its name to the present day.

It is said in a work, חרבות ירושלים, "The Ruins of Jerusalem" (see farther in the historical part, under the year 5386), "that forty years previously, i. e. 5346, the Muphti of Jerusalem, a very great enemy of the Jews, caused the Synagogue to be closed, and had it changed into Al Maraga; and to this day we have not been able to obtain possession of it again; and this holy place is unfortunately transformed into one of a degraded and profane use. At the present time (in the year 5386, 1628), the Cadi, a terrible extortioner, was prepared to cause several shops to be constructed out of the hall and front of the Synagogue, in order to rent them out to Mahomedans, and to make a mill out of the closed Synagogue, Al Maraga. When the officers of the congregation were informed of this, they presented a petition to the Cadi, that he might not so desecrate the holy place, the more especially as it was their lawful property, obtained by purchase, and exhibited to him at the same time the legally signed documents in their hands; but he did not desist from his intention till he had made them give him 1000 grosh = 250 ducats = 500 dollars. Thereupon he himself gave them another legal testimonial that this Synagogue had been already, for more than one hundred years, perfectly legalized property of the Jews, by whom it was built up for a Synagogue, wherefore no one is empowered to contest it with them, or to disturb them in their possession of it."

There is nevertheless no doubt but that, notwithstanding the 1000 grosh and the title deed of the Cadi, this proposition was nevertheless carried into effect at a later period; since the formerly closed Synagogue, Al Maraga, was turned into a mill, as it is even now; and in the outer hall, all along the front side, were erected a number of shops, although they happen to be at present the property of the Jews.

The whole court, therefore, with the exception of Al Maraga, has ever since remained uninterruptedly the property of the Ashkenazim, and used by them as their Synagogue.

In the year 5450 (1690), there arrived in the Holy City a very pious man called Rabbi Yehudah Hachasid (i. e. the righteous), a native of Poland, but who had resided a long time in the neighbourhood of Frankfort-on-the-Maine, accompanied by many distinguished and pious Rabbis from Germany. He was chosen as the chief of the Jerusalem Ashkenazim, and commenced to enlarge, adorn, and improve the Synagogue buildings, whence they were called the Synagogue of Rabbi Yehudah Hachasid. But this precious chief was, alas! soon carried off by death, and the congregation was plunged, through the plague, want, poverty, and distress, into the most melancholy and terrible condition, which compelled them to borrow money on these buildings from the Mahomedans at an enormous rate of interest. Their distress became constantly greater and greater; the capital grew apace, through the unheard-of rate of interest, to an enormous amount; wherefore their chief, the venerable Rabbi Moshéh Hakkohen, undertook himself, about the year 5465 (1705), a missionary journey into Germany, to represent the terrible condition of the pilgrims to their brothers abroad, in order to institute for them a collection on a large scale. Rabbi Moshéh actually met with such sympathy among the German Israelites, that, through the honourable collectors at Frankfort-on-the-Maine, there was raised, in various collections, altogether the sum of 25,600 ducats. But even this large amount was no longer sufficient to free the Jerusalem congregation from debt, since the enormous rate of interest never allowed them to extinguish the capital; and these poor people were continually tormented in the most terrible manner by their insatiable creditors, although, in point of fact, the debt had been paid off severalfold already.

Things were in this state when the Mahomedans suddenly assailed the Synagogue on Sabbath, the 8th of Marcheshvan, 5481 (about 1st of November, 1721), set it on fire, and burnt up whatever was combustible, together with all the books and the rolls of the law (ספרי תורות), of which there were forty in the buildings, which latter also would surely have fallen likewise a prey to the fearful conflagration, had they not been constructed out of large and heavy stones. They also seized the officers and the most respectable members of the congregation, and threw them into prison; they then took possession of all the buildings, driving the Ashkenazim away out of them. These unfortunate people, driven to despair, fled precipitately, in all directions, some to Hebron, some to Zafed, and others beyond the limits of Palestine. Thenceforth no Ashkenazi durst to show himself in Jerusalem. The Mahomedans, the creditors of the congregation, took possession of everything: they made use of the outer court of the Synagogue as a dung and rubbish heap, so that there arose here by degrees a natural dung and rubbish hill. All the cellars and other subterranean structures, likewise, were filled up completely with dung and rubbish.

In the year 5572 (1812), when a fearful epidemic raged in Zafed, and in all Galilee, about twenty Ashkenazim ventured to flee to Jerusalem in disguise. They now were suffered to live in quiet and undisturbed in the Holy City, partly because they were unknown, and partly, perhaps, because the hatred and persecuting spirit of the Mahomedans against the Ashkenazim had abated, as three or four generations had passed away since the above occurrence. In the year 5576 (1816), efforts were made, through the intervention of the respectable and rich Israelites at Constantinople, to obtain a firman (decree) from the supreme government of Turkey, to permit the Ashkenazim to have a roll of the law ספר תורה in their Midrash at Jerusalem, and that the Mahomedans should not in future be allowed to make any claim against the Ashkenazim then residing in the Holy City, on account of the old indebtedness of their predecessors. This concession obtained, caused a constant increase of the number of German Jews in Jerusalem, so that they soon felt the want of a Synagogue. A mission was accordingly sent, in the year 5596 (1836), to Mahmud Ali Pacha at Alexandria, with a respectful petition, to grant them the permission to reoccupy the property of their ancestors, and to rebuild the ruined ancient Synagogue. At the same time petitions were presented to the Austrian and Russian consuls resident there, to employ their influence with the Pacha to obtain for us the desired privilege. I gave myself all possible pains to address this request to these gentlemen in a powerful and touching petition, so that nothing might be left undone to obtain our wish; and we must offer our thanks to these worthy men, who felt sincerely for this noble cause, and actually employed all their influence to induce the tolerant Pacha to be favourable to our petition. He immediately sent, in the most gracious manner, a firman to the congregation, that no creditor should be empowered to make any more demands against the property of the Ashkenazim, since the debt had become outlawed through the lapse of time, wherefore they were permitted to take possession again of their former property, and to rebuild their Synagogue.

On Thursday, the 19th of Elul, 5596 (September, 1836), the matter was judicially decided; the Ashkenazim were permitted to enter the precincts which had hitherto been denied to them; the buildings so long closed were reopened; and they commenced at once to remove the dirt and rubbish, which required several weeks to accomplish; after which the work of building was undertaken. This was done with such zeal and industry, that already on Sabbath, New Moon of Shebat, 5597 (about February, 1837, consequently in a space of eighteen weeks), the Synagogue, being completed, was consecrated amidst the greatest solemnities.

At a later period, all the other structures, terribly ruined as they had been by the savage Arabs, were restored, and thoroughly rebuilt, and are now in good condition. Even Al Maraga would also have been taken possession of, had it not been that the government was taken away again from the tolerant Mahmud Ali Pacha, through which cause much that was good and noble remained unaccomplished.

This holy building was then closed, and no divine worship held therein for the space of one hundred and sixteen years, two months, and three weeks, which had never been omitted before since its foundation, five hundred and seventy years anterior to its reconsecration.

In clearing away the rubbish at the rebuilding of the Synagogue, &c., there was found a very handsome and deep cistern, cut out of the solid rock. It was without water, but there were found in it a number of gold coins. I discovered, however, none among them which belonged to antiquity; they were of modern times, and were German and Polish gold coins (ducats), none of which were more than 300 to 400 years old.

POSTSCRIPT TO THE SYNAGOGUES OF THE SEPHARDIM.

In these Synagogues is also bestowed a Jewish elementary education. It is indeed very simple, still very correct and good, and considerably better than with the Ashkenazim. But the higher school, where the child obtains instruction in the Talmud, holds a higher rank among the German than the Portuguese: and we can soon distinguish whether a child has been educated in one or the other Talmudic school; since the Ashkenazim endeavour to improve the child more than the others in sharp and deep thought and wit.

THE LENGTH OF DAYS IN PALESTINE.

The longest day, the 21st or 22d of June, is here, at Jerusalem, fourteen hours and ten minutes, that is to say, from sunrise to sunset, without including the twilight, which is of four hours' duration, two in the morning and two in the evening; so that there is but, on the above day, five hours and fifty minutes perfect night. The shortest day, the 21st or 22d of December, is nine hours and fifty minutes; the twilight three hours; and the actual night therefore eleven hours and ten minutes. I subjoin a table of the increase and decrease of the days, in accordance with careful and oft-repeated observations made by myself.

Month	Day	Day	Month	H.	M.
March.	21	21	September.	12	
	26	16		12	10
	31	11		12	21
April.	1	10		12	24
	5	6		12	33
	10	1		12	44
	15	27	August.	12	54
	20	22		13	03
	21	21		13	05
	25	17		13	13
	30	12		13	20
May.	1	11		13	22
	5	7		13	27
	10	2		13	34
	15	28	July.	13	40
	20	23		13	46
	21	22		13	48
	25	18		13	51
	30	13		13	55
	31	12		13	56
June.	1	11		13	57
	5	7		14	
	10	2		14	03
	15	27	June.	14	06
	20	22		14	09
	21			14	10

Month	Day	Day	Month	H.	M.
Sept.	22	21	March.	12	
	25	18		11	53
	30	13		11	42
October.	5	8		11	32
	10	3		11	22
	15	27	February.	11	12
	20	22		11	2
	23	19		10	55
	25	17		10	50
	30	12		10	42
	31	11		10	40
November.	5	6		10	33
	10	1		10	27
	15	27	January.	10	21
	20	22		10	15
	23	19		10	12
	25	17		10	9
	30	12		10	5
December.	5	7		10	1
	10	2		9	57
	15	28	Dec.	9	54
	20	23		9	51
	21			9	50

PART II.

תוצאת הארץ

OF THE PRODUCTS OF PALESTINE IN THE ANIMAL, VEGETABLE, AND MINERAL KINGDOMS.

INTRODUCTION.

If we compare the present nature of Palestine, and the poverty of its productiveness, with the former flourishing condition of this holy land, it would appear to us as though all the powers of nature join unanimously in the complaint issuing from Zion, "How have we been destroyed!" (Jer. ix. 18.) Of a large portion of the former natural products, we find no more any trace; and those yet remaining are mostly in a very miserable condition. Still we cannot avoid recognising, judging from these feeble remains, the ancient and blessed Palestine, as much as the magnificent ruins of a destroyed fort give us proof of its former strength.

I have accordingly described in the following chapters whatever I have been able to ascertain respecting the animal, vegetable, and mineral products of Palestine; and if I have mentioned, among others, such species as no longer exist there, it was done because I have sufficiently convinced myself, after many years' investigation in the Holy Land, that several occidental commentators and translators of the Bible and Talmudical works have not rarely erred in respect to these things, and that I believe that I have been enabled, with God's blessing, to rectify completely the errors thus committed.

CHAPTER I.

ANIMALS.

CLASS I.—MAMMALIA.

CATTLE בקר, Al Bakar. Oxen, as well as cows, are in the worst condition in Palestine. They are employed in all sorts of field labour, and are killed only when they are completely worn down, and useless for any work wherefore no beef fat is obtainable in all the country. Only in the vicinity of Zafed are seen, although very rarely, some fattened cattle; but even their flesh is tough and tasteless.

Sheep כבש, Al Charub,* however, are very plentiful. The greater portion of these useful animals have fat tails, weighing from eight to ten pounds, and the fat of which is as well-flavoured and good as that of geese. The rams, who all have horns, are even still larger and stronger than the females. The beef-cattle being so poor, mutton is almost exclusively eaten; and as the domestic supply is not sufficient, many sheep are imported from abroad, chiefly from the countries beyond Jordan, such as Belka and Al Ledja, and from the Euphrates. In the month of Kislev, 5605 (December, 1844), a large quantity of sheep were even imported into Jerusalem from the town of Musi in Kurdistan.

* Onkelos undoubtedly meant sheep in his paraphrase to Gen. xxxiii. 13, giving "hundred Kesitah" with במאה חורפן Chorephan (derived from the Arabic Charub, hence Chorb, or Chorph), a hundred sheep, or purchase by barter, which is a nomadic custom and mode of trading still in vogue. (See also Onkelos to Gen. xxi. 28.)

Goats עז, Al Djidi, which are nearly all black, are certainly lean; still their milk is good and inodorous. From the skins of these animals are manufactured the water-bottles, which are used for the conveyance of water, oil, and milk. The greater part of these bottles, however, are made from the skins of the larger and stronger goats, which are raised in the environs of Hebron. These last are a peculiar species, are of a brown colour, and are called Djidi Mamri. (Compare with Gen. xviii. 1.)

Gazelles איל, Al Gazl,* are very plentiful. In the country around Ramla and Lod are seen entire herds of these beautiful animals; they are eaten by the Israelites also.

Deer צבי, Al Tabi, are a small species of fallow deer, and are mostly found on the mountains of Ramah, Bethel, and in the vicinity of Jordan. Their fawns are often raised, on account of their beauty, in the houses of the more respectable inhabitants for amusement. Their flesh has a taste very much like that of pigeons.

Yachmur יחמור, is left untranslated by Saadiah, who renders it simply, in Deut. xiv. 5, with Al Yachmur. It denotes a species of wild goats; but I have never seen any specimen of them.

Chamois אקן, Al Badn; these fleet animals, which greatly resemble the he-goat, are quite common in the mountains of Lebanon. The Persian version calls them Kuz-Chuhi, i. e. "mountain rams."

Dishon דישן, according to Onkelos, Rima, "unicorn." I do not venture to decide whether this explanation be correct, or that of the Persian Targum, which translates with "mountain goat." Otherwise the unicorn is at present entirely unknown in Palestine, although, according to Bereshith Rabbah, chap. xxx., a young Rima was seen

* It is highly probable that the European word gazelle is derived from this Arabic root.

there in the time of Rabbi Chiya; and it is only still to be found (?) in eastern Africa and India.

Forest Ox, Buffalo תאו, Al Djamush. These stout and fat animals, which are eaten by the Jews also, are as large as an ox, and are met with in great numbers in the vicinity of Lake Semechonitis, or the Waters of Merom, of Joshua xi. 5, and of the cities Akra and Cheifa.

Giraffe זמר, according to Saadiah and the Persian translation, Al Sirafah, does no longer live in Palestine, but in Southern Africa.

Camel גמל, Al Djemal. These animals, which are quite common with us, are employed for the carrying of heavy burdens. There is, however, another species of camel, called Al Adgin,* which have thin feet, a small head, and but one hump; they are able to run very fast; but this they can accomplish only on a level road, and a sandy soil, but by no means in mountainous districts. They are for this reason frequently employed on the road between Gazza and Egypt, which leads through sandy plains; but extremely seldom in Jerusalem, as it is surrounded with many mountains.

The Hare ארנבת, Al Arnab; these animals, which are eaten by the Turks, are quite plenty.

The Cony or Rabbit שפן. Of these there are two species; the one is called Al Avavi, and is like the European stable rabbit, and is eaten; the other, however, Al Wabr, is larger than the first, and lives in whole troops on the mountains and the clefts of rocks. The last appears to be merely a wild subspecies of the first.

The Hog חזיר, Al Chanzir; these animals, notoriously odious to the Turks, are extremely rare in Palestine; but

* Whence the Chaldean version of Isaiah lx. 2, of בכרי מדין Hogené הוגני "Camels of Midian." The commentators to Bereshith Rabbah to Gen. xxvii., translate incorrectly הוגנין with עירים *foals*, as it should be "small camels."

in the same proportion the wild hog is met with more frequently than elsewhere, and it causes great devastation on vineyards, fruit-trees, and the products of the field. These destructive animals increased considerably and to a dangerous extent during the years of Ibrahim Pasha's government, since he did not permit the Bedouins to have any arms. They are most numerously met with on Mount Tabor, in the vicinity of Hebron, the Lake Semechonitis, and finally among the canebrakes which grow on the shores of the Dead Sea.

The Weasel חלד, Al Chuldi; this animal, so well known elsewhere, is quite rare with us. The Persian translation renders it An Gurb, "the cat."

The Mouse עכבר, Al Far, is very numerous, as well as the rat.

The Tortoise צב, Al Selchefi, is found quite plentifully near Hebron. The Arabs also call a species of lizard Al Tzab, exactly like the Hebrew word rendered tortoise.

The Hedgehog אנקה, Al Konpud, which name the Arabs also apply to the porcupine, a subspecies of which the hedgehog is (compare Isaiah xxxiv. 11). Many hedgehogs, which are eaten by the Turks, are found between Tiberias and Zafed.

Koach כח. The Arabic version of Saadiah gives this word with Al Chardun, which denotes a species of large lizards, which inhabit ruins and the open field. Their length, the tail included, is one foot. They keep their head in constant motion, and are quite numerous in Palestine. Their excrement is employed in Egypt for dyeing red. I also heard the Arabs call this kind of lizard Al Tab, nearly the same as Tzab צב. (See above.)

Tinshemeth תנשמת is given by Saadiah with Al Sambaras, i. e. the crab, which animal frequents the rivers of Palestine in large numbers, but is not eaten by the Mahomedans. Rashi, however, and other commentators on the Scriptures, translate it with *toulpe,* modern French, *taupe,* or the mole, called in Arabic Al Far al art,* which means literally earth-mouse. These animals are very numerous, especially in the level district of Sharon.

My researches regarding the nature of this animal led me to important observations, which I cannot pass over in silence. In Talmud Babli, Moëd Katon, 6 *b*, the mole is described as אשות Ashuth, an animal which has no eyes. Many non-Israelite naturalists have sought to cast ridicule in their literary productions upon this statement of the Talmud, and to designate it as an error, the result of ignorance, since the mole is actually supplied with eyes, though they are small and so closely overshadowed by the hair which is attached to the brows, that they can be discovered only with difficulty. So long as I lived in my native land, Germany, the above statement of the Talmud was to me also an incomprehensible riddle, which grieved me the more, since on the one side I could not contradict the truth, whilst on the other I could not comprehend why our learned Talmudists, who display in all branches of natural history an astonishingly thorough knowledge of their subject, should have remained strangers to the nature of the mole. But since I have resided in the holy land of our fathers, on the native soil of our Talmudists, I have become convinced to my great joy that these Talmudic sages have nowise erred, but that the oriental Ashuth אשות is so different from the European mole,

* I believe that the לחפור פרות Lachpore Payroth, is the same as פרות Paroth, from the Arabic Farah, mouse, plural, Faroth, Hebraicé Paroth, mice; hence לחפור פרות "for the digging mice, or moles." [The Arabic root here found in Isaiah must not surprise the inquirer; since in the intercourse subsisting between neighbouring nations, nothing is more natural than that occasionally some expressions or forms should pass from one language to the other, especially if they be cognate dialects.—TRANSLATOR.]

that the two have scarcely any resemblance with each other.

There are namely two species of this little animal in Palestine, both of which the Arabs call Al Far al art; the one is nothing but the ordinary field-mouse; the other, however, is the oriental mole proper, or the Ashuth of the Talmud. It looks very much like a newborn kitten, and is two spans in length, has a large, thick and round head, two small openings for the ears, *but no eyes whatever.* Its four teeth, as it has no lips, are always strongly visible, as though it had its mouth open; the two lower and larger teeth, which stand so close to each other as though they had grown together, are very long and sharp; whereas the two upper and smaller ones, with which it tears off the roots under ground, are short and connected with the nose. Its fore-paws, with which it digs up the ground, resemble those of the European mole. It has no tail. These noxious animals are hunted after by the peasants. But they are not rarely brought alive to Jerusalem, where they are sold, since their blood is said to possess wholesome properties.

In order that European naturalists might be able to convince themselves that the statement of our Talmudists is correct and true, that the Eastern mole has actually no eyes, I was induced to send a specimen of this little animal to Munich, the capital of Bavaria.

The Frog צפרדע, Al Akruk, is very plentiful in the country. (In Baba-Bathra, fol. 73 *b*, occurs the word אקרוקיתא "the female frog," evidently from the Arabic.)

The Lion ארי Al Zbe, is not met with in the Holy Land; but in the wilderness through which the road to Egypt lies, lions are often seen.

The Monkey קוף, Al Setun, is at home on the frontiers of Egypt, and only trained monkeys are occasionally brought to Palestine. The Adné Hassadéh אדני השדה of

Kelaim, viii. § 5, is, according to my opinion, the Ourang Outan.*

The Tiger נמר, Al Nimer, is met with on the banks of the Jordan in the vicinity of Jericho, as also on Mount Tabor and Lebanon. When, in consequence of the destruction of the holy city of Zafed, in the year 5594 (1834), that part of the town inhabited by the Jews remained deserted by them during the space of six weeks, a tiger was seen in that place. The Arabs are in the habit of kindling fires around their tents at night, in order to keep off the tigers, which dread nothing so much as fire.

The Wolf זאב, Al Dzib, is very common in Palestine; but is most frequently met with in the environs of Banias and Chaspeya.

The Fox שועל, Al Shagl. Several species of this animal are found in the Holy Land.

The Hyena צבוע, Al Tebbé, inhabits the mountains of Judah, Lod, and Galilee. This beast, so dangerous to human life, and which has so great a propensity for the exhumation of corpses, has been met with even on Mount Olivet, the burial-place of the Jerusalem Jews.

The Bear דב, Al Dib, is found in the mountains of Lebanon, Chermon, Carmel, Tabor, Banias, and Chaspeya.

The Horses סוס, Al Faras, are remarkably fine and handsome in our country.

The Ass חמור, Al Chmar, is found in large numbers. But the also so-called Wild Ass ערוד Al Paré (comp. with Peréh, Jer. ii. 24), is also at home with us, especially on the mountains of Edom. The wild species are used by the Arabs as food.

The Mule פרד, Al Bagla. This beast of burden is to be met with in large numbers.

The Dogs כלב, Al Kelb, with us, run about without a

* Joseph. Bell. Jud. b. vii. ch. xxv, makes mention of a root called Baraas, which grows in the vicinity of the town Machur, which has much in common with the Adné Hassadéh of Yerush. Kelaim, viii. 5.

master; wherefore they do not enter the houses, but remain constantly in the streets; but they are so quiet, that they even do not bite the passers-by, should they happen to tread on them. It is a remarkable fact, that, although our dogs are constantly exposed to the burning heat of the sun, and cannot, moreover, find water anywhere to quench their thirst, a case of canine madness (hydrophobia) is unheard of among them.

The Cat חתול, Al Kata, is likewise not raised in the houses, but lives without an owner in the street; but this adroit thief knows perfectly well how to steal into the houses by descending from the roof, and to carry off with the utmost cunning whatever is not carefully locked up.

CLASS II.—AMPHIBIA.

The Tortoise צב, Al Selchefi. (See page 289, same article in Mammalia.)

Koach, see ibid.

Letaäh לטאה is, according to Saadiah, Al Etaia in the Arabic of Egypt, the same which is called, by the Palestine Arabs, Al Abubrish; it is the *small* lizard, which is, the tail included, not more than a span in length, and is found in dwellings. The Persian translation, "wangas, i. e., the tortoise," is evidently wrong, since the Talmud speaks of the "Zanab Haletaah," the tail of the Letaäh, which is not applicable to the tortoise.

The Snail חמט, Al Chalson, is given by Saadiah with Al Charba, a species of large lizard. I once found such an animal in the garden which is by my dwelling. It was near three fingers thick, and a foot long, the tail included, which, however, occupied nearly half the length of the animal. Its hue was grass-green, with golden yellow spots; but it changed its colour several times, especially when it was angry. After I had caught it, its whole skin became golden yellow, whereas the former yellow spots became white. Its back was like that of a fat fish, thick and pointed, and its skin furrowed. But its eyes were the most remarkable thing in the animal: it could, namely, look at two objects at the same time; for instance, with one eye it could see an object to the right, and with the other something to the left, or could look with one upward, and with the other downward. The little creature I had captured was therefore a chameleon, which possesses all these peculiarities. But when I questioned an Arab neighbour concerning the name of my prize, he answered Al Charba, which, nevertheless, is the word with which Saadiah translates the Chomet or Snail of the Bible.

The Frog צפרדע, Al Akruk. (See above.)

Serpents נחשים, Al Chivi, are plentiful in Palestine, especially those called house snakes. These remain occasionally for years and days with their young in the same house, and go in and out without injuring any one. I have seen snakes of this kind which were three feet long and three inches thick. Some years ago a serpent was met with on the road to Jericho, which was more than six feet in length, and as thick as a man's arm, and was of a black colour. When the travellers had cut it down, the blood streamed from it as though they had butchered an ox.—The following fact will prove that the warning given by our Talmudists, not to drink water which has been standing in an open vessel (Terumoth viii., § 4), is really deserving of attention. A person in Tiberias drank some water thus exposed, and was soon after a corpse. It had no doubt been poisoned by a serpent, which had drunk from the same.

It is a phenomenon bordering on the miraculous to see many Arabs and Egyptians handling with their bare hands the most poisonous snakes, jumping and capering about, and playing with them as with a string, whereas any one else would be instantly bitten if he were merely to touch these dangerous animals. It must, however, not be supposed that they only practise thus with serpents which they have previously tamed or rendered innocuous by depriving them of their poisonous fangs; for they carry on this incredible sport even with such strange serpents as are brought in from elsewhere, and which they can to a certainty never have seen before in all their life. It is, as said, an exhibition which appears preternatural.

The Crocodile עקרב הגדול, Al Buda, is met with on the shore of the Mediterranean, near Cheifa and Cæsarea, but is not above two feet in length.

CLASS III.—BIRDS.

The Eagles נשר, Al Nisr, of which the greatest variety are found in Lebanon, build their nests on the highest rocky pinnacles of this mountain.

Peres פרס, Al Ekab, is a species of vulture.

'Ozniah עזניה, Al Enka, i. e. Long-neck, is likewise a kind of vulture, which has a long neck and legs, and stands nearly four feet in height. These three kinds of birds are solely found in the Lebanon and the land of the Druses.

Daäh דאה, Al Chadah, is a species of bird of prey, as large as a goose. I have often seen such a one flying down on the roofs of the houses of our town, to fetch his prey from there.

Ayah איה, Al Zada, i. e. the hunter, denotes a species of falcon, which are trained by the Arabs for hunting. There are several kinds of this species to be met with in Palestine.

The Raven עורב, Al Kak. Besides the usual raven, there is here a smaller species, called Zarzir. (Compare Bereshith Rabbah, chap. lxv.)

The Ostrich בת היענה, Al Neam, lives in the wilderness on the frontiers of Egypt. In a Persian translation before me, the ostrich is termed an Shetur Murdj, the camel-bird.

Tachmos תחמס, Al Chtaf, i. e. the bird of prey, a species of owl.

The Cuckoo שחף, Al Hakub, from its call, Kub-ku-ku. The Persian translation has An Shechin (see Tinshemeth).

Netz נץ Al Basi, a species of falcon, which is trained for hunting, and is especially found, in very large numbers, in the country of Diarbekir, on the Tigris.

The Night-Owl כוס, Al Bus, dwells in ruins. The mournful cry of this bird is clearly heard by night in Jerusalem, more particularly, alas! on the holy temple mount.

Shalach שלך, Al Semag, i. e. fish, which means, therefore, the fish-catcher, is found numerously near Lake Chinnereth.

Yanshuf ינשוף, Al Bashak, a species of owl or night-owl. The Persian translation gives An Laglag (see חסידה Chasidah).

The Bat תנשמת, Arabicé, Dir Lil, i. e. Night-bird.

The Pelican קאת is called by the Arabs Al Djemal al Bachr, i. e. the sea-camel, because it is the largest water fowl. Saadiah and the Persian translation give this word with Kuk, which is the bird Kiik (Kik?) mentioned in Talmud Sabbath, fol. 21 *a*. Its Hebrew name קאת Kaäth "disgorger," is derived from the circumstance that it can disgorge from its crop or sack which it has under its throat, whatever it has swallowed into it, be it water, fishes, worms, &c. This bird has been frequently observed on the sea of Chinnereth.

Racham רחם, Al Srakrak, is a bird which is found in the Egyptian desert, more particularly, however, in Northern Africa; it is of the size of a dove, and its Arabic name is derived from its crying *srakrak* when it flies. (See Chulin, 63 *a*, and Onkelos.)

The Stork חסידה, Al Laklak. There are two species of this bird, the one white, the other black, and both are frequently met with in the country about Gazza. The Persian translation has rendered it with An Sepd Murdj, i. e. The White Bird.

The Parrot אנפה, Al Babgah, is not a native of Palestine, and is carried thither as a curiosity by the Turks.

Duchiphath דוכיפת, is translated by Saadiah with Hadhud, the double-comb, the Lapwing.

The Swallow עטלף, Al Senuna. The Persian translation has it An Shab Ferach, night-bird or bat. On the shore of the Mediterranean are found large masses of sea swallows, which have white spots on the breast; whence the expression in Tosephtah of Chulin, ch. iii., סינוניא לבנה The White Senuniah, the swallow with white spots.

The Quails שלו, Al Kuta. Of these fat birds, which are as large as a pigeon, there are such quantities in the neighbourhood of the Jordan, and in the country to the east of the same, that they almost cover the face of the land. The Arabs throw stones at them when they are on the wing in order to kill them.

The Dove יונה, Al Chamam. There are two species of this bird, the House Dove and the Field Dove. It is esteemed as sacred by the Mahomedans, wherefore they do not eat it. In the country of the Druses, in Lebanon, is found a large species of wild pigeon, which is probably alluded to in Talmud Chulin, 139 *b*, under יוני הדרסיות Yoné Hadrisioth, which would almost lead me to suppose that the Druses existed already in the time of the Talmud.

The Domestic Fowl תרנגול, Al Dik. There are in Palestine ordinary and Indian fowls, the latter of which are called Al Dik India, or Dik al Chavash. In the isle of Cyprus there are such large and fat fowls, that they are even celebrated in all Palestine. We have, however, no Guinea fowls.

The Goose or Duck אווז, Al Awas. Except on the seashore in the vicinity of Zidon, Beirut, and the frontiers, no geese or ducks are met with. Wild ducks are found on Lake Chinnereth.

Peacocks תוכיים, Al Fawas, are not found in Palestine, and are only imported from abroad. The Malays, the inhabitants of Malacca, call these birds by their Hebrew name Tukiim.*

The Partridge עגור, Al Chadjla, is used as food by the Jews. The Hebrew name 'Agur is perhaps derived from its peculiar cry, "gur, gur." In the vicinity of the ancient Beth-Choglah, now Beth-Chadjlah, many partridges are found, which circumstance, perhaps, caused the name of the town.

Siss סים, Al Akruk, a species of Crow. See Jonathan to Jer. viii. 7, כרוכיה Keruchiah, i. e. the Arabic Keruk =Akruk.

Koré קורא is given in Bereshith Rabbah with Long-neck, a species of stork, which has a long and thin neck, and of which many are found on the frontiers of Egypt.

In the vicinity of the Jordan and Lake Chinnereth are occasionally seen several kinds of long and thin-necked swans. There is also found there a kind of bird taller than the stork, red in colour, and having a very long neck. I suppose this to be the flamingo. The nightingale also visits the shores of the Jordan. Of the other kinds of the birds of Palestine which are unknown to me, I could obtain no reliable information from the Bedouins and Arabs, because they do not occupy themselves in the least with natural history.

CLASS IV.—INSECTS.

The Scorpion עקרב, Al Akrab, is a native of Palestine; and although not bigger than a very large spider, its sting is nevertheless mortal. About eleven years ago a little girl two years old was stung by a scorpion, and she

* May this not be taken as proof that Solomon's Ophir and Tarshish ships traded to Malacca? since the Peacock is only named in connexion with the voyage to these countries?—TRANSLATOR.

died the same day. The following is the only remedy which can be applied with any degree of success. So soon as the scorpion has stung any one, it runs around in a circle, as if it were confused; it is then to be caught, and fried in oil, which oil is then placed on the wound. The person stung is then saved from death, and escapes with a mere swelling. The greatest number of scorpions are met with south of Jericho, not far from the Jordan.

Centipedes נדל, Al em arba wearbain, are found in Palestine in large quantities. Some are nearly one and a half feet in length, as I have convinced myself by actual inspection; but even on the smallest of these insects I have counted above two hundred legs. Their bite is occasionally mortal. These little animals lay such hold on the human flesh, that they cannot be removed from it without putting a live coal on them, whereupon they immediately quit their prey.

The Bee דבורה, Al Nachal. Hive-bees are not numerous; the more frequent are the wild bees met with. The greater part of the honey used in this country is a syrup prepared out of boiled wine. In the vicinity of Tiberias is found a species of very large bee, called Sbura זיבורא. These little creatures settle down in large swarms, especially at harvest time, and are very troublesome to the people.

The Ant נמלה, Al Namal. There are in Palestine ants of the greatest variety of species, small ones no less than the large winged kind. These domestic plagues, which dread nothing so much as the smell of pitch, are found by troops in the food, and render it unfit for use.

The Hornet צרעה, Al Namus. The species, the sting of which is fatal, is not found in Palestine, it being confined to the frontiers of Egypt, and is there but seldom met with. As these insects fly before the smell of tar, the Bedouins, who are compelled to work in the field when the country is visited by this plague, paint the face, hands, and feet with tar, and are then secured against the sting of the hornets. In the summer of 5598 (1838), Egypt was visited with this indigenous plague, and many human beings lost their lives in consequence.

The Locusts ארבה Al Djardi. These dangerous visiters spread over the country in myriads, though, thank God, but seldom; and when they come they cover the whole surface of the earth, and in a few minutes everything green in the field is destroyed. In the year 5598, I was an eye-witness of this deplorable phenomenon; namely, on Monday, the 25th of Kislev (about the 23d of December, 1837), at one o'clock in the afternoon, there came suddenly a swarm of locusts, flying from the southwest in an easterly direction past the Mount of Olives. They were grass-green, and a finger long. During their passage, which lasted an entire hour, such masses of these little animals fell to the ground that the surface of the soil was covered with them. Fortunately the harvest was long since over at the time, wherefore they could cause no injury. The Arabs roasted many of these locusts and ate them with much relish; so did the Barbary Jews likewise, as they allege to have the traditional certainty that this species of locust is permitted to us in Scripture, it being the Chagab חגב of Leviticus xi. 22. The same visitation was unfortunately witnessed in the year 5605 (1845). On Friday, the 23d of Shebat (31 January), at 1½ P. M., a swarm of locusts, flying from the northwest to the southeast, spread over our land. Their passage lasted about three quarters of an hour. The colour of these locusts was a reddish brown, and they were also smaller and less numerous than the former. They, however, repeated their visit after a few weeks three times, though in less numbers. These guests halted in Galilee and Al Gor, and destroyed the products of nature to such a degree that a famine was almost the consequence. In the month of Ab (August) following, many thousands of Arabs, of the tribe Arab al Anasi, came in consequence to Jaffa and vicinity, from the Syrian Desert between Damascus and Aleppo, with their wives, children, and flocks, in order to supply themselves with the necessaries of life. These famished people gave away their cattle and all they possessed merely to obtain bread. Their intention of staying in our vicinity till the succeeding winter filled all the inhabitants of Palestine with fearful apprehensions.

When, eighteen years ago (1827), the whole of Galilee had the misfortune to be infested with the locust plague, the then governing Pacha, Abd Alla, who resided at Acre, gave orders that each one of his subjects should furnish a peck measure full of these noxious little animals, in order to contribute by this means to their destruction. But this measure was without any good result; another experiment succeeded much better. There is a bird called Al Semarmar, resembling the goldhammer, which the locusts fear as their deadly enemy, and they make their escape so soon as they hear his voice. The Pacha, therefore endeavoured in a cunning manner to entice these birds to come, and this remedy did not fail of being effective, for it was not long before the country was freed from the devastating troop. The south and southeast winds are also destructive to the locusts.

CLASS V.—WORMS.

The Leech עלוקה, Al Alak, is found numerously, especially in the vicinity of Zafed and Jaffa.

The Silkworm תולעת המשי, Tut al Charir, is very largely propagated in the country of the Druses in Lebanon, whence many thousand cwt. of silk are exported abroad.

The Purple Snail, חלזון ארומי, Al Chalsun Achmar, is rarely met with on the sea-shore near Chcifa and Acre.

CLASS VI.—FISH.

In the Mediterranean, Chinnereth, and Semechonitis, as also in the Jordan, are found many kinds of fish, which are nevertheless essentially different from the European ones. Some are found which weigh thirty pounds. In the sea near Jaffa, there is found at times a species of fish which emits a phosphorescent light in the dark not unlike rotten wood. (Compare Job xli. 24.) I even convinced myself that this luminousness continued after the fish had been salted as long as three days, and that the finger, which had some moisture adhering to it after touching the flesh of it, was also luminous in the dark. This peculiar property of the fish is only destroyed when it is put over the fire, or immersed in hot water.

There is found likewise in the sea of Chinnereth a very fat fish, Al Barbud, which has no scales, wherefore it is not eaten by Jews. I consider it to be a species of the eel.

There are two kinds of fish known as שבוטא Shebuta, Al Sabuta, one of which is as large as a hog, and is very fat and well-flavoured. It is not met with in Palestine, and is only caught in the Italian seas, and especially near Fiumé. It is known among the Italians as Tanina. (See Talmud Chulin, 25 *a*, טונס, which Rashi explains with Taninus, Tanina; ibid., 109 *b*; and Sanhedrin, 59 *b*.) The other is a smaller species, has tender flesh, and is salted before being eaten. In Talmud occurs the phrase קולית האספנין (comp. Sabbath, 145 *b*) Kolith Ha-ispanin, in Greek Kolias Κολίας, denotes a species of sea-fish, perhaps the sardelle, and in general all kinds of small salted fish; hence Kolith Ha-ispanan, "salt fish coming from Spain" (Ispanin).

CHAPTER II.

THE VEGETABLE KINGDOM.

In the following chapter it is my intention to enumerate all the vegetable products of Palestine which are known to me, whether they are still existing there, or were formerly to be met with from their occurring in the Talmud. But no surprise must be expressed at the brevity of my description, since it is not my intention to furnish a natural history, but merely an enumeration of the products of the Holy Land.

The Grape-vine גפן, Al Anab, flourishes most luxuriantly in this country, and it is not rare that you meet with vines which are extended so far that thirty men can conveniently sit under the overshadowing of one, as under a tent. The wine obtained therefrom is very good, but somewhat too thick and heavy. Owing to the constantly heated state of the atmosphere, wine does not last long with us, and soon becomes sour. Wine three or four years old is something very rare in Palestine, and brings a high price. The single berries of the grape are at times as large as a walnut.

The Figs תאנה, Al Tin, are small, and are not as large as the Italian. The dried figs are called Al Gragra (Talmudicé גרוגרות Grogeroth). There are also to be met with wild figs, called in the language of the people Adam's figs, because it is said that of the tree which furnishes this fruit it was that Adam and Eve made themselves aprons in Paradise of the leaves, which are more than two feet long, eight inches broad, and two fingers thick,—as the making of aprons was naturally not possible from the ordinary fig leaves. The fruit of this tree, enclosed in a soft shell covered with fine prickles, grows from the midst of the leaves, is in shape resembling a large egg, and is well-flavoured. As this species of fig was originally derived from America (?), it is called in the Africano-Arabic dialect Kirmis Nazari, i. e. the fig of the Christian country.

The Mulberry Fig שקמים, Al Djimis, is a certain species which ripens before the ordinary fig, but has no taste of figs, and is on the whole not good for food. This fruit grows without stem, directly from the wood. The tree bearing it is stronger and taller than the usual fig-tree.

The Pomegranates רמון, Al Riman, which are very abundant, are found of two species, the sweet and sour.

The Olives זית, Al Situn, although plentiful, are small and poor; so also is the olive oil of Palestine very inferior to that of Italy and Provence in France. In the vicinity of Chaspeya, on Mount Lebanon, however, olives grow there as large as a small egg.

The Dates תמר, Al Thamar, of which there are two kinds, are scarce, and then not of the best; and good ones are only found near Damascus. No date-honey is therefore seen any more in Palestine. As the lawful palm branches, Lulab לולב, for the festival of Tabernacles (Levit. xxiii. 40), are used only those which have grown out from the body of the tree the very year they are cut; for when they grow older, the leaves spread apart, and are therefore useless for the ceremonial purpose.*

The Citron, Paradise Apple אתרוג. פרי עץ הדר, Al Athrundj, whence is derived the name of orange, for the citron is a species of orange; lemon, Al Limon; the China orange, Al Portugal; and the orange, Al Orants, i. e. the

* Bedouins have assured me that among the palms there are male and female trees, which they know easily how to distinguish, and that they would not produce fruit if they did not graft the female on the male. (See Pesachim, 56 *a.*) [This phenomenon requires no assurance of Bedouins, as it is universally known. The fruit-bearing olive, too, it is said, requires an unfruitful one near it to produce fruit.—TRANSLATOR.]

golden apple (Prov. xxv. 11), from Mala aurantia, are all, properly speaking, belonging to the orange species. Of all these kinds of fruit, there are very many found in Palestine; but they last not long, and rot away very quickly. Of lemons there are two kinds, the sweet and the sour. Citrons, of which no grafted ones are ever produced here, weigh occasionally more than twelve pounds.

Apples תפוחים, Al Thappach, Pears ענסים, Al Andjas, Peaches פרסק, Al Pharsk, Quinces חבושים, Al Sfarshl, and Almonds שקדים, Al Luz,* both sweet and bitter, are produced in great abundance (see Bereshith Rabbah, chap. xlii.), although the apples and pears are far inferior to the European.

Mulberries תות, Al Thuth, are plentiful. In the garden near my dwelling there is a tree which is twenty-four feet in height. (Sabbath, 144 *b*.)

St. John's Bread חרוב, Box-horn, Al Charub, is produced in abundance with us, but it is dry and tasteless.

Nuts אגוזים. Walnuts, Al Djus, and Hazelnuts לוז? Al Funduk, are rare. But there is a species of long nuts, called Pustuk (Pistachio?), which are green, and have a good flavour.

Chestnuts ערמון, Al Kustul (changing *n* into *l*, for Kustun, castania) are at present not abundant. The chestnut tree is also called Shach Balul, i. e. the Chief Tree, because its wood is hard and very durable.

The Gourd, Wonder Tree קיקיון, Al Krua, of Jonah iv. 10, is scarce; this tree grows so rapidly, that it attains a height of twenty to thirty feet in three to four months. It bears a fruit from which a sweet oil (Ricinus oil, comp. Tal. Sabbath, 20 *b*), which is a wholesome purgative, is

* This shows that Shekadim is synonymous with Luz, as Saadiah translated the first with Luza, wherefore Luz is not to be rendered, as usual, with "hazelnut."

expressed. In the district of Diarbekir, on the Tigris, the Wonder Tree grows abundantly in a wild state.*

Prunes דרמסקן, Darmaskan, the Damascenes, Al Swauda, are not found in Palestine, but are brought hither from Damascus, whence their name. (Of the other kinds of fruits we shall speak hereafter.)

CEREALS.

Wheat חטה, Al Chanta, also called Al Kamch, is grown in abundance, and no other than wheaten bread is met with in Palestine. But the best wheat is grown in the country situated near Gazza, on the Jordan, and near the cities of Kerak and Hauran beyond Jordan, where the grains are particularly large and good.

Barley שערה, Al Seir, is extremely limited in supply, and is used only for horse-feed. Rye, oats, and millet, however, are not grown at all. Rice is produced only in the neighbourhood of Chuli, on the Lake of Merom; it is quite singular in colour and taste, being red in appearance, and swells uncommonly in being boiled.

Pottage or lentils ערשים, Al Adas, are plentiful, and are broader than those grown in Europe. We have, also, a peculiar kind of fruit called Dura, which has nearly the same shape as the lentils, but is quite white, and serves as food for poultry. The Arabs and the common people grind this singular fruit and make cakes of it. Maize likewise is called Dura; this also is used for bread, especially, however, in the vicinity of Chuli, where it is extensively cultivated. Both the last-mentioned grow on thin stalks, which attain the height of a man.

FOREST TREES.

Cedars ארז, Al Ars, are found nowhere in Palestine,

* The Kokos nuts do not grow with us, but are brought hither from Arabia by the pilgrims coming from Mekka. I suppose that the oil of Kik, of Sabbath, ch. ii, § i, is the oil of the Kokos nut.

except on Mount Lebanon. But in Syria, in the vicinity of Aleppo, there are likewise Cedars, though in very limited numbers.

Tidhar תדהר (Isaiah lx. 13), Al Tatar, is a tree which grows near the Jordan, and flourishes for the most part, like the willow of the brook, near water-courses. It grows to the height of ten to twelve feet, and obtains often a large circumference. Its wood is very hard, and brings a high price. It appears to me that it is the one commonly called Box Tree.

The Cypress תאשור, Al Sarui,* is a species of Cedar. It attains a great height, has some fragrance, and the wood is sold at a high price. Specimens of this tree have attained the age of more than a thousand years. It is seldom found in Palestine; in Jerusalem, however, and this on the spot where formerly the holy temple stood, there are several Cypresses.†

The Bay Laurel ארן, Al Ar, is extensively met with in Palestine, especially in the land of Galilee, particularly in the city of Zafed, where our brethren cover their tabernacles on the feast of Sukkoth with laurel branches, which bear a great resemblance to those of the Charub Tree (St. John's Bread Tree).‡

* In Rosh Hashanah, 23 *a*, Teäshur is explained by Saribna, which is similar to the modern Sàrui.

† Bereshith Rabbah, ch. xv., says that Teäshur is identical with Puksinun, which I suppose means Box Wood.

‡ I wish to state here, that, according to my view, the fruit דפנא Daphna, so often mentioned in the Talmud, is derived from the Greek Daphné, which word signifies the Laurel Tree, and has its origin in Mythology. The legend is, that the nymph Daphné being loved by Apollo, and pursued by him wherever she went, became tired of life, and prayed that the earth might swallow her. She was answered; and when Apollo one day was about to embrace her, her feet were suddenly turned into roots, her arms into branches, and he embraced a laurel tree. Hence the Greek name of Daphné for the laurel, and the Talmudic Daphna.

The Acacia (Shittim) Tree שטים, Al Sunt, is found in Palestine of different varieties; it looks like the Mulberry Tree, attains a great height, and has a hard wood. The gum which is obtained from it is the Gum Arabic.

The Red Oak אלון, Al Balut, of our country is larger than that of Europe, and its wood is extraordinarily durable, and furnishes the best charcoal. The acorns growing on this tree are roasted and eaten.

The Terebinth אלה, Al Butum or Ulma, bears a small fruit בטנים, Al Butan, which looks like green peas; it is hollow within, and has a sourish taste. They bore holes in the trunk of this tree, and there issues thence a gum, which is that called Turpentine. Rashi to Gen. xliii. 11, seems not to have known this fruit, since he suspected *Botnim* to be peaches, which are not a natural product of the country, consequently could not have been referred to in the speech of Jacob in the passage cited.

The Birch לבנה, Al Labna, is seldom met with in Palestine.

The Fir Tree, called Al Znober, is found more abundantly in our country.

Gopher-wood עצי גפר, in the Persian translation Zubhai Senobr, is a species of Fir Tree called Al Piniuni, and is found plentifully near Hebron; it grows nearly as tall, and is almost as strong, as the Cedar. On the joints of its branches it has a sort of points, which bear a small nut, called, like the tree itself, Piniuni.

The Myrtle עץ עבות, Al As, is found in Northern Galilee, and especially in the vicinity of Zafed, in such abundance, that they cover the tabernacles with the same. It is from this district, where it is not rare to see Myrtle trees which are fifteen to twenty feet in height, that the holy city of Jerusalem, Chebron, and Jaffa are supplied with Myrtles, as they are not found at all in the country of Judah.

Willows of the Brook ערבי נחל, Al Zafzaf (Ezek. xvii. 5, צפצפה Zaphzaphah), are met with in the vicinity of Jordan, and 2 English miles southwest from Hebron, on the road to Dura (2 Chron. xi. 19), near the Wady Kura. It costs us therefore much trouble to obtain the necessary supply of willows for the feast of Sukkoth (Levit. xxiii. 40); since in the village of Colonia, the former Moza, where this tree was so very abundant during the existence of the holy temple (Tal. Sukkah, 45 *a*), not a single specimen is any more found.

The Thorn אטד, Al Zadr, the wood of which is hard, and therefore used for cabinet-work, grows in abundance in the plain of Jordan. It bears a small and sour plum, called Al Dum, or Al Nebk. Among other smaller shrubs is also met with the sloe-thorn, the fruit of which is better than that of the European kind.

The Broom (Planta Genista) רתם, Al Ritham, grows to a height of about eight feet, and has a hard wood, which makes excellent charcoal; it is found most abundantly in the great desert. To this day there is a valley called Wady Rithma from the large quantity of broom bushes which grow there. (Compare with 1 Kings xix. 4, 5.)

The incorrectness of rendering *Rothem* רתם with juniper bush, as some translators have done, is proved by the fact that not one shrub of the kind is found in all Palestine.

A species of Beech, Al Baks, which has a hard and reddish wood, is also found in our country; also a lighter species, called Al Kikab, which is something like the European ash tree.

The Canes קנה, Al Kazab, which grow on the margin of rivers and in swamps, are thick and often at times ten to twelve feet in height. There is also met with a smaller and thinner kind of reed, which is used for pens by the inhabitants of Palestine.

The Sugar Cane, Al Kazab Mas, is much grown in the

Holy Land, and particularly in the vicinity of Jaffa and Gazza: it grows to the height of a man. As there are no sugar mills in Palestine, and no one understands the art of transforming the sugar cane into sugar, the sweet juice is extracted from the cane merely by sucking it with the mouth.

Cotton צמר עץ, Al Katun, is produced in large quantities in the mountain of Lebanon and the vicinity of Shechem, and is exported extensively to Europe. As we possess no spinning machines, it will appear quite natural that our spun cotton yarn is very coarse.

Flax פשתה, Al Kuthin, is not cultivated in Palestine, but is brought hither from Egypt, and is very fine and valuable. But we obtain a supply from Bengal in India, which is even superior in quality to the Egyptian flax.

Hemp קנבס, Al Kanub, is not found in Palestine, but is produced in the vicinity of the city of Damascus.

Tobacco, Al Dudan, is cultivated to a great extent in the vicinity of Shechem and Zafed, and is of a good quality, although not equal to that of Hungary or Turkey.

The Papyrus Shrub ניר, Al Warak, is only found sparingly in Northern Galilee, on the shores of the Jordan, and has the shape of a large onion, with long leaves. It is a plant consisting of many layers of leaves, one within the other, like the coats of an onion. This plant is not used any more for writing on, as we have plenty of paper imported from abroad.

Jessamine דודאים, Al Jasmin, is a well-known sweet-scented flower. (Compare Rashi to Gen. xxx. 14.)

Cinnamon קנמון, is also found with us. (Compare Echa Rabbethi, fol. 15, col. 4.)

The following names of plants, occurring in the Talmudic writings, I have been able to ascertain.

The Sumach אוג, called the Tanner's Tree, Al Sumak,

does not grow high. It bears a grape-like fruit, which has a sourish taste, and has a remedial power of checking the diarrhœa. The kernels of this fruit are small and red like small lentils. The leaves of this tree are used for the tanning of skins.

Mustard חרדל, Al Chardal, is grown in uncommonly large quantities, especially in the environs of Chebron. In this year (1845) seven pounds Bavarian weight were even sold as low as four cents (two pence sterling). The mustard plant grows to the height of six to eight feet. It appears from Ketuboth, 111 *b*, that in olden times it attained a very great height.

Dill שבת, Al Sabeth, is similar in appearance to the plant called horsetail; it has a somewhat sharp taste, and is cooked up with food.

The Tophach טופח, Al Djillan, is a species of vetch: it produces a fruit resembling large peas; it is black and has the taste of a bean.

Rimin רימין, Al Rimi. This tree produces a thorny fruit, the rind of which is like the apple, half red and half green; it has a sweet taste, and is in size about that of a hazelnut. It has, like the olive, a single kernel. In Egypt, where it grows most abundantly, it is called Al Nebk, and it is a species of sloe-thorn אטד (which see).

The Sorb Tree עוזרדין, Al Serur, bears a fruit resembling a small pear; it has a single kernel, and is not of a very good flavour.

Benoth Shikmah בנות שקמה, are a species of wild mulberry figs, and are called Al Djimis. (See above, art. Shikmin; also Echah Rabbethi, חד גמזין *One* Djimis.)

The Caper נצפה Al Kafar, grows on shrubs, is a finger long, and full of kernels. It is preserved either in salt or vinegar. The kind mentioned in Berachoth, 36 *a*, and elsewhere as קורא, צלף, קפריסין is another species, and unknown to me.

Coriander כסבר, Al Kusbar, although not as good as the European, is produced in large quantities in Palestine.

The Caraway כמון, Al Kamun, of Palestine is larger than that produced abroad.

Cockle זון, Al Suan, is a species of black grain, found growing amidst the wheat; it is very bitter, and makes the person who eats it confused, as though intoxicated.

Sappir ספיר, Al Mas, is a small, broad, and smooth pea, having an agreeable taste.

Cardamons? פורקדין, Al Kurdman, are long and white seeds, which are bitter, and are mostly used for feeding poultry, but are also employed as a remedial agent.

Shaüa שעוע, Al Lubia, is larger than the Mas or Sappir just mentioned; it has a reddish colour, and is well-flavoured and wholesome.

Kishuïm קשואים. This generic name, used in Scripture, for instance, in Num. xi. 5, denotes various kinds of cucumbers and pumpkins, of which the following two are the principal ones: 1, Al Kulwasi, which is red in the inside, and weighs not rarely a hundred pounds, but is as tasteless as large; 2, Al Kara, which is white (Sotah, 10 *a*; Kerithoth, 6 *a*). The usual cucumber, קשות Al Fakus, is long and thin. Melaffin מלפפין Al Chiar, is the name of the usual small pumpkins.

Lettuce חזרת Al Chasa,* is the ordinary head lettuce, of which there are two kinds, the garden and field, or wild salad.

The Endive עולשין Al Hindiv, so called from Hindia =

* While speaking of herbs, I wish to elucidate the Tamcha תמכא of Pesachim ii., § 6, which is generally considered to be the horseradish, but according to my view erroneously, since at this day there grows, to be sure, not in Palestine, but in the Barbary states, an herb Tabga, i. e. Tamcha, by the usual changes of b for m, and g for ch, which has much similarity in taste with the Chazereth or Lettuce. Its leaves are like those of the Karpas; it is an herb resembling the onion. The leaves are not eaten; only the bulb is. The horseradish, however, is, I think, meant by Adal עדל, at the end of Tractate Ukzim.

India, whence it originally came, is somewhat bitter, and resembles the lettuce or chasa. There is also a wild endive, Al Skikara; it is very long, twice or three times taller than the common endive, has a bitter taste, and is eaten with vinegar. In Echa Rabbathi to chap. iii. 42, occurs the phrase אירס נדבי Eres Nidbi, which is the correct reading, as mentioned by Rabbi Menachem di Luzano, in his Maärich, and means "Poison Endive."

The Leek כרשי, Al Kurath, is not found any more in Palestine. The same is the case with the Charob Bean חרוב, Al Chrub. This bean derives its Arabic name, so similar to the Charub tree, or St. John's Bread, from its taste being like that of the kernels of the fruit of this tree.

Turnips לפת, Al Lifth. This name is applied indifferently to both the white and yellow turnip; but in the Egypto-Arabic dialect they have different names for these two species, the first, or the white, being called Al Shalgam, and the other Al Shunder.

Nippuz נפוץ, is a species of radish, and is found of two varieties. One is flat and round, resembles the white turnip, and has an outward reddish skin, and is pungent and agreeable to the taste; the other is long and thin, has a white skin and no sharpness of taste: the last is the צנון Zenone proper; the other is the Nippuz, and is called by the Arabs Al Truf.

Tardim תרדים, Al Salka, is an herb, the leaves of which resemble those of the endive; they are boiled and eaten.

Leünin לעונין, Al Kalaf, is the Greek Chrysolachanon, or Atraphaxis, a kind of spinach.

Cabbage כרוב, Al Krumb, also called Al Sartab, or Kunbit.

The Cauliflower תרובתור, Al Karnibed, grows very high, and has a thick, strong stalk, which often grows to a height of more than four feet. It is reported in Ketuboth,

111 *b*, that formerly this plant grew so tall that they had to employ a sort of ladder to reach the top.

Perishim פרישים, is the same with Chabushim חבושים, Quinces, which see.

Tharmus תרמוס, Al Thurmus, is a sort of large pea-shaped bean, and is bitter. To render it fit for food, it must be soaked in cold water for a day or two; but it requires but little boiling.

Pilsilus פלסלוס, or the wild fig-bean, is so bitter that it cannot be eaten.

Lafsan לפסן, Al Lafsan, and in Greek Sinapi, has a taste like the turnip, and their leaves resemble also each other. It grows to a height of two feet or more. It is not found in our country, but is a product of Egypt. Its seeds are known as the Egyptian mustard.

Melons אבטיחים, Al Batich, are of two kinds—1, the water-melon, Batich Achmar, i. e. the red melon, because it is inside quite red; it is often twenty to thirty pounds in weight: and 2, the sugar-melon, Batich Assar, i. e. the golden yellow melon, the inside of which, consisting of nothing but seeds and water, is unfit to eat.

Rue פיגם, Al Sadabia, is a bitter and acrid herb, and only used as a medicine.

Mallow חלמית, Al Kubisa, a flower-bearing herb.

Talthin תלתין, Al Chalba, is a species of sweet clover, which men can eat in a raw state; its seeds, too, are edible. This herb, which grows extensively in Egypt, resembles the European clover, with this difference, however, that its leaves are longer and more pointed, and that it bears a white flower. Some think that Al Chalba is the Chilef חילף mentioned at the end of Sotah.

Wild Saffron, חריע Al Kartum, grows extensively with us; it is scentless and tasteless, and has nothing to recommend it but its colour.

Indigo אסטים, Al Nil, is an herb which grows in Al

Gor, in the neighbourhood of Jericho. It is boiled down in order to obtain the dye. But the Palestine indigo does not equal that brought from India.

Redwood פואה, Al Pua, is a wood brought hither by the pilgrims from India; it is chipped up and used for dyeing red.

The Poppy פרגין, Al Kaskas, so called because the seed rattles in the dried capsule, is but little cultivated in Palestine, but largely in Syria.

Sesamum שומשמין, Al Sumsum; its seed looks like flaxseed, but is larger. It is good for food, and people prepare from it an excellent oil, suitable both for cooking and lighting. This useful plant grows in large quantities in the vicinity of Lod (Lydda) and Ramla, but is rarely found in Galilee.

Peppermint דנדנה, Al Nané (Yerush. Sabbath, vii. נענע Nanang), has, as is well known, a sharp spicy taste.

Portulacca or Purslain רגילה, Al Ridjla, is an herb which is eaten.

Dardar דרדרים, Al Dardar, is a prickly plant, resembling the nettle; it grows abundantly, especially in the province of Galilee, and is eaten by the peasants residing there. To this species of thistle also belongs

Achbaioth עכביות, Al Akul. Of this herb, which is supplied with prickles, they eat only the inside, which has a sourish taste.

Asparagus ירבוזי, I have never met in this country.

Wild Parsley כוסבר, Al Kusbra, not to be mistaken for Kusbar כסבר, the Coriander described above, is an herb very much resembling the celery, and bears on the top a small green fruit. It is boiled and mixed up with soup.

Chervil כרפס, Al Kraps, is a species of herb resembling the celery.

Lotem לוטם. On the Fir Tree of the country, Znober, there grows a hard, grape-like fruit, wherein the seed is contained. It is called Lotem לוטם Al Chabkrus, and is roasted and eaten.

The Rose ורד, Al Wardi, grows in abundance with us, especially in the level country of Sharon, and in the vicinity of the village of Malchi, situated four English miles southwest from Jerusalem. We have two kinds of roses, the red and the white. The white ones are soaked in water till they have communicated to it the refreshing scent of these flowers. This water is then distilled, and in this manner the fragrant rose-water is obtained. On the surface of this a few fatty drops collect, which are the precious oil of roses; and in order to obtain one ounce of this material, near a hundred pounds of roses are required. In the vicinity of Jericho there grows in the hedges a species of rose called the Jericho Rose, which is especially famous, and is exported even to foreign parts. This Rose has the peculiar property, that, though it has been plucked many years, and has become withered, as may readily be supposed, commences to bloom again so soon as it is put in water, and to expand anew, as though it stood on its green bush in its native land.

Gargar גרגר, Al Girgir, resembles the water-cress, and is bitter and very sharp.

Karshin כרשין, Al Karsin, is a species of lentils having small round kernels resembling peas. They are used for feeding camels.

The Onion בצל, Al Bazal. In Egypt is found a large onion, which is remarkably fine, and has an excellent taste, and is eaten raw. In the neighbourhood of Ashkelon, also, they are particularly good. We have also a wild onion, Al Buzal, which is very large, but unfit for food, and only used for medicinal purposes.

Garlic שום, Al Thum, is quite abundant with us, and is very fine.

Kalokasia? קרקס, Al Kalkas, is a species of potatoe, but

much better. Not rarely tubers are met with, which weigh three to four pounds.

Hyssop אֵיזוב, Al Satr, is found of various kinds. One resembles the sage, is bitter and acrid, is pounded up and eaten as a medicine. There is, however, another kind, which grows in hedges, on thorns, and is not fit to be eaten. It is probably the איזוב יון, the Grecian Hyssop of Sabbath, xiv. § 3.

Cress? שחלים, Al Rashad, is also called the mustard of our country; it is an herb which is of a sharp taste, and is used as a salad.

Black Caraway קצח, Al Kas-cha, consists of small, black seeds, which are kneaded up with the dough, or are strewed on bread, and render it pleasant to the taste, and impart to it an agreeable scent.

Kopher כופר (Spice-pink?), Al China, does not grow in Palestine, but is imported by the Mahomedan pilgrims from Mekka. It is pounded up, and is used by Turkish women to paint their face and nails.

Turkish Pepper פלפל רטוב, Al Pilpil Achdar, i. e. green pepper. There are two kinds, the green and the red. It resembles the caper, and is an acrid herb; it is full of seed, and is pickled either in vinegar or salt water (Yoma, 81 *b*).

Atron עטרון, Al Katran, is a sort of gum which is obtained from the Znober Tree, a species of fir.

Lot לוט (Gen. xxxvii. 25), is, according to my view, the Gum Arabic (Al Samk), which is so abundantly obtained from the chestnut and almond trees.

Sage סלוויא, Al Miriamia, is found abundantly with us, especially on the road to Chebron. The shrub, however, is much stronger, and the leaves longer than the European kind. The infusion of sage is drank as a medicine.

CHAPTER III.

MINERALS.

EARTHS.

In general, all the mountains to the west of the Jordan consist of calcareous earth; and even the stones of these mountains are of this soft substance, lime; and it is not rare to find pieces of lime which weigh above twenty-five pounds. From this cause, that is, because the soil and rocks are soft, it arises that Palestine has so many caverns. These are found more particularly on Mount Carmel, in the vicinity of Beth-Lechem in Galilee, Nazara, and Jerusalem, to wit, on Mount Olivet. The Mount Lebanon also is of limestone formation. This same formation extends likewise to the Great Desert as far as Mount Sinai, for there the granite formation commences, of which Sinai itself consists. East of Jordan also, the soil is in general of a chalk and limestone formation. But in the Lower Hauran (Trachonitis, the district of Argob), Djulun (Golan), and Iturea (Jetur), the ground is composed of basalt stones. To the south of the Dead Sea, near Wady Azy, commences the sandstone formation, which is the character of all the mountains of Idumea, on the east.

CLAY SOIL

Is found in abundance in the vicinity of Hebron, wherefore many bricks are made there, and you see in the village almost no other than brick houses. But as these bricks are not burnt and are merely dried in the sun and by exposure to the air, and as the houses in the East moreover, have no sloping roofs, it does not rarely occur that in a continued rain the houses become softened and tumble in. In Galilee, and particularly in Zafed, where the tops of the houses consist of a covering of clay soil, they must be carefully levelled and smoothed over with a cylindrical roller during rainy weather, to prevent the entrance of the water. If this precaution be omitted, then do the inhabitants incur the danger of being buried alive beneath the ruins of their houses. Hence the custom has always been in those districts to offer up penitential prayers, and to hold a fast during a long continuance of rainy weather. (Orach Chayim, chap. clxxvi., § 11.) In the country of Judæa, however, and especially in Jerusalem, the rain is always regarded as a blissful beneficence of God, promoting the growth of the produce of the earth; and not the least danger need be feared for the houses, since they are built of massive stones, and the roofs are overlaid with a skilfully prepared water-tight mortar called Kisermil. It is prepared in different ways. It usually consists of a mixture of sand, lime, and the residuum which remains in the pan after soap is boiled. This viscid, black-looking mixture is plastered over the roof, and is then beaten with sticks for a day or two till it is dry, and is become nearly as hard as a stone. Another water-tight mass is produced by taking pounded stone, or better yet, pounded potsherds, and mixing it up with eggs, cotton wool, and a little lime and oil. It is more costly than the first, and has a white appearance; and it becomes by exposure as shining and hard as porcelain or glass. Our bathing-tubs, which are placed on the roofs to catch the rain-water, are made of Kisermil. The earthen vessels made in Palestine, as the people are not acquainted with the process of glazing them, are in bad condition and entirely useless for cooking; wherefore we have for the most part metal vessels for culinary purposes.

In the neighbourhood of the village Semach, on the shore of Lake Chinnereth, is found a clayey earth resembling gypsum, of which the best pottery of Palestine is made.

STONES.

I have already remarked that all the mountains of Palestine consist of limestone. Chalk and gypsum we have none with us; they are imported from abroad, and are almost as dear as sugar, although the island of Candia is not far from us. Real marble is also not met with; still there is a species of stone, Al Balat, resembling this substance, found in the mountains of Rama and Ramalah, as also in the vicinity of Jordan, both of a white and a black variety; it is equally as hard and capable of being polished as marble, and is used for flooring houses and courts.

In the environs of Jerusalem are found many flintstones. In our glass-houses, a few of which are near Hebron, they use not, as elsewhere, powdered flint in the manufacture of glass, but a fine sand which is brought from the seashore. In these glass-houses they can make nothing but drinking glasses and bottles; but these fabrics also are so miserably bad, that they cannot sustain the burden of their contents: so that if they are entirely filled, and you attempt to raise them up, the upper part will remain in your hand whilst the lower one will drop away in pieces. They also manufacture in these glass-houses at Hebron all sorts of playthings of glass, such as finger rings, bracelets, &c., which, clumsy and miserable as they are, are sent away to all parts of the world, solely because they are made in the Holy Land.

SALTS.

We have in Palestine a sort of marine salt, which is made in the following manner:—Ditches are dug on the sea-shore, which are filled with sea-water, which gradually evaporates through the heat of the sun, and the dry residuum is salt. In those places, also, where the sea overflows at times the dry land, much salt is found after its recess; this is the case especially in the neighbourhood of Gazza.

The salt obtained around the Dead Sea is very bitter, has a saltpetre-like taste, and when thrown on the fire it melts in part and ignites in part, like ordinary saltpetre. It is very injurious to the eyes, as our sages already observed (Chulin, 105 *b*) that the salt of Sodom blinds the eyes.

Streams are found in Syria, the water in which is salty, and is used for the manufacture of salt. Twenty English miles east of Aleppo runs a large stream called Al Dhab, gold stream, which falls into a large and deep valley, where its waters remain without egress. It, however, flows only in winter, and is entirely dried up in summer. In the month of Tamuz (July), this whole valley is covered with salt. This stream is generally supposed to be the Ahava mentioned in Ezra viii. 15, and I suppose that Dhab is only a corrupted pronunciation for Ahava. In the village of Al Tilp, near this stream, is a very ancient building, which is said to have been the former Synagogue of Ezra. In this village there live permanently but ten Jewish families. But as the air is very salubrious and pure, many of the inhabitants of Aleppo select it as their summer's residence.

NAPHTHA

Is only found in the vicinity of the Dead Sea. At the

recurrence of an earthquake the Naphtha streams down in masses from the mountains on its shores, and it then floats in large pieces on the surface of the sea. This eruption of Naphtha appears to be a sort of lava. At the earthquake of the year 5594 (1834), that substance was seen streaming out in large quantities from all the rocks in the environs of Al Kerak (see Kir Moab). There is also found in the neighbourhood of the Dead Sea, near Nebi Mousa, a species of black stones which burn like coals, probably a sort of stone coal, which are used for cooking by those who travel in that part of the country. These stones have the wonderful property, that, when brought to Jerusalem, they lose nearly altogether their combustible quality, and become, in this respect, pretty much like all other stones.

On the Egyptian frontiers is found a bluish-green Natron, resembling alum, which is dug out of the earth. It has a very salty taste. The best species of this substance is white. It is carried from Egypt to Palestine, and is used here for cleansing and scouring. In Hebron it is also put into the kettle wherein they prepare glass. In ancient times soap was made out of a mixture, of which Natron was a component part. Generally נתר Nether (Jer. ii. 22), given in the English version with Nitre, is rendered by other translators with Chalk, but incorrectly. At present they prepare, in this country, a soap made of lime and olive oil; a great deal of which is manufactured in Jerusalem and exported abroad.

METALS.

Copper. Except in the neighbourhood of Aleppo, no Copper is found anywhere in Palestine. I was, however, told that Northern Galilee and the lower range of Lebanon contain veins of Copper; but no one deems it worth his while to bring to light the subterranean treasures of this desolate country. Otherwise there can be no doubt that this metal would be found abundantly, as Moses said, Deut. viii. 9, "A land whose stones are iron, and out of whose hills thou mayest dig copper." (See also ibid. xxxiii. 25.)

Iron is found in the neighbourhood of the town Dir Al Kamr, which is situated on the Lebanon. The Jews living near this place rent the mines from the Emir, and work them with their own hands; they also make horseshoes out of the metal thus obtained, and send them about through the whole country. On the Egyptian frontier, likewise, copper and iron are obtained.

OF MINERAL SPRINGS,

Which were formerly so plentiful in Palestine, there are but two to be met with at present. The one is the celebrated חמי טבריה, the hot spring of Tiberias, which is a spring almost boiling hot, and has always a strong sulphurous smell, and is at a distance of one mile south of Tiberias. The quality of the water is very much like that of Karlsbad in Bohemia, and Wiesbaden in Hessia, and it is drunk and used outwardly for bathing as a remedy. It is especially efficacious in rheumatic complaints. Abraim Pacha built near the spring a new and elegant bathing house for travellers. There was before that time an old bathing establishment. About a year ago (in 1844) 5604, the aqueduct of the new building was injured, and was rendered quite useless in consequence; still no one thought of doing anything to repair it.* The old house, however, had always a supply of water.

* In the year 5608 (1848), the Galileeans, i. e. the inhabitants of Tiberias, Zafed, and their environs, made a general collection to restore Abraim's bath, and operations were actually commenced to effect it; but the *worthy* Pachalik of Akka cared little about it, and the collection came only from private hands.

The second mineral spring is at Geder (see Rosh Hashanah, 23 *b*; Sanhedrin, 108 *a*; Chulin, 61 *a*), in the vicinity of the river Yarmuch. Here are found remarkable ruins, out of which the hot water bubbles up. It equals the water of Tiberias in heat and the sulphurous odour; but there is no bathing establishment, because the place where this spring bursts forth is a ruin, and the whole country around is a desert.

But the water of Siloah, near the holy city, likewise, I believe myself authorized to reckon among the mineral springs, because it is heavy, salty, and aperient; and I can attest from actual experience the popular belief that those who drink of it habitually are exempt from the chills and fevers which are so prevalent in Palestine.

CHAPTER IV.

DESCRIPTION OF THE CLIMATE OF PALESTINE.

THE promise of Scripture, which says, concerning the land of Israel (Deut. xi. 11), "Of the rain of heaven shalt thou drink water," is still confirmed at this day. In every house almost of Palestine are cisterns, into which is gathered the rain-water which runs down from the roofs. These closed cisterns are deep and broad; they are coated with the kisermil mentioned above, so that not a single drop of water can leak out. The water thus obtained is, —although it may not be expected by those unacquainted with it,—quite fresh, and good for drinking. Nevertheless we have many springs, but nowhere so many as in Shechem, where there are wells in almost every street. In the long absence of rain these springs become dry, no less than our cisterns.

In ordinary years the rain commences to descend in the month of Marcheshvan (October). This so-called first rain (יורה) lasts at times an entire week without interruption, ceases then for a brief space, but occasionally also several days or even weeks, and commences again; but it often is absent till near Adar (March). Then commences the latter rain מלקוש, which comes down with great violence, and lasts the whole month of Adar, and even a part of Nissan (April). But it has been known to continue to the middle of Iyar (May). As soon as the first rain is over, the soil is sufficiently moistened and soft for ploughing and sowing, and the farmer then begins his field labour (comp. Sabbath, 90 *b*). But through the whole summer there falls not a single drop of rain, although the sky is not rarely obscured with clouds. Once during my residence it rained in summer, and this was on Thursday, the 28th Sivan, 5601 (the 17th June, 1841), at a little past midday, when the rain came down quite fast. This unheard of phenomenon caused such a sensation in the whole of Palestine, as though the entire world had been thrown out of its course. This extraordinary occurrence had actually for its mournful consequence the destruction of all the fruit. The more it rains at the proper time, the more blessed and abundant is the product of man's labour; whereas, if the rains remain absent, nothing grows, and the country is then threatened with famine. Such an unhappy time was experienced by the inhabitants of Palestine in the year 5591 (1831), when, in consequence of the absence of rain, the dearth was so great that the price of wheat rose from 1½ to 18 piastres, and the distress caused thereby was boundless.

Rains fall in Palestine mostly with a west, or west-northwest wind; this is succeeded by an east wind, which renders the atmosphere perfectly pure and clear.

SNOW.

In most of the years no snow whatever is seen in Palestine; but occasionally much snow falls in Shebat (February), and lies then several weeks (comp. Yoma, 35 *b*; 1 Macc. xiii. 22). In the year 5604 (1844) there fell a little snow, even on the 22d Nissan (11th of April). In the year 5514 (1753) there fell an immense quantity of snow, and the cold was at that time so intense that in the district of Galilee twenty-five men froze to death near Nazareth. An old man once told me that in that year it snowed even so violently in Sivan (beginning of June), that no one was able to attend Synagogue in Jerusalem on the morning of Pentecost, because the heavy fall of snow during the night prevented every one from quitting his house. Unusual as such an occurrence is, it must nevertheless have been witnessed in former times, as it is reported by the Italian traveller of Leghorn, who journeyed through the country in 5282, that he had seen a monument in a ruin near the village of Brem, in Upper Galilee (although it does not exist now), which bore the following inscription: אל תתמהו על השלג שבא בניסן אנחנו ראינוהו בסיון "Be not astonished if snow should fall in Nissan—we have seen it in Sivan."

The temperature of Palestine averages during the winter, 8°–9° above 0 of Reaumur's thermometer—50° to 53¼° of Fahrenheit. In summer, however, it rises to 21° to 22°, and not rarely to 26°, i. e. 82° to 92° of F. Storms, accompanied by thunder and lightning, we have often, but only in winter. As we have no lightning conductors in all Palestine, the lightning often strikes, and causes some damage.*

Although we have great heat in summer, it is by no means oppressive, as it is tempered by a pleasant and cooling breeze. I therefore found the air of Italy, where this pleasant and cooling breeze is wanting, much closer and more oppressive than that of Palestine. And only now and then, when there is with us no refreshing air, the

* My elder brother, Rabbi Hayim Schwarz, Rabbi of Hürben, called my attention to the fact, that to judge from Tosephtah Sabbath, chap. vii., the Talmudists had a knowledge of an apparatus for conducting away lightning. These are the words: הנותנת ברזל בין האפרוחים הרי זה מדרכי האמורי ואם מפני הרעמים ואם מפני הברק הרי זה מותר "To put iron between young chickens is [prohibited, it being] the superstitious custom of the Emorites, i. e. heathens in general; but to put iron somewhere on account of the thunder and lightning is permitted." But I found yet another confirmation for the correctness of this view in the following, from Talmud Yerushalmi, finis Nazir: אף הדין סערה דחיל מן הדין פרזלא "The tempest also dreads the same material—the iron."

effect of the sun is extraordinary, and the burning heat is nearly insupportable; of which the following may serve as a striking example. Not long since there lay in the yard of my neighbour's house, a metal vessel which was exposed for some hours to the direct rays of the sun; a child came to fetch it away, but burnt its hands so effectually that they became blistered as though they had been scorched with fire.

In those districts where the warm air, being enclosed within the mountains, is not cooled off by the usual breeze, as for example in the vicinity of Jordan and the city of Tiberias, vegetation is much more rank and productive than elsewhere, and there is found the first ripe fruit, both on tree and field, of all Palestine. The heat is particularly great in Tiberias, wherefore you will scarcely see any one properly clad in the summer in this town, since nearly all walk about wrapped up in a sort of large shirt.

The winds of Palestine blow in winter with nearly the same force as in summer, and are pretty uniform and reliable in their influence on the state of the weather; and I may give the following well-founded general data, derived from actual observation, as applicable to this subject. The east wind betokens cold, and causes an interruption of the rain. The west wind brings rain. The north wind interrupts the rain; but should it blow before the rain sets in, it gathers the clouds in large masses and promotes the outpouring of a copious rain, which not rarely lasts for several days under the continued accompaniment of this wind. The south wind brings rain, and betokens warm weather. In regard to the prevalence of the various winds in the different months, the following general observations may be relied on as sufficiently exact:

From Kislev to Adar, December to March, we have the wind from the south or southwest.

From Adar to Tamuz, March to July, the east.

From Tamuz to Elul, July to September, the north; and From Elul to Kislev, September to December, the north-west; so that the wind is most generally from the west. (See Baba Bathra, ii. § 9; also Yerushalmi in the passage cited.)

EARTHQUAKES

Are not rare in Palestine; nay, scarcely a year elapses in which slight shocks are not experienced. In this year (5605), we had two such slight shakings of the earth. But Palestine has unfortunately been often visited by such shocks also as caused the loss of many human lives. As a proof we name the following fifteen:

1, at the time of the King Uzziah (see Amos i. 1); 2, at the time of Herod, in which 10,000 men were killed (see Megillah, 3 *a*, Baba Kamma, 82 *b*); 3, in the year 4075 (315), when the city Rabbath Bné Ammon was destroyed; 4, in the year 4344 (584); 5, in the year 4506 (746); 6, in the year 4509 (749); 7, in the year 4516 (756); 8, in the year 4865 (1105); 9, in the year 4874 (1114); 10, in the year 4880 (1120), in the reign of Baldwin II.; 11, in the year 4930 (1170); 12, in the year 4962 (1202); 13, in the year 5518 (1758), in which calamity the city of Baal-bek, situated at the foot of Mount Lebanon, was destroyed, and, moreover, 140 men lost their lives at Zafed; 14, was the first earthquake which ever I experienced and witnessed; this occurred in the year 5594 (1834); and lastly, 15, the well-known terrible earthquake of 5597 (1837), which devastated the cities of Zafed and Tiberias, with many villages in the vicinity. Earthquakes were formerly more frequently experienced in Syria than even in Palestine especially during the time of the crusades; and the cities of Antiochia (Antikia) and Tripoli (Trablus), were often visited by this terrible scourge. Such a calamity also destroyed Aleppo in the year 5581 (1821), when thousands of human beings perished. The farther particulars I mean to give at another place.

STATE OF THE TEMPERATURE, WEATHER, AND VEGETATION OF THE WHOLE YEAR, ACCORDING TO THE SUCCESSION OF THE MONTHS.

Nissan, April, has for the most part much rain, but only in the first half of the month; strong, and at times cold winds prevail. The commoner vegetables, such as tamarisk, artichoke, and beans, are just now ripe, although barley has attained its maturity long ere this. (See Exod. ix. 31.) In the year 5604, new wheat was brought from Al Gor as early as the commencement of this month; but this is a rare event. The whole surface of the ground is now full of roses and other flowers. When I first trod on the sacred soil in the month of Nissan, 5593 (April, 1833), I was not a little surprised to see the whole vegetation of the valley of Sharon in such a state of forwardness, as it is in Germany, whence I came, not before July or August.

Iyar, May. The rain has long since ceased, and you see not even a little cloud in the sky. The air is pure, and the heat quite moderate. In the district of the Jordan, the wheat harvest has long since commenced, whilst this grain is only half ripe in the other parts of Palestine; but in some parts the wheat is cut before it attains more than half its maturity, and is dried in the sun or by the fire, to produce the so-called green corn, Al Frik. Cucumbers also are now ripe; and in the vicinity of Gazza, the apricot is already gathered.

Sivan, June. The heat increases. The sky is cloudless; the dew inconsiderable. All the fruits of the plum kind are ripe, and all the corn species of the land garnered in.

Tamuz, July. The heat is now very great; the dew is not abundant. Many fruits are now ripe, for instance, apples, pears, water and sugar-melons, also a portion of the grapes.

Ab, August. The great heat continues, but the sky is sometimes overclouded. Much dew. Figs, St. John's Bread, &c., are now ripe.

Elul, September. The heat decreases. The clouds accumulate; and the dew is at night so abundant, that it appears as though it had rained. The grapes, pomegranates, sesamum, quinces, and lemons, are now ripe.

Tishry, October. Temperature about the same as in preceding month. Many clouds. The dew decreases; occasional rains. Olives and dates have attained maturity.

Marcheshvan, November. Many clouds; strong winds and rains. Citrons, China oranges, and other fruit of the orange tribe, as also turnips, and herbs, are now ripe.

Kislev, December. Temperature the same as preceding month. The sowing of grain in the field has already commenced. Although the oranges and kindred fruit have been long since ripe, they continue to mature on the trees, till towards April and May (compare Talmud Sukkah, 35 *a*).

Tebeth, January. Very cold. Almonds are in blossom; most plants and tuberous roots, radishes, cabbages, green onions, which continue in the field till September, are ripe.

Shebat, February. Very cold, with occasional snow and thin ice.

Adar, March. The air becomes of a higher temperature, with occasional strong winds, and much rain. The fruit trees are in blossom; and garlic is ripe, but continues out till June.

PART III.

A SHORT HISTORY OF PALESTINE.

INTRODUCTION.

As in the geographical reference to Palestine, we have been compelled to be content with mere traces, the same will be the case in our historical account of this country. There are nowhere to be met with regular documents in respect to its history, states, and towns; the past seems to have been entirely forgotten; so that the whole country cared, so to say, only for the present, and took no cognizance of what had preceded or was to follow. It is true that some few Arabic historians have written something concerning Palestine, such as Abulfeda and Serif ibn Idrus; but their works have almost entirely disappeared, as was to be supposed would be the case under a government which had not and suffered not a free press. It was only with the greatest trouble that I could obtain here and there an historical document, and I extracted therefrom only what interested me,—that is, what has reference to the Israelitish people, but not the general and to us indifferent accounts and narratives. Reports referring to modern times, I obtained occasionally by way of tradition. Therefore it cannot excite surprise that the historical portion of my book should be so brief and simple.

I divide the same into four periods.

Period I. From the destruction of the temple under Titus, in the year 3828 (68), till the time of the conquest of Palestine by the Mahomedans in the year 4374 (614), consequently a period of 546 years.

Period II. From 4374 to the conquest of the country by the Christian Crusaders in the year 4859 (1099), an interval of 485 years.

Period III. From the year 4859 to the reign of Sultan Seliman the Great, in the year 5280 (1520), an interval of 421 years.

Period IV. From 5280 (1520) to the present year 5605 (1845), an interval of 325 years.

A SHORT REVIEW OF THE DIFFERENT GOVERNMENTS IN PALESTINE IN THE ABOVE PERIODS.

In the year 3828, at the time of the destruction of Jerusalem, Palestine was under the dominion of the Romans.

In the year 4092 (332), under Emperor Constantine, the Greek—Romano-Greek Empire.

In the year 4374 (614), under King Kusarai (Chosroes ?) for a brief space, Persian, but later, again, under the government of the Greeks.

In the year 4397 (637) under Calif Omar, Arab or Mahomedan.

In the year 4502 (742), it was for a short time under the dominion of the Turks or Tartars, but at a later period again under the Arabs.

In the year 4628 (868), under the Califs of Egypt.

In the year 4800 (1040), again under the Turks or Tartars.

In the year 4859 (1099), under the European Christians.

In the year 4947 (1187), under Saladin, Calif of Egypt.

In the year 5004 (1244), under Casiunus, i. e. under Turks or Tartars.

In the year 5051 (1291), under Sultan Asa of Egypt, under Mameluks.

In the year 5161 (1401), under Timurlan, for a short time, i. e., under Mongols, then again under the Mameluks.

In the year 5278 (1518), under Selim of Constantinople, under Ottomans.

In the year 5591 (1831), under Mahmud Ali, Pacha of Egypt.

In the year 5600 (1840), under Abd al Medjid, Ottoman.

Here would well apply the passage from Judges ix. 2: "What is better for you, that seventy men, all the sons of Jerubaal, should rule over you, or that one man should be your master?"

PERIOD I.

FROM THE DESTRUCTION OF JERUSALEM TO THE MAHOMEDAN RULE.

The tragic occurrences accompanying the destruction of Jerusalem and of the temple are sufficiently told in detail in Josephus, the Talmud, and Midrashim, and it is useless to speak of them in this place. I will therefore confine myself to the history subsequent thereto.

Jerusalem was, unfortunately for us, destroyed by the Roman general Titus, in the reign of his father, the Emperor Vespasian. It is doubtful whether the city was completely demolished by the Romans, or whether they did or did not cause the plough to pass over it, as the accounts on this head are very contradictory. Josephus, in his Jewish War, book vii. chap. i., says that the army of Titus pulled down and destroyed the whole city, so that it could not be distinguished any more where it had stood, and that he left standing but a few towers, as a token of his prowess to posterity; but he does not mention that the city was ploughed up. Whereas in the Talmud, finis Taanith, it is stated that the plough was actually passed over the site of Jerusalem, though this ploughing is there mentioned to have been done by Turnus Rufus טורנוס רופוס,

who lived at a later period, at the time of Rabban Gamliel, but not by Titus. In other books, the name of the one who passed the plough over Jerusalem is given as Titus Aniosrufus, or Tyrannus Rufus; and in Yerushalmi Taanith, and Echa Rabbethi, he is called quite briefly Rufus. It would, however, appear that this representation of utter destruction must not be taken so very literally, since we find in several passages of the Talmud—for instance, in Berachoth, 3 *a*, finis Makkoth, &c.—mention made of חרבות ירושלם ruins in Jerusalem; and the very passage of finis Taanith reads כשחרש טורנוס רופוס את האולם "When Turnus Rufus ploughed up the *outer hall* of the temple," which would denote that only the temple was wasted in this manner, but not the whole city of Jerusalem, of which ruins were allowed to exist.

In the year 3844 (84), Domitian, the brother of Titus, ascended the Roman throne. He was a wicked, tyrannical ruler, and in especial hated and persecuted the Jews. He endeavoured to destroy all the descendants of David. It was under him that, as just said, Turnus Rufus pulled down the remains of the temple, and passed the plough over its site. He also pronounced sentence of death over Rabban Gamliel, who was of the family of David, though he succeeded in escaping, as is related in Taanith, 29 *a*. This Domitian was at length slain by his own servants, after he had reigned fourteen years.

In the year 3858 (98) Nerva, a worthy regent, and a humane man, who was at the same time a friend to the Jews, assumed the government. He endeavoured everywhere to improve the condition of our people, and to render more tolerable the oppression they suffered under the Roman proconsuls. He, however, only reigned two years.

He was succeeded, in 3860 (100), by Trajan, who was also a very great friend to the Jews; and he gave them, at the time of Rabbi Joshua Ben Chananiah, the permission to rebuild the temple, of which, however, they neither could nor would make any use, as is circumstantially told in Bereshith Rabbah, chap. lxiv. In his reign there arose in the city of Bither ביתר the celebrated Bar Kocheba, i.e. Son of the Star (Num. xxiv. 17), but later called Bar Kusiba, i. e. son of falsehood. He alleged himself to be the regent (messiah ?) of the Jews, and rebelled against the Romans, and caused a great slaughter among them, but more especially among the Roman and Greek inhabitants of the island of Cyprus. Trajan sent his sister's son, Hadrian, as general to Palestine, to fight against Bar Kocheba; he contended against him for several years, but was not able to defeat him. Trajan reigned eighteen years.

In 3878 (118) Hadrian ascended the Roman throne. In the second year of his reign he at length overcame Bar Kocheba, through means of his general, Julius Severus, who had been previously stationed in Britain (England). He captured the uncommonly large and strong city of Bither, and caused such wasting and destruction in Palestine that they exceeded the misery produced by Titus. He destroyed 50 strong places and 985 towns and villages, and there fell 580,000 Jews by the sword, besides the large numbers who were carried off by famine, fire, and the pestilence, and not counting those who were dragged away into foreign lands, and sold as slaves. Near Hebron, *four* human beings were sold for one seah, about a peck of barley. ["O Lord, behold, and see to whom Thou hast done thus." Echa ii. 20.] Near Bither lay the dead, in a stretch of 18 mills (13½ English miles), for years without interment, till the reign of the succeeding emperor; because Hadrian would not permit the slain to be buried (Yerushalmi Taanith, iv.) This unfortunate war caused the total destruction of Palestine, and is called, in Sotah ix., § 14, Polemos ha-acharon פולמוס האחרון, "the last war." According to Yerushalmi Peäh, vii., not an olive tree was at that time to be found in all Palestine, so entirely was everything destroyed. Under the reign of this tyrant the following martyrs were executed: Rabbi Akiba, at Cæsarea; Rabbi Chaninah, son of Teradion; Rabbi Yishbab, the scribe (Hassopher); Rabbi Chutzphith, the interpreter; Rabbi Elazar, son of Shamua; and Rabbi Judah, son of Baba.

After this devastation of the country, Hadrian had Jerusalem rebuilt, though less than its former extent, and called it Ælia Capitolina, after his own name Ælianus Hadrianus, and Jupiter Capitolinus; whence Jerusalem is called in Greek books Ailia. He also placed on the temple mount the images of Jupiter and Venus נוגה and כוכב, which remained standing 180 years, till destroyed by the Empress Helena, mother of Constantine. Even at this day there is found, on the farthest end of the southern city and temple mount wall, a large stone with the following inscription:*

TITO AEL HADRIANO
ANTONINO AVG PIO
PPPONTIF AVGVR
DDDDD

This stone, however, is placed accidentally upside down, so that the writing has to be read reversed. It would appear that formerly there stood on this spot a monument, to which this stone was affixed; and as it fell down at a later period, the Mahomedans found this large stone when they rebuilt or repaired the city and temple mount wall, and placed it in its present position in the clumsy manner we find it, without troubling themselves about the inscription.

Hadrian also caused a wall to be built around Jerusalem, and allowed no Jews to come even within the en-

* The letters of this inscription are each five inches in height.

virons of the city (Lamen. v. 2). It was only at a later period that they were permitted to go to the surrounding mountains, probably the Mount of Olives, to cast a mournful, sorrowing look towards the seat of their ancient glory. Later yet, they purchased from the Greek and Roman garrison the permission to enter its precincts once a year, on the day of its destruction, the 9th of Ab (August), in order to weep there for their mournful fate, and the fall and dispersion of Israel.

In 3900 (140), Antoninus, son-in-law of Hadrian, became emperor. He was a great friend of the Jews, and lived at the time of Rabbi Judah Hannassi, the author of the Mishna; he was often for a length of time in the town of Rami in Galilee (see above, art. Rimon in Zebulun), and lived on terms of the greatest intimacy with this Rabbi Judah. According to Yerush. Megillah, i., Antoninus privately embraced Judaism. It appears to me that he caused the unburied dead around Bither to be interred, as was stated above. He reigned twenty-four years.

He was succeeded in 3924 (164) by his son-in-law Marcus Aurelius, also called Marcus Antoninus. From Abodah Zarah, 10 *a*, it would appear that Antoninus had a son called Asverus (Severus); if this be well-founded, the prince must have died in his father's time, since the government was transferred to the son-in-law.

Commodus, the grandson of Marcus Aurelius, became Emperor in 3943 (183);* he was a cruel ruler, and an enemy to the Jews.

Septimius Severus, a severe and harsh governor, became emperor in 3955 (195). In the year 3964 (204) he made an irruption into the East, and after several bloody battles effected important conquests, and penetrated as far

* The usual authorities place the death of Marcus three years earlier, 180.

as the Tigris. In the later years of his life, he became more just and humane.

Alexander Severus, a good emperor, ascended the throne in 3985 (225). In 3994 (234) a fierce struggle sprung up in Palestine between the Jews and Samaritans, the former under the guidance of a certain Caudius. This contest lasted so long that Alexander was at length induced to interfere, and restored peace in the country by the execution of many of both parties.

Decius Troanus commenced his reign in 4014 (254); his rule lasted but about 1½ years. He is also called Tarchanianus, and is, according to my view, the Tarchinus טרכינום of Sukkah, 51 *b*, who caused many of the Jews who were settled in Alexandria, in Egypt, to be destroyed. In one edition this passage reads Alexander of Macedon; but this is incorrect, and should be Tarchinus, as it is in the Yerushalmi and Midrash. (See above, Sela Rimmon, in Benjamin.)

Diocletian assumed the government in 4049 (289). He was of mean birth, and a native of Dalmatia; he was carried in his infancy to Syria, and was, according to Bereshith Rabbah, 63, a swineherd near Tiberias, and entered afterwards into the Roman army as private soldier, and rose at last so high that he was chosen Emperor. He lived a long time in the East, at Banias, and caused the Bachr Chams to be dug. (See chap. ii., first note.) At the present day, there is still to be seen in Alexandria of Egypt, the column of Diocletian, 99 feet in height, 28 in circumference, with a shaft of 73 feet in length. It is also called Pompey's Pillar.

Constantine the Great became Emperor in 4072 (312). He was the first monarch who embraced Christianity; the earlier Emperors persecuted and destroyed the followers of this religion in every way and manner, till Constantine and his mother, Helena, professed the same. He caused churches and monasteries to be built in every direction; and also the alleged sepulchre of the founder of their religion was discovered or rather invented by the keen sight of the pious Helena, and supplied with a church by Constantine. He also embellished Byzantium, and called it Constantinople; the Jews name it קושטאנטין or קושטא Costo, or Costantin. The great Roman empire was now divided into the eastern and western; the first is known as the Greco-Romano, the chief seat of the government of which was at Constantinople. Palestine belonged to this, the eastern division, and many believers in Christianity now began to settle in the Holy Land.

At that time there lived at Rome a Jew named Joseph, who went over to Christianity, and acquired thereby much respect with Constantine, and obtained from him the permission to appear openly as converter of the people, and to build churches and monasteries. To carry out his object he travelled into Palestine* as missionary, and commenced to preach publicly in order to persuade the Jews, of whom there were a great many in Cæsarea, Tiberias, Nazara, and Kefr Tanchum, as in fact all these towns were inhabited by Jews solely, to adopt his religion, and he already made a commencement to build churches. But the Jews regarded him not, and would not permit him to construct the like buildings in the places just named. He reported his want of success, on account of this opposition of the Jews, to Constantine, who thereupon imposed on them heavy taxes and fines, and caused a great many of them to be put to

* "Thy destroyers and those who pull thee down proceed from thy own self" (Isaiah xlix. 17), so is the rendering in our sense of this verse; and this then was the first missionary of the destructive kind who came to Palestine. At present there are also many here, who are sent hither from the pious country of Britain. But Constantine is already dead, and no one molests us with small or large exactions or contributions as fines for contumacy. The times *do* change!

death. Constantine reigned till the year 4102 (342). See Abn Ezra, end of Daniel [should be 4097 (337)].

In the year 4098 (338), there was held a great synod of many Christian clergymen, in order to discuss the character of Jesus of Nazareth; and all agreed to deny him all divine attributes, and that he could be declared nothing more than a prophet.

Constantius commenced his reign in 4099 (339). At that time there lived a large Jewish population in Zippori (Safuri), who showed themselves disobedient to the Emperor; in consequence of which, he attacked them, and out of revenge for their disobedience, he caused the city to be demolished; since that time it is but a miserable small village.

In 4125 (365), Julian, called the Apostate, assumed the government. He was a very great friend of the Jews. In the second year of his reign, he gave the Nahssi of Israel, i. e. the chief religious authority, who was at that time Rabbi Hillel, a great-grandson of R. Judah Hannahssi, and who lived at Tiberias, the order to rebuild the temple at Jerusalem. Preparations were actually made to carry this resolve into effect, when the sudden death of this good prince frustrated the measure, and the work was left unaccomplished. Julian was an ardent persecutor of the Christians, and repealed all the contributions and taxes with which Constantine had burdened and punished the Jews, and in short abolished all unfavourable laws with regard to our people.

Valentinian ascended the throne in 4128 (368); he was likewise a humane man, and especially kind to the Jews. In the twelfth year of his reign, 4140 (380), he commanded to surround Jerusalem with a new wall, and promised to make liberal expenditure for this purpose; but he died in the same year, and this project was also frustrated.

Theodosius I. commenced his reign in 4140 (380). He

was a persecutor of Arian Christians, but a friend to the Jews; and he made it known in all his empire that they should have everywhere unrestricted freedom in the exercise of their religion, and that no one should place any obstacles in their way.

Arcadius commenced his reign in 4155 (395); he also was a wise ruler and a friend to the Jews.

Theodosius II. reigned in 4172* (412); he was cruel and inimical to the Jews. In the eighth year of his reign (4180?) he ordered all the Jews to be driven out of Alexandria in Egypt, and commanded that all the contributions and donations which were collected for the Nahssi† of Palestine, for the purpose of defraying the general benevolent objects among the Jews, and the promotion of the study of the law and similar purposes, should be delivered into the imperial treasury.

In 4288 (528), Justinian the Great became Emperor. He was a very wise and good prince, and a friend to the Jews. In the year 4316 (556), a bloody contest arose between the Jews and the Christians residing in Cæsarea, in which very many, nearly all of the latter, were destroyed. Justinian had the matter investigated, and declared that the Jews had been in the right.

Maurice reigned in 4344 (584); he was a good and mild prince. At this time, the East was visited by many and violent earthquakes; through which means the building commenced by Julian on the temple mount, was thrown down. The benevolent Maurice sent Jewish builders from Constantinople to Jerusalem to restore it.

Heraclius reigned in 4373 (613). He was engaged in war with the Persian King, Chosroes II. (Kusarai). The Jews in Tiberias, Nazara, and the inhabitants of the

* Too late by four years.—TRANSLATOR.

† He nevertheless did not reside any more in Palestine, but in Babylon, although he bore the name נשיא הארץ "The Prince of the Land."

mountains of Galilee, were for the Persians. Chosroes penetrated as far as Jerusalem, which he besieged a long time, and took it at length in the month of Sivan, 4374 (June, 614), by assault. He caused a terrible destruction in the same, destroyed all the churches and monasteries, and carried the Christian Patriarch away with him as prisoner of war. About 20,000 Christians lost their lives in this catastrophe; those that remained were likewise carried away into captivity by Chosroes. He next conquered all Palestine, Syria, and Egypt, and carried off in every place a large number of Christians as slaves.

Heraclius and his son Constantine now advanced with a large army and attacked Chosroes furiously; they penetrated as far as Gazza, when the Persians took to flight. At last, however, peace was concluded. Heraclius again obtained possession of Jerusalem, where he would not allow a single Jew to take up his residence, and endeavoured, moreover, to persecute and to destroy them everywhere; for his sharp-sighted court astrologer* had predicted to him, from an inspection of the stars, that his empire should soon fall into the power of a circumcised nation, which he interpreted to be the Jews, but he knew not that the Arabs (Mahomedans) were likewise circum-

* Even to this day this notable personage has great influence in the courts of the oriental rulers; and in difficult cases, he is requested to deduce and read the decision and judgment in the premises from the dear and innocent stars. So, also, did the astrologer of Serif Pacha, of Damascus, as late as 5600 (1840) read quite clearly and truly in the stars, that the wicked gluttonous Jews of that place, had butchered and eaten up the old father Thomas (of which occurrence, I may perhaps say something hereafter); and this oracular decision was so evident, as the light of the sun, stars rather, to the just and tolerant Pacha, that he undertook the most stringent measures against the Jews, by torturing and imprisoning them without any better cause than this unreasonable suspicion. (Compare Jud. v. 20.)

cised. Jerusalem, therefore, remained attached to the Greek empire till 4397 (637).

A SHORT REVIEW OF THIS PERIOD, AND OF THE SITUATION OF SCIENCE AND OF THE LEARNED DURING THE SAME.

After the destruction of Jerusalem, the seat of the Jewish sages, the Sanhedrin, was first in Jabné (Jamnia), but was afterwards transferred to Galilee, to wit, Usha, Shafram, Beth-Sheärim, Zippori, and Tiberias. It was in the three last-named towns, in the times of Rabbi Judah Hannahssi, who compiled the Mishna, about 3979 (209). He died soon after, and his son, Rabbi Gamliel, succeeded him in the Nahssi dignity. He was succeeded by his son Rabbi Jehudah Nessiah, and he, in the year 4118 (358), by his son Rabbi Hillel, who was the last Nahssi in Palestine. The seat of the later Nessiim (chiefs), as also that of the most learned men, and of the sciences and wisdom in general, was the land of Babel, as it had become by degrees soon after the death of Rabbi Judah Hannahssi. The principal cities where the Jewish colleges flourished, were Sora, Nahardeä, and likewise Pumpaditha. Rabbi Yochanan, a scholar of Rabbi Judah Hannahssi, compiled the Talmud Yerushalmi (Jerusalem Talmud) about the year 4030 (279). Rab Ashi, however, compiled the Talmud Babli (the Babylonian Talmud) in Babel, about the year 4129 (367); but the work was not closed till the year 4260 (400).

We know but little of the learned men of Palestine after the decease of Rabbi Hillel. But in the year 4280 (420) there was a slight difference between the Nahssi and the ריש גלותא Resh Gelutha (chief of the captivity), who was next in rank after the Nahssi, for which reason he left Babel and went to Palestine, where he was received as chief by the learned men of that country.

Since, as I have related, the Emperor Maurice sent, in

the year 4344 (584), Jews from Constantinople to Jerusalem to reconstruct the buildings on the temple mount, which had been thrown down by the earthquake, it would appear that at that time there were but few Jews in Jerusalem and vicinity, or else there would have been no necessity to send others thither from so great a distance.

The situation of our people during this period, was not continually the same, but always in accordance with the disposition of the reigning sovereign; since, as already related, some of them were eminently friendly, whilst others were equally bitterly inimical to the Jews, and they, accordingly, were either favoured or persecuted, as the whim of the moment dictated.

PERIOD II.

FROM THE ACCESSION OF THE MAHOMEDANS TO THAT OF THE EUROPEANS.

In the year 4374* (614) there lived in Medina, in Arabia, Mahomed ibn Abdallah, descended from Keder, son of Ishmael (Gen. xxv. 13), who had taken possession of Arabia and the neighbouring countries. Mahomed had two secret counsellors, who assisted him in the construction of his new system of doctrines and belief; these were Aliman Mam Ali, of Jewish descent, and Turchman, a Christian; hence it resulted that the Koran contains many rules bearing analogy to Jewish ideas, for they were derived from Mam Ali.

Mahomed had an astrologer at his court called Bucheran, who was a very great enemy of the Jews, and urged

* It is not easy to give the precise year of the Chadjra (the flight of Mahomed), since all authorities are not agreed in this respect. In general, the year of the text is assumed. In a Hebrew work, out of which I have drawn largely, the year 4384 (624) is given. The Mahomedans reckon this year 5605 (1845) as the 1261st of the Chadjra. If we now calculate their years in general at 355 days, as they have no leap year, we shall have only about 1226 solar years, which would give us the year 4379 (619 of the Christian Era) as the year of the Chadjra.

the prophet constantly to persecute and exterminate them entirely, so that Mahomed at length listened to the proposition, since he had without this already a hatred towards them, because they had not aided him in his campaigns according to his expectation; wherefore the whole Jewish population under his rule, ran great danger of being entirely cut off. Rabbi Shallum, son of the then Resh Gelutha, in Babel, perceiving this dreadful predicament, went to Mahomed, and offering him his submission, friendship, and services, endeavoured to enter with him into a friendly compact. Mahomed accepted his proposition with pleasure, conceived a great affection for him, and took his daughter, a handsome young girl, for wife; he made him also a general in his army, and gave him the name of Abu Bachr al Chaliva al Zadik, literally: The father of the maiden, the descendant of the righteous; this means, that of all his wives, who were either widows or divorced women, this one was the only one who had never been married before, and then she was the granddaughter of the celebrated chief of the captivity; therefore, the descendant of the righteous. This occurrence induced Mahomed to give up his terrible intention to destroy the Jews in his country, and thus did Rabbi Shallum save his people.

Abu Bachr and Aliman now resolved among themselves to remove the dangerous enemy of the Jews, Bucheran. One evening Mahomed, Bucheran, Aliman, and Abu Bachr, were drinking together; the latter two soon saw that Mahomed and the astrologer were strongly intoxicated, and lay stretched out in a deep and profound sleep. Abu Bachr thereupon drew the sword of Mahomed from its scabbard, cut off therewith Bucharan's head, and put the bloody sword back into its receptacle, and both then lay themselves down quietly near Mahomed to sleep. When Mahomed awoke and saw his friend lying decapitated near him, he cried out in a fury: "This terrible deed has been done by one of us three in our drunkenness!" Abu Bachr thereupon said quite unconcernedly: "Let each one draw his sword, and he whose weapon is stained with blood, must needs be the murderer!" They all drew their swords, and that of Mahomed was completely dyed with fresh blood, which proved thus clearly to his satisfaction that he had murdered his friend. He was greatly grieved at this discovery; cursed and condemned the wine which was the cause of this murder, and swore that he never would drink any more, and that also no one should do so who wishes to enter heaven. This is the cause why wine is prohibited to the Mahomedans.

At a later period, Mahomed learned the whole transaction, and that his father-in-law was the perpetrator of the bloody deed; wherefore, he lost his favour, and he would not permit him to come before him. Abu Bachr went thereupon and conquered sixty places, which had not yet submitted to Mahomed, and presented them to him, through which means he became again reconciled to him, was received in favour, and remained thereafter at court.

Mahomed urged his conquests to the north and west; made war against Heraclius and his son Constantine, captured the country around Antiochia, Armenia, a part of Asia Minor (Anatolia), and Palestine. Jerusalem, however, continued in possession of the Greeks. Mahomed reigned 11 years, and died in 4385 (625); he was succeeded by his father-in-law, Abu Bachr, but he survived him but two years, when he also died.

In 4387 (627), another father-in-law, Omar ibn Kataf, ascended the throne. In the tenth year of his reign (4397) he appeared before Jerusalem with a large army. He besieged it, and after producing great distress thereby in the city, it surrendered to his arms. He then made a treaty with the Greek inhabitants of the city, that they should pay him a ransom for their lives, and send an annual tribute. He commanded to rebuild the temple, and appropriated several pieces of ground, the proceeds of which were destined to defray the expenses and keep it in repair, which is continued to be done to this day. He built, accordingly, the great Mosque al Sachara, of which I have spoken above. He also conquered the whole country around Damascus and Ispahan, which is a part of Persia. Egypt was taken by his general Omar ibn Aleaz, as also the city of Alexandria, where he burnt the celebrated library, through which learned posterity suffered an irreparable loss. This conquest of Egypt put an end to the government of the Mameluks, and it came under the rule of the Califs, and so it remained till the country was conquered by the Tartars in 4502 (742). In 4400 (640), Omar built the present al Mazr and called it Al Kairo, which means, "care, pains, sorrow;" since this building cost him much trouble, care, and labour. In the town of Pastat, the ancient Zoar (for which see the Appendix), he prohibited and prevented a terrible ancient custom, which was prevalent among the Greeks of that place. They used, on the day when the Nile begins to rise, to take a handsome young woman, to dress her in the most costly and brilliant attire, to lead her to the river under accompaniment of music and dancing, and then to throw her into the water; since, according to their opinion, the Nile would, in reward for this beautiful sacrifice, rise higher and higher, and scatter its rich blessings over the land. Omar reigned 15 years.

In the year 4402 (642), Osman (or Othman) ibn Afan assumed the government. He was a son-in-law of Mahomed. In the year 4406 (646), he took the island of Rhodes, and in 4413 (653) the island of Cyprus, from the Greeks.

In 4413 (653), the Calif Ali ibn Abu Talbih, also a son-in-law of Mahomed, who had slain his predecessor Osman, succeeded to the throne. The Persians, and many other Mahomedans, regard this Ali also as a prophet, equal to Mahomed. Even at the present day there are two sects of Mahomedans; one is composed of those who only believe in and acknowledge Mahomed as a prophet, and the other of those who ascribe the same honour to Ali. These two sects always are inimical towards, and persecute each other. In Syria and on the Lebanon there are likewise several Mahomedans who belong to the sect of Ali.—Under him the Mahomedans conquered the whole of Anatolia, and penetrated as far as Africa and Spain. He was succeeded, in 4419 (659), by his son, Calif Chazan ibn Ali.

Calif Maëvia ibn Sefian began his reign in 4434 (674). Under him there were constant wars and contests among the great men of the state, concerning the califate, and it was always doubtful whether he should be able to maintain himself on the throne or not.

In 4435, Calif Abd al Maleki assumed the government. He made a treaty with the Greek Emperor of Constantinople, Justinian II. He built the city of Ramla, and several other towns in that neighbourhood. The district of Abu Gosh (see above, Kirjath-Jearim), is to this day called Belad Beni Amaleki, perhaps in allusion to this Calif. In his time, in 4459 (699), there ruled in Irak and Babel yet another Calif, Chadjadj ibn Jusif. Abd al Maleki was succeeded in 4467 (707) by his son, Calif Walid I., ibn Abd al Maleki.

In 4502 (742), the country was invaded by innumerable hordes of Tartars, from the vicinity of the Caspian Sea. They were called Turkemans; hence the name of Turks. These conquered the whole of Syria, Cappadocia, and Palestine, and caused everywhere terrible devastations. The Arab Califs made war against them, and drove them out of the country; they, however, came back a third time, as I shall relate hereafter, till at length the Arabs and Turks became united, by the latter assuming the Koran and the Mahomedan religion, and formed, as at this day, but one nation, only that the former are called Arabs or Ishmaelites, and constitute the greater portion of the inhabitants of Palestine; whilst of the others, called Turks, but few are in our country, whereas in Turkey, in Europe, the population is mostly composed of them.

In 4523 (763), there reigned the Calif Al Mansur, who built Bagdad, the modern Babylon.

In 4546 (786), the Calif Harun ar Rashid (i. e. the just) became ruler, and reigned till 4569 (809). He completed the building of the city of Bagdad, commenced by Al Mansur. In 4557 (797) there arose a terrible war between the Saracens and the Arabic tribes in Palestine, through which means Gazza, Ashkelon, Sarifea צריפין, and Beth-Gubrin were entirely destroyed.

In 4572 (812), the Mahomedans attacked and slew the ecclesiastical chiefs of the Christians in Jerusalem.

In the year 4573 (813), ruled Calif Almamans ibn Harun, until the year 4603 (843).

In 4628 (868), there reigned Sultan Ibn Achmad ibn Tulun over Egypt. In that year the Tartaric hordes made another irruption, and conquered Palestine and Egypt. Sultan Ibn Achmad had constant wars with them: he reigned till 4644 (884).

In 4729 (969), there reigned the Calif Maëz, of the Fatimite family. This name was borne by the Califs of Kairuan, a country to the west of Egypt, in the neighbourhood where Carthage formerly stood (see Appendix). He conquered Egypt, Palestine, and Syria, and had his seat in Cairo (Al Mazr).

Calif Al Chakim, the third of the Fatimite family, became sovereign in the year 4756 (996). He was a great enemy to the Christians, and persecuted them everywhere.

In the year 4776 (1016), he advanced with a large army against Jerusalem, and drove away the Tartars, who yet occupied the same. He also destroyed totally the church which Constantine had built over the so-called place of Jesus's sepulchre. His reign extended till 4781 (1021).

The pilgrims who came from the west (Europe) to Palestine, and beheld these persecutions, painted them in strong and glaring colours on their return to their native countries, and moreover calumniated the Jews, as though these had contributed much to produce the enmity and persecution of the Christians on the part of Al Chakim. These and still other falsehoods and calumnies increased the hatred and the persecution towards the Jews in European countries; and when at a later period the *pious* crusaders from the west went eastward, to snatch the Holy Land from the power of the Mahomedans, they found ample opportunity to execute a pious and holy vengeance on these poor Israelites, as I shall relate somewhat more circumstantially hereafter.

In 4781 (1021), his son Calif Dahir ibn Chakim became sovereign. He was a friend to the Christians, and permitted them to rebuild their destroyed church.

In 4800 (1040), the Tartaric hordes made a third irruption under their leader Seldjuk, who was of the tribe Hildokiao. This chief was uncommonly successful in his conquests: he made war against the Egyptian Calif, and conquered Syria, and Jerusalem with its environs. He bitterly persecuted the Christians in the Holy City, and they had to endure terrible exactions, and were compelled to submit entirely to his arbitrary will.

In 4859 (1099), the Arabs under the Egyptian Calif again acquired Jerusalem and the surrounding country, and drove the Tartars away from there, and thought themselves secure in possession of the city, when suddenly a new enemy came over them, with whom they had to wage a long and bloody strife. This enemy was the Europeans of the West, who in that very year entered the land of Palestine and conquered it.

A SHORT REVIEW OF THIS PERIOD.

There exist but few documents concerning the situation of the Jewish literati and literature in Palestine of this period. But at the time of Mahomed, the most distinguished and learned person amongst the Jews, Rabbi Yizchak Ha-Gaön, resided in Babylon. The title of Nahssi had at that time been given up for that of Gaön.

In 4521 (761), there arose a serious contest in Babylon between the Resh Gelutha, and the celebrated Rab Acha, of Shabeché, the author of the Sheëlthoth שאלתות, through which cause the latter was not chosen as Gaön, wherefore he quitted Babylon and repaired to Palestine, where he ended his days.

In 4543 (783), there lived in Beth-Zur, a town not far from Hebron, a man by the name of 'Anan ענן, a scholar of the then Gaon, Rabbi Yehudaï, of Babylon. He had observed in his scholar that he had neither affection for, nor faith in our tradition as an exposition of the written law; wherefore he ('Anan) could not be chosen either as Resh Gelutha or Gaön. He returned, therefore, to his native country, Palestine, and formed a new sect, the leader of which he became, by openly preaching against our system of tradition. The sect of the Sadducees, who only adopted the written law and rejected the tradition, had gradually fallen entirely into decay after the destruction of the temple and Jerusalem, and had become nearly dissolved. But the appearance of 'Anan gave them new life, and they soon increased and spread extensively in Palestine, Egypt, and North Africa. In Palestine, they had yet another learned chief, Sheich Abu al Ferag, who wrote a work, bearing his own name, concerning the principles of his sect, and which contains much that is absurd and blasphemous. He is the same Abu al Ferag who is frequently mentioned in the Opinions of Maimonides תשובות הרמב"ם. Anan had a wife who was called Al Meälma, i. e. the learned, the instructress, who was acknowledged chief of his sect after the death of her husband, and was consulted in all cases of doubt; and as everything was decided according to her opinion and practice, it came to be customary to ask among the sect, "How did Al Mealma on that occasion? or what was her practice in that case?" and every one looked up to her for guidance. When, at a later period, Rabbi Joseph Ben Ali became Nahssi in Africa, he used every effort to suppress this sect in all directions,—so that it was nearly dissolved, and but few vestiges are found thereof at the present time; since all that is left are the few Caraites קראים, who only acknowledge the written law, are partly descended from the ancient Sadducees, and are found in several places in Asia and Egypt. We find mentioned in Abn Ezra's Commentary on the Pentateuch, several ridiculous expositions of many passages of Holy Writ ascribed to a certain Anan; it would, therefore, appear that he also had composed a commentary on the books of Moses.

In general the situation of the Jews, under the rule of the Mahomedans, was quite favourable, and considerably better than under the Greeks, since the former are naturally more favourably inclined to Judaism;—so that scarcely any persecution took place in this whole period. Only when the Calif Omar ibn Kataf banished, in the year 4398 (638), the Christians from Tiberias, the same fate was soon meted out to the Jews, and they also had to quit this place.

PERIOD III.

FROM THE REIGN OF THE EUROPEANS TO SULTAN SELIMAN.*

When the inhabitants of Europe learned, in 4856 (1096), how great the oppression and persecution were which their coreligionists had to endure in the Holy Land at the hands of the Mahomedans, they resolved to make a campaign thither by their united forces, in order to snatch the Holy Land from the power of the infidels. In consequence of this resolve there assembled an immense number of warlike pilgrims from Germany, France, Spain, Britain, and Italy, composing a mass of all sorts of men, who all hastened to the East in a pious and holy rage,—others, indeed, for the mere love of plunder,—to take part in the holy war; wherein, therefore, it was quite natural that the pious and holy priests should play a principal part. This, however, was a terrible and tragical period for all the Jews residing in the above-named countries; since these pious pilgrims had, at present, the best opportunity to give full vent to their hatred and fury against our poor and helpless people, and to enrich themselves at the same time with their wealth and possessions.

Especially in Germany an innumerable host of Jews, entire congregations, both little and great, both old and young, were butchered in cold blood, and their earthly possessions confiscated by the saints. Only those who would consent to join Christianity, the only saving church, could remain unmolested; but few, indeed, availed them-

* I would merely remark, that I have taken the events of this period, for the most part, from an Eastern Hebrew work; should it, therefore, be found that there are some differences respecting the names and chronology, when compared with European histories, I would, nevertheless, give the preference to this work, which was composed on the spot where the events occurred, and appears on the whole to give an authentic and true account.

selves of this dishonourable means of saving their lives! These are the persecutions of 4856, called among us גזרות התנ"ו; but it is not my province to speak of them more circumstantially. A complete account of these dreadful events is found in the book of Chronicles of Rabbi Joseph, the priest, a native of Italy, known as דברי הימים לר' יוסף הכהן.

The number of these warlike pilgrims was about 600,000 men; they took their journey by seven different routes (Deut. xxviii. 25). They were led by Godfrey of Lorraine, and many distinguished princes. They pursued their difficult and dangerous route through Constantinople, Anatolia, Antiochia, Trablus, Beirut, Zidon, Zur, and Akko. Their near approach produced a panic and frightful terror among the inhabitants of Jerusalem. The Egyptian Calif, who had but recently only taken it from the Tartars, commanded to place the city in a state of defence, to strengthen the wall of the city, and to supply it with brave troops, and with everything requisite, with arms no less than with an ample store of provisions.

In 4859 (1099), on the 7th of June (Tamuz), the pilgrims came at length before Jerusalem by way of Ramla. The large number of 600,000 had already melted down to 40,000, so that but 1 out of every 15 had remained alive and come before Jerusalem; the remainder had been carried off on the long journey by the plague and other diseases, hunger, want, and the sword of the enemy. But even among the 40,000 that remained, there were but 20,000 warriors who fought on foot, and 500 horsemen; whereas in Jerusalem there was a garrison of 40,000 brave soldiers. The city was now formally put in a state of siege, and the Mahomedans defended themselves bravely; but still Jerusalem was taken by assault on the 11th (19th?) of July אב; Godfrey and his brother Eustace (Iyostakea?) were the first to scale the wall, and descending therefrom into the city, forced the gates, when the whole army of the pilgrims poured in, and caused a terrible massacre, so that Arab historians write that the horses waded up to their bellies in human blood; and scarcely any one was spared and saved alive. Godfrey was thereupon acknowledged and crowned by the pilgrims as king of Jerusalem. They next gradually conquered all Palestine and Syria; but they had to carry on everywhere constant battles with the Califs of Egypt, in which they (the Crusaders) were nearly always victorious. In a battle between Godfrey and the Calif, which was fought in the vicinity of Ashkelon, it is said that 100,000 men of the Egyptian army were left dead on the field. The pilgrims made also some conquests on the east side of Jordan.

They had thus possession of nearly the whole country; they built cities, towns, villages, monuments, churches, and monasteries, and gave them arbitrarily biblical names, through which means, if one should regard these names as correct and authentic, the geography of Palestine would become entirely obscure and confused. Many of these names are even retained in the journal of the travels of the Rabbi Benjamin of Tudela. The great bridge over the Jordan, which is at present called Djisr abné Jacub, was built by the Crusaders in the reign of Baldwin IV. The city wall of Jerusalem also was newly repaired by them, or rather nearly rebuilt; and they remained 88 years in complete possession of the land, as I shall relate farther.

When the people in Europe learned the conquest of Palestine, all were rejoiced, and every one wished to be himself able to participate in such holy expeditions, which caused five more to be undertaken.

In 4907 (1147), the second great expedition to Palestine took place, led by the Emperor Conrad III. of Germany, and Louis VII. of France.

In 4930 (1170), there reigned in Egypt King Saladdin (Salheddin Yuseph ben Ayoub), who united Palestine with his own government, and severed it from the Califate, and founded a separate kingdom, independent of that of the Califs, that of the Ayoubites, which lasted till 5010 (1250), when the kingdom of the Mamelukes commenced.

Saladdin, however, marched, in 4947 (1187), with a large army to Palestine, and made war against the then Christian King Guy (Guido), of Lusignan. A great battle was fought not far from the village of Chittin, near the mountain called Kurn Chittin, in Lower Galilee (for which see Chapter II); the Christians were defeated with a terrible slaughter, and King Guido was taken prisoner. Saladdin pushed on to Jerusalem, which he besieged, and soon began to batter and throw down its walls. The besieged, seeing that they had no prospect of a successful resistance, surrendered to him, paid him a contribution, and they were permitted to march out unmolested; whereupon many left Jerusalem with their families. Saladdin now put a garrison in the same, caused all steeples and bells to be destroyed, and the churches and monasteries, to spite the Christians, were converted into horse stables for his army; but he paid all possible respect and reverence to the buildings erected on the temple mount, for instance the Mosque Al Sachra, and other structures intended for the purpose of devotion. All the cities and towns of Palestine surrendered to him; so that he put an end to the Christian kingdom of Jerusalem.

The following are the kings who ruled in Palestine during the Christian period:

1, Godfrey of Boulogne (Bouillon), or of Lorraine; after his death there reigned, 2, his brother, Baldwin I.; after him, 3, Baldwin, called di Burgo; after him, 4, his son-in-law Fulgo; after him, 5, his son Baldwin III.; after him, 6, his son Almeric; after him, 7, his son Baldwin IV., who was afterwards afflicted with a terrible leprosy; so that even in his lifetime the government devolved, 8, on his nephew, his sister's son, Baldwin V., but who was yet a mere youth; after the death of both these, the government came into the hands of, 9, Guy of Lusignan; his queen was called Sybilla; she was a daughter of King Almeric, and was also the mother of Baldwin V.; Guy was defeated, as related above, by Saladdin, and thus lost his kingdom. The leaders of the Christian armies elected, nevertheless, after this from among themselves, as king, 10, Henry of Campania, who, however, soon afterwards fell out of a window in Ptolemais (Akko), and thus died.

Although the reign of the Europeans was thus dissolved in Palestine, several crusades were nevertheless undertaken in Europe, in the hope of recovering the lost dominion over the Holy Land, which was not accomplished, though several great victories were obtained here and there over the Mahomedans, and several towns were captured. But all this availed nothing to recover that power which they had formerly possessed.

In the year 4949 (1189), the third expedition was undertaken; the leaders in this were Frederick I. (Barbarossa), Emperor of Germany; Philip Augustus, of France; and Richard I. (Cœur de Lion), of England. They conquered Armenia and Syria; but the Emperor Frederick was drowned whilst bathing, and was buried in Antiochia. The Emperor Henry also undertook, in the mean time, an expedition with a very large army; but he lost his courage and his love for the Orient, and returned home without reaching Palestine. The other pilgrims moved on towards Akko (Acre), and besieged it. Saladdin came with an immense multitude of men, and attacked the Christians;

but the siege and the war lasted a long time; victory, however, at length declared in favour of the pilgrims, and they conquered Akko and other cities, though they could not long maintain possession of them, as they were always again taken away from them; but during all this time Jerusalem remained in the hands of the Mahomedans.

In 4962 (1202), on the 30th of May (Sivan), there was a terrible earthquake, which has scarcely ever been equalled in the East; it lasted, without interruption, nearly three days, and destroyed the greater portion of Akko, the residence of the Christian kings, as also, almost totally, the towns of Tyre, Arkos (ערקי), Trablus (Tripoli); besides which destruction, a large number of human beings perished. This calamity was followed afterwards by an equally terrible famine; after this the land was visited by a fearful plague; by reason of all which the Christians could not sustain themselves in the country as an independent kingdom. (Jud. v. 20.)

In 4977 (1217), the fourth expedition was undertaken, not as before, by land, through Asia Minor, but by sea, under the guidance of Andrew II., King of Hungary.

In 4979 (1219), there reigned in the Holy Land, Melech al Madem, whose seat was at Damascus. He caused the city wall of Jerusalem to be demolished, sparing only the Kallai (fort), in order to afford to the Christians in future no central stronghold in Palestine.

In 4983 (1223), the fifth expedition, at the head of which was the Emperor Frederick II., was undertaken. Frederick took Palestine from Saladdin, and his son Kurdius, who resided in Jerusalem, had to seek safety in flight. The Emperor having thus conquered Jerusalem and several other towns, replaced King John, who had been chosen king after the death of Henry of Campania, and who had been driven from Jerusalem by the Mahomedans, into his royal dignity. King John gave thereupon his daughter

Julia to Frederic for wife, and presented him in perpetuity with the kingdom of Jerusalem. The Emperor was accordingly crowned in the Holy City as King of Jerusalem; and it is upon this ground that all the Roman, or rather German emperors, have, since Frederick's time, borne the name of King of Jerusalem, and the House of Hapsburg bear it even now, though only as Emperors of Austria. It is well enough understood that this empty title confers no power whatever.

In 4999 (1239), the barons and knights then in Jerusalem commenced to restore and rebuild the destroyed city wall, and to repair in particular the fort Kallai. But the Amir Da-ud of Al Kerak, surprised the city, captured it, and slew a great many Christians; he also caused all that had been built to be again demolished.

In 5003 (1243), the Pisans (Italians), again undertook to restore the fort; but in the year following, 5004, the hordes of Karismians (Turks and Tartars), made a fourth irruption into Palestine under their king, Kasiumi; they took Jerusalem, caused a terrible slaughter among its inhabitants, and destroyed all that had been lately built up, together with the sepulchral church.

In 5008 (1248), the sixth and last crusade was undertaken; at its head was Louis of France. He took Egypt on his route, in order to defeat first its king. He found there that a conspiracy had broken out against the family of Saladdin, who had lost the government, which had devolved on the Mamelukes, who then began to rule, as I shall narrate somewhat more in detail hereafter.

In 5025 (1265), the Tartaric hordes made their fifth and last irruption, and killed a great many persons in Jerusalem.

In 5040 (1280), there ruled in Palestine the Sultan Seif Eddin, the Calif of Egypt.

In 5046 (1286), or rather, as appears to me more correctly, in 5051 (1291), there ruled here the Sultan Mahmud ibn Kialian, who caused several buildings to be erected in Jerusalem, and had constructed the northern pool without the city, as stated above when describing the pools, as appears from the inscription on the same, "SULTAN MAHMUD IBN KIALIAN SANE 693;" and as I have already noticed that the Chadjra commenced with 4479, and as 693 Mahomedan are only about 672 years, the date of the construction of the pool must be 5051 (1291).

In 5051, Asa Sultan Mameluki, King of Egypt, appeared with a large force before Akko and Trablus, and captured both, and killed a great many Christians, and destroyed entirely their dominion and power in Palestine, which has remained ever since, to our own times, in possession of the Mahomedans.

The proper duration of the Christian kingdom in Palestine was 88 years, as I have stated already; but their entire expulsion did not take place till 104 years later: consequently, the whole Christian period lasted 192 years.

Palestine was thus under the government of the Mamelukes, and continued so for 227 years, till it was conquered by the Ottomans.

I consider it proper to say something concerning the origin and descent of the latter. In the year 4970 (1210), when the terrible Gengis Khan, the king of the Tartars, conquered nearly the whole of Asia, and overcame all the kings and princes of that portion of the world, devastated their lands, and destroyed their cities, many of these princes saved themselves by flight, and settled in distant, uncultivated, and unpeopled districts, in steppes and deserts, in order to be safe against the all-destroying tyrant, Gengis Khan. Among these fugitives was a certain prince, the grandfather of the later named Osman or Ottman, whose descent some trace directly to Ishmael, son of Abraham, others to Japheth, son of Noah.

In the year 5060 (1300), when the Tartaric hordes, in one of their fearful inroads, robbing and murdering, caused destruction in every direction, Eladin, prince of Guna, (?) in Eastern Asia, fled before them, and left his country in the hands of a brave warrior who sojourned there, by name of Ottman or Osman, who was a grandson of the prince who had fled before Gengis Khan. The people of Guna elected Osman as their chief and king, in order to take the field against the marauding hordes. He was so fortunate in his campaigns that he overcame them; after which he gradually extended his conquests, penetrated to the West, defeated the Greeks, and conquered all Anatolia (Asia Minor). He took up his seat at Brusa, a city in the present province of Kodavenkiar, not far from Mount Olympus, in Asia Minor. His successors, the Ottoman rulers, constantly increased their dominions by conquest, till they acquired an immense extent, as I shall tell hereafter. This chief, then, is the ancestor of the celebrated imperial house which rules to this day in Constantinople, and hence the names of Ottoman Empire and Ottoman Emperors.

In 5162 (1402), Tamerlane (Timour Lenk), king of Samarkand (Samrchand), in Mongolia, conquered all Persia and Central Asia, and penetrated to the west as far as Anatolia, which he conquered, together with the whole of Syria and Palestine, and he destroyed and devastated everything wherever he appeared. Among others, the strong and celebrated city of Baal-bek, in Coelesyria, was destroyed by him, and it continues to this day in ruins. Bajazet (Biastus), of the family of the Ottomans, king of Anatolia, made war against him; but Timour defeated him, and, having made him prisoner, he enclosed him in an iron cage, and carried him about with him wherever he went, and he was compelled to eat under Timour's table what was thrown down to him. It was probably an old heathenish custom to treat conquered chiefs after this fashion. (See Judges i. 7.) After Timour's death, Mahmed Ismaeli I., the grandson of Bajazet, conquered all the countries and territories once possessed by Timour. Mahmed was a distinguished warrior, and very fortunate in his battles and conquests, by which he gave his dominions an immense extent, so that in 5175 (1415) he penetrated even as far as Salzburg in Tyrol. Palestine also reverted to the dominion of the Mameluke kings of Egypt.

In 5213 (1453), Sultan Mahmed II., the ninth in descent from Ottman, appeared before Constantinople with an immense army, and captured it by storm on the 29th of May, after a siege of fifty-four days. He caused a terrible slaughter among the Greeks, the inhabitants of the city, and made an end of the Greek part of the Roman Empire, which had been maintained there 1121 years, namely, from 4092 (332), when Constantine the Great rebuilt the city of Byzantium, and took up his residence there. Sultan Mahmed himself made Constantinople the capital of the Ottoman empire, and it has continued to be so to our own days. He also conquered nearly all Western Asia, and extended his power over a great portion of Europe, so that he conquered twelve kingdoms and more than a hundred large and fortified cities; and he was very fortunate in his wars. He attacked also the isle of Rhodes; but here his luck forsook him, and he was beaten back by the Greek inhabitants of that island, and he was not able to take it. Palestine also remained attached to the kingdom of the Mamelukes.

In 5278 (1518), Sultan Selim I., a grandson of Mahmed II., consequently the eleventh in descent from Ottman, made war against Sultan Kampison, king of Egypt. Near Aleppo, in Syria, a battle was at length fought between them. Kampison had a large army of Arabs and Mamelukes; but Selim conquered through means of his janissaries, and the Arabs and Mamelukes were put to flight, and Sultan Kampison, who was in his seventy-sixth year, and in the sixteenth of his reign, fell in this battle, the first and the last which he had ever fought. Palestine came, therefore, under the dominion of the Ottomans, and it has continued so ever since. Selim concluded a treaty of peace with the inhabitants of Trablus, Zidon, Beirut, Akko, and Damascus. He then moved on to Jerusalem, and ascended the Temple Mount, where he exhibited the reverence due to the sacred spot. Thence he took up his route to Egypt, and made war against Sultan Tumubera Diadoro, whom the Mamelukes had appointed as their king after Kampison's death, and defeated him, and had him hanged on a gallows. He also took the whole country of Egypt, and thus made an end of the Mameluke domination. Egypt came thus under the power of the Ottoman, as it has remained till the latest time, as I shall tell at the conclusion of this narrative. Selim conquered yet other kingdoms and provinces, and penetrated, in 5279 (1519), as far as Vienna, where, however, he met with a severe defeat. He died in 5280 (1520), and his son Seliman ascended the throne.

A SHORT REVIEW OF THIS PERIOD.

The following will prove that even at this early period German Jews must have lived in Jerusalem. The noble family of Dalberg in Worms is one of very ancient date, and has been in existence probably from eight to nine hundred years. It so happened that a son of this family had a great inclination to travel, in order to see the world and learn various languages, especially the Arabic; wherefore he resolved to visit the East, and came at length to Jerusalem. But, by reason of the long journey, the money with which he had provided himself became exhausted, and he was in the greatest distress, since he became sick, had neither money nor acquaintance, and knew not the language of the country, in order to make himself understood. He was lying despairing, dangerously sick and emaciated, in the open street of the city; but none of the passers-by took notice of him, either because they could not or would not understand him; till luckily a Jew came along, who had a knowledge of his language, and heard him say, "If people only knew who I am, and the character of my family and of my father, they would surely have compassion on me, for my father is able to repay manifold any kindness shown to me." The Jew, who was a German, had him immediately brought to his house, procured him medical assistance and good nursing, treated him as became his high station, and took such excellent care of him that he speedily recovered. He kept him also a long time after that in his house, and had him thoroughly instructed in the Arabic language. The young cavalier now reported to his father the whole occurrence, how a Jew had saved him almost from death, and become his benefactor, and that he had to thank him for his life and existence. The father was greatly rejoiced to hear from him, and sent out a large sum of money to enable him to return, and showed himself in an eminent degree grateful to the benefactor of his son, who thereupon returned happily to his native land. Soon after the father died, and left him great wealth. He wrote down this event in the family annals, and left a command to all his descendants for ever to do the Jews kindness, and made it a custom in Worms, that at each marriage or funeral procession among the Jews, two servants of the noble house of Dalberg should march before the same with silver-headed staffs in their hands, as a mark of honour and respect. This custom was observed several centuries in Worms.

When Jerusalem was taken by storm in 4859 (1099), by the pilgrims, there was among the generals one of the house of Dalberg, and he recollected the command of his ancestor, to show the Jews kindness, and especially that it was to a Jew of this place that he and his whole family owed their existence. He therefore endeavoured, so far as possible, and with all his power, to save the Jews from the fury of the conquerors; he took many under his protection, and sent them away to his own home, to Germany, and gave them possessions, houses, and fields, where they could live quietly and in peace. He also caused the Jews who fell in the conquest of Jerusalem, to be interred under the protection of his division of the army.

Some years before I left my native land there appeared a little work, written by one Dalberg, which spoke extremely kindly and sympathizingly for the Jews; the author partly referred to the above event, and said plainly that it is his duty by inheritance to speak only well of Israel, and to render them all possible service. "Send thy bread on the face of the waters, for in the multitude of days thou wilt find it again." (Eccles. xi. 1.)

In the year 4930 (1170), R. Benjamin of Tudela, travelled through the Holy Land, and I extract from his journal merely the number of Jewish inhabitants whom he found in the following places, which will give us some means of judging of their extension and condition. In Antiochia there were about 10 Jewish families, whose business was the manufacture of glassware; in Ludkia were 200; in Gebal, the modern Djebl and ancient Biblus, 150; in Beirut, 50; in Zidon, 20; in Zor (Tyre), 400, who had several ships navigating the sea; in Akko, 200; in

Cæsarea (Kisrin), 10 Jewish and 200 Cuthean; in Lod, but 1, who was a dyer; in Nablus, 200 Cuthean; in Beth-Gubrin, 3; in Nob, 2, dyers; in Ramlah, 30; in Jaffa, 1; in Ashkelon, 200 Jewish and 300 Cuthean; in Jezreël, 1, a dyer; in Shunem, which is Turun, דליש גברא לריש* 300; in Tiberias, 50; in Gush-Chalab, 30; in Damascus, 3000; in Jerusalem, 200, who dwell near the Tower of David מגדל דוד; altogether, 4,858 Jewish, and 700 Cuthean families, which would give us about 30,000 individuals; whereas, at present there are scarcely half as many in the country. R. Benjamin's mentioning neither Zafed nor Hebron, should lead us to the conclusion that at his visit no Jews lived in these places.

The celebrated Nachmanides רמב"ן, who travelled in 5027 (1267) to Jerusalem, wrote to his son in Spain† among other things as follows: "Jerusalem has about 2000 inhabitants, among whom are 300 Christians, who have escaped the sword of the Sultan; but there is scarcely a Jew among the whole; for when the Tartars captured the city in 5025 (1265), many of the Israelites lost their lives, and the remainder fled to Shechem. I only met two brothers, who have farmed the dyeing business from the commander of the city; and there are scarcely ten

* This name is incomprehensible to me; wherefore I believe it to be an incorrect reading, and that it should be "de les chevaux legers," as perhaps a troop of light-armed horsemen were stationed there. Perhaps he alludes by Turun, to Turanus, which is 10 English miles from Tyre, in the direction towards Banias, which was built by the Christians; or perhaps the modern village Turan, near Chittin (which see); but neither can be identical with Shunem, as must appear evident from its position.

† This letter is appended to the celebrated תורת האדם (The Law of Man) at the end of שער הגמול "The Division on Recompense," also a work of the learned Ramban. At the conclusion to his commentary to the Pentateuch, he gives a touching picture of the situation of Jerusalem as he found it.

persons who meet at the house of the dyers to hold divine service. I have urged them to found a general Synagogue of their own; for as the city is, so to say, without owners, and there is no priority right of possession, whoever takes possession of any house, dwelling, or court, (to be sure they are all in ruins,) it becomes and remains his property. We afterwards found a very handsome ruinous building, with marble columns and an elegant cupola; we instituted a collection to restore it to answer as a Synagogue; we then commenced the rebuilding, and sent for the ספרי תורה books of the Law to Shechem, whither they had been conveyed for safety; and now we have a handsome regular Synagogue, where public divine service is held; for there are constantly arriving here brothers and sisters in the faith from Damascus, Aleppo, and the whole surrounding country, in order to see the ruined temple, and to weep and mourn over it."

At that time there lived here the learned Rabbi Moshéh de Leon, who found the manuscript of the Zohar, composed by R. Simeon Ben Yochai, which was concealed in a cave not far from Miron.

In 5082 (1322), there was here the celebrated Astori Hapharchi איש תמרי הפרחי, the author of Caphtore Vapherach כפתר ופרח, a description of his seven years' travels and investigations in Palestine. At his time there was already a large Jewish population in Jerusalem, Beth-Sheän, and in Eglon, at the east of the Jordan.

In 5171 (1411), a large Jewish pilgrim society was formed, of distinguished, pious, and learned men in France and England (?), consisting of more than 300 persons, in order to travel to Jerusalem. The king then reigning there showed them every honour and respect, and permitted them to build themselves Synagogues and colleges. The celebrated scholar, Rabbi Jonathan Hakkohen,* was likewise one of this society of pilgrims. (See end of the book שבט יהודה.)

CONCERNING THE GENERAL CONDITION OF THE JEWS DURING THIS PERIOD.

When the Christians conquered Jerusalem and Palestine, the situation of the Jews became extremely miserable, and many thousands were butchered by the holy and pious pilgrims. But after awhile, when these same Christians were attacked and persecuted in their turn by Saladdin, they were not able to be any longer persecutors of the Jews; these then extended themselves gradually over the country, and lived happily and contentedly under the protection of the Egyptian rulers, as will appear from the number of souls in the year 4930; and, as a general rule, the statement which I have made above will be found confirmed, that the Mahomedans of that time cannot be regarded as enemies and persecutors of the Jews. Under Sultan Saladdin they had great privileges and liberties; for he was a particular friend to our people, and he caused it to be made known throughout his dominions, that every Jew should have the liberty to settle unmolested in Jerusalem, and should enjoy all the rights of freemen. Jerusalem accordingly received a large Jewish population; but when the Tartars, particular enemies to the Jews, at a later period, made an inroad into the city, the Jews had

* It appears that there is an error as to the time stated by the Shebet Yehudah in which this society should have been formed, since Rabbi Jonathan Hakkohen could not possibly have travelled to Palestine in 5071, as he lived more than two hundred years before that date. I would, therefore, correct קע"א 171, i. e. 5171, with חתקע"א, which error occurred by dropping the two ת; this would give us the date 971, i. e. 4971 (1211); and in truth Rabbi Jonathan lived about that time. [This solution of the question will also remove the question of Jews being in England at the time of the pilgrimage, which may have been in 1211, but not in 1411.—TRANSLATOR.]

to endure many persecutions. The later Ottomans also were no persecutors of the Jews. Selim had, as his physician and confidant, Rabbi Joseph Hamon; and was likewise a friend and benefactor to the Jews.

PERIOD IV.

FROM THE REIGN OF SULTAN SELIMAN TO THE PRESENT TIME.

Sultan Seliman the Great, the son of Selim I., ascended the throne in 5280 (1520). He is also called Seliman Abu Alim; and he was the greatest and most distinguished regent of the whole Ottman family. His empire extended from the far east, and the far south, to far in the west, as far as the town of Weissenburg in Hungary, and he penetrated even, in one of his expeditions, up to the city of Ratisbonne (Regensburg), 8 miles south of my birth-place, Floss, in Bavaria. In the year 5297 (1537), he caused Jerusalem to be enclosed with strong walls, after they had been broken down and ruined for a space of 318 years, since 4979, as related above. He also caused the aqueduct of En Etam to be built, which fact also was stated above in its proper place; as also the southern pool in the Wady Djurad (see above in the description of the pools). He also built, in 5300 (1540), the walls of the town of Tiberias. He was likewise a very great friend of the Jews, and gave them all the privileges they required, and conferred on them several public employments and offices; and one of them was made commander of one of the city gates near Zion, in 5283 (1523). He was no less the friend and encourager of science, and he gave to his learned personal and court physician, Rabbi Mosheh Hamon, son of the Rabbi Joseph Hamon, who had been physician to Selim, the order to translate for him the whole of the Scriptures and the Jewish prayers into the Arabic tongue; and the prayers especially obtained great approbation from him. The learned Rabbi Tham, son of Rabbi

David Abn Jechia, who was court physician, was his favourite, and stood in high esteem at court. Seliman reigned 46 years. After his death, the Ottoman empire began gradually to decline, and could never again attain to the same extent which it had acquired under him. His successors were but little distinguished for their deeds, so that there is but little to be told of them, and I therefore will only enumerate them in succession.

In 5326 (1566), Salim I., the son of Seliman the Great, ascended the throne. In 5334 (1574), Amurad III.; about 5350 (1590), Mustapha I., who was declared, in 5378 (1618), to have forfeited the throne, and in his place Osman II. assumed the government, in 5378; he was murdered in 5382 (1622), when Mustapha I. again obtained the government, but for one year only; and in 5383 (1623), Sultan Amurad (IV.) ascended the throne. He was engaged in a war with the king of Persia in 5392 (1632). As his army took its march through Syria, his general sent a written mandate to the cities of Aleppo, Damascus, Zidon, Zafed, Akko, &c., that they should give free quarters to his men, and supply them with everything necessary through the three months of November, December, and January (Kislev, Tebeth, and Shebat). This order bore, as might naturally be expected, especially hard upon the Jews, since the *preference* is always shown to them on all such occasions, and they are oppressed and plundered more than other classes of the inhabitants. It happened, unfortunately, that there was a great dearth in the country, since the harvest had been very scanty, and every one was in the greatest distress. The Pacha of Akko, who was a great friend to the Jews, received an order to provide quarters for 2000 horsemen in Zafed, Zidon, and their environs; but he replied, that not one of the army should dare to come within his territory, since, with the great distress already existing, the country could not possibly be troubled with such guests: and that, in case of persistence, he would be compelled to employ force to repel the invasion of the country under his charge. He actually called together an army of 40,000 Bedouins and Arabs, and placed them on the frontiers; he also sent 2000 men to cover Zafed, and prohibited every one to go near the houses of the Jews, or to harm the least of their property, or to demand anything from them. All the troops could not find convenient quarters in the town; and as it was the rainy season, they could not camp out, they were even quartered in the mosques, whilst all the dwellings of the Jews and the thirteen roomy Synagogues were spared. The general, who had taken up his winter quarters at Damascus, did not think it prudent to employ force to obtain his demands, and sent, therefore, none of his troops to be quartered in Palestine; and the whole country was spared the presence of those troublesome and terrible guests, through the favour of the Pacha for the Jews, whilst they carried out their full measure of oppression and tyranny in Damascus and Aleppo.

In 5408 (1648), Abraim ascended the throne, but was murdered the year following; and in 5409 (1649), his son, Mahmed IV., ruled in his place. Mahmed had to quit the throne, after reigning thirty-eight years, in 5447 (1687), in favour of his son, Salim II., who was succeeded by his son, Mustapha II., in 5451 (1691). Sultan Achmed III. assumed the government in 5459 (1699), who was dethroned in the thirty-first year of his reign, and thrown into prison. In 5490 (1730), Sultan Ottman ascended the throne; and in about 5510 (1750), Sultan Mustapha III.

In the year 5542 (1782), Sultan Selim became head of the empire, but was afterwards murdered. During his reign, in 5558 (1798), Napoleon Bonaparte, the general of the French army, invaded Egypt, and, having conquered it, he pursued his march to Palestine. He arrived at Gazza, where he fought a battle with Abraim, Bey of Egypt, and Achmad Djizer, Pacha of Akko (St. Jean d'Acre). On the 25th of December, 1799 (Kislev, 5559), he captured Gazza. The Jews of this place had to endure a great deal from his soldiers, so that many were induced to escape by flight. On the 6th of March, 1800 (Adar, 5560), he came to Jaffa, where he ordered 4000 Turkish soldiers to be executed. His route of march was then directed to Jerusalem, in consequence of which a terrible consternation, a perfect panic prevailed there. The Jews of the Holy City were, in the mean time, in the greatest danger of being all slain by the Mahomedan inhabitants; from which they were saved by the presence of mind and wise demeanour of their chiefs, the learned Rabbis Algazi and Mejuchas. They were accused of standing in secret correspondence and in a treaty with Napoleon to deliver the city into his hands, through fraud and cunning; and, as the Mahomedans actually believed that all the resident Jews of Jerusalem were spies and traitors, they had secretly resolved among themselves to kill all the Jewish inhabitants, so soon as Napoleon should march upon Jerusalem. This resolution was, however, revealed and communicated by a Mahomedan, a confidant and friend of our ecclesiastic chief, to the Rabbis; and, as it was already universally known that Napoleon had resolved to march towards the Holy City, there was scarcely more than a step between the Jews and death (1 Sam. xx. 3). Our chief, therefore, had at once a proclamation made throughout the whole city, that all the Jews, from the greatest to the smallest, should assemble in prayer in front of the west wall of the temple (כותל המערבי), in order to entreat God for protection and aid for the city against the French army. This order was at once obeyed, and an immense multitude assembled to perform their devotion, to pray for the welfare of the city and its inhabitants. The Rabbi then called upon the chiefs of the Mahomedans to commence at once to make a new rampart and bastion around the fort, the Kallai, and stated that all the Jews were ready on the spot, no one to be spared, to labour with all their might. This was actually done; and even this high chief, a venerable, gray-headed man, stood with shovel in his hand, labouring on the fortification, digging and working with the greatest industry, through which, as one will naturally conceive, all Jews were stimulated to be active. The Mahomedans now saw clearly that it was nothing but calumny and falsehood to accuse the Jews of a treasonable intention, since they proved themselves the true defenders and protectors of the city and the country; nay, they thought much better of them in consequence, as they afterwards asserted that the general prayer of the Jews before the "Mourning Wall" had saved the city.

Napoleon had already reached Ramléh with his overwhelming army, to march on Jerusalem; but he suddenly altered his plan, the reason of which step is unknown, and took up his march towards Akko, and left Jerusalem untouched, where the joy was indescribable, and people asserted that this sudden change was owing to the Jewish devotion, for which cause they were greatly esteemed by the Mahomedans. On the 18th of March, Napoleon appeared before Akko, and on the 15th of April (Nissan), he fought a great battle near Mount Tabor, where his generals, Kleber and Murat, defeated the Turkish army, and put them to flight. A division of the French army then marched towards Tiberias and Zafed, where the Jews were greatly maltreated by the French. Napoleon now commenced the siege of Akko, which was occupied and defended by the Turkish forces, under Djizer Pacha, and the English, under Sir Sydney Smith. The siege lasted till the 21st of May (Iyar), when he was compelled to raise it, as he was attacked on all sides, and was suffering from want; besides this, the plague broke out fearfully in his army, and he was therefore no longer able to maintain his position. Enraged, he now commenced his return to Egypt, and, appearing before Jaffa, he ordered the city wall to be demolished, and, quite inhumanly, he caused his soldiers who were sick with the plague, and whom he had left here behind when he moved on to Akko, to be poisoned, that he might be rid of them, and that they might be no incumbrance to him on his return march, or rather his flight to the south. He thus fled to Egypt, and soon after returned to France. Nevertheless, this short expedition had much of interest and influence for Palestine; since the spirit of the Arabs became thereby somewhat more animated, particularly in military matters, for they saw the conduct, the mode, and ways of civilized troops in campaigns, battles, and sieges; and I often heard the Arabs here express themselves, "Yes, Napolis and the French have opened our eyes."

Sultan Mahmed II. came on the throne in 5568 (1808). He commenced to give his government a direction somewhat more akin to that of civilized states, to which the abolition and execution of the Janissaries, of whom he caused 100,000 to be butchered in 5588 (1828), greatly contributed. A part of these troops, however, who were natives of Palestine, formed the garrison in the Kallai; and even these had to quit the fort and city; and at present the name of "Ginitsheris" is banished from the whole empire. But this monarch had also many tyrannical traits, which he permitted himself to display against several rich Jews at Constantinople, of which I shall speak more hereafter.

In 5584 (1824), the inhabitants of Jerusalem rebelled against Seliman, Pacha of Damascus, because of the terrible exactions which he practised against them. At that time there was a garrison of about 500 Arnauts (Harnuwut) in the Kallai. The inhabitants of Jerusalem represented to the commander in the fort, that they were engaged in a contest with the people of Beth-Lechem; and they therefore requested him to march with his Arnauts, in connexion with the men of Jerusalem, against the rebel people of Beth-Lechem. The commandant did not think of any deception, and leaving but very few men in the fort, moved with his Arnauts, in company with the men of Jerusalem, on the 17th of Tamuz (June), out of the city, on his way to Beth-Lechem. Scarcely, however, was he gone, when suddenly several brave Arabs surprised the fort, drove out the few Arnauts who formed the garrison, and took possession of the same. They then fired several cannons as a signal to their fellow-citizens who served as soldiers for the time, and who were outside with the commandant, that the city and fort were in the power of the inhabitants. The commandant asked his seeming auxiliaries why the cannons were fired; but they professed to know nothing of the matter. At last, however, he found out, when too late, that he was terribly deceived, and he saw clearly that he had lost the city and fort. The people of Jerusalem were far too powerful for him to think of entering the city with his handful of men by force of arms. His supposed allies now returned, and denied him all ingress; and after all had safely arrived within the town, the gates were closed, and the commandant saw himself compelled to leave everything behind him, and to move with his Arnauts by degrees as far as Damascus. Jerusalem was thus left to the will and pleasure of several Mahomedan rebels, and our people had to submit to manifold exactions.

The event was soon reported to the Sultan in Constantinople, and he gave Abd Allah, the Pacha of Akko, orders to take Jerusalem by storm from the rebels. He therefore moved on to the Holy City with a strong force, in the month of Tishry, 5586 (September, 1825), and took up a position on the west side thereof, opposite the Kallai, and commenced to bombard the fort, which, however, returned his fire in such a manner that he was speedily compelled to give up this position, and he encamped then on the Mount of Olives. He next commenced to fire terribly into the city, as he had now a safe and sure point of attack, the distance from the Kallai being too great, and the Mount of Olives being too remote to be reached by cannons and bombs from the fort. But something incredible occurred in this bombardment, and I could myself, I confess, scarcely believe it, if I were not firmly persuaded of its truth, and could assure all my readers that it actually so occurred. Thousands on thousands of cannon-balls were thrown into the city without doing the least harm, and they appeared to have lost their destructive power. They fell everywhere, in the courts, houses, and dwellings, without killing or wounding any one. Children played in the open court-yards and places; and they often saw a terrible cannon-ball suddenly fly in their midst without touching one of them, and falling harmless near their feet. My friend was sitting in company with several others, when suddenly a ball came flying through the window over their heads, and remained fixed in a hole in the wall left there for ventilation, in the opposite direction; had it rebounded it would have caused a frightful havoc among the persons assembled there. The balls occasionally passed between people sitting near each other, without injuring any one. At length the people became so indifferent to the bombardment, that they walked fearlessly about the streets, so strong was the conviction that a higher Power protected Jerusalem. But a single mishap, of no importance, occurred during the whole siege. My friend, G. A——, was sitting on his roof, when all at once a ball fell near him, and, as it exploded, a splinter struck his foot, causing a severe but not dangerous wound; he was soon restored, however; but to this day he feels in a slight degree the effects of the injury, when walking. This person was the only Jew injured; but the other inhabitants likewise, whether Mahomedans, Christians, Armenians, Greeks, &c., remained uninjured.* The bombardment lasted nearly two weeks. The Pacha was astonished to find that he neither perceived any injury or destruction in the city caused by his cannons and bombs, nor that he was offered any capitulation on the part of the besieged. He thus saw that his bombardment was quite fruitless, and could not explain it in any other manner than that a higher Power protected Jerusalem. He therefore offered favourable terms to the city. Negotiations were now commenced, and on the 22d of Tishry (October), the gates were opened to him, and he had a peaceable entry. The people of Jerusalem surrendered to him both city and fort. He placed in the latter some troops, remained some days longer in town, and then moved off with his army without molestation to Akko.

In the year 5592 (1832), Mahmud Ali, pacha of Alexandria in Egypt, declared himself independent of the Sultan of Constantinople. His son, Abraim Pacha, moved suddenly with a large force towards Palestine, and took, without almost any resistance on the part of the adherents of the Sultan, Jaffa, Jerusalem, Nablus, and Chaifa, and placed Egyptian soldiers as garrisons in the same, and appeared next before Akko, which was occupied by Abd Alla Pacha, and besieged it a long time, and took it finally by storm, carrying away the Pacha as prisoner to Egypt. He gradually now occupied all Palestine, Syria, Arabia,

* May not this little execution have been owing to unskilful gunnery? —TRANS.

and Nubia, together with a part of Anatolia, and even penetrated as far as Smyrna, and was about making a conquest of Constantinople, when his progress was stayed by the European powers, and he was bidden to content himself with his southern possessions, and give up his advance to the north. He now commenced to introduce civilization in his dominions, instituted regular courts of law and proper officers of justice, and restrained the wild Bedouins; but he more particularly extended his protection over the strange Europeans, called here the Franks, gave them all rights, and even privileges, and would not suffer them to be exposed to the arbitrary proceedings of the Mahomedans. He conferred on the consuls ample power, and the privileges and respect due their station, so that the name of Frank was in a measure a title of nobility, especially as he had not to pay any poll-tax or contributions, nor could be held to labour for the state.

In the year 5593 (1833), he conquered completely the eastern part of Palestine beyond Jordan, called Al Ledja (where he had several severe contests with the Druses), Al Djedr, Hauran, &c. Soon after, he ordered the Arabs and Bedouins to furnish him recruits for his army, on the plan of the European states, and proceeded to organize a formal conscription in the country. This was, however, an extraordinary and unusual measure, since it is not the oriental custom to raise troops after this fashion. The Arabs and Bedouins of Palestine resolved, therefore, with one voice, to refuse him this concession, and came to an understanding among each other to organize a revolution in the land against Abraim Pacha. Unfortunately, he was at that time absent in Alexandria, and the whole military force in the country was exceedingly small; so that the rebels had to use but little exertion to overcome the same, and to get possession of the fortified places and the whole land, which in consequence became disturbed.

All the roads were unsafe, and highway robberies were openly committed, since immense bands of Arabs and Bedouins collected together and roamed through the country. Their principal plan and aim was the capture of Jerusalem, and to obtain possession of the Kallai, which is the strongest fortified point, and contained the chief garrison. The whole of the mass was divided into four divisions, to conquer—1, Galilee, i. e. Zafed and Tiberias, with their environs; 2, Nablus (Shechem); 3, Hebron; and 4, Jerusalem and the Kallai.

In the beginning of the month Iyar, 5594 (May, 1834), word was brought that these bands were gradually approaching Jerusalem, and had already made their appearance on the mountains not far from the city. On the 16th, therefore, the city gates were closed, and the siege commenced; and at midnight of the 22d, the town was taken by the rebels by assault,—the first one which I ever witnessed. Whilst a part of the rebels penetrated into the city through a subterraneous canal, the others scaled the wall, and others battered down the gates, and thus obtained possession of the town. The soldiers, observing in the moment of the assault that they were unable to oppose the rebels with any degree of success, withdrew into the Kallai, and left everything to the assailants. What a terrible night was this for us all! The echoing of the voices of thousands of warriors,—of men, women, and children, who all raised their wild Arab war-cry in the gloom of the night, at the storming of the city; the tumult of the retreating troops; the lamentations of the defenceless, abandoned inhabitants, who heard already in their midst the shouts of the infuriated conquerors,—all presented a most mournful scene.

At daybreak we observed that the whole city was completely filled with an innumerable mass of the rebels, great and small, women and children. We thought indeed that we were all lost, in being exposed to the licentiousness of such barbarians; and some houses and courts were already broken open and plundered: when suddenly the herald or crier of the rebel leader, a just and venerable Bedouin, who in this matter might perhaps put to the blush many European generals, proclaimed throughout the city that Mislamin, Yehud, and Nazrani might remain perfectly quiet and in peace, since no one should be molested; and, if any one of his subjects should dare to violate this order, he should be summarily dealt with according to military rule. We felt ourselves partly saved and happy through this proclamation. The soldiers, indeed, made, a few hours afterward, a small sortie from the fort, in which many of the rebels fell, and others were taken prisoners; but they nevertheless could not maintain themselves, and had to withdraw again within the fortifications. The rebels now commenced to fire against the Kallai; but they had no cannons, consequently they could do no execution. The commandant, a venerable and philanthropic man, who was particularly on terms of friendship with many Israelites, could easily have opened a heavy fire upon rebels; but he would not employ the cannons against them, as they were all within the city, which he was desirous to spare. Although now they fired on the Kallai from the city, they were unable to approach the fort any nearer, not to mention that they could not scale it. As they then found that it was impossible for them to obtain possession of the fort by open violence, they endeavoured to undermine it; when suddenly the joyful news was noised about, on the afternoon of the 28th, that Abraim Pacha had arrived at Jaffa from Egypt, with a very large force, and was reported already as being near Jerusalem. This news scattered the whole rebel army, so that in a few hours scarcely one man of the whole could be seen in Jerusalem, as they had fled towards Burak and the mountainous district near it. On the 29th, in the morning, Abraim Pacha actually arrived, with his large army and heavy artillery; and then only did we breathe freely again, since we were in the greatest anxiety and terror the whole preceding week, notwithstanding the proclamation of the rebels.

The Pacha made, after a few days' rest, several rapid expeditions against the rebels at Burak, and they suffered on each occasion a severe defeat, and many were captured and imprisoned; the remainder then moved farther to the south, and united themselves with their confederates at Hebron and its vicinity. Abraim Pacha then restored order, appointed in Jerusalem and its environs new judicial officers, placed troops in the country, and moved against Nablus, where he again defeated the rebels, and put a garrison therein, and caused the principal instigators to be executed. Order and quiet were likewise restored in Galilee a few months later, through the chief of the Druses, called the Amir Abshir. But the most obstinate were the rebels in Hebron and its neighbourhood, as their numbers constantly augmented, since the Arabs to the east of Jordan also joined them, and, making common cause with them, formed quite a formidable army. They rejected all summons made to surrender by Abraim Pacha; till at length he surprised them, on the 28th of Tamuz (July), with a force of nearly 20,000 men, and caused a terrible defeat, accompanied with a fearful loss of life, among them. Hebron suffered severely, and was given up for several days to the license of the soldiers, on which occasion the Jews were great sufferers, as I shall mention more fully, under article "Hebron." From this place Abraim Pacha extended his expedition of conquest to Kerak, and chastised its inhabitants, who had destroyed his whole garrison stationed in the fort of that city; their sheich was taken prisoner, and executed publicly in Jerusalem. The same fate overtook several others, who had all been engaged as authors of the revolution. Abraim restored peace and order in every direction; and, after the lapse of two or three months, he was again lord over the whole country. Soldiers were quartered everywhere among the Bedouins, all sorts of arms were taken from the Mahomedan inhabitants of both town and country, and only the strangers, the Franks, were left in possession of their weapons; houses also were visited with extreme rigour; a close search was instituted, to effect this end; and Abraim Pacha became at length so greatly feared in the whole country, that his very name was a terror to the wildest Arabs. The entire land enjoyed, in consequence of this, such security that highway robberies were scarcely to be heard of any more, and everything commenced to flourish. People could travel unmolested, day and night, in perfect security in every direction, and this even among the wildest Arab tribes. He also abolished and prohibited, under severe penalties, the onerous and exorbitant so-called *Kafaar*, which means transit toll, which was not a fixed tax, but an arbitrary exaction, which every villager, every sheich, every Bedouin, demanded at pleasure from every traveller or wayfarer at every village,—I might almost say from every one met in any division of a village, even from a Bedouin working in the field; and it was accompanied with the grossest maltreatment of the plundered individual. The Israelites obtained permission to rebuild their ancient but ruinous Synagogues, and all their rights were conceded to them. In the year 5599 (1839), an English consul was permitted to reside at Jerusalem, and all the usual immunities were accorded to him, while hitherto a European consul was scarcely ever suffered to reside there. But Palestine was now compelled to furnish regular recruits to the Pacha's army.

In 5600 (1840), Abdul Medjid ascended the throne of

the imperial house of Constantinople. After the death of Sultan Mahmed, Abraim Pacha again commenced to extend his dominions beyond the fixed limits assigned to him, and already made some conquests to the north of his government from the territory of the Sultan; whereupon England and Austria joined the Turkish army to oppose Abraim's progress. In 5601 (1841), they besieged Akko, and in a very short time this town, as also the whole of Syria and Palestine, were again in the possession of the Sultan. Abraim fled to Egypt, and his whole army was dissolved, every one returning to his home; and thus all the possessions which he had in Asia reverted to the Sultan, so that only his African territory remained under his sway. The Arabs and Bedouins had their arms restored to them, and Palestine again began to retrograde, and to relapse into its former state of insecurity, since the Arabs obtained anew the privilege of not furnishing any recruits, and of not being compelled to be civilized by force; the roads, or more correctly speaking, the whole country, was rendered anew insecure, and the Franks were deprived of many of their former privileges. Nevertheless, much of the good and beautiful which Abraim had introduced was retained. Many consuls were appointed for Jerusalem, and now there are six of them resident there, namely, Russian, Austrian, English, French, Prussian, and Sardinian.

In the year 5604 (1844), the French consul obtained the imperial permission from Constantinople to hoist his national flag. But when he was about to display the same on his roof, in company of the Pacha of Jerusalem and several of the principal officers, a general insurrection took place among the Mahomedan inhabitants against the Pacha, and they employed violence, through which means several persons were wounded, to prevent the unheard-of outrage of displaying any other flag in the Holy City except that of the Crescent. The Pacha seeing that the mass of the people was too great, he yielded so far as not to have the flag hoisted. And although several of the rioters were afterwards arrested and severely punished, the Mahomedans nevertheless maintained their ancient right, and the permission was revoked by the imperial authority; and thus no consul is at this day permitted to display or hoist his flag in Jerusalem.

A SHORT REVIEW OF THIS PERIOD.

In the year 5283 (1523), a learned Italian of Leghorn travelled through the country, and he gives the Jewish population as follows: In En Sethun, a village not far from Zafed, where at present no Jews live, 40 families, with a Synagogue, wherein were kept 21 copies of the law ספרי תורה; in Zafed, more than 300 families, with 3 Synagogues; in Alma, a village 5 miles south of Kedes in Naphtali, where no Jews reside at present, 15 families, with 1 Synagogue; in Gith (Gath Chepher), 40 families; in Nablus, 12; in Hebron, 10, with 1 Synagogue; in Jerusalem, 300, among whom 15 German; in addition, there lived in Jerusalem more than 500 widows; in Kefr Anan 30, with 1 Synagogue; in Beirut, 20, with a small handsome Synagogue; and in Damascus, 500, with 3 Synagogues. He also says: "Tiberias is quite destroyed, and entirely depopulated." The whole would give us 1267 families, which, with the 500 widows in Jerusalem, would probably constitute a population of about 18,000; consequently, considerably smaller than at the visit of Rabbi Benjamin of Tudela in 4930 (1170).

(In the original, there follows here a list of 28 Rabbins who succeeded each other in Jerusalem from the year 5250 till 5605, which, not being of interest to the general reader, is omitted in our translation.)

In the year 5385 (1625), in the reign of Sultan Amrad,

there lived in Jerusalem the just and kind governor Machmad Pacha, who granted the Jews all possible privileges, so that they had their own properties, both houses and fields, and lived in the greatest security, contentment, peace, and happiness. When suddenly a rapacious and tyrannical Arab, who was blind in one eye, called Ibn Paruch, purchased the post of Pacha of Jerusalem from the chief of all Syria and Palestine, the Pacha of Damascus,—as it is nothing strange to sell offices to the highest bidders. Ibn Paruch came thereupon, on the 26th day of Tebeth (January), to Jerusalem, with an escort of about three hundred armed men, and deprived the benevolent Machmad Pacha of his office. The situation of the people now took a woful change, as Ibn Paruch tormented them terribly, and made heavy exactions, especially from the Jews, and often caused the most respectable men, the principal officers of the congregations, to be thrown into prison, and compelled them to satisfy his unheard-of demands through means of cruel treatment, which often brought them to the verge of the grave. Thus, for example, he ordered the Synagogue to be surprised during divine worship on Sabbath, the 11th of Elul, of the above year, and caused fifteen venerable men to be taken from the same to prison as hostages; and they were not liberated until he was paid 11,000 grush, or 5500 American dollars. These scenes and exactions followed each other so often, and became so general, that the Jews were gradually exhausted, and could contribute no more money to satisfy this monster's desires; they had to part with all their gold and silver articles, and everything of value; and at length, to save their miserable lives from the tyrant, they were compelled to borrow of their Mahomedan fellow-townsmen the sum of 50,000 grush, for which, though obtained for but a short time,—till they could obtain relief from their benevolent brothers abroad,—they had to promise the exorbitant interest of 20,000 grush, wherefore their indebtedness amounted to 75,000 grush, or 35,000 dollars. Many endeavoured to escape with their oppressed families by flight; they left everything behind, glad only to save their lives; but the tyrant placed guards in every direction, so that no one could leave the city; and even when a corpse was carried out for interment, it was examined, to discover whether or not it might be one feigning death endeavouring to make his escape.

The Jews nevertheless succeeded, in almost a wonderful manner, to communicate in secret their dreadful situation to their brothers in Constantinople, and to pray of them to announce at court the raging of this hyena. The Sultan was greatly incensed at hearing the news, and commanded the Pacha of Damascus, also an insatiable extortioner, immediately to depose Ibn Paruch; who nevertheless endeavoured, partly by artifice and the interest he had, and partly by means of considerable bribes and presents, to prevent the Pacha from carrying the imperial will into effect; and mainly gained his point by showing himself openly as a rebel against the Sultan, inasmuch as he captured, on the 22d of Kislev, 5386 (December, 1626), the Kallai, in which lay in garrison some troops of the Sultan, under command of an Aga. This affair made him still more formidable; and having thus little to fear from outward force, he commenced to tyrannize yet more cruelly in Jerusalem; and he caused occasionally the most venerable and aged Israelites to be dragged to the scaffold, and the hangman stood with the axe in his hand, the rope was already fastened round their necks, and it only needed his diabolical nod to hurry these honoured fathers into eternity; and all for the great crime that they were not able to furnish him any more money. So that every one was tired of life, and sighed for death as a deliverer from an insupportable burden.

But at length as report said (which, however, seems to want confirmation), the Sublime Porte again gave orders to the neighbouring Pachas to attack the tyrant, and to deliver him into prison. Those Mahomedans, however, who were most intimate and best acquainted with him, related afterward the following as the real cause of his precipitate flight. One night he had a dream, when he saw standing before him a venerable old man wrapped in a purple cloak, who was about to slay him. Ibn Paruch in great terror asked him who he was, and why he appeared so inimical to him, to which the apparition answered, "I am King David; and know, tyrant, that if thou quittest not the city instantly, and if thy eyes close themselves here again in sleep, thou shalt surely die." Ibn Paruch awoke trembling, and caused the treasures which he had obtained by robbery to be collected together, as far as this could be done, in the greatest haste, and loading several camels with gold, silver, and other precious things, he fled away suddenly and hurriedly, on Tuesday, the 12th of Kislev, 5397 (December, 1627); and thus was Jerusalem saved from the power of this monster, to the general joy and gratification of all its inhabitants.

This remarkable occurrence I have taken in extract from a printed document, entitled חרבות ירושלים, "The Ruins of Jerusalem," printed in Venice, in 5388 (1628), in which this event is told circumstantially, and quite at length. The document was written and signed by the chiefs of the Jewish people at Jerusalem, and given as an authorization to the messengers who had been sent to Italy to make collections in behalf of the Holy City, which had been reduced to indigence through the acts of the tyrannical Ibn Paruch.

THE REMARKABLE HISTORY OF PHARCHI.

In the year 5560 (1800), there lived in Akko a distinguished, pious, and rich man, called Rabbi Hayim Pharchi, whose family belonged to Damascus. He was famous throughout the East not only on account of his great wealth, but also through his virtuous and generous course of life. He stood in high esteem at the imperial court of Constantinople; and the choice of all the Pachas in the whole of Syria depended on him. Whomsoever he proposed at court was appointed and installed, so that he might be considered in a measure as the ruler of all Syria. Nothing also was undertaken by the Sublime Porte in the East without first informing him of it. His house was the asylum for all the distressed and the sufferers of all nations and religions. Nothing but justice and equity could be executed in the whole land; because all the officers and authorities dreaded this just and excellent man too much to do anything wrong. In him the house of Israel in Palestine had, so to say, a pious and faithful regent, who protects his people in every possible manner, and bestows on them all kinds of benefits, and endeavours that all shall live happily under his sway. He knew nothing of oppression and exclusion, not to mention persecution.

There lived also at the same time in Akko the tyrannical Pacha, Achmad Djizer, of whom I shall have to say more hereafter; he endeavoured to accuse the above noble philanthropist of treasonable devices: he accordingly had him arrested, and put out one of his eyes, and cut off the end of his nose. The court at Constantinople was informed of this terrible deed of infamy, but was not able to act against the tyrant, because it was feared that he would employ this as a pretext to organize a rebellion against the Sultan, and indeed there was ample evidence to make this intention a matter of certainty almost. But Achmad died soon after, and his place was conferred on Seliman Pacha. Pharchi had a distinguished Mahomedan friend, who died suddenly, with his wife, and left quite a young child, only a few years old, called Abdalla, who was without any protectors, and was therefore educated in the house of the noble Pharchi, who viewed him as his own child, and had him instructed in all the necessary scientific branches; and in addition to this, Pharchi caused that Abdalla was appointed Pacha of Akko, after the decease of Seliman. He at first viewed Pharchi as his father, and followed his guidance to execute justice and equity in the land. But as early as one year after assuming the government, he commenced to act counter to this advice and instruction, and was reproved occasionally on this account by his venerable guardian. Abdalla now observed that he stood in his way, and that he would be a check on the exercise of his mere will and pleasure, and resolved therefore to get rid of him. He endeavoured first secretly to accuse him of treason and other charges, to find thus an opportunity to lay violent hands on him. The confidants of Pharchi revealed to him the terrible purpose of his ungrateful ward, and advised him to save himself by flight. But he declined doing this, and he answered magnanimously that his flight would call down on all the Israelites of Palestine the greatest persecution, and might indeed cause their entire extermination, since the Pacha might be induced through his escaping, to wreak his fury on this innocent people. He added, that he was prepared for everything, and would bear patiently whatever might occur, in order to save thereby, or at least to benefit in some degree, his own people.

Now it happened, on Thursday, the 28th of Ab, 5579

(August, 1817), which the pious Pharchi kept as a fast day (as the eve of the New Moon of the month Elul), and as he was about to take his supper, that an officer with his soldiers suddenly entered his apartment; his death-warrant was read to him, in which he was condemned on account of treason, and with the offence that his private Synagogue was built higher than the mosque of Akko, and several other diabolical charges and crimes; and this sentence was instantly executed.

The day following his house and court-yard were ransacked and plundered, and a large quantity of gold, money, silver, and other valuable articles were carried to the Pacha, the monster and parricide. The corpse of this martyr he did not even permit to be interred, but ordered it to be cast into the sea; and when, the day following, it was carried again on shore, he ordered it to be taken out far into the sea, and then to be thrown into the water. The pious widow of Pharchi fled in all haste towards Damascus, but died suddenly on the road, and was buried in Zafed; and suspicion was entertained that she had been poisoned by the furies who surrounded the Pacha.

This deed of terror excited universal consternation and mortal fear in all Palestine, especially among the Israelites; and the parricide now showed himself openly as the persecutor of the Jews in the Holy Land, and exercised such acts of violence and abomination among them, as are not perpetrated by cannibals and savages. My friend S. M., who lives at present in Jerusalem, was at that time an active and courageous young man, who often went to Akko as dragoman, that is, interpreter, with commissions from the Russian Jewish congregation of Zafed, and in consequence came frequently to the house of the ——— consul. A few days after the above tragical occurrence, he had to attend to some business for the congregation, and therefore visited Akko, and the consul's house among others. All at once, Abdalla came in, and was received very friendly by the consul, who was his bosom friend from early youth, as both had been at the same time brought up by the same nurse. They went together into a side room, and had a confidential conversation. S. M. perceived that something very important was being discussed between them, and had the courage to approach softly and to overhear them. The substance of what reached him was, that the Pacha requested his faithful foster-brother not to interfere, in his consular capacity, with his own affairs; that he had no intention to touch the foreigners who were under the consul's protection; but that he desired of him not to put any obstacles in his way, in the manner he intended to proceed with the other Jews. The *worthy* consul had *humanity* enough not to refuse any favour to his brother, and promised him faithfully not to make any representations whatever to him in this respect, notwithstanding his great influence. The Pacha then continued: "I mean, on the coming Saturday, during divine worship, to surprise the Synagogue, and to hang up before the same, on the instant, the spiritual chief of the Jews, A. J. I intend, also, to proceed in the same manner at Zafed, to capture, during worship, the three richest among them (giving here their names), to hang them, and to confiscate their property." My friend S. M. having thus listened to this frightful conversation, moved quietly from the spot he had occupied. The Pacha soon after took his leave; S. M. of course did not give the consul the least cause to perceive that he had heard what was going on; he thereupon concluded his business, and then left him. But he hastened to the chief, A. J., and revealed to him in secret the danger in which he was, and advised him to escape on the instant by flight, without communicating the least to any one of the whole affair. The advice was followed; A. J. disappeared suddenly, and no one, not even his household and friends, knew what had become of him, or whither he had gone. S. M. hastened next with equal speed to Zafed, and revealed the secret to the three proscribed rich men, who also disappeared suddenly in the same mysterious manner, and no one could tell where they were. The Saturday at length came; no one knew anything of the fatal plan of the Pacha, and all assembled as usual in the Synagogue at Akko. Suddenly the troops made their appearance with a gallows' frame before the Synagogue, and they entered to seize A. J., in order to hang him. But he was not there, and could not be found all over the town. The Pacha now commanded to seize another respected man in his stead; this was done, they beat him cruelly, and dragged him, though perfectly innocent, to the gallows, to hang him up. But the Pacha said he would pardon him, if he would become Mussulman, and confess the Koran. The other, in his fright, assented, and was thereupon liberated. But he afterwards fled the city, despising the Koran and the Prophet, and lived again as a faithful Jew.

In Zafed, also, the prior resolution of the Pacha was proceeded with; but the three rich men destined to be hanged had likewise disappeared, and could nowhere be found. He therefore ordered all the Jews of the place to be locked up in the castle, a small Kallai, and demanded of them an exorbitant ransom, which they were unable to furnish; so that they were compelled to sell even their garments, and whatever of value they possessed, in order to obtain their liberty. He also exacted much from the Jews in Tiberias and Akko. But Jerusalem and Hebron, being in the southern part of Palestine, belonged not to the Pachalik of Akko, but to that of Damascus, and the Jews residing there were spared for the present; they, however, had to endure since then other persecutions and exactions, when the monster at Damascus opened wide his fiery and deep jaws, and threatened to swallow up everything. Subsequently to the above related event, no one was secure in life and property in Galilee, on account of the tyrant Abdalla, till the excellent Austrian Jewish consul-general at Aleppo, the well-known Baron of Picciotto, employed the influence he had with him to restrain him in his barbarous procedure against his own brothers in faith.

In Damascus dwelt the three brothers of the martyr Pharchi; they were the most distinguished and honoured men of the whole surrounding country, not only through their wealth and their extensive commerce, which was carried on to all parts of the Orient, but also for their great influence in Constantinople and other large cities and towns, and they were likewise famed for their honest and noble conduct.* Their names were Seliman, Raphael, and the youngest Mosé Pharchi; the last mentioned died in 5600 (1840), through the torture inflicted by Serif Pacha, as one of the accused for the murder of Father Thomas, in which this excellent man was, among others, charged with having taken part in the slaughter of that old priest, to make use of his blood at the celebration of the Passover. When these men learned the deplorable death of their beloved brother, they resolved to be revenged on his murderer, even at the greatest sacrifices. Through their great influence at Constantinople they succeeded in obtaining a firman (a decree), signed by the Sheich al Aslam,† literally, the chief of the faith, authorizing them

* One who knew this excellent family maintained that this name Pharchi, "the Blooming," from Perach, "flower," was quite appropriate, since among them was to be met with whatever was beautiful, great, noble, and religious, in the greatest flourishing state of development. Alas! that at present the flowers are nearly all fallen.

† This personage is the chief ecclesiastic of the Turks, on whose judgment and supervision of the whole ritual of the Moslems, all jurispru-

to take hostile measures against Abdalla. It was a small matter with them, on account of their immense wealth, to engage Seliman Pacha of Damascus, Mustapha Pacha of Aleppo, and two other minor Pachas, who were under the jurisdiction of these two principal ones, with their soldiers, to take the field against Abdalla. A large force having thus been collected, the expedition passed over the Jordan in the month of Nissan, 5581 (April, 1821). Abdalla marched out against the advancing Pachas; and a battle took place at the bridge over Jordan called Djisr abné Yacob, in which he was defeated, and he fled in haste, retreating to Akko. The brothers Pharchi now took possession of all Galilee, deposed the officers appointed by Abdalla, and appointed others in their place. The victors next laid siege to Akko, where the famine rose to such a height, that a single egg was sold at 70 grush,* which at that time was near six dollars, and a sheep at 900 grush, or 78 dollars. The siege was continued for fourteen months, during which period the Pharchis supplied the place of the Pacha in the country, and acted as governors. But it was decreed that Abdalla should not yet meet his deserts, and he was permitted to have a few years more indulgence. He succeeded, through treachery, to have the worthy Seliman Pharchi poisoned, through which means he died suddenly in the month of Nissan, 5582 (April, 1822). Mustapha Pacha likewise showed, by his acts and conduct in battle, that he was not true to the cause in which he had embarked. Raphael Pharchi was therefore induced, shortly after the decease of his

dence depended. The Sultan himself cannot alter his decision, and his signature is considered equal to that of the Emperor.

* The grush or piaster has no fixed exchange value; at present, it is 4 cents, 50 grush being 1 ducat, or 2 dollars; some years ago, even as many as 60 were only worth a ducat. In old times, this term denoted a coin nearly in value a Spanish dollar,—at another time the half of this, or 50 cents.

elder brother, to withdraw with Seliman Pacha to Damascus. Mustapha, it is true, maintained the siege till the month of Sivan (June), when he also withdrew to his own government.

Abdalla saw himself thus freed from danger from that quarter, and had only now to fear the action of the Porte, and therefore requested Mahmud Ali, the Pacha of Egypt, to act as mediator between him and the Sultan. The Egyptian Pacha now employed all his influence to obtain the pardon of his compeer of Akko. The Sultan was greatly astonished to learn all the above proceedings, which were perfect news to him, since he had never been before informed of the tragical end of Pharchi of Akko, nor of the Damascus expedition against Abdalla, as the firman of the Sheich al Aslam was obtained without any knowledge on his part, and procured of the Divan (the council of ministers), through the great influence of the Pharchi and their very rich Saraf or court-agent, Rabbi Bechor Karmona. The Sultan was so incensed at this, that he banished the Sheich al Aslam from Constantinople, as he dared not to have him executed, but inflicted the punishment of death on the Saraf in the month of Tamuz, 5582 (July, 1822). But the greatest and the real crime which induced the Sultan to this execution was, that the worthy Rabbi Bechor was too rich, and that he desired to appropriate to his own use the alleged criminal's great wealth. Abdalla was thus saved a second time; but instead of being grateful to Mahmud Ali, he subsequently commenced to defy him, till at length he was induced to besiege Akko in 5592 (1832), when he took Abdalla and carried him as prisoner to Egypt.

A SHORT DESCRIPTION OF HEBRON.

Hebron is called in Arabic בית אל חליל Beth al Chalil, "The House of the Beloved," because Isaac, the beloved son of Abraham, was born and educated here, and, as appears from Genesis xxii. 1, resided also here a long time. It is situated in the portion of Judah, 20 English miles south from Jerusalem, in a valley (Gen. xxxvii. 14). The mountains which surround it are the highest points of the mountains of Judah, and are 2664 feet above the surface of the Mediterranean Sea. It is a small town, or, more correctly speaking, a very large village, which consists of several divisions, each, so to say, constituting a village by itself. It contains several thousand Arabic inhabitants. On its eastern end is the cave of Machpelach מערת המכפלה, Arabic, Al Magr, i. e. the cave. It is also called the Fort of David, and is a very handsome and most ancient structure, built of immense stones, and surrounded with strong and high walls. It forms, in a measure, a fortress. Beneath the surface of the earth is the celebrated cave where the patriarchs lie buried. It is covered over with masonry, having a small opening on the top, through which the Mahomedans constantly lower burning lamps, and maintain there a perpetual light. Above this cavern is a mosque, built at a later date.

Hebron is mentioned but little in history after the destruction of Jerusalem, and I will therefore merely relate the few traces which I was able to find.

When Benjamin of Tudela travelled through Palestine in 4930 (1170), Hebron was entirely destroyed, probably through the wars of the Christians with the Saladdinian kings. He says, "Here is a large church, called St. Abraham; and it was, when the country was still in possession of the Ishmaelites, a Jewish Synagogue." This proves that, during the rule of the Mahomedans, before the Christians came, Jews must have lived there. About seventy years later, when Rabbi Pethachiah of Ratisbonne ר' פתחי' מריגנסבורג, travelled through Palestine, it was already in a measure rebuilt; but no Jews were living in it. At the time of the Nachmonides רמב"ן, in 5027 (1267), some Jews were found here, as he wrote to his son* that he was on the point of going to Hebron to select for himself a spot to be buried in. It appears, however, that they afterwards quitted it again, as Astori, in the year 5082 (1322), says nothing of any Jewish families in Hebron. In 5283 (1523), there lived here but *ten* Jewish families. When, in 5300 (1540), the celebrated Rabbi Jechiel Ashkenazi went to Hebron, he found in it many Caraites. He founded there a Jewish congregation; and it appears that he purchased a Synagogue, which exists to this day, and belongs to the Sephardin (Portuguese), from the Caraites. About twenty-five years ago there came several messengers from the Caraite congregation at Constantinople, to lay claim to the said Synagogue, alleging that it was originally their property; but they were easily and soon confuted, for they could not establish their allegation. Since the time of R. Jechiel to our own day, Hebron was uninterruptedly inhabited by Jews.

In 5594 (1834), Hebron met with a heavy calamity, since it was taken by storm on the 28th day of Tamuz (July), by Abraim Pacha, and given up to his soldiers for several days. One can better imagine than describe the scenes which were then enacted. Nearly all the Mahomedan inhabitants fled into the depth of the mountain range, but the Jews could not do this; besides which, they entertained but little fear, since they could not be viewed as rebels and enemies by Abraim, wherefore they fell an easy prey into the hands of the assailants. When the Pacha marched out to take Hebron, a petition was presented to him by the officers of the Jewish congregation in Jerusalem to take these unfortunate people under his protection, which he faithfully promised to do; but, notwith-

* See above, Period III., year 5027.

standing this, they were not spared at the taking of the town, so that five Jews were purposely murdered, and all their property which had not been buried under ground was either stolen or destroyed in the most wanton and cruel manner. Abraim did then indeed place a guard around their quarter of the town, but it was too late; and he said, "Whatever is already in the hands of the conquerors, the soldiers, cannot be demanded back again of them;" wherefore the whole Jewish community was sunk into poverty.

One of the leaders of the Hebron rebels was the Sheich Abd al Rachman, who had his seat not far from the town Al Dura (see p. 113, Art. Adoraim). He had been for several years previously the principal personage of the environs, as far as the Dead Sea and the Djebl (Mount Seir). When Abraim Pacha had conquered the country, he fled, and the Pacha appointed in his place the Mutzelim, Abu Suwat, who had been even before this time an enemy of Abd al Rachman, and he therefore acted inimically towards those of his family who had been left behind. But when the government of Abraim came to an end, in 5601 (1841), the banished chief again appeared, greatly respected and with increased power. He also acquired anew a strong party, and became again the Sheich of the whole district. He thereupon caused Abu Suwat to be publicly executed in Hebron, and acquired gradually such authority that the Pacha of Jerusalem did not think it prudent to venture putting a check on his proceedings and actions; and the name of Abd al Rachman sounded more fearful and was more respected than that of the Sultan. The whole vicinity was at that time quite secure, and one could, with the greatest safety, travel among the Arabs and Bedouins; because they were strictly prohibited to rob or to make their usual exactions, since this *right* belonged to the Sheich alone. He was exceedingly cunning, and never missed making the capture of those he pursued in a witty and ludicrous manner, and he was particularly fortunate in his expeditions. So it happened that on his flight he was caught by the soldiers of Abraim in such a way that they had got hold of his red terbush:* he nevertheless succeeded in eluding their grasp, merely leaving the empty terbush in their hands. Towards the Jews he permits no ill-treatment; but he is a most insatiable leech, as scarcely a day passes on which some demand is not made, which, though not presented as an extortion, comes in a worse shape yet—in that of a request or petition, with an understanding that a threat may be added to enforce compliance. And, as his whole family, from little to big, imitate, each for his own benefit, the magnanimous head of the house, it is almost impossible to live among such leeches; and actually the greater part of the Israelites of Hebron have left it and settled in Jerusalem.

In the year 5605 (1845), Abd al Rachman's two brothers rebelled against him, and laid claim to his government, that is, they wanted the right to plunder: they procured adherents, and a regular partisan warfare ensued; in consequence of which, Abd al Rachman was driven out. He next collected some Arabs, and had several bloody fights with his brothers; and it appeared that his good luck had forsaken him. But at length his star again became in the ascendant, through which, or rather through his heavy gold, he succeeded to induce the Pacha of Jerusalem to take his part, who then marched against Hebron with a large force, in the month of Sivan, 5606 (June, 1846). He took the town after several skirmishes, and reinstated Abd al Rachman in his government. On this occasion the Jews suffered severely, many were dangerously wounded

* A peculiar long cap which the Turks wear, though it is not much used among the Arabs, who adhere to the turban.

at the taking of the town, and deprived of all their property. The two rebel brothers took to flight, and have not been heard of up to the time of writing this, in 5609 (1849). Abd al Rachman governs therefore unopposed, and is very industriously engaged in filling up the great deficiency in his heap of gold, which had become diminished through the war with his brothers, by his usual exactions from those subject to his rule.

Hebron has two congregations; first the Sephardin, containing about 60 families, who have a very ancient Synagogue, as I have stated already; and secondly the Ashkenazim, consisting solely of about 50 families, since many of them have left and moved to Jerusalem. This congregation, however, has been in existence only about thirty years. Still, they have two Synagogues, one built thirty years, and one fifteen years ago.

A SHORT DESCRIPTION OF ZAFED צפת, ARABICE, AL ZAFED.

This little town is situated on the summit of a high mount, in the mountains of Naphtali, in one of the handsomest districts of the whole country, with a very wide prospect all round, and with a clear and pure atmosphere, wherefore it is naturally very healthy. The name of the town is nowhere mentioned in Scripture, and it was therefore undoubtedly built at a period subsequent to the biblical records. Josephus, in his Jewish War, Book ii. chap. xxv., mentions a town Seph or Zeph, in Galilee; unquestionably our modern Zafed. So also we find in Yerushalmi Rosh Hashanah, ii., a town צְפַת Zefath. But except in these two places, I could find no vestige of the name in any other book of antiquity. So also I find no mention of Zafed in all the middle ages before 4947 (1187); since the celebrated historian, Rabbi Joseph Hakkohen (דברי הימים לר' יוסף הכהן), relates, that at the battle of Chatun, the Christians fled as far as the fort of

Safid, undoubtedly Zafed, where a small and ancient castle yet exists. In the year 4930 (1170), when R. Benjamin of Tudela travelled through Palestine, he mentions no Jews as residing in Zafed. Only in the year 5250 (1490), it commenced to be inhabited by Jews uninterruptedly to the present time; and since then the most distinguished and most learned men were residents of it. About the year 5330 (1570), the number of the Jews was so uncommonly great, that they had seventeen Synagogues, among which, one belonged to the Ashkenazim; they had even a Jewish printing office, that of R. Abraham Ashkenazi, in Zafed, Birié, and En Setun, two villages yet existing near Zafed, although no Jews now reside there. I myself have seen a Midrash *Agur* printed in Zafed in the year 5386 (1626). It would appear that the Jewish population had at that time reached its greatest extent, and commenced then gradually to diminish. In 5518 (1758), Zafed was visited by an earthquake, through which 200 houses were destroyed, and 140 Jews lost their lives. Those who escaped, deprived of their shelter, left it in consequence, settled elsewhere, and only 50 Jewish families remained behind. In 5520 (1760), there were yet standing five Synagogues. In the years 5525, 5537, and 5540 (1765, 1777, and 1780), many Jews from Poland settled in Zafed, and it began to flourish a little in consequence of this immigration. In 5572 (1812), all Galilee was visited with a frightful pestilence, and in Zafed the mortality was so great that scarcely one fifth of the entire population escaped with life. Many fled to Jerusalem; but the plague, having been carried thither by the fugitives, broke out subsequently there also, and raged with violence. It was only after the lapse of several years that Zafed recovered in a measure; and the Jews lived very happily under the protection, or rather government, of the noble R. Chayim Pharchi, of Akko, until the tyrannical Abdalla Pacha commenced his misrule there, in 5580 (1820).

In the year 5594 (1834), during the rebellion of the Arabs and Bedouins against Abraim Pacha, Zafed suffered from a fearful calamity. On Sunday, the 8th of Sivan (June), a very large number of Arabs and Bedouins from the environs of Zafed, aided by those from the east of the Jordan, suddenly surprised the Jewish quarter of the town, and wasted and destroyed everything to such a degree that I am not able to paint accurately the scene of devastation which then ensued. Everything was carried off which could possibly be removed, even articles of no value; boxes, chests, packages, without even opening them, were dragged away; and the fury with which this crowd attacked their defenceless victims was boundless. One of the Bedouins in his eagerness dragged off so heavy a box that he was a corpse after a few hours in consequence of the violent exertions he had made. A good old Arab woman, who lived near the Jewish quarter, reproved her son for his barbarous proceedings against his worthy neighbour, who had always shown himself so friendly towards him, and begged him to spare the same. But the Arab became so incensed at this reproof, that he gave his own mother such a blow that she soon after expired.

The Jews in consequence left everything behind, and fled into the open country, some going to Birié, others to En Setun, and others to Miron, where they found here and there some old acquaintances among the Arabs, who had compassion enough on them to permit them to take shelter for the moment in their courts, although it was merely under the bare sky, naked as they were, and deprived of all their possessions. There lay thus a crowd of several hundred men and women, old and young, nay, women who were expecting to become mothers, or who had just given birth to a child, all intermixed, with scarcely any garments to cover their bodies, since even their clothes had been stripped from them by the savages, and with scarcely a drink of cold water to quench their thirst. Nevertheless, on account of the very old acquaintance subsisting between them and many of their protecting Arabs, who at the same time were probably moved by the hope of a hundred-fold return, they received here and there in a few days a little Bedouin bread, the so-called Pitta, which is scarcely fit to eat, and this in such small quantities, that each individual obtained daily as much as the size of three fowls' eggs. This miserable situation continued for six weeks, to the 22d of Tamuz (July). In addition to all this suffering, they were kept in constant danger of their lives, as it was all along reported that they were all to be killed by the roving band who had first attacked them; and they had thus to dread, the whole of this fearful time, that every day, every hour, might prove their last. Several, however, of the Jews, especially the Ashkenazim, who were perfectly familiar with the Arabic language, and thoroughly acquainted with the customs and habits of these Arabs, had the courage to procure the poor dress of the Bedouins with a few arms, through which means they resembled the robbers so thoroughly that they could not be recognised, and they therefore could mix freely among the miserable rabble, and commence plundering in their turn; they had thus a good opportunity to go to their own dwellings, and recover the gold, silver, and money, which they had hidden under ground. While thus occupied, they often were met by the real robbers, and they had then to divide the booty equally and fairly with them; and it thus happened that many a one of these pretended Jewish robbers broke into his own house, where, but a few days or even hours before he had dwelt happily as the head of the family, surrounded by those dear to him, and now sat as a marauding Arab, in the midst of *such* society, speaking ill, quite indifferently and in a merry mood, of his own people, in order to play successfully his dangerous part, although his heart might be torn and bleeding all the time, and being compelled, after ransacking all, to divide his own property with these bloodhounds. Nevertheless, much was saved in this manner which otherwise would have been lost.

The whole Jewish quarter was thus demolished, and was uninhabited during full six weeks, so that wild beasts began to take up their abode in the same, and on the return of our people they actually found a tiger in a ruined cellar. As might be expected, many were greatly misused during this scene of rapine, others were wounded and maimed, and several were actually slain. The Synagogues were particularly exposed to the fury of the assailants; the rolls of the law were trodden upon and cut in pieces; Tephillin and Tallethim were used as straps and coverings for their cattle; books were torn into shreds; in brief, everything was blasphemously destroyed, so that even a cannibal might be ashamed of such doings.

During nearly all this time the robber-troop remained in Zafed, first, in order to be able to search often among the ruins, in the hope of finding yet something not before discovered, till at length not a bit of wood was left, and doors, windows, and boards were all torn away; and secondly, to divide, by degrees, their booty among themselves. They were perfectly safe and unmolested; for they had learned that Abraim Pacha was, at the moment, so much occupied at Jerusalem and vicinity with his enemies there, that he could not go into Galilee. They also took the precaution to guard all the roads, and placed sentinels everywhere, so that the poor prisoners could not give any information abroad of their pitiful condition. But "behold, the Guardian of Israel slumbers not and sleeps not;" and the chiefs of the congregation succeeded, notwithstanding the vigilance of the Arabs, to send an account of all that had occurred to the consuls at Chaifa, Akko, and Beirut. These now united as one man to inform Abraim Pacha at once of these events, and they represented to him the great danger in which the poor Jews were, and asked of him to interpose by force without delay. But as it was then impossible for him to make a campaign in Galilee, he commanded the chief of the Druses, Amir Abshir, with whom he stood in friendly relations, to advance in all haste to save the unfortunate Jews from the power of the Bedouins.

Abshir therefore appeared suddenly in Zafed on the 22d of Tamuz, with a strong force of Druses, and the Israelites were relieved; they now returned, but found everything totally ruined and destroyed. But a new scene was now enacted, as severe measures were demanded against the robbers. Many of the Bedouins belonging to the east side of Jordan saved themselves by flight; still, many of them were taken by the Druses. The most respectable Mahomedans of Zafed and its environs were arrested as the authors of the outrage, and some of them were afterwards publicly executed, and whatever could be found of the stolen property of the Jews was restored. Every Jew was believed, when saying that he recognised this or that Arab among the robbers. The person so accused was instantly arrested, and punished with blows till he at last confessed and gave up his booty. Even many of the richest and most respectable of the Arabs were arrested, loaded with chains, and punished, upon the mere assertion of a very poor and common Jew. The word of a Jew was regarded as equal to the command of the highest authority, and severe punishment was at once resorted to, without any previous investigation, without any grounds or proofs. In this manner much of the stolen property was discovered; since many, in order not to be exposed to the violence of the Druses, delivered up everything of their own accord. The Jews were now required, by order of the Pacha, through the intervention of the consuls, to make out a correct list of all they had lost, of whatever they missed, and to indicate the true value of the same, and to hand it in to Abraim Pacha through means of the European consuls. The losses thus ascertained amounted to several millions of piasters.* Abraim devised a plan to collect, by force, gradually, a sum equal to this amount, from the inhabitants of the country. It was divided into several terms of payment; and the Jews actually received a part of their losses. But through later mishaps by which the land was visited, such as earthquakes and deficiency of harvest, it became impoverished; and not long afterwards Abraim lost the government, everything got into confusion, and thus the Jews were repaid scarcely one-fourth of what they had lost. The whole Jewish community of Zafed is accordingly impoverished.

Finally, the terrible earthquake of the 24th of Tebeth, 5597 (January, 1837), destroyed Zafed completely. On this occasion 1500 Jews lost their lives, and were buried with all their possessions in a moment of time. The few who escaped alive settled elsewhere; and the town only commenced to recover a little, and to be rebuilt and again inhabited, after the lapse of several years. In addition to this, when, in 5598 (1838), Abraim Pacha was engaged in a violent contest with the Druses, these surprised Zafed suddenly in the month of Tamuz, at the

* For the value of these coins of account, see note, page 395; at 4 cents the piaster, the property thus lost would be at least 80,000 dollars,—a moderate estimate, even with the acknowledged poverty of the people.—TRANSLATOR.

same time of the year in which they had appeared four years before as protectors and defenders, plundered and ill treated the Jews yet remaining there, and thus destroyed completely the last vestige of their prosperity. Under the present government, Zafed is left entirely exposed to the pleasure of the surrounding Bedouins and Arabs, and its Jewish inhabitants lead a constant life of terror.

There are at present two congregations in Zafed; 1, the Sephardim, numbering about 130 families, with one Synagogue; and 2, the Ashkenazim, numbering about 200 families, also with one Synagogue.

A SHORT DESCRIPTION OF TIBERIAS.

טבריה, IN ARABIC, AL TIBARIA.

This town is situated on the western shore of the Lake Chinnereth. Its name is derived from that of the Roman Emperor Tiberias Cæsar,* who reigned in the year 3718, A. M., 110 years before the destruction of the temple. In Tal. Megillah, 6 *a*, are found several opinions as to the name of the town which formerly stood on the site on which Tiberias was built. According to some, it was Rakbath רקת; according to others, Chamath חמת (Josh. xix. 35). After the destruction of Jerusalem, it was the seat of the most learned Jews; and the last Sanhedrin, and the latest Nessiim, till about the year 4125 (365), had their seat there. Near this city stood formerly a castle, mentioned in Yerushalmi Abodah Zarah, iii. "When Rabbi Jesi died, the castle of Tiberias קסטולין דטברי fell in." It was still standing in the reign of Baldwin IV.

* So says Bereshith Rabbah, ch. 31, that Tiberias has its name from King Tiberias; Alexandria, from King Alexander; and Antioch, from King Antiochus. There is also mentioned, ibid. 20, a woman from the house Tibrinus בית טברינוס, which I suppose to signify the town of Tiberias.

I could find but few traces of Tiberias during the middle ages, only that in 4398 (638), all the Jews and Christians were driven out by the Kalif Omar ibn Kataf; but when the Christians conquered the country at a later period, Jewish inhabitants were found in it, and Rabbi Benjamin of Tudela reports there already 50 Jewish families. A little while prior to this, it was the seat of the most distinguished scholars and grammarians of all Palestine, who had an academy there, מדרש גדול, as reported by Ibn Ezra to Terumah. It was destroyed in the subsequent wars of the Christians with Saladdin; and it was still uninhabited in the year 5283 (1523), as only 12 houses were standing in it. Sultan Seliman had it surrounded with a wall in 5300 (1540), and it commenced to revive a little, and to be inhabited by the most distinguished Jewish literati; but it was again destroyed in 5420 (1660).

In 5502 (1742), the celebrated pious Rabbi Chayim Abulafié, of Smyrna, settled there, and had the city wall restored at his own cost; and it was again inhabited by Jews through the exertions of this distinguished man. Soon after, Tiberias had to endure a severe contest and siege from an Arab tribe of that neighbourhood, at which R. Chayim and his small Jewish population distinguished themselves; on account of which, he was nominated chief of the city by the Mahomedan inhabitants, as a mark of respect. This distinguished family of Abulafié has produced a large number of the most learned men. At the present day it flourishes in Jerusalem, Tiberias, and Damascus, and contains the wealthiest men in the Jewish congregations in these cities.

In 5540 (1780), many Polish Jews emigrated from their own country and settled in Tiberias.

In 5594 (1834), during the Arab rebellion, the Tiberias Jews suffered the least. The rebels locked them up in their quarter of the town, and demanded an immense sum of money. The prisoners perceiving in what danger they were, surrendered at once all they had without the least hesitation, according to the advice of the wise king, "It is a time to lose" (Eccles. iii. 6), and were then liberated, and no farther extortion was practised. But when Abraim Pacha overcame the rebels, they preferred their demand to him, again according to Solomon, "It is a time to gather in," and all the extorted property had to be restored to them.

In 5597 (1847), Tiberias was almost entirely destroyed by the great earthquake of the 24th of Tebeth, when nearly 500 Jews perished in the ruins; the city wall also fell down. Afterwards the city gradually recovered, and it is now nearly rebuilt, but the wall still lies in ruins.

Tiberias has two congregations; 1, the Sephardim, with a handsome Synagogue and 80 families; and 2, the Ashkenazim, with two Synagogues and about 100 families, who are all Poles and Russians. The Jewish inhabitants of Tiberias enjoy more peace and security than those of Zafed.

A SHORT REVIEW OF THE EGYPTIAN KINGDOM.

As Palestine was a long time under the dominion of the rulers of Egypt, I deem it not entirely superfluous to take a brief view of this country.

Up to the year 4400 (640), Egypt was a part of the Romano-Greek, i. e., the Eastern Roman Empire. In this year it was conquered by the Kalif Omar ibn Kataf, and it thus came under the protection of the Mahomedan Kalifs. In 4628 (868), Tartaric hordes, composed of Turkomans and Turks, overran the whole of Western Asia and Egypt, and they obtained possession of the country, until the year 4772 (1012), when the Kalif Al Chakim, of the Fatimite family, defeated them, whereupon the

Kalifs governed Egypt until 4930 (1190), when Saladdin arose, united Palestine with Egypt, formed a particular state, that of the Saladdinites (Ayoobites), and severed it from the Kalifat. In 4980 (1220), ruled Sultan Nadjmadin, one of Saladdin's family, who formed the corps of the Mamelukes, similar to the Janissaries at the Ottoman court. But they rose against the family of Saladdin in 5010 (1250), and chose a king out of their midst in 5014 (1254), Turan Shach Mameluki, and maintained the government two hundred and sixty-four years, till 5278 (1518), when Sultan Salim I., of the Ottoman family, conquered Egypt, and caused the last king of the Mamelukes, Sultan Tumubera Diadoro, to be executed. The country came thus under the government of the Ottoman emperors of Constantinople, or more correctly speaking, under that of the Beés (Beys), also a species of Janissaries and Mamelukes, who always ruled the land, but more particularly the *governor*, for the time being. These Beés obtained their greatest power and renown under Ali Beé, in the year 5526 (1766). In 5559 (1799), Napoleon Bonaparte conquered Egypt, and it came, though for a brief time, under the power of the French, on which occasion the Beéis lost much of their renown and power, till at last, in 5580 (1820), Mahmud Ali Pacha caused all the Beés to be executed, and thus procured himself the sole dominion over Egypt. It is now independent of the Ottoman power, and forms a state by itself. In 5609 (1849), this Pacha died at a very old age, and as his son Abraim had preceded him to the grave several months, the government is now in the hands of his son Abbas Pacha.

APPENDIX

TO THE HISTORICAL PART.

CONTAINING TRAITS OF THE CELEBRATED DJIZER, PACHA OF AKKO, ANECDOTES CONCERNING THE JUDGMENT OF SEVERAL KADIS IN PALESTINE, ACTS OF THE SHEICHS, ARAB AND MAHOMEDAN LEARNING, ORIENTAL WIT, ETC.

1. THE PROHIBITED TRANSIT TOLL.

Soon after Achmad Djizer Pacha had assumed the government of Akko, he prohibited the so-called *Kafar*, or transit toll, which every village took upon itself to exact from all passing through it. But in order to convince himself whether he was obeyed or not, he undertook frequent journeys through the country, accompanied by a small force. Before he entered a village, he would send some one in advance, to discover whether he would be allowed to pass unmolested, or whether the Kafar would be demanded. If he was actually detained, he himself came up quite indifferently, and pretended to be a mere stranger to the matter, until he had in person convinced himself fully that the prohibited Kafar was actually demanded; when the greatest offender in the matter was instantly seized and hung up on the spot in the public street, and suffered to remain suspended a long time as a terror to the others. Such scenes were enacted in many villages and towns. All this produced such a dread among the Arabs and Bedouins, that so long as this Pacha ruled, the Kafar was not heard of any more.

2. THE TENDER FEELING OF A TYRANT.

Through Achmad Djizer's unexampled severity and fearful cruelty, which he exercised everywhere, in all relations, and for the smallest trifle, such fear and anxiety were excited among the Arabs, that the whole country was quiet and secure, and the robber Arabs and Bedouins conducted themselves as peaceably as lambs. You could travel by night through the whole country without being molested by any one. A respectable citizen of Akko went one evening to take a walk outside the town, and met at a great distance from it, an Arab woman, who was pursuing her way quite alone. He asked her, whether she had no fear to walk alone at so great a distance from the town; to which she replied, "Thanks be to Alla, so long as he keeps alive our Efendi (Lord), one is safe everywhere." The citizen had the next day some business at the Pacha's, and anxious to compliment him upon his being so generally feared throughout the country, he related to him the answer of the Arab woman. "What!" he exclaimed, in a rage, "thou venturest to terrify the poor woman to ask her whether she has any fear to walk alone! since she must have felt some little fear in the moment when thou didst put the question to her." And he had him executed on the spot, out of a tender compassion and pity for the poor Arab woman, who must have experienced some fear.

3. THE JEWISH KILLER (SHOCHET) AS EXECUTIONER.

One day the Jewish Shochet of Zafed was at Akko. Suddenly there came some Guwassés (servants) of the Pacha, to seek him, with the command to appear before his highness without delay. He was greatly terrified; for he could form no idea why he was so suddenly summoned, and augured nothing good. When he had been speedily conducted before the Pacha, one may imagine his surprise to see a Bedouin lying bound, and to hear the Pacha giving him the command to slay this man, since he was a practised killer. The Jew knew well enough that he should always be regarded by the friends, acquaintances, and adherents of this Bedouin, as his murderer, and would therefore never more be sure of his life, since the offence could only be atoned for by a vengeance of blood for blood. He therefore fell on his knees before the Pacha, and had the presence of mind to free himself from the execution of the unpleasant order by a ready invention. "I am, gracious Lord," he said, "a poor man, the father of a numerous family, whom I support in a very humble manner by my office of killer; if I, however, were to obey thy august command, to slay this Bedouin, I would not be fit any more, according to our Talmudic rules, to act as Shochet; because the hand which once has shed human blood, can never again slay cattle for the food of man, and I should thus be without bread for myself and family, and we would be sunk into the greatest distress." The Pacha was deeply moved on hearing the words of this poor head of a family, and said, "If this be so, then go thy way, as I will not deprive a poor man entirely of his bread;" and he seized the sword, and cut off, himself, the head of the Bedouin, out of pure compassion for the killer.

4. THE RIGHT PROOF.

One day the Pacha stood at a window in his palace at Akko, and observed that a soldier asked of an Arab peasant woman, who was selling milk, ten paras' worth (about one cent) of her commodity, which he obtained and drank up. When the woman asked for her money, he averred that he had not yet received the milk, and would only pay when she had duly furnished him with it. The woman cried aloud that he had already drunk the milk; but he maintained the contrary. No one was present who could appear as witness; but the Pacha had seen everything, without being perceived by them. He had both thereupon summoned before him, as though he knew nothing of the whole dispute, and asked unconcernedly, for what they contended, when they told him their story. The Pacha demanded an oath from the soldier, who swore that he had not drunk the milk. The other, who from the evidence of his eyes knew the contrary, said then that an oath is no certain proof to discover the truth; but that he knew of a surer and entirely reliable evidence, to wit, that the man's stomach should be ripped open: if now the milk be found, he should pay the Arab woman the ten paras, and have to defray the expenses of being sewed up again himself; but in case no milk be found, he need not pay the money, and the woman should defray the cost of sewing him up. The Pacha's method of proving the fact was at once executed, the milk was found undigested in the soldier's stomach, and the woman received her ten paras.

5. THE SOLDIER'S MEAL.

The Pacha came once accidentally into the barracks at Akko, and heard in the kitchen a great quarrelling and disputing among the soldiers. He stepped furiously into the kitchen, and without asking the cause of the quarrel, he grasped the first soldier whom he could lay his hands on, and pitched him into the large kettle in which the food for the soldiers was prepared, and which happened then to contain boiling rice; after he had boiled for some time, he was taken out, and had to be eaten by his quarrelling comrades in the presence of the magnanimous Pacha. What a horrid meal!

6. THE WALL OF PARADISE.

There raged at one time a frightful epidemic among the Mahomedans in Palestine, whilst nearly all the Jews were spared. This circumstance excited such envy and hatred among the former, that they resolved to kill all the Jews; but they were secretly informed of this design. But what could these unprotected people do to stay the fury of the inhuman monsters? They therefore sought safety in the all-powerful material, which is so potent from sunrise to sunset—money. They promised the Kadi a considerable sum if he would frustrate the evil design. He ordered the Jews to remain quiet and without fear, and he would promise to grant their request. The succeeding day he preached a sermon to the people, telling them that he had been grieved a considerable time, and wondered why only the pious Mussulmans were so terribly visited, whilst the unbelievers were spared. But the preceding night Mahomet had appeared to him in a dream, and comforted him by saying, "Take courage, thou faithful believer! know that for these several years past, the wall of Paradise needeth repairing; but this year it fell down altogether. In order to rebuild it quickly, the labour of many believers is needed; this, therefore, has caused the great mortality among the faithful. It is therefore clear that the unbelievers must be spared, for they cannot be permitted to enter paradise." When the Mahomedans had heard this joyful news from the mouth of their holy preacher, they were rejoiced, and wished even to die, and they desisted from their purpose of laying hands on the Jews, because they were not worthy to die in the general mortality, as perhaps, through the crowd of the deceased hurrying onward, some of the unbelievers might by accident attain to the dignity of being admitted among the labourers on the Paradise wall.*

7. THE JEW FOUND IN AL CHARIM.

In the year 5593 (1833), soon after my arrival in Palestine, it happened that the Mahomedans found one morning, at their entering their great mosque on the Temple Mount, Al Charim, a young Jew, who had remained there the whole preceding night, and had made great havoc among the costly lustres, lamps, lanterns, and the like—whatever, in fact, he was able to destroy. But it was speedily perceived that he lacked reason, and was not much less than downright crazy. The furious Mahomedans, however, fell upon him, and he was dragged out, thrown into prison, and cruelly beaten the whole day, all of them thinking it a religious duty to ill-use him. Every one, therefore, who passed by, and every one who could get near him, deemed himself obliged to strike him, in quality of a faithful believer. He was, therefore, beaten with cudgels, sticks, hands, and fists, besides being kicked; and it was almost a wonderful thing that he was not torn to pieces by them, and killed on the spot; but the latter alternative was purposely avoided, as he was destined to be reserved for something yet better and higher,—a punishment yet more agreeable to Alla. The rage of the barbarians went so far that every Jew who was at that time seen in the street was ill-used, and it was feared that they would have to suffer a general assault of the

* If the pious Germans, French, and Spaniards had had likewise such correspondents from Paradise, when, in the year 5108 (1348), a fearful plague raged also among them, and spared the Jews (see *Zemach David*, part 2d, year 5108), who might have informed them that the wall of Paradise had then fallen down, and pious Christians were wanted to repair it, surely those frightful slaughters and persecutions would not have taken place. Perhaps the Mahomedans are nigher to Paradise than the others, since they have several correspondents there.

faithful. This state of things lasted several days, until, fortunately, the Egyptian troops arrived, on their march to the seat of war in the North, and, stopping a few days, restored quiet and order. The day on which the awful criminal should be publicly burnt had almost been determined on already; but it was resolved first to inform the lord of the land, Mahmud Ali of Egypt, and to obtain his sanction and confirmation, which no one doubted would be readily given. But the Pacha answered briefly, "that the guards of Al Charim were responsible, and greatly deserving of punishment, in so carelessly executing the duties of their office; and that the Jew should be set at liberty, since the sacred law which interdicts the entrance to Al Charim to a non-Mislamin, under punishment of death, that is, to be burnt, is inapplicable in the present instance, because the Jew is also circumcised, and is thus somewhat akin to the Mislamin; that he could not indeed be permitted to enter freely the sanctuary; nevertheless he is not liable to the death penalty." The pious believers looked greatly surprised when they heard this resolve, but they were compelled to let the malefactor go at large.

8. THE BARGAIN VOID IN LAW.

A merchant of this city once bartered several chests of indigo (in Arabic Al Nil), with another merchant, for sugar. But, before delivering the indigo to the purchaser, it rose greatly in value, and he sought for some device to declare the bargain void. The other merchant, however, maintained, as was natural, that the trade was perfectly fair; and, as the other would not deliver up the indigo, he saw himself compelled to go to law. In the mean time the defendant went privately to the Kadi, and promised him a considerable sum if he could annul the sale, although there was no pretext for such a proceeding. On the day fixed for the hearing of the case, both parties appeared before the Kadi, to hear his judgment, whether the sale should be set aside. The judge gave thereupon the following wise and just decision: "Indigo is *blue;* sugar, on the contrary, is *white;* therefore they are almost of opposite colours, and in nowise similar, wherefore they cannot be bartered against one another; and the sale is accordingly declared null and void."

9. THE POISONED COFFEE.

Some years before Mahmud Ali had assumed the government, and the Arabs had the ability and power to tyrannize over the Jews, a very rich Jew of Constantinople emigrated hither. The Mahomedans ardently desired to find some pretext against this rich man, in order to extort money from him, according to their fashion. One day a Mahomedan, accompanied by a Bedouin, leading two camels loaded with charcoal, entered the courtyard of the Jew, and said that, as no doubt he was in want of coal, he would spare him the trouble to go to market for it, and brought therefore to his house two heavily loaded camels with this necessary article. But the Jew, fearing some evil, made some excuses—was very grateful for the kindness of the other, yet averred that he could not make any use of it, as he was well supplied already. But all subterfuges were in vain, and the Mahomedan forced him fairly to take the coal; and when the other asked after the price, he answered, "Never mind, give what you think the article is worth. Yet, as thou camest but lately in our holy city, it is no more than becoming that thou shouldst invite us, as faithful fellow-citizens, into thy house, and entertain us with pipes and coffee,* until the camels be unloaded by the servants." "Let it be so," answered the rich man; and, opening the door of

* The oriental custom of entertaining strangers.

his saloon, he told them to enter. Coffee and pipes were brought in; they drank and smoked, spoke of indifferent things, when suddenly the Bedouin sunk down as dead, and gave no signs of animation. The Mahomedan jumped up from his seat in a great rage, and addressed the Jew with a loud voice—"Murderer! what hast thou done? Thy coffee is poisoned! Shall we tolerate the Jews among us, that they may lay plots against our lives? This murder shall be washed out by the blood of all the Jews." The other protested his innocence, trembling, with tears in his eyes, saying, "Have I not drunk myself of this coffee? How, then, can it be poisoned?" "Then must the Bedouin's cup have contained poison," was the furious reply of the other. The Jew adduced all sorts of proofs of his entire innocence. At length the Mahomedan was moved, and said, "My friend, I indeed pity thee and all the Jews of the city; but I can think of only one remedy by which thou and thy people can be saved. Have thy court-yard immediately locked up, so that no one from without will be able to enter. I will employ all possible means to suppress this affair and keep it a profound secret; and this evening I will send thee two confidential persons, who shall fetch away the corpse and bury it in all secrecy; and in this way thou and thy brothers will be saved. But to effect this a large sum of money is necessary, which I am sure thou wilt readily and willingly furnish on the spot." The trembling Jew esteemed himself happy that the matter could be settled with money, and gave immediately the sum which the Mahomedan had demanded, large as it was, with great willingness and with the utmost unconcern. The other went away, and the corpse was left lying in the saloon. After sunset two Bedouins arrived with a large sack, in which they thrust the corpse, took it on their shoulders in profound silence, and walked away greatly terrified. But scarcely were they a few steps distant from the house of the rich man, when the dead Arab jumped out of the sack; and the Jew now learned for the first time that the whole affair was a gross deception, contrived merely to extort from him the large sum he paid for his ransom.

10. THE GRAVE OF MOSES.

The Mahomedans make annually a pilgrimage in the spring to the grave of Moses, which is about 20 English miles to the east of Jerusalem, and nearly 7 from the western shore of the Dead Sea. A highly respected and learned Mahomedan, the Sheich, or rather preacher in the great mosque on the Temple Mount, is in the habit of visiting me constantly, and gives me many an explanation concerning Mahomedanism. I asked him one day, how it were possible that the grave of Nebi Musé could be on the spot indicated, since it is explicitly said in Holy Writ, that the true grave is on the east side of Jordan, whilst the monument of Nebi Musé is to the west of the same. He thereupon told me: "I will make thee acquainted with a tradition which many of our own learned men and many of the faithful do not know. Listen—it is now about eighty years ago, when there lived here a distinguished and pious dervish, i. e. a simple devotee, who spends his time in spiritual and religious contemplations and acts; this saint was continually grieved concerning the great fatigue and danger to which the faithful were exposed in going over the Jordan, to make their pilgrimage to the grave of Musé, which is on the eastern side. He therefore thought on means to avert this necessity, midst fasting, bathing, and prayers; but he could not succeed; and it lasted a long while before he was answered by Alla. At length, however, Mahomed appeared to him in a dream, and said to him, that his prayer had been accepted, and that he (Mahomed) had obtained from Alla the favour to be permitted to transport the whole grave to the western shore of the Jordan, in the vicinity of Jerusalem, in order to save the pious pilgrims of the Holy City and its environs the great fatigue and danger of travelling over the Jordan. He showed him also in this dream the exact spot whither the holy grave was to be transferred. Soon after a monument was erected on the spot indicated by the dervish by the pious faithful, and this is the now well-known Nebi Musé on this side of the Jordan. Art thou now satisfied, asked my credulous Mussulman informer, to find the grave of Musé on this side of the river?"*

11. HOW THE BEDOUINS CROSS RIVERS WITHOUT BRIDGES.

In the rainy season, the little wadys often swell and become great rivers, overflowing their banks, and thus prevent any one from passing to the other side for several days. When they begin to grow a little shallow, and the travellers are tired of waiting longer, a set of very tall and strongly built Bedouins make their appearance, and as it is their business to transport men and baggage across the stream, they undress themselves completely, take the traveller, who embraces their head quite firmly, on their shoulders, and wade through, whilst the water often stands up to their breast, and place their burden safely on the other shore.† When in this manner all the travellers are transported, the small packages are carried over, and then the cattle are driven through; after which all the things are repacked, when the journey is continued.

* If Mahomed has the power to transport graves, it would be advisable for him to transpose himself his own grave from Mekka, in Southern Arabia, to some more convenient northern Mahomedan possession, in order to spare his followers so long and dangerous a journey.

† These carriers may truly say with the Psalmist (lxvi. 12), "Thou hast caused a man to ride on our head, we have come into (fire and) water, and thou hast led us forth happily."

With the greater rivers, for example the Southern Jordan, where there is no bridge, and which is not fordable even in the latter part of the summer, the ferriage is managed by the Bedouins with their cattle and baggage in the following manner: the smaller cattle, such as sheep and goats, are all cast into the river, and they then swim over of their own accord; the camels, however, which are not able to wade the Jordan because it is too deep and rapid, and as the great length of their legs prevent them from swimming, are driven close to the edge of the water, where they are made to kneel down, and their feet are then tied together with strong cords, so that it is impossible for them to raise them or to stand erect; they are then pushed into the water by the Bedouins with all their strength, and they are thus forced to swim over. They present indeed a most curious and ludicrous means of ferriage. With their head and hump out of the water, bobbing up and down as they are accustomed to do in walking, unused to the fluid element, and feeling themselves, though manacled, carried forward, their spirit seems to be occupied with the business of crossing over; and the whole appears to be to them a great mystery, as they indicate by constant, impatient growling. When they have arrived safely on the opposite side, their bonds are instantly loosened, and they jump up, as one might say, quite joyfully, in having successfully accomplished their toilsome voyage.

Men and baggage are ferried over in a yet more singular manner. They take eight to ten water-skins, made of goat-hides, blow them full of air, tie them together on a square framework composed of several stout poles; on these they place some pieces of wood and boards as a floor; they fasten next the water-skins under the frame, and this *artistical* ship is thereupon launched into the water, and its cargo placed on it. The inflated water-skins prevent this frail vessel from foundering, and the crew then scull it over with their sticks to the other side of the stream. As may be imagined, this conveyance is not very safe, and it often happens that those who trust themselves to it make on it their last voyage, as they land from it in eternity. However, it is in this wise that the poor Bedouin knows how to help himself in various positions; and if he does not understand how to propel his vessel by steam, he can at least prepare his conveyance by filling the water-skins by the breath of his own mouth.

12. MISLAMIN.

The name Mislamin, Mussulman, is etymologically derived from the root Salem, "perfect, complete, enlightened, faultless," or a man who has attained perfection in all his relations. The title or expression Malim, "master, or doctor," is a term of offence to the Mahomedans, wherefore they are never addressed by it. Should a Mahomedan be called or addressed in this manner unawares, he asks very angrily and offended, Ana Malim, "Am I only a master or learned man?" You have then to apologize, and to say that this offence was committed without thought, without any intention of wounding his feelings. The salutation Selam Alikun, "Peace with you," should only be used among Mussulmans, but not from a non-Mahomedan to a Mahomedan, unless to offend him and be offended in turn by his rude reply. A non-Mahomedan has to address a follower of the Koran with Alla vi, "God be present." Selam should be used only by and to a Selamen, Mislamin. The only pity is, that the poor Mislamin is perfect already at his birth, and thus brings his perfections with him in the world like the animal, wherefore he has no necessity for any cultivation or improvement. But in modern times it appears that the Mahomedans do not regard themselves any more as so completely perfect, and are not so particular with the different titles, and tacitly submit to be styled once a while "learned, doctor, or master."

13. HOW A NON-MAHOMEDAN CAN WORK IN AL CHARIM.

As the Mislamin now considers himself perfect in every point of view, it is quite natural that he holds it derogatory to his dignity to learn any trade; hence you seldom find among the Mahomedans, and this among the poorest classes, any mechanics; the rarest of all do you find them masons and carpenters, which trades are mostly supplied by Christians, and latterly also by Jews. If it is now the case that something has to be repaired in Al Charim, and the pious faithful are under the deplorable necessity to entrust this work to a Kafr, or unbeliever, in this instance always a Nazrani, because no Mislamin can be found to execute it properly, and the Jews not being permitted, according to their own Mosaic law, to enter at present the holy place, on account of the want of purification (see Num. xix. 13 and 20), and as they are thus compelled to permit a Kafr to enter, they do it in this way: a black African dervish, belonging to the guard of the sanctuary, appears at the gate of the Temple Mount, takes the Nazrani on his shoulders, and bears him, running rapidly, to the spot requiring repair, the whole room in which he has to work being covered and hung round with carpets or coverlets, on which he is set down; and he is prohibited, on pain of death, to touch the bare floor in any manner. When the work is completed, he is again taken up on the shoulders of a dervish, and carried out at a running pace. As may be expected, all the places whither the Kafr has been carried must afterwards be purified by holy incense, scented drugs, and rose-water, of the *Misma* of the Kafr. Nevertheless, in this respect also the faithful have become more indulgent, and are not so averse as formerly, to come in contact and closer connexion with unbelievers, especially if these are their creditors, or they expect to obtain favours from them.

14. THE MODE OF WORSHIP OF THE ASHKENAZIM BEFORE THEY WERE PERMITTED TO HAVE A SYNAGOGUE.

As I have told already in the description of the Ashkenazim Synagogue, they commenced only as late as 5572 (1812), to be again seen in Jerusalem, which they formerly did not dare to do. When their numbers gradually increased, and the Mahomedans appeared to have already laid aside some of their hatred towards them, incurred on account of the indebtedness of their ancestors, they hired a small place as a Midrash, and even took courage to hold worship therein; but they could not venture to carry thither a ספר תורה "A Roll of the Law," without the sanction of the chief civil authority; for to do so without previous permission being obtained would have been regarded and punished as a grave crime. But as it is impossible to hold a regular public worship without a Sepher Torah, they procured a small one, which was put up in the form of a large book, that is, they put it in between covers, and thus placed it among the other reading books, and it was hardly distinguishable from them. When they read out of it, and when it was necessary to remove it from its cover, they had, as may expected, to close the gates of the court-yard, and to place guards around, that no Mahomedan might detect them at their terrible crime, the great sin of reading the Word of God. But through some oversight the matter became known to the Mahomedans. One day, therefore, while the gate was closed, during their reading the Sepher, they all at once heard a loud knocking at the door, when they put the book hastily in its cover, and placed it in the usual spot among the other books; immediately there entered a considerable number of the most respectable Mahomedans, connected with the administration of justice, to convince themselves by personal inspection of the crime committed by the Jews. They, however, saw no Sepher Torah, and the terrified worshippers maintained that they had no *Asara Kilmat* (literally "The Ten Words," meaning the Ten Commandments, by which name the Arabs designate the whole Roll of the Law, as well as the *Tephillin* and *Mezuzah*), out of which to hold public reading. But the others asked why they found the doors of the court closed? To which the malefactors replied, that they had done it on account of the dogs, which run freely about the streets, who otherwise would rush in and disturb them in their devotions. The Mahomedans now searched in all corners, but never once thought that what they sought for was standing before their eyes among the other books. They, however, went away both furious and confounded, since they were convinced that a Sepher must be in the place of meeting though they had not been able to discover it. When the inquisitors had thus left, the congregation again closed the doors and finished the reading. The day following the owner of the place came to the president of the community and said: "We know for a certainty that you have an Asara Kilmat in your Midras, out of which you read in public; but a higher Power must protect you to make it invisible, since we could neither see nor find it: give me now a considerable sum of money, and I will effect that no search shall again be made in your meeting-place; because, if I, as proprietor, am indifferent whether such a sin is committed in my house, and that it is so degraded, it must be a matter of indifference also to the other worshipful Mahomedans." The president gave him what he demanded, and they had now nothing to apprehend to be again molested by the visits of the authorities.* At a later period the congregation

* It thus appears that the gravest prohibition, the greatest crime may be winked at by the pious believers, through means of a Bakshis, i. e.

applied to the supreme government at Constantinople, when they obtained a *firman* (decree) to be allowed to read publicly in their Midras out of the Sepher Torah; and in 5597 (1837), they obtained at length permission to rebuild their ancient Synagogue, when they restored the solemn public worship in the usual manner.

15. PERJURY AND TREASON.

In the year 5586 (1826), when the people of Jerusalem had rebelled against the Pacha of Damascus, and the city was besieged by Abdalla of Akko, the Pahkid, i. e. the President of the Jewish Congregation, was one day in his room, when an officer of the rebels unexpectedly entered, and requested him to go into a private room with him, as he had something of importance to communicate in secret. The Pahkid rose trembling, and led him into a side-room, when the rebel ordered him to lock the door, and, seating himself near him, spoke as follows: "I entrust thee a secret, and ask thy advice at the same time, because thou art a very sensible man;" and indeed the Pahkid was considered as a very intelligent man, and many sought his counsel at every opportunity. "But know that, should this affair be discovered, my wife* shall be prohibited to me, if I do not take revenge on thee by taking thy life." The terrified Pahkid then said, "I pray thee, do not communicate to me thy dangerous secret, and seek advice from some other person." "No," replied the rebel, "none can counsel me as well as thou;—be still. I have observed that we shall not be able to defend our city, and the Pacha

a present or gift, although it must be proportioned to the greatness of the crime or prohibition.

* This is the greatest and holiest oath of the Mahomedan, holier and greater than to swear by Alla and the Nebi, since in case he violates this oath he is not permitted to enter the house where his wife resides, wherefore she is at once considered as divorced and at liberty to marry another man.

is sure to take it soon. I am therefore resolved to disguise myself and to escape by flight, so as not to fall into the hands of the Pacha; but I know not in what way I shall be able to save my money and ready means, and to carry it securely beyond the city." To this the Pahkid replied: "To do this there is but one way: the Armenian and Greek convents here have strong connexions in Constantinople, and have at the same time friendly relations with the Pacha, and have therefore nothing to dread from hostilities or persecution. Carry thy money to them, take a draft for it on Constantinople, and thou canst then receive it back there with perfect ease and security." "Taib, taib, taib katir" (good, good, very good), was the other's reply. "This is well advised. Thou seest thus that I was right to ask thy good and sage counsel; but, if thou valuest thy life, keep silence, so that no one hears the least of this." He thereupon left him. A few days after this he brought along another dreaded rebel, and both rushed furiously into the Pahkid's apartment. "Kelb!" (dog) cried the first, drawing his sword, "I will murder thee on the spot! Thou hast betrayed me. I have heard already to-day my intention discussed in public places, and my whole plan is frustrated." "Chansir!" (hog) roared out the other, placing the point of his weapon against his breast, "I will slay thee! Thou knewest the whole intention of this traitor, that he would leave the city to its fate, merely to save himself and his money, and thou hast kept the matter a secret, and said nothing of it to the city authorities; but all you Jews are such traitors." Thus one cried out "betrayer," the other "traitor;" the one threatened to kill him because he had revealed the secret, the other because he had not. The poor Pahkid was quite beside himself, and said, "I swear by God that I have not spoken a word of thy business; and, as regards thy accusation of high treason," addressing the other, "how could I know that his intended escape was not with the knowledge and consent of all the other leaders?" They, however, pushed him about among them, and he was terribly maltreated, whilst they swung over him their naked weapons in a menacing manner, and the pitiable Jew thought that his last hour was certainly come. Still he exclaimed, "Surely I cannot be guilty of both charges; I have either revealed the secret or not, but to do both is impossible." But they continued their beating a long time, till at length the enraged Arabs made the proposition that he might succeed in atoning for this twofold crime by the payment of money; and they then insisted that he should give to both parties interested a large amount of ready cash on the spot, in order to repair the injury he had done them. The Pahkid, seeing that it was a plot, merely contrived to extort money, and the whole transaction was nothing but a falsehood and base deception, was not slow in paying over what was demanded, and was very thankful that nothing else had been intended when his sage counsel was demanded, with no other view than to find a pretext against him for an extortion. But he had to keep silence, as the rebels were of the highest rank, and held even judicial appointments, and had, consequently, everything their own way.

16. THE FAITHFUL TESTIMONY.

In the year 5606 (1846), when the Sheich Abd al Rachman was engaged in a violent contest with his brothers for the government of the large district of Hebron, he brought it at last so far by his influence, or rather the power of his money, that the Pacha of Jerusalem took his part, who thereupon marched with a large body of men against Hebron, to reinstate Abd al Rachman by force of arms, and to make war against his brothers, as also all the city, which had taken their part. The Pacha was now earnestly urged by the consul-general in Beirut, and the consuls in Jerusalem likewise, not to molest the Jews at Hebron, who had joined neither party, but kept themselves quite neutral, and to use all possible means that they should come to no harm at the taking of the hostile city. The Pacha promised this faithfully, and assured them that their recommendation should be strictly complied with. Some days had now elapsed since he had marched against Hebron, and we had received no tidings whether he had succeeded, and that the city was taken, or whether he had received a check from the strong party within it, and was yet compelled to continue the siege: when one morning we saw quite unexpectedly several articles exposed in the streets of Jerusalem by the soldiers, which evidently had been plundered from the Ashkenazim at Hebron. These things consisted of clothing and furniture, which were known to belong to the German Jews of that place; and there were even copper and tin cooking utensils, to which the just prepared food yet adhered. This then was the first evidence that we had that the city must already be in possession of the Pacha, since his brave army had behaved so gallantly there. At a later hour we learned that, on the preceding evening, the city had been taken by assault, and that, therefore, during the same night the plundered property had been carried hither in all haste, since it was offered for sale by the soldiers at break of day. The Jews of Hebron had been grossly ill-used, beaten, and wounded; one old man had his hand shot off; some houses were clean plundered out; and it was on the whole a terrible scene which the military enacted there in their wild licentiousness. When their fury had abated a little, which probably was when there was nothing more to be plundered, the magnanimous Pacha made his appearance with his august escort in the house of the President of the Jewish community, to receive his thanks for the noble protection (perhaps for their not having been all killed) which had been afforded them. But, not satisfied with mere thanks, he asked the Jews, or rather commanded them, to give him a written testimony that they had not suffered the least harm; that the noble Pacha, true to his promise which he had made to the consuls, had taken them and their property under his paternal protection, although at the very time the stolen property was offered publicly for sale in Jerusalem by his faithful soldiers; and as it was sold very low, and much under its value, many a kind-hearted Jew here bought in much of it, so as to be able to restore it afterwards to its impoverished owners. No one ventured to remonstrate with him at this outrageous falsehood which he demanded from the Jews as a faithful testimony, when the warm blood of the wounded was yet running before the eyes of the tyrant,—when he yet saw the destruction which his bloodhounds had caused. But all this was mere sport which his brave warriors had had with the Jews, who might therefore, nay, ought to give him an honourable and faithful testimonial of his kindness. He nevertheless had some little fear that the certificate given by these unfortunates might not for all this paint in sufficiently bright colours the noble protection they had received; and in order also to spare them the trouble of writing, he had the magnanimity to order his secretary to draw up the required paper, in his own style, and required of the directors of the congregation merely to sign their names, and they had only to pay 50 pieces of gold (1000 piastres), as a fee for the writing. But there was one of the managers to whom it was impossible to subscribe this lying certificate. And why he more than the rest? From the simple cause that he lacked the hand with which to write his name, because it had been shot away by the infuriated assailants. Can cannibal chiefs show more beautiful traits of character?

17. A SEQUEL TO THE FALSE ACCUSATION AGAINST THE JEWS OF DAMASCUS, IN 5600.

This charge of murder arose from the sudden disappearance of a certain Father Thomas, who lived there a long time as a Catholic priest, and it was reported that the Jewish congregation of that city had murdered him to mingle his blood with the Passover bread, though the festival was celebrated long after the disappearance of this priest, wherefore his blood must have possessed a peculiar property if it could be kept so long without being spoiled. The torture and the tyrannical proceedings of the chief of Damascus, Serif Pacha, which he practised against that unfortunate congregation, were indeed stayed by the interference of the supreme authority of the state; but as no trace of the body of Father Thomas could ever be found, notwithstanding the most careful and diligent search, the suspicion that he had been made away with by the Jews has always remained, although the fact could not be proved.

About four years later, a Christian boy at Alexandria, who had been seen for the last time at the house of a Jewish merchant, suddenly disappeared. As may be expected, the suspicion fell again on the poor Jews, that they had murdered him according to their custom; and the consequence was nearly a riot of the Christians of Alexandria against the Jews. But the tolerant Mahmud Ali Pacha interfered by force of arms, and protected the unfortunate. To pacify, however, in a certain degree, the excited Christians, and since a suspicion was attached to the Jews, because the boy had been last seen in the house of one of them, he ordered them to use all possible efforts to trace him out; set them a long term when they should be held to answer the charge against them; and gave them all possible protection to carry on the investigation in every direction. The Jews were nevertheless in the greatest perplexity, as the problem was a most difficult and important one to discover the lost boy. They had therefore recourse to the power of money, the potent general solvent, and they promised a large reward to any one who should produce to them the missing child. And they were actually right in this mode of proceeding; for a compassionate young man, one of the rioters, who pitied the hard fate of the unfortunate Jews, after he had heard of the large prize offered by them, promised to deliver them from their dilemma, in order to obtain the reward. He only required a few sensible men among the Jews as also a few men as a guard for his protection to accompany him, and then set out on his search. When he had come to a Greek convent at a considerable distance from Alexandria, he said, "Here is the boy, as he has been taken under the protection of the holy and pious fathers." It, however, required a great deal of trouble and stratagem to get the boy to come out of the precincts of the convent, which, however, the young man at last succeeded in by the address with which he entrapped the priests; and as soon as the boy was outside, he was at once firmly detained by the escort. But it would not have answered any good purpose to employ force; since these saints were fully capable to murder the boy and conceal his body sooner than let the innocence of the Jews be proved. In brief, however, the boy was delivered up to the Jews in Alexandria perfectly sound and well; and every one was thus clearly and fully convinced that the whole was nothing but a wicked contrivance to have a pretext to torture and persecute the helpless Jews. What a commentary this on the conduct of the servants of the sole saving church! The young man then obtained the promised reward, when he said, "O ye unskilful Jews! give me a greater prize, and I will procure you the body of the long-since-consumed Father Thomas of Damascus, fat and sleek as he was years ago." But the poor Jews were glad enough in the happy finding of the boy, not to require the reproduction of the other party, and for fear of stirring up the nearly forgotten affair, they left it untouched, although they were greatly blamable for so doing.

When I learned these particulars at a later period, I took all the pains possible to reveal this mystery to the world. But I could not succeed, from various causes; first, because I could not be on the spot, Alexandria; and secondly, and this more especially on account of the very large sum which the discoverer demanded, which he did probably, because he would in all likelihood not have been safe any longer in the country, and in every other place else where he would have come in contact with monk or friar, who might have been interested in the business; and he was therefore compelled in a measure to demand enough means to procure himself an asylum abroad. This flagitious act was therefore passed over with indifference, and remains a mystery to the world.

18. THE PASSOVER SACRIFICE קרבן פסח AMONG THE SAMARITANS, THE ANCIENT CUTHEANS OF 2 KINGS XVII.

This is not the place to speak circumstantially of the whole nature of this sect; and I only mention a striking and remarkable ceremony which they practise, namely, the passover sacrifice. In the month of Nissan, but not on a certain and fixed day, they all assemble, little and great, on their holy Mount Gerizzim, not far from Nablus (Shechem). At present these people are only found in that city; but some hundreds of years ago they had also a large congregation at Cairo, as I derive from a work of the celebrated Ben Zimra (Radbaz רדב"ז). They bring out a sheep, which is slain by their ecclesiastical chief, whom they call "the high priest" כהן הגדול. They then dig a pit, in which they make a fire, and it is then covered over with sticks of wood; and on these the entire sheep is laid without being opened, with skin and hair, and thus roasted, or rather nearly burnt; and when it is sufficiently done, they all seize it like hungry wolves, and consume it, each one endeavouring to get something from this holy meal. They often get to fights and blows in so doing, and this ceremony will give us some idea of their entire practical religious life, since they allege that thus they fulfil the behest of the law in Exodus xii. 9. And can they really call this a family feast, nauseous as it is, and a token of which is carried off in welts on their backs, faces scratched, and bleeding noses? And nevertheless the Cutheans call themselves the true and actual Israelites, who alone live strictly according to the laws of the Holy Scriptures, and assert that they alone have the proper and correct interpretation of the law, whereas they call us ignorant in all this.

I have to remark something which strikes me as peculiar among them. They call God *Ashima*, and they use this term whenever the name of God is to be pronounced in the Bible or their speech. But this word Ashima occurs in 2 Kings xvii. 30, as the idol of the men of Chamath (not of the Cutheans, who worshipped Nergal), which first was, according to Talmud Sanhedrin, 63 *b*, in the shape of a goat. The modern Cutheans are, however, of a mixed class, as they employ an image resembling a bird, much like a dove (see Chulin, 6 *a*), which is carved of wood, and put on the top of their rolls of the law which are written in the Syriac (Samaritan character), and out of which they read a short passage every Sabbath somewhat after the fashion of our modern reformers. The just-cited passage of the Talmud avers that Nergal, the idol of the Cutheans, was a cock, a bird, therefore, having nothing in common with the goat; and as nevertheless the Samaritans use the word Ashima, which denoted the goat, the idol of the Camatheans, it proves that they are of a mixed descent, and not pure Cutheans merely.

19. THE ELEMENTARY SCHOOLS OF THE MAHOMEDANS IN JERUSALEM

Are in a most miserable condition, and it is easy to deduce therefrom the degree of the sciences and cultivation which prevails there. They present to the enlightened man, especially if he should have visited the schools in civilized countries, or still more if he has been educated there, a most striking and melancholy spectacle. In many streets you will find small, damp, and dark cellars, having no windows, and in which the light is only admitted through the door, which always stands open. In these there is spread on the floor a large, miserable straw mat, and on this are seen sitting, with their legs bent under them, in a circle, ten to fifteen boys, from five to twelve or even fifteen years old. In the middle stands a teacher with a long stick. Nearly every boy has before him a small wooden board, on which are drawn a few Arabic letters; and in this manner do they receive the rudiments of their education, which actually amounts to no more than a very little knowledge of reading and writing the Arabic; wherefore you will find but few citizens here who are able to read and write their native language.* Whoever, now, is able to do this is considered as belonging to the higher classes. The chief object of the education in the schools here described is to teach the scholars to say by heart the formula of prayers, or rather to sing them, as they are nearly all recited in a singing tone. You can hear even

* And there are therefore in many streets small shops, in which are seated learned persons, who form a sort of Arabic writing office, where any one can be served for a compensation, in case he wants Arabic reading and writing done.

at a great distance the tumultuous and loud shrieking of these boys. One thing is quite curious to remark, that all these boys, as well at their prayers as their other exercises, keep up a constant shaking backward and forward, as is often done by our Jews when praying or studying. This habit is also observed in adult Mahomedans during their devotions, and it appears therefore that it must be an old oriental custom.

It may readily be imagined that the teachers themselves have no necessity for any high scientific and moral cultivation, in order to impart the required amount of instruction; and I can assure the reader that I have met in these institutions with teachers who were quite blind or otherwise crippled; and it would appear that if such an unfortunate being is no longer able to earn his bread by begging in the public streets, he endeavours to accomplish this by becoming a teacher. I even found these schools kept in a large cellar, so to say, a vault, in the middle of which there is a Wely, or the monument of a saint, a pious dervish, or of a sheich. The scholars sit, or rather lie around this grave, and obtain their education, as a *memento mori*. The constant loud cries of these boys once excited my curiosity as I was passing by, to see what it all meant, and I looked through a small window into the place whence the sounds issued. I can assure the reader that a shuddering seized me at what I saw. A damp, heated atmosphere, an almost sepulchral odour, rose towards the spot where I was standing, and I could hardly observe the scholars, as my stepping up to the window had deprived them of the only light which they had. I could not prevail on myself to remain a few minutes even to take a closer observation of this most dreary schoolroom, and for my own part I would rather stay in a common stable, than in this subterranean, frightful school, held in the receptacle of the dead. Is it then wonderful that these Mahomedans are so far behind the Europeans? whence are they to learn anything of scientific culture? Their reading is confined to the written Koran, since printed books, which come from Kafers only, from unbelievers, are held in no esteem by them. To show what idea of geography they have, I may state that a very learned dervish, who had made many journeys, told me that he had travelled from Sudan (Central Africa), in a few weeks by land to the East Indies, as they are not far from each other.

The Mahomedan in general ridicules the European, that he displays so much interest for such stupid and useless stuff. If he sees a foreign scholar or traveller showing some curiosity in behalf of a scientific subject, or making a measurement, a calculation, or a drawing, he exclaims, in a tone of derision, "*Heida mushnem*,"—*he is mad*. They tell me often that they can have no idea, what interest such things can have for any man, that he should make long and distant voyages by sea and land, to obtain information of such nonsensical subjects. What can I answer them? Shall I give an idea of colours to one who is born blind? an explanation of sounds to one born deaf, of which he can form no conception? One can say with truth of the Mahomedans with Solomon, "I say that an untimely birth is better than he. For he cometh in with vanity, and departeth in darkness, and his name shall be covered with darkness." (Eccles. vi. 3, 4.)

20. THE COFFEE-HOUSE, KAFFANÉ, IN JERUSALEM.

It is perhaps not entirely uninteresting to read a description, or sketch rather, of an oriental coffee-house, as this will give us also some idea of the state of civilization among the Mahomedans. Near the Bazaar, which is at present used as a corn-market, on the corner of the *Zuk*, the market where there are shops for various kinds of goods, stands a large and old building, through which there is a passage-way, which, as it passes through a number of houses, shortens the distance considerably to pedestrians, as it enables them to dispense with a long circuit on the outside. This passage forms also the coffee-house in question, though it is in a very miserable condition. It is, at the same time, a large and very old structure, resembling greatly a ruined church, has a high cupola, and pillars and boxes on both sides. In the centre is a hearth, on which there stand large copper urns filled with boiling coffee. Close to them sits the landlord squatting on the ground, who has near him a quantity of very small coffee-cups, piled up one on another, and a row of the so-called argilé,* as also a pair of iron fire-tongs, called masha, with which he is ready to serve every one that smokes with a burning coal. On the sides are a sort of benches, which are covered with narrow straw mats, and which serve the guests as seats. The passage is so narrow, that those who pass through often knock the coffee-cup out of the guest's hand, and not rarely scald thus both lips and chin, or crush with their feet the pipe-bowl of some smoker; or it happens that the passer-by is thrown down through means of the long tube, which gets entangled between his feet or legs, and pulls down to the ground at the same time the smoker from his elevated seat. All this causes naturally many curious scenes. In the corner of a side-box sit usually some Arnaut soldiers, playing draughts and dice, with looks and gestures well calculated to excite the fears of the bystanders. The games often cause them to quarrel and fight among themselves, and thus all present are in danger of their lives.

* This is a tobacco-pipe, to which is fitted a vessel containing water, through which the smoke is driven, before it reaches the mouth, by means of an elastic tube, rolled up in a coil, several yards in length. This produces a constant bubbling and boiling noise in the water during smoking.

In the background you hear the neighing of a wild horse, the bleating of a sheep or a goat, and the braying of an ass, which some of the guests have brought along with them; and thus the coffee-house serves also as a sort of stable, and the landlord acts as hostler, taking care of man and beast in the same moment. At the entrance there is hung up in a bag a very young child, perhaps but a few months old, screaming with all its might, being left there by its faithful mother, an industrious Bedouin woman, whilst she attends to her business in the market, and wishes to spare herself the trouble to carry it in her arms. Near the door, on the bare earth, sleeps a tired Bedouin, covered like the drunken Noah in his tent, with his face turned to the ground, and who attracts the attention of all present by the harmonious sounds which he makes in his sleep. On the other side lies a small hillock of charcoal, from which the fire is fed, and on which sits a Bedouin woman with her dear half-naked boys. The attention bestowed on the guests is very simple, and is confined to coffee without milk or sugar, the argilés, and at most a glass of cold water in addition. In the month of fasting, the Rhamadahn, this passage, as is also the Kaffané, remains closed during the day, as a token of penitence and fasting; but during the whole night it is so thoroughly crowded that one is scarcely able to squeeze his way through. The other parts of the year it is closed at sundown.

The Kaffané answers also as an exchange, and many a trade is driven there between the Arabs and Bedouins.

If we now cast a look on and contemplate the most forlorn condition in every respect of the Holy City, we cannot avoid asking with the prophet, "Is this the city of which they said, She is the perfection of beauty, the joy of all the earth?" (Lam. ii. 15.) For all that, this very miserable condition is the greatest consolation the believer can have, "for the word of our God will stand for everlasting." (Isa. xl. 8.) And we see quite clearly that his words are being fulfilled when he said, "As I have brought over this people all this evil, thus will I bring over them all the good which I have spoken concerning them." (Jer. xxxii. 42.) "For the Lord hath comforted Zion, he hath comforted all her waste places, and maketh her deserts like Eden, and her plain like a garden of the Lord; joy and gladness are found there, thanksgiving and the voice of song." (Isa. li. 3.)

21. THE DERVISHES, SAINTS, SHEICHS.

I will now give a brief description of this singular class of men. The proper meaning of the word Dervish is an innocent, who, so to say, knows nothing which has the least traces of wrong and injustice, and is therefore quite childlike. The main business of the Dervishes is praying and preaching; and thus you will frequently see and hear them in public places and the open streets, teaching the people morals with a loud voice. Their exterior is by no means inviting, their whole dress consisting of a long and loose shirt, which is very dirty, not having been washed perhaps for a year, over which they have a broad leathern girdle or rope; and add to this a cudgel in their hand, and you have the attire of this class. Their feet are bare, their head is uncovered, and many have their hair hanging down in a disordered, wild state on their back, and a long beard; and they thus present more the aspect of terror than sanctity. Their second business is begging; and many gather for themselves, under holy pretences, a considerable quantity of money. They are regarded by the faithful as though they possessed a superior power, and knew future events. Some few holy (i. e. unintelligible) words written by them on a bit of paper are said to guard the possessor against all things, though surely not against superstition and stupidity. The manner of their devotion is very curious, and has much in common with the ancient followers of Baal, as stated in 1 Kings xviii. 28. They utter fearful sounds by producing a rattling noise with throat and breast, so that often the blood runs out of their mouth; besides, they keep up an uninterrupted moving backward and forward, till at length they fall down on the ground quite exhausted, in entire unconsciousness. Near my dwelling lives such a dirty, miserable saint, and I am often disturbed half the night through by his edifying devotion; but he has in addition a sort of tambourine, which he strikes, and this *pleasant* music forms a glorious harmony with his frightful rattling and guttural noise.

Their food is said to be most miserably limited, if a person might depend on their own assertion; but their looks by no means confirm this; and let no one therefore believe that their abstemiousness is real; the whole is mere deception and mere outward appearance, assumed to obtain thereby the means of support. But little confidence can be reposed in them. Many of them are nothing else than hypocrites, deceivers, and rogues; and you meet among them real wits, who, when they find a person who understands them, say distinctly that, as they have no occupation, they make it their business to point out to the world the way to heaven. One came to my door to beg, with snow-white beard and hair, and actually represented an old man; but I soon discovered that it was a deception, and that the hair was only dyed, he being a young and active fellow.

It is now some years since a respectable Mahomedan died at Damascus; he had a large funeral procession, which was preceded by two Sheichs, quite naked, without any covering whatever. These were to represent the image of innocence, and therefore were to appear thus as the first pair in Paradise, without shame. What a religious sentiment!

They are also wonderful physicians. I saw once in the public street a sick woman whom a holy Sheich endeavoured to cure by wonder-working prayers and conjurations, whilst he made a terrible smoke with a panful of coals, on which he sprinkled some spices.

Stupid and simple as this class of men appear to be, they still are not rarely enabled to deceive the worshipful Pachas and other state officers. It is now some years past when a very holy Dervish revealed to the Pacha of Jerusalem, having had a prophetic vision, that a great treasure was buried near the pool of Burak. The Pacha immediately sent thither some troops, and they dug deep with might and main to discover the hidden treasure; but the prophet had in the mean time escaped, and like that for which they dug, remained invisible thereafter.

In the same manner they dug, several years back, by order of the Pacha, near the hot spring of Tiberias, upon the assertion of a holy Sheich, to find there a lump of gold. But there seems to have been an error in the prophetic knowledge of this saint, since instead of the gold they only found a large stone.

22. HOW THE MAHOMEDANS VISIT AL CHARIM.

In addition to the usual hours of devotion, especially on Friday, the Charim is visited on three different occasions, to wit:

1. At a marriage, which, however, only takes place in the evening; the young people about to be married are placed under a species of tent made of linen, which resembles an inverted chest, and you can only see the feet of those who are under it. This canopy is carried by slaves, and those who are thus protected have to measure their

steps by those of the bearers, and are thus in a measure dragged along. Alongside of these slaves walk others with lighted torches made of pitch; then follows a man playing on a large kettle-drum, accompanied by several who play on a species of bagpipe, the shrill and braying tones of which are extremely offensive to the ear. Next follow the friends and relatives of the bride and groom, and after them a tumultuous mass of men and boys, young and old, all mixed up together, the shouting of whom is heard nearly all over the city. In this manner the procession moves on to Al Charim, where several religious ceremonies are performed, and some prayers recited, and after about half an hour, they return home as they came.

2. At a funeral, which is for us a most mournful and afflictive ceremony. Says the prophet Jeremiah, vii. 30: "They have placed their abominations in the house on which my name is called, to contaminate it;" and (ibid. xvi. 13), "With the carcass of their abominations and detestable things they have filled my inheritance." The corpse is placed in a coffin, and is accompanied by the friends and relatives, Dervishes, pious Sheichs, several of whom carry long palm-branches, and many other persons, and is thus carried forward amidst continual humming, and prayers half chaunted in a deep and low voice. Oftentimes I could hear only "Hu Alla," He is God; and the whole prayer consists of nothing but these two words, which are repeated innumerable times. In this way the funeral proceeds to Al Charim, where the coffin is placed on a stone destined for this purpose, and after some prayers are recited, it is carried for interment without the city.

3. At a circumcision. This ceremony has no fixed time as to the age of the boy, only that it must take place before he is thirteen years old, which was the age of Ishmael at the time of his circumcision (Gen. xvii. 25).

The boy, and often several at once, are gaily dressed up with all possible ornaments, and seated upon a horse likewise caparisoned, and led through the city accompanied by a large concourse of people, on which occasion the magnificent kettle-drum and the sweet bagpipes must not be wanting. At length Al Charim is reached, when, after the recital of some prayers, the procession returns home, where the operation is performed, generally by a barber. Nearly the whole following week, till the wound is healed, they have merry-making and feasting in the house of the circumcised both day and night. The circumcision is, however, but imperfectly performed, and by no means after the Jewish fashion; wherefore the Mahomedans can well be called "the uncircumcised circumcised," and I would apply to them the prophecy of Jeremiah ix. 24: ופקדתי על כל מול בערלה, properly rendered, "And I will visit on all the uncircumcised circumcised."

23. THE GREEN COLOUR AMONG THE MAHOMEDANS.

According to a tradition of theirs, the green colour is considered holy among the Mahomedans. Only Serifs (saints), and especially those who have made the holy pilgrimage to Mekka, are allowed to wear a green turban and a green cloak; but this is strictly interdicted to any other, especially to a non-Mislamin, and is considered as an infringement on their religion, and as blasphemy, and therefore severely punished. For this reason they call the prophet Elijah "Al Chatr," the Green; and the spot where he is said to have shown himself, according to their tradition, is also called "Al Chatr." It is now some years ago that a highly respected English lord was ill-treated in the public street of Constantinople, because the pious believers observed that he wore green pantaloons. Soon after my arrival in Jerusalem, my mother-in-law stood one day near the door of my house, when suddenly a furious Mahomedan rushed upon her with a drawn dagger, and she was only able to escape the deadly weapon by a precipitate flight. Her offence was, that she wore for her head-dress a green shawl.

But of late they are not so particular any more, thanks to the enlightened policy of Mahmud Ali, of Egypt; still it would not be advisable to appear even now with a green garment, if one would not desire to be exposed to a brutal persecution on the part of some fanatical Arab.

APPENDIX,

EXPLAINING MANY NAMES OF COUNTRIES, NATIONS, TOWNS, OUT OF PALESTINE, WHICH OCCUR IN THE HOLY SCRIPTURES, AND IN THE TALMUDIC WRITINGS, OF WHICH MANY HAVE HITHERTO REMAINED QUITE OBSCURE, BEEN INCORRECTLY EXPLAINED, OR HAVE REMAINED QUITE UNKNOWN.

I COMMENCE with the descendants of Noah enumerated in the Scriptures, in Genesis x., and 1 Chronicles i., and explain at the same time the various commentaries and Targumim, such as Onkelos, Jonathan, Saadiah, to these names; also the views of the Talmud and of the various Midrashim concerning the same.

"The sons of Japhet were Gomer, Magog, Madai, Javan, Tubal, Meshech, and Tiras." (Gen. x. 2.) Jonathan ben Uziel, by the by, not the same who translated the prophets, explains these names with אפריקא גרמניא המדי" מקדוניא ויתיניא אוסיא תרקי.

AFRICA אפריקא.

It appears very strange to translate Gomer with Africa, since it is well known that this part of the world was peopled by the descendants of Ham, as I will prove hereafter, but not through Gomer, the son of Japhet. There is also a curious narrative in Talmud Tamid, 32 *a*, that Alexander of Macedon, consulted the wise men of the south זקני הנגב, that is, those of Lod (see page 134, article Lod), as to the best manner in which he could reach Africa, but that these represented to him the difficulty and the almost impossibility of the expedition, since the "dark mountains" הרי חשך were in his way. This surely cannot refer to Africa proper; because Alexander had been there, prior to that time, when he conquered Egypt, before he marched to Syria, and consequently had no necessity to inquire about the way and the means of getting thither; neither do we find any dark mountains between Palestine and Egypt.

This would seem to indicate clearly that another Africa is meant here; and it is now our business to solve this difficult question, and to ascertain its whereabouts; but I believe that I have ascertained it, after taking all possible pains to aid me in the discovery.

I will cite, for this purpose, several passages from the short history of Josephus written in the Hebrew* language [and known as Josippon]. At the conclusion of the twelfth chapter he relates, "Thence, i. e. the country of the Amazons, where women bear the rule, Alexander pursued his route three days farther, when he came to a very dark district. Thence he moved into the land of Karas and Kariksam כרש וקריקסם, which already belonged to the kingdom of Persia." In the ninety-sixth chapter he says (as is also stated in his Bell. Jud. b. vii. c. 27), "that, at the time of Titus, the Roman emperor, there lived a people in the mountains of Ararat אררט called the Allauni. This people being compelled to emigrate, by a

* Although there exists a general doubt concerning this book, that it was written by the celebrated Josephus Flavius, since it contains so many contradictions to his great work, and embraces, moreover, many narratives and stories which can scarcely be ascribed to Josephus: still, we know that this learned man also wrote a history in the Hebrew language for his own nation, as appears clearly from the preface to his Antiquities. It is certainly very doubtful whether it be the one we have still in our possession or not; nevertheless, we can use much of it as a credible auxiliary, to explain, by this means, the names of many lands, towns, nations, &c.; and should even the historical part, the narrative itself, be doubted or called in question for various reasons, the nomenclature remains, notwithstanding all this, reliable and correct.

severe famine, as they were not able to find enough to live on in their own country, left their mountain fastnesses, in which, as they maintained, they had been inclosed by Alexander, and turned to the land of Midian, and plundered every place whither they came. The king of Ararat went out to battle against them; and when Titus heard this, he resolved to undertake a war against this people, the Allauni." From all this it is evident that the ancient territory of the Amazons, and the dark mountains, must be sought for only in the mountainous country of Ararat, not far from Circassia (Kirkassia), consequently in the northern portions of Syria.

The Taurus mountain is, as is universally known, a very high, and at one time almost an inaccessible chain, so that in olden days it was almost considered impossible to cross it to the opposite side; and it was necessary to seek a passage through its gorges and narrow passes, which might be regarded almost as subterranean channels, with the greatest labour and no inconsiderable danger; and as the sunlight was naturally excluded from these gorges, clefts, and passes by the high and steep mountain peaks and rocks, they are quite dark and dreary; and hence, there can be no doubt, arises the appellation of the "dark mountains" הרי חשך, as they are called in Zohar to Behaalotecha, folio 148, טורי (קרדו) אררט הם הרי חשך "The mountains of Kardo (Ararat) are the dark mountains." It says farther to Num. xxii. 23, טורי חשך הררי קדם אקרון, "the dark mountains mean the eastern mountains;" which phrase embraces also all those situated north of Palestine, since all Syria, Aram, the Euphrates, and Pethor פתור, though all north, are called קדם the East, and hence the mountains are styled "the eastern ones." This, therefore, was meant by the wise men of the South, that, on his way to Africa, the dark mountains of the Taurus range would oppose obstacles to his advance, since he could pursue no other road than that which leads through its dark defiles and passes.

We have now to look for our Africa beyond the Taurus, and I think that I may maintain with certainty, that, under the name of Africa, the ancients understood the country and provinces which were situated beyond the fearful and high mountains of Taurus; and we find, at this day, in the district called Arabkir* (?), the town of Devrighi (Devrikioi), which has a strong trace of the name Africa in it. In the Greek and Roman period this district was called Cappadocia.

As a farther support of my view, let the following suffice. We read in Yerushalmi Baba Meziah ii., Bereshith Rabbah xxxiii., and Vayikra Rabbah xxvii., that Alexander of Macedon came into the land of the king of Kizia; and in Midrash Yalkut Tehillim xxxvi., the same is told with the addition, "behind the dark mountains." This Kizia is undoubtedly the Kizica (?), the later Kezina (Gizenenica?) in Pontus, not far from the Black Sea, mentioned in Josephus's Antiquities, book xiii., ch. 17(?). In the above-cited passage of Vayikra Rabbah it is said, "the kingdom of the women was in Cartagina," which is an incorrect reading, and should be "Caragina," to wit, Charachiné (?).

All this, therefore, proves clearly that all these countries and nations, mentioned in the expedition of Alexander, were in the north of Asia Minor.

To the northeast of the just-mentioned district of Dev-

* In the books and maps accessible to the translator, he finds the district called *Roum*, and the town has the name Devrikioi, and is situated in latitude 39° 14′, longitude 38° 16′ east of Greenwich. But may not the Targum allude to Phrygia thus, A-phry-ki, especially if we consider that the Rabbins often commence words with א *a* as a superfluous letter? for example, Aktispun, Cesiphon; Aspamia, Spain; and that the final *a* is but a Greek termination, and is not a part of the root? To reach Phrygia from Palestine, mountains have to be passed.

righi commences the country of Circassia; and I think that this name retains a trace of Girgashi, since, according to the assertion of the Midrash, this Canaanitic nation emigrated to *Africa*, and settled there (before the arrival of the Israelites under Joshua), and Circassia is not far from the supposed ancient Africa of the Rabbins. It is also said farther in Sanhedrin 94 *a*, that the Ten Tribes were partly banished to Africa; and, according to Echa Rabbethi, to ch. i. 13, they took their route, when they wandered into exile, through Armenia. This also agrees closely with my hypothesis, that we must seek for this Africa in Armenia.

The above Karas of Josippon appears to me to be that at a later period called Karzan (Charzan), the capital of which was Colchian, on the River Usis. I believe that this is referred to in the 16th chapter of Rabbi Nathan, when saying that Rabbi Akiba travelled to אכוליא קורצא Achulia of Kurza, to wit, the town Colchian in Charzan; since we find that Rabbi Akiba often journeyed to the northern countries, for instance Galatia (see farther article Gallia) and Africa, as we are told in Rosh Hashanah, 26 *a*.

It is, therefore, sufficiently proved that there was a second or northern Africa, which is also mentioned in Yerushalmi Shebiith ix., and which was peopled by the sons of Japhet, whilst the Africa of the south belonged to the sons of Ham, as is said in Sanhedrin, 91 *a*, "that Africa was peopled by the sons of Canaan, who was a son of Ham;" wherefore, then, there is every reason to conclude that the country occupied, according to Jonathan, by Gomer, was the northeastern portion of Asia Minor.

Josephus, Antiquities, b. i., ch. 7, explains Gomer with Galatia, also a northern territory, not far from the supposed Africa (Devrighi); which, therefore, also agrees with Jonathan. See also Jos., Antiq., b. xviii., ch. 6, which agrees with my opinion relative to the "dark mountains."

There was also, it is true, another district in the north called Phrygia, of which I shall speak hereafter, the name of which strongly resembles Africa, wherefore they might be deemed identical; but I do not deem this hypothesis so well founded, and more hazardous, and must insist that my views already given are more reliable and correct.

GERMANIA. גרמניא

As late as the middle ages, there stood in the Taurus mountains, on the western bank of the Euphrates, a town called Germania. The environs of Tarshish, the modern Tarsus (which see), were also formerly called Caramania. Even at the present day, there is the town of Caraman, west of Tarsus, and between it and Konieh. It must, therefore, not be taken for Germany or Ashkenaz, of which we shall treat hereafter.

It is curious that Jonathan should render Magog with Germania, whilst all other commentators so render Gomer.

In Yoma, 10 *a*, it is said, "Magog is Kandia," קנדיא, which is, without doubt, an incorrect reading, since Kandia is a much later name than the time of the Talmud for the island of Crete, also called Telechina, and could therefore not have been known to the Talmudists as Kandia. Accordingly, I am certain that it should read קודיא Kudia; and we actually do find this reading very nearly, גותיא Guthia for Kudia, in Yerushalmi Megillah i., and the Targum to 1 Chronicle i. 5 (?). In the Russian language Gittai signifies China, and the Nankeen cloth (a species of cotton goods) is also called Gittai, because it comes from China; and I would derive this name from Katcheou, a river and district of China; which country I therefore presume is meant under Kudia, Guthia (Kandia), and to be understood by Magog.

Joseph., Antiq., b. i., ch. vi., explains Magog with Scythia, a people which formerly was scattered over Syria. They held, a long time, possession of Beth-Shean, and hence it was called Scythopolis.

HAMDIJI, המדיי

i. e. Media; and even at the present day there is in Kurdistan the town of Hamdan (Hammadan), the ancient Ecbatana, which is, according to the tradition of the Jews, the ancient Shushan of Esther i. 2. They point out there the monument of Queen Esther and Mordecai, which is a magnificent building, in which there is at the same time a Synagogue. I presume that Hamdatha, the father of Haman (ib. iii. 1), was born in this town, whence he obtained his name. In Ezra vi. 2, it is called אחמתא Achmetha. In Yoma 10 *a*, it is said: מדי זו מקדונא "Madai is Makduna," which does not mean Macedonia in Greece, but the ancient district of Mikdunia, in Mesopotamia, which was reckoned as belonging to Media. So also does Josephus, Antiq., b. xx., ch. ii., say, that in the neighbourhood of Nisibis there stood formerly the town of Antiochia, which was also called Mukdania, because it had been built and was inhabited by Macedonians. This Antiochia must not be mistaken for either of the other two of the same name, of which we shall treat farther down.

MAKEDONIA. מקדוני'א

This means Macedonia, which borders on Morea, in Greece. In Yerushalmi Megillah i., it is said יון הי'א אוסם "Javan is Uses;" and in Targum to 1 Chron. i. 5, the reading is אוביסוס Ubesos, which I suppose to be the ancient and celebrated city of Ephesus, in Anatolia. Its ruins are still to be seen, a day's journey south of Smyrna.

VITHINIA. ויתינ'א

The same version for Tubal is given in Yerushalmi Megillah and Targum to Chronicles. I suppose that reference is made to Bithinia or Asia Minor (Anatolia), the V only being substituted for B. In Yoma 10 *a*, the reading is בית אונייקא Beth Uneika, doubtless Bith-inicia, *k* being as usual put for *c* [as Okionos for Oceanus]; as Bithinia is synonymous with Bith-inicia.

Josephus, Antiq., b. i., ch. vi., translates Tubal with Iberians. Some suppose that Tobolsk in Siberia (northern Russia) is derived from Tubal, who, as it is said, settled there.

USIA. אוסיא

The other commentators read מוסיא Musia, which is, however, all the same, viz., Mysia, since Mysia, Lydia, and Phrygia, are all denoted under the general term of Asia (Minor), whence afterwards the whole eastern quarter of the globe was termed Asia. I take, therefore, Usia (Usaiah) to stand for Asia.

Josephus, Antiq., b. i., ch. vi., explains Meshech with Cappadocia, also in Asia Minor (Anatolia).

THARKI, תרקי

Refers probably to Turkestan in Tartary, whence the Turks emigrated, at a later period, to the west. Or, perhaps, we should be empowered to understand by this term Thracia (Thrace, exchanging as above *k* for *c*, and read Theraki), in Asia Minor (Anatolia); and indeed Josephus explains Thiras with Thracia. In Yoma and Yerushalmi Megillah, it is rendered Persia by some authorities.

Saadiah translates, in his Arabic version, as follows:

Gomer with Al Tharak, probably Turkestan; Magog with Al Agog; Madai with Al Madath; Javan with Al Aliunani, "the Hellenists, Greeks," as we also read in Yerushalmi Sota (?) vii. קריין שמע אלוניסתין "They read the *Shemang* in the Greek language (*Elonisthin*);" Tubal with Al Ziz, which is unquestionably an error, and should be צין Zin, i. e. China, which is so called in ancient works, as in the book Kusari; Meshech with Al Krasan, a Persian province, Khorassan, in which there is to this day the large city of Charasan, in which there live many and respectable Jews. It is now about twenty years since the Persians attacked them, plundered their property, and slew many of their number, and drove away the remainder, so that at present no Jews whatever live there. Thiras he gives with Al Pars, Persia.

Some suppose that Gomer signifies the Crimea, the peninsula of the Black Sea.

"And the sons of Gomer were Ashkenaz, Riphath, and Togarmah;" which Jonathan* renders with אסייא ופרכוון וברבריא.

ASIYA. אסייא

See article Usia, p. 455; it appears, therefore, that, according to Jonathan, Meshech and Ashkenaz denote the same territory, since both are explained by *Asia*.

Josephus, in his Antiquities, says: "Ashkenaz are those called by the Greeks Rhegenians," which term is unknown to me.

PHARCHEVAN, פרכוון

Stands probably for Phargavan or Phargaun, which is Phrygia, in Asia Minor. To Phrygia belonged Phricia, Pararius, Isaoria, and Diallus. Josephus says Riphath signifies Paphlagonia in Anatolia.

BARBARIA, ברבריא

Is probably to be looked for in North Africa, the mo-

* This explanation is probably that of the Yerusalem Targum, which, however, is the same with Jonathan, only that in the copies of the men of Jerusalem there were found different readings in this version, and they were hence designated as the Targum Yerushalmi [which appears as a fragmentary work in our usual editions].

dern coast of Barbary. In Siphri to Deut. xxxii. it is said, "In Tunis, Barbaria, and Mauritania, people go openly naked." There was, however, another district, as also a town, Barbaris, beyond Euphrates, which Jonathan may have considered as Togarmah. According to Ezekiel xxxviii. 6, Togarmah must be situated in a northern direction from Palestine. Josephus says that the Greeks call Togarmah Phrygia.

In Bereshith Rabbah, ch. xxxvii., Ashkenaz, Riphath, and Togarmah are given as Asea, Chadeb, and Germania, and Rabbi Berachiah renders the last "Germanikea." So also does the Chaldean Paraphrast render Jer. li. 27, "Ararat, Mini, and Ashkenaz," with Kardo, Churmini, i. e. Urmini or Armenia, and Hadeb.* In Kiddushin, 72 *a*, Chabor of 2 Kings xvii. 6, is expounded as being חדייב Chadjeb, or Chadeb. This Hadeb or Chadeb is the country of Adiabené, east of Tigris, which was once governed by Queen Helena, mother of Monobazes (Izates).† There also is the town Ardibel (Arbela), famous for the battle in which Alexander of Macedon routed the Persian King Darius.

It is ridiculous to understand by Ashkenaz and Germania the Germany of the present day, although the Jews in general called Germany Ashkenaz. I shall say more on the subject hereafter, and explain whence this general appellation is derived.

Saadiah translates Ashkenaz with Al Zkalbh, probably

* In Yerushalmi Shebiith i., there is the incorrect reading הדיית Hadijith for הדייב for Hadjib.

† The learned reader will perhaps recollect that both mother and son were converts to Judaism. The Talmud speaks often and in just praise of these worthy proselytes. Especially is an anecdote told of the King Monobazes, that he distributed his treasures of corn in a year of famine, excusing this deed of charity by stating that he wished to heap up treasures imperishable, where his fathers only gathered transitory wealth.—Transl.

the Slaves, Slavonians; Riphath with Al Faringh, the Franks; and Togarmah with Al Brgan, the Burgundians.

"And the sons of Javan were Elishah and Tarshish, Kittim and Dodamin," which Jonathan gives with אלס וטרסס אכזיא ודורדניא.

ALAS. אלס

In the former district of Lamatis, in the most southern part of Anatolia, at present Itchiil, situated on the Mediterranean, and forming nearly an island, to the southwest of Tarshish, was the district of Alusa, having a town of the same name, and is unquestionably the one referred to by Jonathan.

TARSAS. תרסס TARSHISH. תרשיש

There are many difficulties to be removed before we can properly determine on the position of this celebrated town. In Genesis, the passage of which we now speak, describes it as an appendage of the possessions of Javan, whose descendants settled themselves for the most part in western Asia and eastern Europe (Asia Minor and Greece). Jonah (i. 3) wanted to fly to Tarshish on board of a ship which departed from Joppa (Jaffa), consequently to a city on the Mediterranean. We nevertheless find (1 Kings xxii. 48, and 2 Chron. xx. 36) that King Jehoshaphat had ships built at Ezion-Gaber, on the Red Sea, to go to Tarshish and Ophir. So also Solomon had vessels built at the same port to go to Ophir (1 Kings ix. 26–28). It seems next to impossible to assume that it was customary to make a voyage to Tarsus, the Tarshish on the Mediterranean, from Ezion-Gaber on the Red Sea, which would make it necessary to circumnavigate the whole of Africa, whereas from Joppa the voyage, as it was intended to be done by Jonah, could be made both quickly and easily.

I therefore maintain that the Scripture speaks of two

towns called Tarshish, of which we have sufficient and satisfactory proofs and references.

The Tarsus, or Tarshish, of Genesis, is a town in the territories of the descendants of Javan, and is without doubt the modern Tarsus, in the ancient country of Cilicia, the Kilikia קיליקיא of Yerushalmi Challah, finis, and situated on the Mediterranean. In its neighbourhood are very large ruins. There live at present in Tarsus about twelve Jewish families, who lately emigrated from Aleppo (Haleb). Now it was this town to which Jonah fled.

But there must have been another Tarshish on the Red Sea; and it appears to me that either Tarshish and Ophir signify the same, or that they were at least near to each other; for it says, in 1 Kings xxii. 48, "Jehoshaphat made ships of Tarshish to go to Ophir for gold," and in 2 Chron. xx. 36, in the same narrative we read, "to Tarshish."

I have therefore no doubt that Ophir is the same mentioned among the sons of Joktan, along with Shebah and Chavilah (Gen. x. 29), whose possessions were in Arabia, as I shall explain hereafter; but they spread out by degrees till they crossed the Red Sea, and settled on the coasts of Africa, so that we must look for Ophir and Tarshish only in that portion of the world. Some even go so far as to derive Africa from Ophir. Even at the present day there is the country of Sofala, in the south-eastern part of Africa, situated opposite to the island of Madagascar. There is found a mountain called Afura, which, as does also the whole country of Sofala, produces much gold. There are also found in that vicinity ivory, monkeys, and peacocks, which, as we read in 1 Kings xi. 22, came from Tarshish. No one can doubt that Afura bears a resemblance to Ophir; and hence we may assume that Tarshish was situated in that vicinity, wherefore it was proper to despatch the ships trading thither from Ezion-Gaber on the Red Sea.

I have discovered a singular proof from the Chaldean paraphrase of Jonathan that there were two places named Tarshish. We find the northern one, on the Mediterranean, mentioned in several passages of Scripture, for instance, Jonah i. 3; Isaiah xxiii. 1, &c.; lxvi. 19; Ezekiel xxvii. 12–25; xxxviii. 13; and everywhere Jonathan explains it with מדינת ימא "the maritime country"—"the sea-port;" since it is situated on the Mediterranean, and the environs almost form an island. But when he has to comment on the Tarshish which was situated near Ophir, in the three passages, 1 Kings x. 22; xxii. 48, and Jeremiah x. 9, he renders it with Africa אפריקא; from which it is clear that the Tarshish of Ophir was, according to this ancient paraphrast, in Africa.

No argument can be drawn from the length of the voyage, which lasted three years (1 Kings x. 22), that therefore the distance must have been much greater than from Palestine to Sofala; since navigators in those days moved very slowly along; and perhaps the greater part of the time was consumed in gathering the articles for which the expedition had been fitted out.

The assertion, therefore, of many learned men, that Tarshish means Spain, is entirely incorrect; and it was quite absurd, not requiring any contradiction even, to assert, as has been done very recently, that California should be the ancient Ophir.

ACHSIA, אכזיא

Is an incorrect reading, and should be אבויא Abuia, as in Yerushalmi Megellahi it is written אביה, which letters can be pronounced the same as אבויא; either, therefore, Abbiah or Abuiah, is perhaps put for Appia, the Forum Appii, which was distant seven miles from Rome, and was once a considerable city in Italy. So also we read in Siphri to Num. xxiii.: "This (Roman) empire had four considerable towns besides Rome, namely, Abbia, Alexandria, Carthago, and Antiochia."* Jonathan therefore assumed Kittim to be synonymous with Italy. The same is said in Bereshith Rabbah xxxvii., that Kittim signifies Italy. Onkelos to Num. xxiv. 24 translates it with "the Romans,"—and there was actually in ancient Latium a town called Cittim, which is a clear proof that the Kittim had settled there. Jonathan to Ezekiel xxvii. 6, explains Kittim with Apilia, probably Apollonia in Macedonia. It would appear partly from 1 Mac. i., that Macedonia was called the land of the Kittim.

DURDENIA. דורדני'א

In 1 Chron. i. 7, we read Rodanim in place of Dodanim. It appears from Isaiah xxi. 13, that Dedan was settled in Arabia. There is also at the present day in Yemen, the southern Arabia, the city of Dadan, situated on the Arabian Sea.† But in the district of Epirus, Macedonia, there are found a canton and town named Dodona. The Chaldean translation to 1 Chron. i. explains Rodanim with רדום חמין ואנטיוך Radum, Chammin, and Antiuch. Radum is the island Ruad (Rhodes?), (see farther, article Arvadi); Chammin is Chemath, the modern Chamé, and Antiuch is Antiochia; and all these places are not very far from each other.

Saadiah explains Elisha with Al Mezizh, which I do not know how to elucidate; Kittim with Al Kabrus (i.e.

* Josep., Bell. Jud., b. iii. ch. 3, says, "Antiochia was the third city in the Roman Empire."

† In the vicinity of that Dadan, about one day's journey east from Aden, on the Arabian Sea, stands to this day the town of Duan, and north of this another called Juan: they are without doubt the Dan and Javan mentioned in Ezekiel xxvii. 19 along with Dedan.

the island of Cyprus;* and there is actually at this day a town called Kittim in that island; and this proves that the Kittim settled in many places, since we find also a town of that name in Italy. The same appears to have occurred with other nations, whence, then, resulted the various explanations and diverging views concerning the names of the sons of Noah; since the same tribe very often occupied different territories.) Dodanim Saadiah gives with Al Adnah, unquestionably the town of Aden in Yemen, not far from the Red Sea, of which I shall speak more hereafter. This view of Saadiah confirms what I have stated, that Dadan in Arabia is identical with the Dodanim of the Bible.

"And the sons of Cham were Cush, Mizraim, Put, and Canaan;" which Jonathan explains with ערביא ומצרים ואליחרוק וכנען

ARABIA. ערביא

It is most singular that Jonathan should render Cush with Arabia, which is in Asia, when it is generally assumed that this name is identical with Abyssinia or Ethiopia, or in general terms Central Africa. But we must recollect that there are two countries which went by the name of Cush,—the one actually in Asia, in Arabia, and the other, as generally understood, in Africa. Cush in Africa is mentioned in 2 Kings xix. 9; Isaiah xviii. 1; xx. 3; and Psalm lxviii. 32. Cush in Arabia, and other parts of Asia, is spoken of in Habakkuk iii. 7; Zipporah,

* This may serve to explain an uncommonly obscure passage of Sanhedrin 106 *a*. It says: וצים מיד כתים "And ships of war shall come from the shore of Kittim" (Num. xxiv. 24); אמר רב זו ליגיון אספר is explained by Rab to mean "the legion of Asper." This is the correct reading, as cited in the book 'Aruch. I presume that אספר is = אי ספר the island of Sephar, Cyprus, the ס being put for צ, and the legion of Cyprus is then supposed to be the correct version of צים of כתים. Whence then it appears that Rab thought Kittim to signify the island of Cyprus.

the wife of Moses, a Midianite, is called a woman of Cush (Num. xii. 1); Jonathan to Jeremiah xiii. 23, translates Cushi with "Indian." (The Indian fowl is called in Arabic, Al Tik al Chabash, and Al Tik al Hind, i. e. the fowl of Chabash, Abyssinia, and of India.) The same version is given to Isaiah xi. 11. We read also in 2 Chron. xxi. 16, of "The Arabs that were near Cush." It is indeed singular that Rabbi Joseph, in his Chaldean version, should render this with וערבאי די על תחומי אפריקאי "And the Arabs who were on the coasts of Africa." I also have heard Persian Jews who have emigrated to Palestine, say that the country of Shirwan, on the western shore of the Caspian Sea, is called Cush by the Israelites who live there. It therefore appears that, according to Jonathan, Cush, son of Ham, did not settle in Africa, but in some part of Arabia. The second Targum, or the later Paraphrast to the book of Esther, translates, From Hodu to Cush, מהודו דמערבא ועד כוש דמדינחא "India in the west to Cush in the east," which certainly is a most singular statement; [perhaps the terms were casually transposed, or, we might render it from the west side of India to the east of Ethiopia.—Trans.]

ALICHERUK, אליחרוק

Is unknown to me; but I suppose that the town of Al Kargah, of Upper Egypt, west of the Nile, is meant here. It is also called by the Arabs, Al Djirdji; and if this be the synonyme for Alicheruk, Put's residence was in the vicinity of Ethiopia.

Saadiah explains Cush with Al Chabasha, which is the name at present given by the Arabs to the whole of Middle Africa, Abyssinia (Ethiopia), and Nubia; Mizraim with Al Mazr, which is the Arabic name for all Egypt as well as the town of Kairo; Put is given with Al Thapth, probably referring to a large valley in Nubia, called Wady

Thapujuth. In Shemoth Rabbah, x. and xiii., it is said that the lands of Egypt and Cush touch and border on each other. In Ezekiel xxx. 5, there is mentioned in connexion with Cush, Put, and Lud, also Chub, of which latter no farther account is given in the Bible. Nevertheless, after much seeking, I found in Shemoth Rabbah to Exod. xii., that the Israelites travelled forty years in the wilderness of Chub, and in chap. xxiv. it is said explicitly מדבר שור הוא מדבר כוב "The wilderness of Shur is identical with the wilderness of Chub."

"And the sons of Cush were Seba, Chavilah, Sabtah, Raamah, and Sabtechah, and the sons of Raamah were Sheba and Dedan," which Jonathan explains with: סיניראי והנדקי וסמדראי ולובאי וזינגאי ובני דמוריטי (זמדגד) זמרגד ומזג:

SINERAI, סיניראי

Is probably the land of Senaar, between Egypt and Nubia.

HINDEKI, הנדקי

Means India. We find two countries called Chavilah, the first on the borders of India and Persia, which is also mentioned in connexion with Eden (Gen. ii. 11); and Strabo likewise calls the inhabitants of Eastern Arabia, on the Gulf of Persia, "Chavilatai," from Chavilah; and it is this which Jonathan calls India: the other country of this name is the one belonging to a son of Joktan, mentioned in connexion with Ophir in Gen. x. 29; so do we also read that the sons of Ishmael dwelt "from Chavilah to Shur" (ibid. xxv. 18); consequently, we must look for this in the southern part of Arabia (Yemen); and at the present day there is a territory in that country called Al Chulam, which name greatly resembles Chavila.

SEMIDAI (SAMDAI). סמדאי

I suppose this to mean the district of Sandi (changing

m into *n*) in Nubia, as also the town of that name which is situated there. Nevertheless, there is found in southern Arabia, on the Red Sea, the town of Sabata, which has much resemblance to Sabtah, and it is therefore quite likely that Sabtah may have settled there.

LUBAI, לובאי

Signifies the country of Lybia, to the west of Egypt. In Yerush. Kelaim viii., it is said that Lub (Lybia) לוב is Egypt; but this only refers to Egypt in its most extensive meaning, which includes the Lybian country, and the passage quoted then only asserts that it borders on Egypt.

ZINGAI, זינגאי

Means probably the country of Zing, which is Zanguebar, east of Ethiopia.

MORITI, OR MEVARITINOS, מוריטינוס OR מוריטי

See farther down, article "Anamin."

SIMDIGAD, OR SEMARGAD, זמרגד OR זמרגד

Jonathan translates in the same manner (1 Kings x. 1), the Queen of Sheba, with Queen of Semargad, probably deriving this name from the Smaragd (emerald), which was found in abundance in that country; and even at the present day this precious stone is frequently met with in Upper Egypt, not far from Chabash. It was probably this jewel which the Queen brought to King Solomon (ibid. x. 2).

MESAG, מזג

Appears to me to denote Mozambique, situated to the south of Zanguebar.

I have already remarked above, article Dodanim, that there is at present a city of Dadan in southern Arabia, which is certainly derived from said Dedan, and may be assumed as the country where this tribe settled.

In Yoma, 10 *a*, it is said Sabtah, Raamah, and Sabtecha are סקיסתן Sekistan, a name unknown to me; but it may signify the Scythians [Scykistan], the chief settlements of whom were on the Caspian and Black Seas.

Saadiah translates Seba with Al Seba; Chavilah with Al Suila, probably Sofala (see above, Tarshish); Sabtah with Al Sagava, the Zingai of Jonathan, by leaving out the *n*; Raamah with Al Kaiko, probably the district Al Mikoko, northwest from Zanguebar. In the book of Eldad the Danite, in his description of the country whither the Israelites were banished, he says, "Beyond the river of Cush בעבר לנהר כוש (meaning, perhaps, the Niger*), in the land of the Ludin and Kako," referring, probably, to the Raamah of Saadiah. Sabtecha he gives with Al Damdem (unknown to me); Sheba with Al Sand, the Samdai of Jonathan; and Dedan with Al Hind, India.

"Babel, Erech, Akkad, and Calneh, in the land of Shinar," are rendered by Jonathan with בבל רבתי והדס ונציבין וקטספון בארעא דפונטוס.

THE GREAT BABEL. בבל רבתי

(Daniel iv. 27.)

The following is a very short description of this once so celebrated city. It was situated about 50 English miles south of the modern Bagdad on the Euphrates, and was 60 English miles in circumference. Its walls were 300 feet high, and 87 thick. In the middle of it stood the Belus Tower (Jer. li. 44), which was 600 feet high; and some believe that it was built on the old Tower of Babel (Gen. xi. 5). There was likewise by the royal palace the hanging garden: it was 300 feet in height, and was

* Might not the Upper Nile in Abyssinia be understood by the "river of Cush?"—TRANSLATOR.

regarded as one of the seven wonders of the world. In the centre of the city stood the palace of Nebuchadnezzar, which, so to say, formed a city by itself, and was 10 miles in circumference. A hundred gates and fortifications afforded entrances into the same. The dams erected on the Euphrates were also very remarkable works of art; they protected the city against an overflow in the highest stage of the river, and always supplied it with an abundance of water, when the stream was even at the lowest point. Coresh (Cyrus) of Persia conquered it from the Babylonians, but did not destroy it; but at a later period, in the reign of Arthachshastha (Artaxerxes), it was destroyed in part. Alexander of Macedon intended to restore it, and to bring it back to its former splendour; and he commenced to repair and rebuild the dams, and had put 10,000 men to labour on this work, when the whole plan was frustrated by his death.

At the time of the destruction of Jerusalem by Titus, Babel was yet standing, but shorn greatly of its ancient grandeur and importance. It commenced at that period to decline gradually; and in the year 4072, A.M. (312), in the reign of Constantine, it was already bereft of all population, and only a few of its walls were yet standing, which the kings of Persia employed as enclosures for their hunting ground. At present it is an immense heap of ruins. "But wild beasts of the desert shall lie there; and their houses shall be full of owls; and ostriches shall dwell there; and monkeys (satyres) shall dance there." (Isaiah xiii. 21.) "And Babel shall be changed into heaps of ruins, the dwelling of serpents, an astonishment and a hissing, and be without an inhabitant." (Jer. li. 37.)

In the midst of the site of Babel there is met with, so to say, a mount formed out of glazed bricks; it is, at its base, 2000 feet in circumference, and is 198 feet high. On the summit there is a pillar 37 feet high. To the west of it is a ruinous structure 500 feet in length, which is two stories in height, the upper one being more than 100 feet high, and the lower 60, although this also was equally elevated with the other, only that it is now buried nearly one-half in sand and rubbish. On the upper story there are pillars, which evidently served for the support of a third story; and some maintain that it is the remains of the ancient tower of Babel.

HADAS, OR HEDES. הדס

The present Orfa (see farther, article Ur אור), was called in the time of the Romans Edessa. In Ezra iv. 9, occurs the word ארכויא "Archevites," that is, men of "Erech."

NEZIBIN, נציבין

Is the town of Nizibin (Nisibis), 30 miles east-south-east from the town of Mardin, in the eastern part of the district of Diarbekir. Many Jews reside in this place, and they point out here the grave of Rabbi Jehudah ben Bethera (Pesachim, 3 *b*; Sanhedrin, 32 *b*). Rabbi Petachiah also says, in his travels, that in Nizibin is the Synagogue of the just-named Rabbi.

KETISPUN, קטספון
(Vayikra Rabbah v.)

Was formerly an important city in the modern Diarbekir. Josephus (Antiquities, b. xviii. ch. ix.), calls it Ctesiphon.

PONTOS, פונטוס

Appears very singular when applied as an explanation to the word Shinar, since Pontus did not belong to Babylonia, which is evidently synonymous with Shinar, but was situated on the shore of the Black Sea, of which country the celebrated Aquila (Akilos, the proselyte) עקילוס,* who translated the Holy Scriptures into the

* In Echa Rabbethi, 58 *c*, the Targum Onkelos is referred to, which is incorrect, and should be עקילים Akilis; since the former only trans-

Greek, was a native (see Torath Kohanim to Levit. xxv). I therefore prefer to adopt the exposition of the Targum Yerushalmi, who translates, בארעא דבבל "In the land of Babel."

In Yoma, 10 *a*, it is said Erech is Urichus, אוריכום. Rabbi Benjamin of Tudela speaks of a city existing in his time which he calls Rachia, which is probably the town mentioned in the Talmud, although Rabbi Benjamin himself thought it identical with Calnéh. It is farther stated there, "Calnéh is גופר Gofer;" another reading has it, "גופר נינפי Gofer Ninphé," meaning, no doubt, the modern Djober on the Euphrates, north of the town of Hit. Ninphé is of mythological origin, and stands for Nymphé. It is stated in Rosh Hashanah, 26 *a*, "In Babel is a bride כלה called Ninphé." The name כלנה Calneh is then explained as כלה נאה "Callah Noah, beautiful bride," and hence the town Nimphé Djober is fittingly regarded as Calnéh. Rabbi Benjamin of Tudela says, "Al Jubir is Pumbaditha." In Ezekiel xxvii. 23, we find Canneh, with *l* wanting, assimilated by double *n* for Calneh. Jonathan on that verse explains it by Nezibin. It is also stated there אכד זה בשכר "Akkad is Bashchar," for which see Chapter IV.

Saadiah leaves Babel, Akkad, and Calneh untranslated, but gives Erech with Al Beram, which is unknown to me.

"Nineveh, Rechoboth-Ir, Calach, and Ressen," are translated by Jonathan with נינוה פלטיאת קרתא פריות (Yerushalmi has חרית) תלאסר. The same explanation is given in Bereshith Rabbah xxxvii.

NINEVEH. נינוה

Not far from the Tigris, opposite to the town of Mosul,

lated the Pentateuch, and this in the Aramean dialect, but not the passage mentioned there, nor in the Greek, as stated by the Midrash.

are pointed out the ruins of Nineveh. This formerly celebrated city held almost the same rank with Babel. Near these ruins, on a mount, is a large building, which the Turks call Nebi Juna, i. e. the prophet Jonah, since they, although erroneously, believe that there is the grave of this prophet, which is pointed out by others in Galilee.

There is yet another unfounded tradition prevailing in that vicinity; since the people point out, not far from Mosul, a large and old structure, in the village Alkus, which they allege to be the grave of Nahum of Elkosh, and relate, that when the people of Nineveh fell back again into their course of former vices, after the mission of Jonah, Nahum was sent thither to summon them to repentance, and predict their certain downfall; that, farther, the persons so threatened with punishment assailed him, and called him a deceiver and false prophet, because Jonah had already prophesied their destruction, which nevertheless was not accomplished; in consequence of which he was murdered by them, and this place where he was buried was named Alkus after him. Now, although Nahum actually predicted the downfall of Nineveh, which seems to be the chief subject of his book, the tradition in question is entirely fabulous and absurd; since his grave is accurately pointed out at Tanchum, (p. 188, which see,) and the town of *Alkezi*, near Tanchum, of which he was a native, was yet standing in the time of Hieronymus. His remains are, therefore, interred near his native place, but not beyond the Tigris, after having fallen under the murderous assault of the Assyrians. We must admit that Rabbi Benjamin of Tudela says in his travels: "At Ashur, i. e. Mosul, there is a Synagogue of the prophet Obadiah, one of the prophet Jonah, and one of the prophet Nahum the Elkoshi;" but he says nothing about his having been murdered or buried there.

PALTIATH KARTHA, PERAJOTH (CHERITH) (חרית) פלטיאת קרתא פריות.

In these names Jonathan gives us no clue to their ascertainment, as he renders the Hebrew words merely into the Chaldean, wherefore his paraphrase has here no geographical value. Rechoboth-Ir in Hebrew is identical with the Chaldean Paltiath Kartha—the City of Streets; Calach כלח he considers as Kelach קלח branch or sprout, which is in Chaldean Perioth or Cherith.

THELASSAR. תלאסר

See farther the article of this name.

In Yoma, 10 *a*, we read "Rechoboth-Ir is a town on the Euphrates near Meshan. Kelach is a town on the Euphrates near Bursif. Ressen is Aktispun." The most southern part of Mesopotamia, i. e. the country between Euphrates and Tigris was formerly called Mesa (for Meshan); which was therefore a city or district situated on the Euphrates, now unknown. The same is the case with Bursif. It appears from Sanhedrin, 109 *a*, as also Bereshith Rabbah xxxvii., that Bursif, or Bulsif, was a place not far from the former town of Babel; Kelach likewise must have been therefore either a city or district in the vicinity of this town, on the banks of the Euphrates. "Aktispun," see above, article Calneh.

It is also said there, "Ashur is Siluk; this means probably the ancient Seleucia. Josephus, Antiq., b. xviii., ch. xii., calls it Silicia, not far from Ctesiphon."

Saadiah renders Ashur with Al Muzl, and to this day Mosul is called Ashur by the Jews; Rechoboth-Ir, with Rachbah al Kiryah, i. e. the town Rachbah, which signifies unquestionably the modern Rahabeh, on the Euphrates, ten English miles south from Kerkisieh; Calach with Al Ablah, which is unknown to me; Ressen with Al Medain, which is the present town Amadia, about eighty English miles northwest from Mosul, where many Jews reside.

Some are of opinion that the town Chaluan, between

Irak Arabia and Persia, is the ancient Calach. At present there is nothing left standing of Chaluan; still it may be the modern Chalchocenia west of Shuster.

"Ludim, Anamim, Lehabim, Naphtuchim, Puthrusim, Casluchim and Caphtorim." (Gen. x. 13, 17.)

Onkelos renders Caphtorim with קפטקאי Kepotkai, which is the name of the modern Dimiat (Damietta), an inconsiderable town on the eastern branch of the Nile, where it falls into the sea. This place is therefore known under three different names: Caphtor, Kapotka (see Ketuboth, ch. xiii. § 11), and Dimiat (Damietta).

Jonathan renders the verse with גיווטאי מריוטאי ליווקאי פנטסכינאי נסיוטאי פנטפולוטי פילוסאי.

GIVATAAI. גיווטאי

This appears to me to be the original name of Egypt, from *Givtai*. The wandering race called Gipsies in English, are called by the Arabs "Gibtis;" the word "Kopts," found in European books, is incorrect, for the proper term is Gibti, whence then Egypt is derived in all probability; and these Gipsies were originally inhabitants of that country. The name of *Zigeuner*, as they are termed in Germany, is probably derived from Zoan צען, pronounced in Arabic with Gain, *g* instead of Ain; hence Zoan makes Zogan, and then Zoganer, Ziganer, or Zigeuner. See also the explanation of Saadiah. In Talmud Sabbath 115 *a*, and Megillah 18 *a*, we find גיפטית Giptith to mean Egypt.

MARTIYOTEAI, OR MARYOTAAI. מריוטאי

This is the district of Mauritania (see Siphri to Haazinu; Jebamoth 63 *b*). Josephus calls the country of Put, Moriti, in which is the river Put, of the same name with the country.

LIVAKAAI, ליווקאי

Is quite unknown to me. But may it be taken for

Lybia? But this is already mentioned by the author under Lubai.

PANTASCHINAAI, פנטסכינאי

Signifies the district between Gazza and Raamses (Pelusium), once called Kasiati Kadsai. (See farther down, article פנטפולוטי Pantapuloté.)

NASYOTEAI. נסיוטאי

I am inclined to correct this by substituting ו W for נ n, and read Wasyoteai, since to this day Central Egypt is called Wastani.

PANTAPULOTE. פנטפולוטי

I believe myself authorized to maintain that the commencing syllable פנט Pant, as also in the above Pantaschinaai, is not to be considered as a name, but as denoting a country or district, equal to the Arabic *Belad;* since even at the present day there is a place on the Nile, twelve English miles above the town of Siot, called Man-Falut, and I, therefore, think that Pant-Puloté, from its evident resemblance, means as much as the district of Puloté or Falut.

PELUSAAI.* פילוסאי

This signifies the city of Raamses, since Jonathan translates it in Exod. xii. 37 with Pelusin. (See also Yoma, ch. iii. § 7.)

The Yerushalmi has pretty much the same explanation of the above names as the T. Jonathan, with only an occasional deviation and a transposition of the letters.

Saadiah explains Ludim with Al Thanisiim, which is Zoan, since Onkelos translates Zoan of Num. xiii. 22 with

* In my copy, this word is found in the Tar. Yerushalmi, but not in Jonathan.—TRANSLATOR.

Tanis, the ancient Thanis. This will confirm my supposition as given above, article Givataai; since Jonathan and Saadiah, rendering Ludim respectively Givataai and Thanis (Zoan), refer to the same people, the Gibti or Gipsies; and the Yerushalmi Terumoth viii. asserts the Ludim to be cannibals, a charge even yet laid against the wandering tribe called variously Gipsies, Zigeuner, Bohemians, Egyptians, Gitani, in the several European languages. Anamim he translates with Al As-chandraniin, which is Alexandria; Lehabim with Al Behanasiin, which is the present Banha, a place on the eastern Nile, twenty English miles north from Cairo; Naphtuchim with Al Pirmi-un, which is the village Bermin, about five English miles west from the Nile, and eighteen English miles south from Fium (Pithom); Pathrusim with Al Bimiin, probably Fium (see farther, article Pithom); Casluchim with Al Zaidin, which is the southern part, or Upper Egypt, and called at present even Al Zaidi; and Caphtorim with Al Demiatin, the modern Dimiat (Damietta, as above, in Caphtorim).

I will take this occasion to explain some few other names belonging to Egypt. Gichon, גיחון of Gen. ii. 13, is left unexplained by Rashi, whereas he gives Pishon פישון with Nile. It appears, however, that the former might be taken for the Nile, since even at present the inhabitants of Chabash (Abyssinia) call the Nile Guchan. Josephus, also, in his Antiq., b. i. ch. i., translates Gichon with Nile, and supposes Pishon to be the Gusan, or Ganges in India. Nevertheless, there is a river named Gachun in northern Persia, which flows to the north and falls into Lake Ural, and is, perhaps, the Gichon mentioned in Eden.

On און of Gen. xli. 45, called in Ezek. xxx. 17, *Aven*,*

* In Pesiktah Rabbethi, chap. xvii., it is said to Isaiah xix. 18: "At that time there shall be five cities in the land of Egypt speaking the language of Canaan, one shall be called Ir-Hacheres;" the following are the cities, עיר החרס עיר השמש · נוון אלכסנדריא · נוף מנפות · תחפנחס חופיינס · ועיר

is also termed נא אמון No Amon (Jer. xlvi. 25; Nahum iii. 8); we ascertain this identity, because Jonathan renders No Amon with Alexandria, which is the same as that given for On by Saadiah; though Jonathan translates כהן און the priest of On with רבא דטנים the chief of Tanis, which would give us Zoan for On, and consequently not No Amon.

Goshen גשן of Gen. xlv. 10, is given by Saadiah with Al Sdir. In Upper Egypt, on the eastern bank of the Nile, is a town named Al Dir, and opposite to the same, at the distance of about a day's journey, is a place called Gashn, and it is therefore to be assumed that according to Saadiah the country between Dir, called by him Sdir, and Gashn,

החרס סרק אני ועיר שמש אילו פילוס. Here are some typographical errors, which should be thus corrected, נוון Navon, is undoubtedly incorrectly put for No Amon or Aven נא אמון or און, and is then said to be Alexandria; "Noph is Manpuach" is also wrong, and should be Memphis מנפים (*n* for *m*); the ruins of which ancient city are still to be seen about ten English miles south from Al Cairo; the same explanation is given by Jonathan to Jer. xxxiv. 1, "Noph is מפס i. e. Memphis;" [Isaiah xix. 13, "the chiefs of Noph" he gives with אינש מכים, which is incorrect and should be מפים or Memphis;] "Tachpanches is Chuphaines" is incorrect and should be Duphaines דופיינים, i. e. Daphné, which was situated in the Delta of the Nile, not far from the sea; or it may be Tuphaines טופיינים, and would then signify Thebes, which was in Upper Egypt, on the left bank of the Nile, where at present immense ruins are found, and which many hold to be No Amon, since a temple of Amon stood formerly in Thebes. "Ir-Hacheres is סרק אני" Serak Ani; this is an extremely obscure term, since we know of no town resembling this name. I think we ought to read סרבאני Sarbani, since there is a lake called Serboni, situated near the sea, about midway between Al Arish and Dimiat, and it is probable that formerly a city of the same name may have been situated there, and been the "Ir Hacheres" of Scriptures. עיר השמש Ir Hashemesh, "the city of the sun," is Heliopolis, the Greek synonyme of the Hebrew; in Jer. lxiii. 13, it is called Beth-Shemesh, "the house of the sun." The ruins of Heliopolis are still seen five miles north from Cairo. The passage quoted should then be rendered, "Ir-Hacheres, Ir-Hashemesh, No Amon or Alexandria, Noph or Memphis, Tachpanches or Daphné (or Thebes); Ir Hacheres is Serboni, and Ir-Hashemesh is Heliopolis."

is the land of Goshen. But it is hardly likely that this land was situated so far to the south. There is, however, pointed out at the present time, a village called Gishan, about a day's journey northeast from Cairo, which marks more probably the position of Goshen. We also find that Joshua conquered a land, Goshen (Joshua xi. 16); but I could not succeed in tracing it out, as it is scarcely to be believed that the Egyptian district of that name is alluded to.

Pithom פיתום (Exod. i. 11), is translated by Saadiah with Al Fium, and is the modern Medineth al Faium, two days' journey south from Cairo, and three-fourths of a day's journey from the western shore of the Nile. It was the birth-place of this celebrated and learned man, who is hence called Saadiah al Fiumi. According to the statement of Herodotus, the Greek historian, Patanus (Pithon) was near the town פי בסת Phi-Beseth (which see); but this would place it much farther north than Fium. Jonathan also translates Pithom in this passage most surprisingly with טאנים Tanis.

Raamses רעמסס (ibid.) In the Coptic (Gipsy) dialect, *Rem* signifies a man, *Shoss*, a herd; whence then the name of the place Rem-shoss, because the sons of Jacob, the shepherds, were settled there. Saadiah gives it with "En-Shems," i.e. Ir-Hashemesh-or, Beth-Shemesh, Heliopolis, (see above, art. On); Jonathan, with Pilusin פילוסין, which is perhaps the present Telfeis, which is about a day's journey north-northeast from Cairo.

Zoan צען (Num. xiii. 22), is given by Onkelos and the pseudo-Jonathan to this passage, and the real Jonathan to Isaiah xix. 13, with Tanis. Saadiah, however, gives it with Pastat al Mazra, which is the name of a most ancient city on the western bank of the Nile, opposite to Cairo, and is identical with Zoan, according to a tradition generally received; and they point out there the ruins of a handsome palace of the regent Joseph, the son of Jacob, which is often visited by our pious fellow-Israelites as a worthy relic, especially in the month of Elul (August and September). No Jews, however, reside there at present, but it is only recently that many resided there. I once saw a *Get* (a letter of divorce), which was dated "Pastat of Egypt, called the old Mitzraim, situated on the river Nile," בפסטאט מצרים דקרו לה מצרים הישנה דעל נהר נילוס.

Seveneh סונה of Ezekiel xxx. 6, the most southern town of Egypt, Siené, is at present the town of Sina on the Nile, not far from the frontiers of Nubia, though it is a little to the northeast of the site of the ancient Siené. It appears very curious that the towns of Dir and Goshen, which are south of Siené, are supposed by Saadiah to mark the bounds of the land of Goshen, which would have been in Nubia, if the hypothesis of the learned Gaon be correct, which it is evidently not, as said above under Goshen.

Phi-Beseth פי בסת (ibid. 17), the ancient Bubestus, is said to have been situated far to the north, in the Delta of Egypt. Josephus, Antiq., b. xiii., chap. vi., says: "The Jewish Temple (the house of Onias בית חוניו Beth Chonio of Menachoth, 109 *b*) stood in Leontopolis, which was called Bubasté in the ordinary language of the country." But in his Bell. Jud., b. vii., chap. xxxvii., he says that this temple was 180 stadia, or 22½ English miles, from Memphis, which would place it considerably more to the south than the first statement.

Sin סין (ibid. 16), is said to mean the vicinity of Pelusium. (See above, art. Raamses.)

Pathros פתרוס (ibid. xxix. 14), was the former city of Pathuris, in Upper Egypt, not far from Thebes, wherefore the whole of the environs were named Pathiritis. At present, no vestige of the place is to be found.

"The Hivite, the Arkite, and the Sinite," v. 17.

Arki, Arkite ערקי, is probably the village Arki, situated seven miles north-northeast from Trablus.

Sinite סיני is explained by Jonathan with אנתוסאי Anthosaai, probably the modern village of Ortoso, which is near the sea, fifteen English miles north from Arki. Targum Yerushalmi gives these words with טריפולאי, Tripolaai = Tripoli, or Trablus, and כפרוסאי Kaphrosaai, i. e. Capros = Cyprus. In Bereshith Rabbah, chap. xxxvii., Arki is explained to be ארקם דלבנון Arkam on the Lebanon, which is so far correct that the village Arki stands on the northwestern point of the Lebanon. Sini, he says, is ארתוסאי Arthosaai, which appears to be a more correct reading than the Anthosaai of Jonathan, since the modern name is Ortoso, not Ontoso. In the same manner does Saadiah explain Sini with Al Trablsiin, which is Trablus.

"The Arvadite, the Zemarite, and the Chamatite;" these Jonathan renders לוטסאי חומצאי אנטיכואי.

Lutaseai לוטסאי is Laodicea (?), which is also called Dussi al Djededa. (See Chap. I., article Zedad.)

Chomezaai חומצאי; this is the modern Chams on the Ahzy River. (See Chap. II., Note 1.)

Antichoay אנטיכואי is in Arabic, Antakia; it is situated ten English miles from the sea, and is an unimportant town on the Ahzy. About forty Jewish families live there. The paraphrase of the Targum Yerushalmi אנטוכיא מן בבל "Antiochia from Babel" is inexplicable to me. Bereshith Rabbah, chap. xxxvii., says, החמתי היא פיפני "Chamathi means Epiphania;" in Pesachim 42 *a*, the place is given פפוניא Pephonia; it is at present a small town called Chamah, twelve miles north from Chams, and is likewise situated on the Ahzy. At present no Jews reside there; but it is only twenty years since the sheich of the place laid to their charge false accusations, and had them expelled from there. The greater part of them thereupon settled in Damascus. (See Chap. I., art. לבוא חמת.)

Yerush. Megillah, i., says, ארודי היא רודוס Arvadi is Rhodos; this is not the island of Rhodes, which I will mention hereafter, but the very small island of Ruad, which lies somewhat north, opposite to the town of Ortoso, where the Eleuther falls into the sea.

Saadiah also gives the above in the same manner, Al Arudiin, Al Chemaziin, Al Chamauiin.

"ZIDON, GERAR, LESHA."

Jonathan gives Zidon with Bothanias* בותניים; this word was entirely unknown to me. But fortunately I found in the Chaldean translation of Rabbah Joseph of 1 Chron. i. 13, וכנען אוליד ית בותניאס הוא דבנא ית צידון הוא בוכרי דכנען "And Canaan begot Bothanias, who built Zidon, and was the first-born of Canaan," whence it appears that Zidon was also denoted as Bothanias.

Lesha לישע is explained by Jonathan with קלדהי Kaldahi; it ought to be קלרהי Kalrahi, i. e. the former Callirrhoé, which was spoken of above in the portion of Reuben.

Saadiah explains Gerar with Al Chaluzia; Jonathan renders ברד Bared (Gen. xvi. 14), and מדבר שור the wilderness of Shur (Exod. xv. 22) with Chaluzah; whence we may infer, that the whole southwestern part of Palestine, up to the vicinity of the Red Sea, was called Chaluzia, since Gerar, which was between Beersheba and Gazza (see article Gerar, Chap. III.), was still named Chaluzia.

"ELAM, UZ, CHUL, GETHER, AND JOKTAN."

Our Targumim give us no explanation of these names; but Saadiah gives Elam with Al Chus-sthan, no doubt the modern Chosistan, which is north of the gulf of Persia, and is a district belonging to the kingdom of Persia. The city of Shuster, which is held by many for the former Shushan of Esther i. 2, lies in thisd istrict. Those who take this view found it upon the assertion of Daniel viii. 2, who states, "I was in Shushan, which is in the land of Elam;" since Shuster is in Choristan, which denotes the

* My edition has Cothanias.—TRANSLATOR.

country of Elam, according to Saadiah. But the generally prevailing tradition, that Hammadan (which see) is the former Shushan, is in direct contradiction with the first assumption.

Ashur is rendered by Saadiah with Al Muzl (see Mosul, p. 471); Aram with Al Armin, i. e. Armenia; Uz with Al Gutah, the modern Al Ledja, which is beyond Jordan (see above, ch. iv., article Bashan); and they actually point out there the grave of Job, who lived in the land of Uz (Job i. 1), though the Chaldean version of the book of Lamentations renders Uz (iv. 21) with Armenia. In Echa Rabbethi we read עוץ זו פרס "Uz is Persia."

Chul he gives with Al Chula, in Coelesyria. (See above, Chap. II., article לבוא חמת.)

Gether he translates with Al Gramkah, which name I think myself authorized to trace in Kirmanka, a city and district in Kurdistan.

Joktan he gives with Al Kachtan. In Mahomedan books there are mentioned among the Arab tribes, "Ad, Thimud, Djurchim, Midian, Amalik, and Kachtan." It therefore appears that Saadiah supposes this Ishmaelitish tribe of Kachtan to be descended from Joktan, through an intermixture with the same.

Chazar-maveth חצר מות, is no doubt the present town Al Azarmuth, one day's journey to the east of Aden in the country of Yemen.

Hadoram הדורם, is, according to a certain tradition, the city of Senaar, the capital and residence of the king (the sheriff) of southern Arabia (Yemen).

Uzal אוזל, is also, according to a certain tradition, the town of Zanaa, which is to the north of Mocha, in the vicinity of which the celebrated Mocha coffee is produced, and where about one hundred Jewish families reside. In Zanaa, also, many Jews are found.

Mesha משא, is rendered by Saadiah with Al Meka, and

Sephar ספר with Al Medina; both towns being the well-known sacred cities of the Mahomedans.

Har Hakkedem, the Eastern Mountain, הר הקדם, is given in the Persian version with Kuh Ahl Arab, i. e. "the mount of the Arabian people," or, more properly, "of the Arab community, assembly," the Persian Ahl being synonymous with the Hebrew קהל congregation of assembly.

EXPLANATION OF SEVERAL OTHER NAMES MENTIONED IN SCRIPTURE.

Nod נוד (Gen. iv. 16). Some suppose that this means India, and that its name of Hoda הודו stands for Hondu הונדו, i. e. נוד Nod.

Jubal יובל (ibid. 21). There is a little island in the Red Sea, in a southerly direction from Mount Sinai, which is called Djubal; it is possible that Jubal settled there.

Ararat אררט (ibid. viii. 4). Onkelos, Jonathan, and Saadiah explain this with Kardo, a mountain chain in Armenia. Jonathan says, טורי דקרדון שום טוורא חד קרדניא ושום חוורא חד ארמיניא "The mountain of Kardon; the name of one mountain is Kardania, and of the other Armenia." This gives us two chains, and both are understood under the general name of Ararat. Three days' journey north from the town of Sacho, which is about one day's journey north from Mosul, is a very high mountain, called Djebl Djudi, to which the Turks of the neighbourhood make annual pilgrimages about the month of Tamuz (June), and illuminate it with a multitude of torches in the evening, so that they can be seen even as far south as Sacho, though a three days' journey distant. The Turks assert that it was on this mount the ark of Noah remained standing, and that Calif Omar had it taken down, and built a mosque of the materials thus obtained.

Nevertheless, west of the city of Erivan there is a very

high mountain, called by the Turks Agri Dagh (Dagh being the Turkish name for mount or mountain), and by Armenians Machis. Its elevation is 16,254 feet above the level of the Caspian Sea, and 13,300 above the plain on which it stands. The inhabitants of the country say that the ark of Noah rested there; and in Etshmiazin, 3 English miles to the northwest of Erivan, they point out a board which is alleged was a part of this ancient structure. At the foot of this mountain is a little village called Arghuri; in Armenian "argh" means "to plant," "uri" a "vine branch;" and the name is therefore derived from the vineyard which Noah planted, which is alleged took place near this village. Josephus (Antiquities, b. i., ch. iv.) relates, that the place where Noah left the ark is called, in the Armenian dialect, Apobateria, which means "the going out;" and that there were boards of the same in that place. In book xx., ch. ii., he says, "that, in the neighbourhood of Kerun, there are found boards of Noah's ark."

Casdim כשדים (ibid. xi. 31), were descendants of Kesed כשד, who was of a later date, and was the son of Nahor (xxii. 22); they were also called Chaldeans, in Talmud כלדאי Kaldaé. According to Homer, the original seat of the Chaldeans was in the north, near the Black Sea. Afterwards they were removed by an Asiatic king to Mesopotamia to fertilize the land; and it was here that they became so extended and powerful, that, at a later period, they assumed the government and power of the Assyrian empire, and were themselves the rulers of the country. This view will explain the passage of Isaiah xxiii. 13.

Ur אור is at present called Urfa, and is a day's journey east from the Euphrates, in the country of Diarbekir. They point out here the house of Abraham, as also the site of the furnace wherein he was cast by order of Nimrod. On this site is at present a pool, or little lake, in which are a great many fish, which, however, the pious Mahomedans will not allow to be touched, out of reverence for Abraham.

Charan חרן (ibid.) is probably the village Charran, situated in a desert district, about 20 English miles south-east from Urfa. It stands near the river Gallab, which runs from Urfa to Charran. They show here a strong tower, called the Tower of Nimrod; also the grave of Terach, the father of Abraham.

Elassar אלסר (ibid. xiv. 1) is at present unknown; but it appears from the book of Judith, i. 6, that it was not far from the Median kingdom, near the celebrated town of Ecbatana, the modern Hammadan. (See above, Hamdiji, p. 454.)

Shuach שוח (ibid. xxv. 2) is probably the country now called Sachai, situated to the east of Batanea. (See above, article Bashan, p. 220.)

Pethor פתור (Num. xxii. 5). According to Rabbi Benjamin of Tudela, Pethor is the same with באליץ, i. e. the modern Bales or Blis, on the Euphrates, east of Chaleb (Aleppo); and he found there still standing the (astronomical) tower of Bileam.

The land of the Zidonians ארץ צידונים (Josh. xiii. 4) was formerly called Phœnicia, and in Bereshith Rabbah 90, פנוקיא Phœnukia; it extended from Sur to Trablus. I will mention a few towns of this district.

Arpad ארפד (2 Kings xviii. 34) is of the same signification with Arvad (which see), by changing *p* for *v*. Properly speaking, Tyre was also called Arad, since on old Tyrian coins there was found the inscription of מלך אל ארד Melech al Ard, "King of Ard," which is Zor or Tyre.

Berotha ברותה (Ezek. xlvii. 16) is called Beritha in Jos., Bell. Jud., b. vii., ch. xx., and in the Life of Josephus,

p. 520. It is fifteen English miles north from Zidon, and is a considerable sea-port town. Here reside about fifty Jewish families, who have a very ancient Synagogue.

Chethlon (ibid. 15) חתלון, is probably identical with the ruins of Athlun, situated on the sea-shore four miles south from Surafend. (See above, art. Zarephath.) It is possibly the same with Hithlo היתלו, spoken of in Niddah, fol. 9 *b*, which is termed in the Yerushalmi of the same treatise Ayithlo עייתלו; only that it would be most surprising that the ancient boundary of Palestine should never have extended farther north than this point.

Berothai ברתי (2 Sam. viii. 8), is the present Biri on the Euphrates, about two days' journey to the northeast of Chaleb. This town was situated in the territories of the King of Aram-Zobah, whose capital and residence is said, according to a tradition, to have been the city of Chaleb, wherefore it is called by the Israelites Aram-Zobah. This district furnished much copper, as is apparent from the passage cited; and now there is a mount, one English mile west from Chaleb, called Djebl Anchas, i. e. copper mountain, where it is possible much copper was obtained.

Betach בטח (ibid.) is called Tibchath טבחת in 1 Chron. xviii. 8. There is about eighteen English miles west from Chaleb a town called Metach, which is, perhaps, identical with Betach, by changing *B* into *M*, which is frequently done.

Chelbon חלבון (Ezek. xxvii. 18) is the village Halbun, about ten English miles to the northwest of Damascus. It furnishes even at the present day remarkably good wine, as it is said also in the passage cited.

Rezeph רצף (2 Kings xix. 12) is the present village Razapa, two days' journey east from Chaleb, near the Euphrates.

Eden עדן (ibid.), (Ezek. xxvii. 23). Jonathan explains

this with חדיב Chadeb. I have already stated that this signifies Adiabené, in the vicinity of Ardebil. About five English miles south of this place is, even at present, the village of Daibuiné, which appears to bear some similarity to Chadeb and Adiabené.

Thelassar תלאסר (ibid.), perhaps for תל אשור Tel Ashur, "the high, mountainous Assyria," which would then denote the country around Adiabené.

Sepharvaim ספרוים (ibid. 13), was the ancient city of Siffara, on the Euphrates, in Mesopotamia.

Hena הנע (ibid.), is the present town of Anna, on the Euphrates, situated on the road from Chaleb to Bagdad.

Ivah עוה (ibid.), is the district of Avadiah in Persia.

Cuthah כותה (ibid. xvii. 24). As late as the time of Nachmanides (the רמבן Ramban), there still existed a large town, called Chuth, between Charran and Mosul, as he states in his commentary to the Pentateuch at the end of section Noach. It is, properly speaking, the birthplace of Abraham, as Maimonides (רמבם Rambam) states in his Moreh, "that Abraham was born at Chuth, and opposed the idolatry of the people of the place, who worshipped the sun." It is also said in Baba Bathra, fol. 91 *a*, "that Abraham was hidden three years in Chuth and seven in Kardo (Ararat), on account of the general persecution which then prevailed." I have already stated that many have sought for Chuth in the vicinity of Zidon, since the Samaritans (Cuthians) claim to be of Zidonian descent. (See Jos., Antiq., b. xiii., ch. xvii.)

Kir קיר (ibid. xvi. 9), is probably the river Kur, which has its sources east of the Black Sea, runs eastwardly and falls into the Caspian Sea near Salian. Probably the country near it is the Kir of the Bible.

Karkemish כרכמיש (Jer. xlvi. 2). It is called קרקסיון Karkission in Echa Rabbethi to ch. i. 18, and is the present town of Kerkisieh, on the River Euphrates, where it is joined by the stream Chabur. (See כבר Chebar.)

Thiphsach תפסח (1 Kings iv. 24) is the town of Thaphsaki, to the north of Kerkesie, on the Euphrates.

Tadmor תדמור (ibid. ix. 18). On the road from Damascus to the Euphrates, about two days' journey northeast from the former, are found the ruins of Tadmor or Palmyra, in a sandy desert. Thus also is it said in Sabbath, fol. 30 *b*, "The inhabitants of Tadmor dwell in a sandy country." These ruins present remarkably large, beautiful and magnificent remains of hoary antiquity, and are equal to the ruins of Baal-bek. Among others is found a ruined structure of marble, having the appearance of a Synagogue, which is called כנסת שלמה "the Synagogue of Solomon."

The river Chebar נהר כבר (Ezek. i. 1). We find two rivers, now Chabur, having this name. The one rises in the country of Diarrabiar and falls by Kerkisieh into the Euphrates. The other, Chabur, rises to the southwest of Lake Van, and joins the Tigris between Chesan-Cherfa and Djezrieh. I have no means of ascertaining to which of the two streams Ezekiel refers.

Thel Charsha תל חרשא (Ezra ii. 59) is probably the village of Tel al Chansa, for Charsa, situated between Mosul and Nisibin.

Apharsathechai אפרסתכאי (ib. iv. 9) denotes, as it is said, the inhabitants of the former province Parætacena in Media.

Beth-Arbel בית ארבאל (Hosea x. 14; see also Chap. III., article Arbel) is perhaps the modern town of Ardebil, to the west of the Caspian Sea, famous for the battle (of Arbela) in which Alexander of Macedon overcame the Persian King Darius. Several Jews formerly resided here, but there are none left at present.

Chilmad כלמד (Ezek. xxvii. 23). Jonathan explains

this with Media, and means probably the ancient district of Charmanda (changing *R* for *L*) in Media.

Chelam חילם (2 Sam. x. 16) is stated in ancient documents to be the town of Alama, east of Jordan on the canton of Argob, and is perhaps identical with the fortress of Ulama in the land of Gileäd, often mentioned in the book of the Maccabees.

Pul and Lud פול ולוד (Isa. lxvi. 19). I believe that Pul signifies the country of Pamphilia, near Cilicia, in which the city of Tarshish is situated, which is mentioned in the passage cited in connexion with Pul. Or, it may be the country of Paphlagonia, near Pontus. Lud, however, I presume to be Lydia, which is to the south of Mysia, the capital of which was Sardes, where the well-known immensely rich King Crœsus once resided.

In Talmud and Midrashim occur the following names, concerning which I believe it requisite to give some account.

Ludkia לודקיא (Sabbath, 119 *a;* Menachoth, 85 *b;* and in Pesiktah Rabbethi, where it says, "Ludkia belongs to Suria" סוריא), is the little town of Ladikieh, situated close to the sea, sixty English miles to the south of Antakia. Until within six years several Jews lived here; at which time they removed to Damascus, Chaleb, &c. There is found here an old Synagogue.

Cuchelith כוחלית of Kiddushin, 66 *a*, is, perhaps, the country Calkis כלקים, mentioned in Yerushalmi Megilla i., and possibly, also, the קוכליקום Kochlikos of Megillath Thaanith xii.; it is the desert district Calchis, not far from Antakia, or possibly the environs of the town of Colossæ, on the banks of the Lykos in Phrygia.

Bagris בגרים, mentioned in Megillath Antiochus, the history of Hanukkah, as a city built by Bagris, general of Antiochus Epiphanes, is probably the very old destroyed Kallai or fort, called Bagris, which is situated on the road from Chaleb to Antakia.

Kesipha כסיפא, mentioned in Vayikra Rabbah v. as the extensive district of Kesipha, is perhaps identical with Casiphia of Ezra vii. 17, and is probably the very large plain situated east of Chams, in the direction of the Euphrates, where is found a mount called Djebl Chesaphia.

Piska פיסקא, of Yerushalmi, end of Bikkurim, is probably Pisidia, near Galatia, in Asia Minor. In Pisidia was a second Antiochia, the ruins of which are shown at the present day, near the small town of Jalabatz.

Kepudkaé קפודקאי (see above, article Caphtorim), is probably Cappadocia, in Anatolia, substituting, as usual with all words of Greek derivation in the Talmud, the ק *k* for the Latin *c*.* Formerly many Jews lived there.

Cathphi כתפי (see Rashi to Exod. xiii. 16). I deem this to be the present Turkish district Kotavenkiar, in the northern part of Anatolia; its capital is the town of Brusia.

Rodos רודוס, mentioned in Yerushalmi Abodah Zarah, ch. iii. צלמא דרודוס, "The image of Rodos," so also in Midrash Shemuel xix. This image is the celebrated Colossus, which stood in the Grecian island of Rhodes. It was considered one of the seven wonders of the ancient world.

Italia of Greece איטאליא של יון of Bereshith Rabbah 66, I suppose to be Calabria (the קלברי of the same book, 23); it is a part of that which was formerly called Magna Græcia, "Great Greece," and is extremely fertile. In it is the sea-port town of

Perandissin פרנדיסין, of Erubin, ch. iv. § 1, the ancient Brundusium, and the present Brindisi.

Paltilum פלטילום (end of Makkoth; but in Echa Rabbethi, ch. v. 18, it is called פיטלילום Pitlilus). It is, according to the passages cited, one hundred and twenty mill, or ninety English miles, from the city of Rome. In

* Which, however, was no doubt always pronounced like K by the ancient Romans.—TRANSLATOR.

the commencement of the Life of Josephus, also in Antiq., b. xviii. ch. viii., it is called Puteoli, and by the modern Italians Pozzuoli; or it is, perhaps, the modern Pitigliana, where a tolerably large number of Jews reside.

Athuna אתונא of Bechoroth 8 *b*, and Echa Rabbethi i. 1, is the ancient and famous city of Athens in Greece.

Tiria טיריא of Vayikra Rabbah xxx., and Midrash Shemuel viii., is the formerly celebrated Troia (Troy), the ruins of which in Anatolia, opposite the island of Tenedos, in the Archipelago, are visible to this day. It may also be the town Tirra, likewise in Anatolia, about three days' journey from Smyrna (Ismir). Here reside many Jews, who have an old Synagogue.

Karthigna קרתיגנא of Menachoth, 110 *a**, (Yerushalmi Sabbath vii., Yerushalmi Sanhedrim xii.) signifies the ancient well-known Carthage in North Africa, near where the present Tunis stands.

Kiriah קריה of Tosephtah Maaser Sheni iv., I believe to be the present town of Cirena, in North Africa, in the country of Al Barka, to the east of the state Al Trablos (Tripoli). Many Jews reside in this vicinity.

Terbanth טרבנת, of Yerushalmi Megillah iv., is the very ancient city of Derbent, on the western shore of the Caspian Sea; it has remarkably old and strong fortifications, which were built at the time of Alexander of Macedon. Many Jews are yet living here at the present day.

Buli בולי of Yerushalmi Shekalim vii., and Abodah Zarah 42 *b*, is probably Constantinople (Byzantium), as it

* אמר רב מצור ועד קרתגני מכירין את ישראל ואת אביהם שבשמים מצור כלפי מערב ומקרתגני כלפי מזרח אין מכירין לא לישראל ולא לאביהם שבשמים "Rab said, From Zor to Karthagné they know Israel and their Father in heaven; from Zor towards the west, and from Karthagné towards the east, they know neither Israel nor their Father in heaven." I believe that here an exchange of names has taken place, and should be "from Tyre to the east, and from Karthagné at the west," since these were the respective positions of Tyre and Carthage.

was also called by some Buli, whence the Turkish appellation, Stamboul.

Beth-Balthin or Biram בית בלתין זו בירם (Rosh Hashanah, 23 *b*, and Sanhedrin, 108 *a*, עיני רבתי דבירם "the large spring of Biram"). To the north of the town of Hitt, on the Euphrates, the entire Jewish congregation of which consists of none but Karaites, on the caravan route from Damascus to Bagdad, and not far from the river Euphrates, is found the large and wonderful spring of Biram. It has three openings, from one of which issues forth sweet and hot water, as in Tiberias; from another, very cold water, greatly charged with salt, so that salt is found after it evaporates; and from the third issues Petroleum (earth-pitch) or Naphtha: this is gathered up and sent off all around the whole of the vicinity, where it is chiefly used in building, instead of lime and mortar, whence the houses of the district, and particularly those in Hitt, have quite a black appearance.*

Galia גליא (ibid. 26 *a*), is generally believed to be Gallia, Gaul, or France; but it can scarcely be supposed that Rabbi Akiba should have travelled so far as France, and his journey to Galia is spoken of in the passage cited. I therefore hold it to be more reasonable to believe that Galatia in Asia Minor is here referred to, which was situ-

* I believe that this will enable us to expound the difficult passage of Gen. xi. 3, והחֵמָר היה להם לחֹמֶר "And the slime served them for mortar" (English version); and I suppose that this Chemar is nothing else than the Naphtha, since it is used even at the present day for building purposes, to cement the stones together, instead of mortar made of lime. Saadiah actually translates it with Al Kaphr, as he has rendered also the בכפר which occurs before in Gen. vi. 14; which clearly proves that Saadiah understood by Chemar the same substance as under Kopher, to wit, the earth-pitch or Naphtha. I am induced to believe that בארות חמר (ibid. xiv. 10) do not mean clay-pits, since בארות signifies wells, springs, and is not identical with בורות pits; and that hence the *slime* must be something fluid, something rushing from a source,—unquestionably, therefore, "Pitch, naphtha wells, or springs."

ated not far from the river Halis.* It is likely enough that Rabbi Akiba, who often journeyed to the north (of Palestine), for instance to Africa, in the passage cited above from Rosh Hashanah, to Charzan, as in Aboth of Rabbi Nathan xvi., may also have travelled to Galatia, which was likewise in the north. I nevertheless found a passage in Yebamoth, fol. 63 *a*, which almost clearly proves that Galia means Gaul or France; the words are אפילו ספינות הבאות מגליא לאספמיא "Even the ships which go from Galia to Ispamia" (Spain), i. e. vessels voyaging between countries not far remote from each other, and which consequently have not to come over a long distance. This, however, leaves us no other way of explaining it, except to assume Gallia, Gaul or France, to be the Talmudic Galia; and after all, it is possible that Rabbi Akiba may have undertaken a voyage to France.

Bagdath בגדת, of Kiddushin, 71 *b*, Ketuboth, 7 *b*, is the city of Bagdad, on the Tigris, which the Kalif Al Mansur built, or rather rebuilt, enlarged, and beautified (since it was in existence several hundred years before), in the year

* The author introduces the following, which I append as a note: "I have ascertained from ancient documents, that the language of the inhabitants of that country has a strong resemblance to the German. As Rashi says to Deut. iii. 9, 'The Emorites called it (the Hermon) Senir,' that it resembles the German Schnee, English Snow—hence Snow Mountain—and that the word is (almost) identical in the languages of Canaan and Germany. A colony is said to have gone from Galatia and settled in the West, Germany and France. As I have already observed, p. 453, there was in that district a town called Germanie, or Germania (see above, article Germania); so were the settlements of Ashkenaz likewise in the north (of Palestine), as has been stated already; and it would appear likely, that from there emigrations took place to Germany proper; whence, then, the name of Ashkenaz for Germany; since it was actually peopled by a colony out of Galatia, Ashkenaz, or Germania. The names of Ashkenaz and Germania, occurring in Scripture and the Targumim, cannot possibly be rendered with Germany (Deutshland) of the present day; nevertheless, the usual nomenclature is not without a good reason, as has been just exhibited."

4523 (763). There reside at present a very large number of Jews in Bagdad, under their chief, the so-called Prince of Babylon נשיא של בבל, who is in great esteem with the authorities of the place.

Sardia סרדיא, of Bereshith Rabbah xxxiv., is the island of Sardinia, in the Mediterranean.

Britania בריטאניא of Pesiktah Rabbethi xv., is Britain, England.

Astherkanith אסתרקנית, of Bezah, 39 *b*, "salt of Astherkanith," Baba Bathrah, 20 *a*, Menachoth, 21 *b*, is probably the town of Astrakhan on the Caspian Sea, where much salt is obtained.

In Baba Bathrah, 56 *a*, Keni קני of Gen. xv. 19, is explained with נפתוחא Naphthucha. This is surely an incorrect reading, and should be נותיא or נותייה or נבטיא, and means נביות Nebaioth, i. e. the Nabathians (see Chap. IV., article Nebaioth). The princes of Kedar נשיאי קדר of Ezekiel xxvii. 21, is rendered by Jonathan with רברבי נבט "chiefs of Nebat," i. e. Nebathia, since Kedar and Nebaioth are almost synonymous, or at least placed often in juxtaposition. (See also Bereshith Rabbah xliv., and Yerushalmi Shebiith vi.)

There is farther mentioned in the same passage, Ardiskos ערדיסקוס, also used as an elucidation of Keni; but we find this name as a town not far from Tob Ain (see ch. iii, article עין טוב, in Erubin, 29 *a*; wherefore I think we ought to read דרמוסקוס Darmoskos, for Ardiskos, i. e. the environs of Damascus, which is also called דרמשק Darmesek (1 Chron. xviii. 5); and actually the above-cited passage from the Yerushalmi Shebiith has Damesek instead of Ardiskos, which confirms my hypothesis.

ADDENDA.

SOME ACCOUNT OF THE SO-CALLED YEHUD CHEBR AND THE TEN TRIBES.

UNDER the name of Yehud Chebr are generally understood the descendants of Heber the Kenite חבר הקני, the father-in-law of Moses, or Jethro. "Now Heber the Kenite, who was of the children of Chobab, the father-in-law of Moses, had severed himself from the Kenites" (Jud. iv. 1); they are also called בני רכב Bné Rechab, "the Rechabites"—"These are the Kenites that came of Chemath, the father of the house of Rechab" (1 Chron. ii. 55). They abstain from wine, and only dwell in tents (Jer. xxxv. 8, 9). In Pesiktah Rabbethi xxxi., it is said ארץ הסינים בני יונדב בן רכב "The land of Sinim (of Isaiah xlix. 11), is the land of Jonadab the son of Rechab." From Bereshith Rabbah lii., it appears clearly that Sinim is the land תימן Theman (the south), or Yemen in Arabia, which is verified to this day. There are many traces of them at present; but they live entirely isolated, will not be recognised, and shun, or rather hate, all intercourse and every connexion with the other Jews. They have nevertheless not escaped the searching look of our brothers.

They only sojourn in Arabia, and for the most part on the western shore of the Red Sea, and are engaged solely in the raising of cattle. In the vicinity of Junbua, a seaport on the eastern shore of the Red Sea, they are found at times labouring as smiths, and have commercial connexions with other Arabic tribes, that is, they barter with them. They are called Arab Sebth, i. e. Arabs who keep the seventh day Sabbath, and are generally esteemed and feared; so that they form, so to say, a gigantic people, whose power and greatness excites fear. They only speak Hebrew and Arabic, and will form no connexion or acquaintance with the Jews; and should they be recognised as Jews, or if one should enter into conversation with them on the subject, they will quickly deny their origin, and assert that they are but of the common Arabic descent. They will not touch another Arab, much less will they eat anything with him, even those things which are permitted to Jews; and they always stand at some distance from the other Arabs, should their barter trade at times bring them together, so as not to come into any mediate or immediate contact. They always appear on horseback and armed, and people assert that they have noticed the fringes, ציצית, commanded in Scripture on their covering and clothing.

In the time of Abraim Pacha, when the country was everywhere secure, and men were able to travel in all direcions without being molested, two Jewish mechanics, the one a tinsmith and the other a silversmith, left Zafed with their tools, in the hope of finding employment among the distant Arabs. They in consequence crossed the Jordan, and went in a southeastern direction towards the mountains of Hauran. They actually obtained there much work among Arab tribes, and stayed some time among them. They could eat only bread, butter, honey, oil, and similar permitted things, and they thus sat one evening apart from the Arabs who were eating, to take their supper by themselves. Several Arabs on horseback had come from the south, in order to barter with the tribes of the district. They remarked those who sat eating isolated from the others, and asked, why they sat apart, and why they had a different meal from the others, and who they were? They were told that these men were Yehud (Jews). "But," asked the strangers in return, "do you believe that we have never seen any Yehud before, that you wish to impose on us these dwarfs as Yehud? We often barter with the Yehud Chebr; but they are a giant race, and it is impossible that these little creatures can belong to the same family. Besides, no Yehud would ever eat anything with another Arab, or come in so close a connexion and contact with you as these." The Arabs of the district had then to explain to the strangers that there are actually many other Jews besides the Yehud Chebr, although they differ from them.

They are occasionally seen in Palestine, but very seldom, and then, as it were, in secrecy and unrecognised. Some even say that several have been met with in Jerusalem, but they never make themselves known; although the reason of this singular silence, and this anxious desire to escape detection, has remained hitherto a profound secret; at the same time it is clearly ascertained that they are Jews in every sense of the word, live according to our laws, and are also somewhat acquainted with our learned men. It is now some years ago that two Ashkenazim of Tiberias went into the cave where the worthy martyr, Rabbi Akiba, lies buried. Just as they were coming out of the cave, there passed by two Arab horsemen, who observed them. The Arabs addressed them in Hebrew, and asked them what Zaddik (pious, righteous man,—this being the name by which the Arabs and Bedouins designate our ancient and modern learned men) lies buried there; and when ansewred, Rabbi Akiba, they descended from their horses and went into the cave. The two Ashkenazim without heard them utter a touching and mournful prayer in the Hebrew language; and they asked them, on coming out, who they were; to which they answered, "We are Yehud Chebr; but we adjure you, by the name of the Holy God of Israel, that you tell not soon after your return home in Tiberias that you have seen us, and only speak of it after some time, when we are away from your district and distant from your environs." With these words they hastened away and soon were out of sight. It seems, therefore, that they were afraid, in case the account of their appearance had been divulged in the city, of being perhaps overtaken, and thereby probably compelled to make themselves fully known.

They have also a chief among themselves, who is almost regarded as a regent.

About twenty-five years ago, the serif of Zanaa (see above, Uzal) resolved to make a pilgrimage to Mekka. It is usual to make this pilgrimage by sea: they sail up the Red Sea as far as Djida, and proceed thence by land to Mekka. But this serif resolved to make the whole journey by land. He supplied himself, therefore, and all his large retinue and escort, with everything requisite for this long journey; as, however, their road lay necessarily in part through the great sandy desert, they soon got into the greatest difficulties, for they lost their way, and roamed about, and could not find any egress. They were already in the greatest distress and danger, all their provisions, especially water, were consumed, and they saw clearly that they must perish, since they were constantly wandering in the desert, without the means of extricating themselves: when they had at length the happiness to come to a somewhat more fertile district, which convinced them that they had traversed the greater part of the desert. They now pushed eagerly forward, though nearly famished, without strength and longing for water; but they could find no vestige of inhabitants. But towards sunset they observed at a distance, so to say, a whole town of tents. This revived them, and they hastened on with the last remains of their strength, since they now hoped to be among their brothers, the Arabic tribes. They soon came near a very large and beautiful tent, and the leader of the advance of the caravan called out with a very loud voice: "For God's sake, water! water! we are all famishing this moment." Thereupon, a very tall Arab came out from the tent and exclaimed in an angry tone: "Kelb (dog), who dares to cry so loudly in the hour of devotion?" The Mahomedan then told him of the great danger of the company, and begged him to give them a little water. But the other asked: "Dost thou know where thou art now, and where thou hast lifted up thy voice so loudly? Here is the tent of our worthy Melek (king), and we are even now engaged in our afternoon prayer (מנחה), and thou hast disturbed both him and us with thy outcry in our devotions." The stranger looked into the tent, and saw a whole assembly of venerable gigantic Arabs, who all were standing still, and praying in a low tone of voice (probably the silent prayer of the eighteen benedictions שמנה עשרה). Very soon after, water was offered to the whole assembly, though without touching any of them, and they were then furnished with everything requisite for the pursuit of their journey, and a guide was sent along with them, who showed and described to them the best and shortest route by which they could reach Mekka, where they arrived after some weeks' farther journeying. Upon inquiring who their benefactors were, they were answered quite briefly, "Yehud Chebr."

I learned the above from a trustworthy person of Zafed, who was soon after this occurrence in Zanaa, and obtained the whole account of it from the above-mentioned Serif, who had himself experienced it. He has become, moreover, since then an exceedingly great friend of the Jews, and treats them with the greatest respect.

Of late, much pains have been taken to obtain more reliable particulars of the Yehud Chebr. I, myself, employed all available means to obtain success. At length, myself and some honourable Israelites, who felt the deepest in the matter, agreed to seek out a suitable person who should be able to travel through Arabia as a pretended Mahomedan Arab pilgrim, and to employ every available effort to obtain a correct account of the Yehud Chebr, and to enter into friendly intercourse with them. We at length obtained a man suited to our purposes, an African Jew, named Rabbi Amram, who was then sojourning in Zafed, and who had friendly relations with several Arab tribes, and knew their manners and habits quite accurately, and was thus enabled to enact well the part of a pilgrim. We supplied him with everything requisite, and with documents signed by the principal Rabbis of Jerusalem and Zafed. I wrote him out his line of travel, pointed out to him which road he was chiefly to follow, indicating to him, with all possible accuracy, the places where they have their principal connexions; and supplied him with two copies of my Geography of Palestine תבואות הארץ; upon which he commenced his journey from Jerusalem in the month of Elul, 5606 (Sept. 1846). About a year from that time, I received a letter from him *via* Cairo, dated at Zanaa, in South Arabia, in which he informed me that whilst journeying by land between Aden and Mocha, he was plundered by a hostile tribe of Arabs, but that his documents were all safe; that at present the northern Arab tribes were engaged in mutual strife and warfare, wherefore he was at that moment unable to pursue his journey in the desired direction, and he was compelled to tarry some time at Aden, till quiet should be restored. But that he had learned from a sure and reliable source, that in an eastern direction there is a very uncommonly numerous and extensive tribe of Jewish Arabs, universally called the tribe of Benjamin שבט בנימין, which he would visit after peace should be restored; and that it might be a long time before he would write again, since he would report nothing which is not strictly correct, and found perfectly reliable by his own personal conviction.

THE LATEST ACCOUNTS CONCERNING THE LOST TEN TRIBES.

Before I proceed to give the important accounts concerning the present existence of the Ten Tribes, I will mention the various explanations of the Talmud and Midrashim of the names of the countries and towns whither they were carried by the kings of Assyria.

We read in 2 Kings xviii. 11, "And the king of Ashur carried Israel away to Ashur, and settled them in Chalach, Chabor, and by Nehar (the river of) Gozan, and the towns of Media;" and in 1 Chron. v. 26 is added, "and Harah."

The Talmud Kiddushin, 72 *a*, explains חבור זה חדי״ב "Chabor is Chadeb," and I have already stated above that Chadeb is identical with Adiabené.

It is farther said there נהר גוזן זו גינזק "Nehar Gozan is Ginzak." In the middle ages, there was yet standing a town called Ganzakia, on the most northeastern point of the Lake Ooroomiah, about where the modern village Shebister stands; the vicinity yet bears the name of Adir Beizan, very similar with Gaizan = Gozan. The Jews residing there generally call the district פרס קטן מדי "Little Persia, or Media," wherefore this town is called in Bereshith Rabbah xxxiii. גינזק של מדי Ginzak of Media. But, also, much farther north, on the River Aras, a day's journey before it joins the Kur, is, at the present day, a village named Ganzak (?).

It is stated next ערי מדי זו המדן "The cities of Madai mean Hamdan, or the country around Hamdan, the ancient Ekbatana" (see above, article Hamdaji). Again, it is said, "Some think that the cities of Madai signify נהונד Nehund and the כרך מושכי town of Mushechi, which is near the above." Nehund is no doubt the modern town of Nehavend, one day's journey south from Hammadan; and perhaps Kerach Mushechi is the modern Kirmansho, one day's journey west from Nehavend. It is not likely that the country of Mush, situated to the west of Lake Van, can be understood by Mushechi, because it is at too great a distance from Nehavend.

The Chaldean translation of Rabbi Joseph of 1 Chron. v. 26, renders Hara with טורי קבלא the dark mountain, (see above, article Africa). Some suppose that Hara signifies the country of Aria, by which name the ancient historians denote the land of Media. Chalach חלח is not explained, and there can be no doubt that here is understood the district of Diarbekir, still called Chalah.

Gozan may also denote the Ganges in India; there is, however, this objection: the Bible says, "He carried them away to Ashur," and it does not appear that the Ganges can be considered as belonging to the Assyrian empire, since it never extended thus far.

It would be perfectly ridiculous to look for the Ten Tribes in the countries just named; since these lands, with their various classes of inhabitants, are perfectly well known; wherefore it is impossible to predicate of those who dwell there in the language of Isaiah xlix. 9, "To say to those bound, Go forth, and to those who are in darkness, Be known;" or ibid. 12, "Behold, these will come from afar, and these from the north and the west, and the others from the land of Sinim." There can be no doubt that the exiles left their new places of abode and wandered away into other parts of the world, where they settled.

We may admit that this emigration may have been for the most part eastward into Asia; but Africa also must have received many of the exiles. "And it shall come to pass on that day that the great cornet shall be blown, and they shall come who are lost in the land of Ashur, and those who are cast out in the land of Egypt" (Isa. xxvii. 13). Thus also related the trustworthy אלדד הדני Eldad the Danite, who arrived from there in the west several centuries ago, that many of these tribes reside beyond the river of Ethiopia נהר כוש in the land of the Ludin and Kaka, consequently in Africa. It is said in Yerushalmi Sanhedrin, x., and in Echa Rabbethi, 73 *a*, that many of the Ten Tribes are beyond the river Sambatyon.

I will now proceed to give the latest traces of the existence of one, or rather several Israelitish kingdoms, with independent power, having their own regents, standing armies, and their own coinage; in brief, existing in the greatest power and prosperity.

It is now about twenty-five years ago that a Mahomedan dervish came to Damascus from Eastern Asia, and had with him a gold coin which he was desirous of exchanging for the current money of the country. On the one side was in Hebrew square characters תחת ממשלת אדונינו יצחק המלך, "Under the rule of our Lord, the king Isaac." And, on being asked how he had obtained this money, he told briefly and with great simplicity, without being able to give a correct solution of the various questions put to him, that he had been engaged on a pious (i. e. begging) journey of several months' duration, setting out from Adjim in Persia in a northeastern direction. He reached, so he told, a great, mighty, and flourishing empire, and came to a very large city, where he excited the greatest curiosity through his ridiculous beggary and singular dress, and was summoned one day into a handsome and elegant palace. He found a majestic-looking person sitting on a species of throne, who asked him in the Persian language, whence he came; to which he answered, that he was a Mahomedan dervish, and came from the southwest. The prince then asked, if there were any Jews in the country whence he came, and desired some account of them. The simple dervish knew not that he was speaking to a Jewish prince; and began, therefore, to paint them as a contemptible and weak people, and that it was not worth while to speak much about them. He soon noticed, that the prince was strongly excited at what he told, and appeared to be getting angry at his picture of the Jews. Simple, however, as he was, he was, nevertheless, cunning enough to give another turn to his words, and he now commenced to speak of them in more flattering terms, and praised them as a good and peaceful people, although weak and not independent, and endeavoured to represent them in many respects as a quite distinguished class of men. The prince was greatly rejoiced at this, and commanded, at the concusion of the audience, to give him three hundred pieces of gold. More information than this could not be obtained from the simple dervish. The weight of these coins was about that of a double ducat, and they were made of the purest gold. This, I learned from a creditable person, who had himself obtained one of these coins from the dervish, and had the above from his own mouth.

However defective this description of this ignorant traveller may be, and however much that is fabulous may be in the details, since the dervish, true to the manners of his order, troubled himself about nothing which had no relation to self; it is, nevertheless, certain, that the main part of the story must be true, for these gold coins in question are sufficient proof of the existence of a Jewish ruling prince.

It is also now three years ago that I saw a distinguished Indian dervish in the streets of Jerusalem. I entered into conversation with him, and I observed that there appeared something worthy of belief in his words. I invited him to accompany me home, and conversed a considerable time with him concerning his long and distant journeys into Asia. I endeavoured to draw many things from him, and put to him many and various questions, through which I could speedily notice whether his words were true and not in contradiction with each other; and I almost convinced myself that he was worthy of confidence. He told me that at a distance of four months' journey from the city of Cashmir, in the northeastern part of Persia, in a northeast direction, there is a large Jewish kingdom, the seat of the regent being in the city of Ajulun. Nearly the whole country is surrounded with immensely high and inaccessible mountains, forming a kind of fortified wall—this is on three sides, and on the fourth there is a rocky pass, forming, so to say, a large entrance, where Jewish soldiers are stationed. These Jews have commercial connexions with their neighbours, but it is extremely rare that strangers are permitted to enter the country within the just-mentioned gate. This dervish also related that he had formerly a travelling companion, another dervish, who had travelled in that country, and had been fortunate enough to sojourn for some time in the city of Ajulun, which is situated on the frontier. He told some wonderful tales of the beauty and the splendour of this town, especially of the many and magnificent Synagogues, which, in a measure, are resplendent with pure gold. The inhabitants are all Jews, with the sole exception of their slaves, who are non-Israelites out of the vicinity. He could not recollect any more of what he had told him concerning this Jewish kingdom.

The report brought by this dervish, agrees almost entirely with that of the former one, so that the regent *Isaac*, who bestowed on the first the gold coins, is perhaps the same who lives in Ajulun.*

It is about nineteen years past that the Jewish congregation of Zafed sent a messenger to Yemen, to make there, as usual everywhere, collections for the poor of Palestine. He tarried some time in Zanaa (see above, Uzal), and observed there one day in the Synagogue a remarkable-looking person; and on making inquiries concerning him, he was told, that he had arrived but a few days previously, and alleged himself to be of the tribe of Dan. The messenger expressed the wish to become somewhat better acquainted with the stranger, and had a request preferred to him, either to permit him to pay him a visit, or for the other to call at his lodgings. The Danite accepted the latter proposition, and made his appearance at the house of the messenger on the following day at the precise hour appointed. The stranger was a gigantic and very handsome man, who had something remarkable, honourable, and inspiring in his physiognomy. He had a fine long beard, and his hair, which was black and long, hung down over his back, and gave him a peculiar, noble, and majestic appearance. His costume was partly oriental. Around his body he wore a broad belt, on which was embroidered in large Hebrew letters יהי דן נחש עלי דרך שפיפון עלי ארח, "Dan shall be a serpent on the way, an adder on the path" (Gen. xlix. 17). By his side hung a large and broad sword. He spoke only pure Hebrew, but said very little, and betrayed in his speech a great degree

* The Translator has taken the liberty to omit an anecdote of the adventure of a Calcutta Jew, which is too improbable to meet with credence, although, if a Jewish kingdom does exist in the mountains of India, it might be true notwithstanding its improbability. But the country has been too often traversed to leave space for any large country not yet discovered.

of reserve and caution, and his words evinced much reflection. He lived very sparingly, mostly on bread and water, slept but few hours, and seemed always to be spiritually engaged. He kept himself scrupulously clean, and made frequent ablutions; in brief, his whole demeanour resembled greatly that of the Essenes, as described by Josephus and Philo; and his entire appearance was such that it gave one an excellent idea of the ancient prophets and seers of God.

Immediately after his entering into the messenger's house, he inquired carefully after the condition of the Holy City of Jerusalem, Zion, the destroyed Temple, and the situation of his brothers the Israelites in the Holy Land. The messenger thereupon gave him a vivid picture of them, the Holy City and the Temple. The other fell then suddenly with his face to the ground, and commenced to weep and sob bitterly, and it was near half an hour before he was able to speak again.

The messenger on his part inquired likewise after the situation of our brothers, the children of Dan, but he received merely the brief reply, that they formed an independent state, situated several months' journey from there, beyond the great sandy desert, in an eastern direction, were governed by their own regent, whom they call נשיא Nahssi or prince, and who is the bravest and the most distinguished for piety among them, and that they led a most peaceful and happy life. More than this he did not say. When asked for what purpose he had undertaken the great journey thither, he answered, that he was commissioned thereto by the Nahssi, since they had not received for a long time any account of the situation of their brothers in the west, and wished, therefore, to obtain some reliable information concerning them. The messenger asked, at length, whether he could or would permit him to make the journey with him, in order to visit the children of Dan, and in case this could be done, who was to bring him back again. After a brief reflection, the Danite promised him sacredly to have him restored to his present abode in a few months. But the simple messenger recalled his word, and said, that on account of the business of his mission he could not undertake so distant a journey. This displeased his visiter so greatly, seeing that he broke his word so quickly and easily, that he spoke not another word, rose from his seat and left him on the spot. A few hours afterwards, the messenger repented of his folly, and wished to reconcile him again, and actually resolved to undertake the journey in his company, and hastened into the town in order to seek him; but in vain, as no trace could be discovered of him, and he had disappeared as suddenly as he had come; and it is quite a mystery how he could traverse alone, without cattle or provisions, the great and dangerous sandy desert, filled as it is with serpents and other poisonous reptiles.

When now the messenger came back to Zafed and related his great and unpardonable error, he received many reproofs for it; since he had failed to make use of the best and fairest opportunity to obtain a better knowledge of these brethren, through which means a closer connexion might have been formed with them. Nevertheless, his narrative excited universal interest, and it was resolved to send out an especial mission to the Danites. There lived at that time at Jerusalem, a certain Rabbi Baruch Mosheh, who was an emigrant from Russia, and a very courageous and intelligent man, and who had also some knowledge of medicine. He resolved to undertake this difficult mission, and after being supplied with everything requisite, he set out by way of Alexandria and Cairo, and arrived safely at Zanaa. Here he sought for some one who could accompany him, and succeeded in finding a very pious man who offered to make this dangerous journey in his company.

But he said, "As is well known, the great sandy desert which we have to traverse is infested with poisonous serpents; I am willing to venture everything with thee; but know, that so soon as one of us should be injured, if even ever so slightly, by a serpent or any other reptile, I shall view it as a bad omen, as a signal that we cannot and dare not pursue this journey, and I will then turn about instantly." They now provided themselves with all things possible for their dangerous route, and actually travelled for six days in an eastern direction without any mishap; but on the seventh day a poisonous serpent bit the man from Zanaa. They had the proper remedies with them, by the application of which, his life was saved; but he remained firm to his resolve to return at once, and Rabbi Baruch could not induce him by any persuasion whatever to continue on their way, and he saw himself thus compelled to return with him, and the whole journey was therefore frustrated.*

Although this is not the place, I cannot avoid giving the mournful end of this venerable Rabbi Baruch Mosheh. As said, he was compelled to return to Zanaa, from whence he went to Senaar. The prince (serif) of Yemen, who resided in this city, suffered much from epilepsy, and all the remedies that had been applied by his physicians had failed to relieve him. Rabbi Mosheh, who, as said, was also a practical physician, undertook to cure him, and was in fact fortunate enough to restore the prince almost completely, so that he had no attack for a considerable length of time. The Rabbi thereby became naturally a great favourite with him, through which cause he drew upon

* The author alludes here to the mysterious connexion between the blessing of Jacob to Dan, and the alleged fact of his descendants living in a country to reach which a desert filled with serpents and adders has to be crossed, and also, that the above-named commissary should have had the words in question embroidered on his belt.

himself the envy and hatred of the other physicians, who therefore endeavoured to convince their master by all means that this Rabbi Mosheh was a spy of the Sublime Porte at Constantinople. Although the prince was perfectly well satisfied that the charge was nothing but calumny, he found himself at length compelled to yield, and to promote the downfall of his benefactor. In his palace garden he had confined in a strong cage a ferocious lion, who tore to pieces any one who came near him. The prince one day took a walk with Rabbi Mosheh in the garden, and led him, apparently by accident, but entirely by design, close past the lion, in order to rid himself by his aid of his new physician. The lion jumped up furiously from his lair, as though to tear the intended victim to pieces, but remained suddenly standing still, looked steadily at the innocent man, and laid himself down again. The prince stood astonished, and was now firmly convinced of the innocence of this pious man, since he was protected by the hand of a Superior Power. But the furious calumniators, more cruel than a fierce lion, did not relinquish their persecutions; and they then brought forward new and false proofs of his treason, so that he was necessarily regarded as a most dangerous person for the prince and the whole country, and from the evil consequences of which nothing but his death could save them. The stupid and weak prince saw himself now in a measure compelled to resolve on his destruction, and gave the order, that when he again was about to appear at court, to induce him to enter the garden, where he was to be shot; which command was executed on the following day. It is customary in that country not to inter those who have been convicted of high treason, but to have their bodies thrown into the open field, to be devoured by the birds and wild beasts. Their property also is confiscated by the prince. Rabbi Mosheh's corpse was treated with the same indignity, and it was cast without the city on the same spot where lay the remains of many malefactors. But how were people astonished to find that he lay there for several weeks and still remained untouched by birds and beasts of prey, and whilst these terrible guests were assembled over the carcasses and devoured them greedily, they did not defile the remains of this pious sufferer. The prince heard of this wonderful occurrence, and was now convinced a second time, though, alas! too late, that he had been innocent. He therefore commanded instantly to have him brought into the city, and had him interred in his palace garden as a martyr, with the greatest demonstrations of honour and respect, and had a handsome monument erected on the grave, and permission was given to every one to visit it as a place holy to the memory of a martyr, and it is now known as Zadik Baruch Musé, i. e. the pious Baruch Mosheh, and is generally visited, especially by the Jews of that neighbourhood, as a sacred place of devotion.

This remarkable narrative I obtained from the mouth of a creditable Jew from Senaar, who was an eye-witness of this fearful event, and had often visited the monument to perform his devotions.

Soon after, about twelve years ago, the Russian consul in Beirut received notice from the consul-general of his government at Alexandria, that all the property and effects of this innocent and pious man had been forwarded by the Serif of Senaar to the government of Egypt, in order to transmit them to his relatives, whom he left in Zafed, consisting of a wife and one son; who afterwards were duly put in possession of the property, through the intervention of the consuls.

My friend Moses Jafé, of Hebron, who was sent several years ago as messenger of his city to the East Indies, and who feels much interest for any information which may lead to the discovery of the lost tribes, told me not long since that he had to undertake another mission to that country; wherefore I urged him strongly to take all possible pains to procure us some definite and correct account on this subject. I told him plainly my views of the matter, and pointed out the countries where there had already been discovered some traces of the Ten Tribes. He promised to let me hear whatever he might learn; accordingly, on the 23d of Tishry, 5608 (October, 1847), I received his first letter by the English India mail, and I give it in part literally, leaving out only uninteresting matters.

"Bombay, Tuesday, Elul 12th, 5607.

"I visited the governor of Aden (in Yemen), who received me very friendly, and inquired after the object of my journey. He asked me, 'Why I did not visit the Israelitish kingdom in Africa, which had been lately discovered? I have contributed much,' said he, 'to effect this discovery, and I have already written about it to London. It is not very far from here. About thirty days' journey from the Red Sea, is the large city of *Harar*, about ten days' journey from which is found this Jewish kingdom. They have there a perfectly independent government, a standing army of 200,000 capable warriors, remarkably handsome and numerous Synagogues, are real Jews, and have plenty of gold.' He said farther: 'Although I am no Jew, I believe firmly in the Messiah whom you expect, and who is to found for you one day a universal kingdom, which is never more to be destroyed.'

"'I have also reliable accounts of a Jewish kingdom in China, nay, even of the existence of the wonderful stream Sambatyon, which has hitherto been viewed as a fabulous invention. I have been convinced by creditable men coming from China. I promised them a handsome reward if they could procure me some earth and sand of this river, which they readily promised, as a thing very easy for them to accomplish. But as hostilities have again broken out between China and England, through which all access to the former has been rendered impossible, I have hitherto not been able to obtain what I desired, but I have no doubt to be able to succeed so soon as peace is again restored.

"'The Jewish kingdom in Africa is by no means, as some may perhaps imagine, in Chabash, the capital of which is Kunder (Gondar); for the inhabitants of that country are only, properly speaking, Christians who have retained many customs derived from Judaism. But the country in question is inhabited by real Jews, and is not under the dominions of the Abyssinians (Chabshians), but is ten days' journey distant from Harar, which is also not under the dominion of the Christians.' All the above was communicated to me by the governor of Aden.

"In the same town (Aden), I spoke with a certain Chai Levy, a man of some learning, but quiet and pious, who is a goldsmith by trade, and travels almost every year in the month of Tebeth (January), when the spring commences in Chabash, beyond the Red Sea, in order to attend the "Tent-Fair," held not far from the same. They have, namely, a custom the whole of their summer, which lasts from Tebeth to Nissan (January to May), which season they call in their language *Mashem*, to erect a town of tents or booths, to which caravans resort coming from Kunder, Harar, &c., in order to purchase linen and iron, as their country does not furnish these necessary materials. With the termination of Mashem, the fair is ended, the merchants moving away, each man striking his tent or booth.

"This Chai Levy now told me that, at one of his visits

to the fair, he had seen in the hands of a Jew from Cush (Ethiopia), a book written in a very handsome square letter, also another (?) in the rabbinical character, the so-called Rashi-writing. The caravans from Harar, distant about twenty-five days' journey from the tent-town, who visit the fair, had told him that an immense number of Jews live in their vicinity, with whom these merchants of Harar, in which town itself no Jews live, have commercial relations. He requested me to give him a letter for the Jews of that country, which he would forward through the caravans from Harar; but I declined doing so, because he does not travel again before the coming Tebeth, and it is possible that I may learn something more reliable in the mean time, before I write.

"Have the goodness to speak with the chief of the Jewish congregation at Jerusalem, and tell him that it would be most interesting to send, in respect to this subject, an especial mission to Chabash, by way of Aden, since this is the shortest and best route thither. It would be indeed a great triumph for our faith, קידוש השם, to convince the world of this important fact. I also announced to you that during my sojourn at Aden, I learned that Rabbi Amram, the missionary to the Yehud Chebr, had already arrived at Zanaa, and was resolved to travel to the tribe of Benjamin, dwelling within the wilderness of Theman (Yeman); and as he may not be able to inform you himself of his so doing, I have been requested to do so. He has no intention to travel to Chabash on any account; wherefore, it is necessary to send thither, as soon as possible an especial messenger.

"Yours, &c.,

"MOSES JAFÉ."

I have already stated above that I had also received a

letter from Rabbi Amram at Zanaa, giving nearly the same information which my friend communicated.

REMARKABLE OCCURRENCE.

Three days before receiving the foregoing letter from Bombay, I had a visit from a young Jewish scholar, Dr. Asché, from Prussia, who had resolved and prepared himself for some years before, to undertake a distant journey in order to seek out the traces of the Ten Tribes. He has studied medicine, is acquainted with military affairs, having been two years in the Turkish service as a military surgeon, and witnessed several battles in the Caucasus, and all this merely as a proper preparation for his difficult journey of discovery. He accordingly had arrived a few days previous to my seeing him at Jerusalem, to continue his journey from there. I was quite surprised and highly rejoiced at the intention, the enterprise, and I may say self-sacrifice, of this noble young man. We discussed the subject in its various ramifications, as to the road which he ought to pursue, and I spoke to him also of the Rabbi Amram, the messenger to the Yehud Chebr. My plan was, that he ought to go by way of Egypt and Yemen; but he thought it would be better to go over Djida, Janbula (also called Janbua), when suddenly and quite unexpectedly, but just in the proper time, I got the above letter from Bombay, which gives the route of march for the journey. We were agreeably surprised, and viewed this singular coincidence as a fortunate omen; and two days afterwards, Dr. Asché commenced his travels with a caravan, which was about making a land journey to Cairo. On the 28th of Kislev, 5608, I obtained from him the following letter:

"Cairo, New Moon of Kislev.

"My dear Rabbi Joseph Schwarz:

"I cannot as yet communicate a great deal to you, since I have been compelled to stay hitherto in this place; but this afternoon, at one o'clock, I hope to leave here, under Divine protection, for Suez, and thence by the steam-packet for Aden, and expect to reach it on the 26th of November, 1847. During my stay here, I have been nearly the whole time with the venerable Chief Rabbi, your friend, who inquired particularly after your well-being, and was greatly rejoiced to hear of my intentions, and showed me many writings and documents which prove, beyond a doubt, that there are a great many Jews in Chabash. He told me that at present there sojourns at Aden a Jew, called Rabbi Phineas, who had arrived there from the tribe of Dan. I shall not rest till I have carefully investigated and probed everything. I shall write you again before I leave Aden; and you will favour me by forwarding all my letters thence, and those I may write hereafter from Chabash, according to our agreement, to Vienna. Whenever you visit the 'West Wall' remember me in your prayers, and pray for me, on that holy spot, to the Father of Israel for assistance, protection, and success in my long and dangerous journey; for He who proves the heart, knows that I undertake it only for the sake of his holy Name and the glory of Israel.

"Your obedient servant,

"Dr. Asche."

On the 18th of Adar, 5608, I received the following letter, from which I extract only the most interesting portion:

"Bombay, the 27th of Shebat, 5608.

"RABBI JOSEPH SCHWARZ:

"In reference to many accounts concerning a Jewish kingdom, I have to report that I have spoken here with a credible Mahomedan from Chabash, who has told me wonderful and astonishing things concerning the Jewish kingdom in his country. The residence of their chief, the King Zachlon, is in the city of Shemeän, which is distant twenty-eight days' journey from the town of Ascilé, on the Red Sea. He has an army of one hundred thousand cavalry, and an innumerable host of infantry. This Jewish regent excels all the kings and governors in Chabash in power and renown. The Jews speak three different languages, Hebrew, Arabic, and Chabash. The whole country is very fertile and densely populated, and has many towns and villages. I have already told you in my last letter that our friend, Dr. Asché, had safely arrived at Aden in the month of Tebeth, and it is probable that he has long since departed for Chabash.

"Yours, MOSES JAFE."

On the 10th of Ve-Adar, I received the following letter:

"Aden, 7th of Shebat, 5608 (12th of January, '48).

"MY DEAR RABBI:

"I am still at Aden, but in the coming week I mean to depart, God willing, for Mocha, for there are always vessels which sail for Massua, on the western shore of the Red Sea; from that place I shall have yet before me a journey of twenty days for Gondar, the first place where I expect to meet with Jews. There are various opinions current here concerning the inhabitants of Chabash. Some believe that all the people resident there are Jews proper, that is to say, Caraites; but this is evidently incorrect, for they are only Christians, and others actual pagans, with some Jewish customs. They also practise circumcision. But this cannot be said of those Jews who live farther westward and southward, for they are averred to be Israelites in the amplest sense of the word. I feel very impatient to be able to convince myself accurately, by actual inspection, of the true state of affairs. Rabbi Amram has already commenced his journey to the city of Chaban in Yemen, and I hope that he may be able to discover there some vestiges of the tribes of Israel. Chai Levy, the goldsmith, travels as usual the coming week to the "tent fair," on the other side of the Red Sea; but I mean to take another route, the one by way of Mocha, wherefore we cannot journey together. Should nothing be heard from me in the course of three years, which may the God of Israel forefend, there will, nevertheless, in all probability, be found in the Holy City some one who will again undertake a journey to Chabash. Should you in the meanwhile write to Vienna or London, have the goodness to inform my friends and acquaintances of all particulars. Yours, &c.,

Dr. Asche."

On the 16th of Ab, 5608, I received the following letter:

"Calcutta, 28th Izar, 5608.

"My dear Rabbi J. Schwarz:

"I have obtained reliable information concerning the wonderful stream Sambatyon, in China. The well-known merchant, Signor David Sason, of Bombay, lately sent his son, Abdalla, on business to Canton. He took with him a servant, a worthy, truthful man, whom I have had occasion to become acquainted and converse with at Bombay before his departure. But he remained only one month in Canton, as he was taken sick, and Signor Abdalla sent him hither to be cured. This man told me, that his master, Signor Abdalla, has in Canton a zaraf (a banker or money-broker), who is a distinguished man, and has much commercial intercourse with the Chinese, even in the most remote districts of the country, and he thus becomes accurately informed of whatever takes place throughout the whole land. 'We learned from him,' says my informant, 'that it is a notorious fact, that, two months' journey from Canton, there is a stream which throws out sand, stones, and water during six days of the week, but is entirely at rest on the Sabbath. Beyond it is a large and unknown kingdom. The Chinese of the neighbourhood always cross it on the Sabbath, when it is quiet and can be navigated, with their various kinds of merchandise, which they leave on the shore, as they are afraid to venture inland, and then return to the other side; but on their next return, on the following Sabbath, they either find the money or their goods untouched. This is alleged to be a fact; as the Chinese, who deal with our zaraf, themselves take part in this business.' He also told me, that before he left Canton he learned, that lately there had been discovered in the northern part of China more than 200,000 men, who all wear beards and long curls פאות, who must be Jews, since the Chinese wear neither beards nor side-locks.

"Yours,

"Moses Jafe."

Since the above, I have received no farther details; and my curiosity will be on the stretch till I shall have the good fortune to obtain accurate accounts and confirmation concerning these discoveries, which I shall then communicate immediately to the public.

We have therefore vestiges of the Ten Tribes in four

different localities: 1, In Africa; viz., Chabash, which means not merely Abyssinia, but the whole of Central and Southern Africa; 2, in Yemen; 3, in Thibet, and 4, in China; and it is a truly ludicrous assumption to pretend to find them among the Americans or Hindoostanees, for no better reason than that people suppose they have discovered some traces of Jewish customs among them, and to argue thence that the Israelites had been entirely lost and mixed up with them. Equally cogent would it be to argue that the ape ought to be classed among the members of the human family, because he imitates and copies the same in many of their acts.

"The word of our God remaineth for ever." (Isaiah lx. 8.)

"Behold, days are coming, saith the Lord, that I shall fulfil the good word which I have spoken concerning the house of Israel (the Ten Tribes), and the house of Judah (Judah and Benjamin); on that day shall Judah be assisted, and Jerusalem dwell securely, and this is the name which they shall call it, 'The Lord our right.'" (Jer. xxxiii. 14, 16.)

Amen.

NOTES.

(Page 78.—Art. The Plain of Jordan.)

We find in Siphri, as also in Rashi to Deut. i. 7, בערבה זה מישור של יער "Arabah means the plain of the forest." Jonathan renders it in the same manner במשרא דחורשא. As we cannot ascertain what *forest* is meant here, and as we always understand by *Arabah* the plain of Jordan, I deem myself authorized to read for יער "forest" ירדן "Jordan," or the plain of Jordan. Jonathan no doubt copied from Siphri, but without doubt an incorrect reading.

(Page 99.)

In Joshua xi. 16, the land of Goshen is mentioned between the South הנגב and the Lowland השפלה. We also read (ibid. x. 41), "All the land of Goshen to Gibeon." Although now we are told of a city Goshen in the mountains of Judah (ibid. xv. 51), I have not been able to ascertain where this land was situated. It may, perhaps, have been to the south of Beth-Djibrin, in the district now called Al Hasy, or Henady.

(Page 202.)

Line 13 (Sycamore?) is wrong; and should read, "See article אלה, p. 308."

(Page 211.)

The distance from Djebl Tor (Mount Sinai) to Wady Gaian, or Wady Bierin (Kadesh Barnea), is about 180 to 190 English miles. The usual distance travelled by a caravan during one day is from sixteen to seventeen miles: wherefore the journey from Sinai to Kadesh Barnea can be made in *eleven* days, as stated in Deut. i. 2.

THE END.